T0204643

Global Issues in Patent Law

By

Martin J. Adelman

Theodore and James Pedas Family Professor of
Intellectual Property and Technology Law
George Washington University

Shubha Ghosh

Vilas Research Fellow, Professor of Law, & Associate Director,
Initiatives for Studies in Transformational
Entrepreneurship (INSITE),
University of Wisconsin Law School, Madison, WI

Amy Landers

Professor of Law
University of the Pacific
McGeorge School of Law

Toshiko Takenaka Ph.D.

Washington Research Foundation/W. Hunter Simpson
Professor of Tech Law Director,
Center for Advanced Study and Research on Intellectual Property
Director for Research, Law, Technology & Art Group
University of Washington School of Law

AMERICAN CASEBOOK SERIES®

A Thomson Reuters business

Mat #40756732

American Casebook Series is a trademark registered in the U.S. Patent and Trademark Office.

© 2011 Thomson Reuters
    610 Opperman Drive
    St. Paul, MN 55123
    1–800–313–9378
Printed in the United States of America

ISBN: 978–0–314–19517–3

Global Issues Series

Series Editor, Franklin A. Gevurtz

Titles Available Now

Global Issues in Civil Procedure by Thomas Main, University of the Pacific, McGeorge School of Law
ISBN 978–0–314–15978–6

Global Issues in Commercial Law by Claude D. Rohwer, University of the Pacific, McGeorge School of Law and Kristen David Adams, Stetson University College of Law
ISBN 978–0–314–19993–5

Global Issues in Constitutional Law by Brian K. Landsberg, University of the Pacific, McGeorge School of Law and Leslie Gielow Jacobs, University of the Pacific, McGeorge School of Law
ISBN 978–0–314–17608–0

Global Issues in Contract Law by John A. Spanogle, Jr., George Washington University, Michael P. Malloy, University of the Pacific, McGeorge School of Law, Louis F. Del Duca, Pennsylvania State University, Keith A. Rowley, University of Nevada, Las Vegas, and Andrea K. Bjorklund, University of California, Davis
ISBN 978–0–314–16755–2

Global Issues in Copyright Law by Mary LaFrance, University of Nevada
ISBN 978–0–314–19447–3

Global Issues in Corporate Law by Franklin A. Gevurtz, University of the Pacific, McGeorge School of Law
ISBN 978–0–314–15977–9

Global Issues in Criminal Law by Linda Carter, University of the Pacific, McGeorge School of Law, Christopher L. Blakesley, University of Nevada, Las Vegas and Peter Henning, Wayne State University
ISBN 978–0–314–15997–7

Global Issues in Employee Benefits Law by Paul M. Secunda, Marquette University Law School, Samuel Estreicher, New York University School of Law, Rosalind J. Connor, Jones Day, London
ISBN 978–0–314–19409–1

iii

Global Issues in Employment Discrimination Law by Samuel Estreicher, New York University School of Law and Brian K. Landsberg, University of the Pacific, McGeorge School of Law
ISBN 978-0-314-17607-3

Global Issues in Employment Law by Samuel Estreicher, New York University School of Law and Miriam A. Cherry, University of the Pacific, McGeorge School of Law
ISBN 978-0-314-17952-4

Global Issues in Environmental Law by Stephen McCaffrey, University of the Pacific, McGeorge School of Law and Rachael Salcido, University of the Pacific, McGeorge School of Law
ISBN 978-0-314-18479-5

Global Issues in Family Law by Ann Laquer Estin, University of Iowa and Barbara Stark, Hofstra University
ISBN 978-0-314-17954-8

Global Issues in Freedom of Speech and Religion by Alan Brownstein, University of California, Davis School of Law and Leslie Gielow Jacobs, University of the Pacific, McGeorge School of Law
ISBN 978-0-314-18454-2

Global Issues in Income Taxation by Daniel Lathrope, University of California, Hastings College of Law
ISBN 978-0-314-18806-9

Global Issues in Intellectual Property Law by John Cross, University of Louisville School of Law, Amy Landers, University of the Pacific, McGeorge School of Law, Michael Mireles, University of the Pacific, McGeorge School of Law and Peter K. Yu, Drake University Law School
ISBN 978-0-314-17953-1

Global Issues in Labor Law by Samuel Estreicher, New York University School of Law
ISBN 978-0-314-17163-4

Global Issues in Legal Ethics by James E. Moliterno, College of William & Mary, Marshall–Wythe School of Law and George Harris, University of the Pacific, McGeorge School of Law
ISBN 978-0-314-16935-8

Global Issues in Patent Law by Martin J. Adelman, George Washington University, Shuba Ghosh, University of Wisconsin Law School, Madison, WI, Amy Landers, McGeorge School of Law, University of the Pacific, Toshiko Takenka, University of Washington

ISBN 978–0–314–19517–3

Global Issues in Property Law by John G. Sprankling, University of the Pacific, McGeorge School of Law, Raymond R. Coletta, University of the Pacific, McGeorge School of Law, and M.C. Mirow, Florida International University College of Law

ISBN 978–0–314–16729–3

Global Issues in Tort Law by Julie A. Davies, University of the Pacific, McGeorge School of Law and Paul T. Hayden, Loyola Law School, Los Angeles

ISBN 978–0–314–16759–0

Summary of Contents

Table of Contents

Table of Cases

The principal cases are in bold type. Cases cited or discussed in the text are roman type. References are to pages. Cases cited in principal cases and within other quoted materials are not included.

Global Issues in
Patent Law

Chapter 1

INTRODUCTION

Global patent law refers to the set of treaties and international institutions that govern the patent systems of the various countries that have adopted patent law. There is no such thing as a global patent. A patent is a creature of national law, and an inventor seeking worldwide protection for her creation would have to obtain a patent in every country that offers patent protection. However, global patent law is not just a collection of national laws. While there are important differences across countries in patent rules and enforcement, there is a growing consensus across countries about the importance of patent law for promoting innovation, economic growth, and economic development. The materials in this volume will expose you to the differences and similarities across national patent systems which constitute global patent law.

Our presumption is that you have had some exposure to patent law in a previous course, most likely the patent law of the country in which you attended law school. Presumably, you have already been exposed to a discussion of what a patent is and what purpose it serves. As a time-limited property right, a patent gives the owner the right to exclude others from making, using, selling, offering to sell, and importing the invention claimed in the patent. The patent grant is an important tool for licensing and, when licensing proves difficult, for business litigation. Patent practitioners defend the rights of patent owners so that they can obtain economic value from the commercialization of invention. Patent practitioners also work to secure the rights of inventors by guiding them through patent prosecution, the administrative process through which a patent is obtained. What makes patent practice challenging is that it entails an understanding of the full range of activities in which attorneys engage: litigation, transactions, and administrative law.

1

Your study of global patent law will continue this broad ranging and deep understanding of patent practice. The volume begins with an discussion of treaties, the primary means by which countries coordinate and harmonize their individual patent systems. You will study the Paris Convention, the Patent Cooperation Treaty, and the Agreement on Trade Related Aspects of Intellectual Property Rights. Your study of these treaties will illustrate how global patent practice involves coordinating patent applications across the different national patent regimes in which a client seeks protection in order to maintain priority and the full scope of patent protection across patent regimes. Global patent practice also requires recognizing the differences across regimes and identifying which differences are permitted under international agreements. After your study of treaties, you will look in depth at how the requirements of patentability vary across countries. Different nations have adopted comparable rules for patentable subject matter, utility (or industrial application), novelty, nonobviousness (or inventive step), and enablement. By looking at these differences, there will be greater appreciation for individual national rules and the broader policies that these requirements aim to achieve. With these basic concepts reinforced, you will turn to how global patent practice addresses the challenging questions of litigation, competition policy, and border enforcement. The volume provides a comprehensive picture of global patent practice, combining administrative details, policy analysis, and judicial enforcement.

By studying global patent law, you can become a stronger practitioner of patent law at the national level. You will also obtain a better sense of the policy issues that inform patent practice. By studying how different countries structure their patent systems, you will be exposed to different arguments for how patent rights should be defined and enforced, some more convincing than others. It is important to know how to practice law but also why the law is what it is. Patent law has been the focus of many policy debates and efforts at reform across all countries. A study of global patent law will better inform your understanding your debates and help you to shape your own thinking of what types of patent reform makes sense and why.

Chapter 2

TREATY REGIMES

A. OVERVIEW

Despite the title of this book, there is no such thing as a "global patent." Patent rights are territorial and arise from domestic legislation passed by a nation state. What this means is that an inventor needs to file for a patent in every country in which he or she seeks protection from patent law. In general, owning a patent in the United States does no good if an infringement occurs in Germany. One narrow exception to this rule is the principle of extraterritoriality, about which more later in this book. Under the doctrine of extraterritoriality, a United States patent owner can sue for infringing activity in another country if domestic law allows for such a claim.

Putting aside the principle of extraterritoriality, an inventor seeking protection globally needs to deal with the patent laws of several nation states. There are two main problems with this. The first is procedural and the second is substantive. It would be desirable to have some coordination mechanism that allows an inventor to be able to coordinate patent applications across different countries. Furthermore, once patent rights are obtained in different countries, it would be desirable to have some degree of harmonization of patent laws across different countries. These two problems are dealt with through treaties that would bind the various nation states to harmonization of law. Three treaties guide global patent law: (i) the Paris Convention for the Protection of Industrial Property; (ii) the Patent Cooperation Treaty; and (iii) Trade Related Intellectual Property Systems Agreement (or TRIPS Agreement), which is part of the World Trade Organization. This chapter will focus on each of these treaties.

The Paris Convention for Industrial Property, more commonly known as the Paris Convention, is the first major international treaty to deal with intellectual property. Its primary focus is on trademark and patents. Ratified by eleven European countries in 1883, the Convention has grown in importance over time with the number of signatories at 173 with the joining of Thailand in 2009. The United States joined in 1887. An important substantive provision of the Paris Convention is the principle of national treatment, stated in Article 2. Under the principle of national treatment, a foreign national of a Paris Convention country has to have the same patent (and trademark) protection as a domestic national of a Paris Convention country. The Paris Convention also contains a procedural provision in Article 4. Known as "Paris priority," Article 4 states that a patent application filed in a Paris Convention country shall have the priority date of that filing if the application is also filed within 12 months in another Paris Convention country. The implications of this priority rule, especially under United States law, are explored in the materials below. The World Intellectual Property Organization (WIPO), a division of the United Nations headquartered in Geneva, Switzerland, administers the Paris Convention.

The Patent Cooperation Treaty (PCT) went into effect in 1970. The PCT creates a streamlined process for the filing of patent applications in multiple countries simultaneously. Administered by WIPO, the PCT application consists of a centralized filing of a patent application which allows the inventor to designate several countries whose patent office will review the application. Before the PCT application moves to the national patent offices, it moves through an international phase in WIPO, which results in a report on the patentability of the invention under the laws of the several countries. While this PCT does not harmonize patent law substantively, it does create an important procedural mechanism for obtaining patent protection in multiple countries. All Paris Convention signatories are eligible to be members of the PCT, and as of 2009, there were 142 signatories.

The TRIPS Agreement is a comprehensive intellectual property treaty closely tied to the principle of free trade administered by the World Trade Organization. The TRIPS Agreement went into effect in 1994 and currently has 153 signatories. In addition to the national treatment principle, the Agreement also requires its signatories to recognize the principle of most-favored nation. Under this principle, the nationals of a member state has to be given the same privileges that a signatory grants to nationals of other member states. In addition, the TRIPS Agreement requires that signatories have to amend their intellectual property laws to conform to the substantive minimum provisions of the Agreements. These substantive minimum include such provisions as term of protection and protected subject matter. The Agreement allows member states to create certain exceptions from intellectual property protection so long as these exceptions satisfy the requirements of the Agreement. Finally, the World Trade Organization established a dispute resolution process to resolve claims that a member state is not meeting its obligations under the Agreement. Since developing countries have lagged behind in legal infrastructure, the Agreement does create exceptions for developing countries in the form of timelines for conforming to obligations under TRIPS. The scope of these exceptions has also been the subject of dispute. In November 2001, the WTO ministerial conference adopted the Doha Declaration which recognized some limits on pharmaceutical patents in order to facilitate access to essential medicines. The Doha Declaration illustrates the continued tension between harmonized intellectual property law and differences across TRIPS signatories. The materials below illustrate these challenging issues.

B. PARIS CONVENTION

Article 4 of the Paris Convention gives a priority date based on a patent application filed in one Paris Convention country if the application is filed within one year in another Paris Convention country. For example, if an inventor files a patent application in Germany on April 3, 2009 and then files in the United States on April 2, 2009, then the U.S. application can be given the priority date of the German application. It is as if the U.S. application had been filed on April 3, 2009. In practice, different national jurisdictions have interpreted the priority under the Paris Convention in different ways. The United States has a notable interpretation.

The principal case in the United States is *Application of Hilmer*, 359 F.2d 859 (CCPA 1966). Habicht and Hilmer were two inventors engaged in an interference to establish priority of invention over an aromatic ring system. Habicht had filed a Swiss application on January 24, 1957, and a United States application on January 23, 1958. Hilmer had filed a German application on July 31, 1957, and a United States application on July 15, 1958. Each inventor could take advantage of Article 4, and for the purposes of the interference, Habicht could establish a constructive reduction to practice date of January 24, 1957, and Hilmer, one of July 31, 1957. Therefore, Habicht was the first to invent the claims on which the two applications overlapped. Hilmer proceeded with his application on the non-overlapping claims. The Office rejected these claims on nonobviousness grounds citing Habicht's Swiss application as the prior art under Section 102(e). The Court of Claims and Patent Appeals reversed on the grounds that Section 102(e) allows use of a patent application filed in the United States as prior art. Habicht had filed his United States patent application on January

23, 1958, after the priority date of July 31, 1957, given to Hilmer's application. Under the *Hilmer* doctrine, Article 4 can be used offensively by the inventor to assert an earlier priority date, but not defensively by someone challenging a patent. The doctrine is a controversial, but an accepted one. The CCPA affirmed and extended it to prior art under the old version of Section 102(g) in *Application of Hilmer II*, 424 F.2d 1108 (CCPA 1970). The Federal Circuit has affirmed the *Hilmer* doctrine in *In re Deckler*, 977 F.2d 1449 (Fed. Cir. 1992).

For the European perspective on Article 4, consider the following case. In it, the Enlarged Board of Appeals for the European Patent Office considers the phrase "same invention" as used in the European Patent Convention art. 87(1), which provides that patentees "... shall enjoy, for the purpose of filing a European patent application in respect of the same invention, a right of priority during a period of twelve months from the date of filing of the first application."

SAME INVENTION

Enlarged Board of Appeal, 2001
[2002] E.P.O.R. 17, G02/98

Messerli, Moser, Andries, Davies, Saisset, Teschemacher, Turrini.

On July 29, 1998, the President of the EPO, making use of his power under Article 112 (1)(b) EPC, referred the following point of law to the Enlarged Board of Appeal:

(1a) Does the requirement of the "same invention" in Article 87 (1) EPC mean that the extent of the right to priority derivable from a priority application for a later application is determined by, and at the same time limited to, what is at least implicitly disclosed in the priority application?

(1b) Or can a lesser degree of correspondence between the priority application and the subject-matter claimed in the later application be sufficient in this respect and still justify a right to priority?

(2) If question (1b) is answered in the affirmative, what are the criteria to be applied in assessing whether the claim in the later application is in respect of the same invention as is in the priority application?

(3) In particular, where features not disclosed, even implicitly, in the priority application have been added in the relevant claim of the later application, or where features defined in broader terms in the priority application have been more specifically or more narrowly defined in the later application, can a right to priority neverthe-

less be derived from the priority application and, if so, what are the criteria which must be met to justify the priority in such cases?

* * *

In order to answer question (1a) of the referral as to whether the concept of "the same invention" referred to in Article 87 (1) EPC means that the extent of the right of priority derivable from a priority application for a later application is determined by, and at the same time limited to, what is at least implicitly disclosed in the priority application, it has to be examined in the first place whether a narrow or strict interpretation of this concept, equating it with the concept of "the same subject-matter" referred to in Article 87 (4) EPC, is consistent with the relevant provisions of both the Paris Convention and the EPC. Such a narrow or strict interpretation gives rise to the requirement that the subject-matter of a claim defining the invention in the European patent application, i.e. the specific combination of features present in the claim, must at least implicitly be disclosed in the application whose priority is claimed.

* * *

Pursuant to Article 4H of the Paris Convention, priority may not be refused on the ground that certain elements of the invention for which priority is claimed do not appear among the claims formulated in the application whose priority is claimed, provided that the application as a whole specifically discloses such elements. It follows that priority for a claim, i.e. an "element of the invention" within the meaning of Article 4H of the Paris Convention, is to be acknowledged, if the subject-matter of the claim is specifically disclosed be it explicitly or implicitly in the application documents relating to the disclosure, in particular, in the form of a claim or in the form of an embodiment or example specified in the description of the application whose priority is claimed, and that priority for the claim can be refused, if there is no such disclosure.

* * *

Article 4F of the Paris Convention, first paragraph, provides, inter alia, that priority may not be refused on the ground that an application claiming one or more priorities contains one or more elements that were not included in the application or applications whose priority is claimed, provided that there is unity of invention within the meaning of the law of the country. From the second paragraph of this provision it follows that, with respect to these elements, the filing of the subsequent application shall give rise to a right of priority under ordinary conditions. These elements would then be contained in the application whose priority is claimed in respect of a further application. Since, according to Article 4H of the Paris Convention, an invention for which priority is claimed need not be defined in a claim of the application whose priority is claimed, an "element" within the meaning of Article 4F of the Paris Convention represents subject-matter specifically disclosed be it explicitly or implicitly in the application documents relating to the disclosure, in particular, in the form of a claim or in the form of an embodiment or example specified in the description of the application claiming one or more priorities. This is in line with the purpose of Article 4F of the Paris Convention. The possibility of claiming multiple priorities was introduced into the Paris Convention in order to avoid improvements of the original invention having to be prosecuted in applications for patents of addition. This makes it clear that "element" was not understood as a feature but as an embodiment (Actes de la Confrence de Washington de 1911, Bern 1911, pp. 45 et seq.).

Furthermore, since priority for a claim can be refused under Article 4H of the Paris Convention, if the subject-matter of the claim is not disclosed in the application whose priority is claimed, unity of invention as required under Article 4F of the Paris Convention, first paragraph, must exist between two or more inventions disclosed in the application claiming one or more priorities, and not, as submitted in some statements by third parties pursuant to Article 11b of the Rules of Procedure of the Enlarged Board of Appeal, between an invention disclosed in the application claiming one or more priorities and an invention disclosed in an application whose priority is claimed.

In fact, a narrow or strict interpretation of the concept of "the same invention" referred to in Article 87 (1) EPC, equating it with the concept of "the same subject-matter" referred to in Article 87 (4) EPC, is perfectly consistent with Articles 4F and 4H of the Paris Convention, which are provisions representing substantive law. Furthermore, the requirement of "the same subject-matter" does not contravene Article 4A (1) of the Paris Convention although this provision makes no mention of the subject-matter of the subsequent application. It is, however, generally held that the subsequent filing must concern the same subject-matter as the first filing on which the right of priority is based (cf. Wieczorek, Die Unionsprioritt im Patentrecht, Koeln, Berlin, Bonn, Muenchen, 1975, p. 149). This follows from the very aim and object of the right of priority: the protection from novelty-destroying disclosures during a period of 12 months from the date of filing of the first application is necessary only in case of the filing of a subsequent application relating to the same invention. Finally, such a narrow or strict interpretation is also consistent with Article 4C (4) of the Paris Convention, which provides that a subsequent application concerning the same subject as a previous first application shall be considered the first application if, at the time of filing the subsequent application, the previous first application satisfies certain requirements; there is no reason why in this particular situation the concept of "the same invention" should be interpreted differently.

* * *

In order to assess whether a claim in a later European patent application is in respect of the same invention as the priority application pursuant to Article 87 (1) EPC, a distinction is made in Decision T73/88, and in a statement by third parties pursuant to Article 11b of the Rules of Procedure of the Enlarged Board of Appeal, between technical features which are related to the function and effect of the invention and technical features which are not. This approach is problematic because there are no suitable and clear, objective criteria for making such a distinction; it could thus give rise to arbitrariness. In fact, the features of a claim defining the invention in the form $A + B + C$ do not represent a mere aggregation, but are normally inherently connected with each other. Therefore, if the above-mentioned distinction is to be made, the answer to the question whether the claimed invention remains the same, if one of these features is modified or deleted, or if a further feature D is added, depends very much on the actual assessment of the facts and circumstances of the case by each individual deciding body. Different deciding bodies may thus arrive at different results when assessing these facts and circumstances. Furthermore, as pointed out in the referral of the President of the EPO, it has to be borne in mind that the assessment by these different deciding bodies of whether or not certain technical features are related to the function and effect of the claimed invention may completely change in the course of proceedings. This is the case, in particular, if new prior art is to be considered, with the possible consequence that the validity of a hitherto acknowledged right of priority could be put in jeopardy. Such dependence would, however, be at variance with the requirement of legal certainty.

If the invention claimed in a later European patent application constitutes a so-called selection invention-i.e. typically, the choice of individual entities from larger groups or of sub-ranges from broader ranges of numerical values—in respect of the subject-matter disclosed in a first application whose priority is claimed, the criteria applied by the EPO with a view to assessing novelty of selection inventions over the prior art must also be considered carefully when assessing whether the claim in the European patent application is in respect of the same invention as the priority application within the meaning of Article 87 (1) EPC. Otherwise, patent protection for selection inventions, in particular in the field of chemistry, could be seriously prejudiced if these criteria were not thoroughly complied with when assessing priority claims in respect of selection inventions. Hence such priority claims should not be acknowledged if the selection inventions in question are considered "novel" according to these criteria.

From the analysis under point 8 above, it follows that an extensive or broad interpretation of the concept of "the same invention" referred to in Article 87 (1) EPC, making a distinction between technical features which are related to the function and effect of the invention and technical features which are not, with the possible consequence that a claimed invention is considered to remain the same even though a feature is modified or deleted, or a further feature is added, is inappropriate and prejudicial to a proper exercise of priority rights. Rather, according to that analysis, a narrow or strict interpretation of the concept of "the same invention", equating it to the concept of "the same subject-matter" referred to in Article 87 (4) EPC, is necessary to ensure a proper exercise of priority rights in full conformity, inter alia, with the principles of equal treatment of the applicant and third parties and legal certainty and with the requirement of consistency with regard to the assessment of novelty and inventive step. Such an interpretation is solidly supported by the provisions of the Paris Convention and the provisions of the EPC, and is perfectly in keeping with Opinion G03/93. It means that priority of a previous application in respect of a claim in a European patent application in accordance with Article 88 EPC is to be acknowledged only if the person skilled in the art can derive the subject-matter of the claim directly and unambiguously, using common general knowledge, from the previous application as a whole.

Conclusion

For these reasons the point of law referred to the Enlarged Board of Appeal by the President of the EPO is answered as follows:

The requirement for claiming priority of "the same invention", referred to in Article 87 (1) EPC, means that priority of a previous application in respect of a claim in a European patent application in accordance with Article 88 EPC is to be acknowledged only if the skilled person can derive the subject-matter of the claim directly and unambiguously, using common general knowledge, from the previous application as a whole.

C. THE PATENT COOPERATION TREATY

By its own terms, the Paris Convention is not an exclusive agreement. In fact, the PCT complements the Paris Convention well. Without the PCT, international applicants would have to file an application in each separate country within a year of their first national filing. With the PCT in place, those applicants can instead file a single PCT application. The PCT filing, in turn, designates additional nations where the applicant intends to seek patent rights. At its most basic, the PCT defers nation-by-nation prosecution—also known as entry into the "national phase"-until many months after the priority date. With these additional months, a patent applicant can defer the costs of international prosecution, which can be substantial with translation and foreign counsel fees.

To take advantage of the fee-deferring and timeshifting effect, an applicant files a PCT application with a PCT "Receiving Office." This application is automatically published 18 months after the earliest priority date, which may be the filing date of an application to which the PCT application claims priority. The Receiving Office also automatically performs a prior art search and issues a perfunctory search report without substantive examination. A PCT applicant, however, may request (for an additional fee) a preliminary examination of the claims. This request is also called a "demand" for preliminary examination. Even though this may superficially seem like substantive examination, the preliminary examination report is in fact a nonbinding opinion on the patentability of the claimed invention. In essence, the PCT facilitates a patent filing system, not a patent granting system.

The PCT does not create an "international patent" of any kind. To get patents, applicants still need to apply to each national office. Under the Paris Convention alone, a patent applicant would need to file those multiple applications in other nations within 12 months of the first filing. That process would entail multiple different formality requirements, translations, amendment and publication procedures, and fees. This timeline illustrates the traditional Paris Convention filing system:

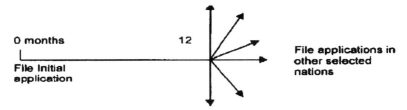

Under the PCT system, the applicant can file a single international application which can then undergo a single preliminary examination. This filing process permits the applicant to postpone entry into multiple nations for up to 30 months from the original filing. The following illustration shows the contrast from the traditional Paris Convention system and highlights the advantages of the PCT filing system. As this shows, the applicant can amend a single application in response to prior art and likely streamline the process of acquiring a patent from the various national patent offices at the end of 30 months. As this shows, the applicant can amend a single application in response to prior art and likely streamline the process of acquiring a patent from the various national patent offices at the end of 30 months:

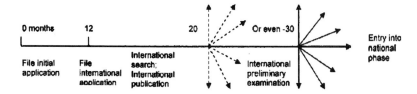

In sum, the PCT can reduce the burden and expense of seeking worldwide protection for an invention. In the long run, the PCT affords extra time beyond the 12 months granted by the Paris Convention. This additional delay in prosecution often gives time for an accurate evaluation of the value of the patent rights eventually obtained. The extra time may also allow applicants to identify potential licensees or other parties interested in the technology before incurring filing fees and costs at the national phase.

STEVENS v. TAMAI

366 F.3d 1325 (Fed. Cir. 2004)

CLEVENGER, CIRCUIT JUDGE.

Christopher J. Stevens appeals a final decision of the United States Patent Office Board of Patent Appeals and Interferences ("Board") granting priority in an interference proceeding to Shigeru Tamai. Because the Board erred in granting Shigeru Tamai the benefit of Japanese Patent Application No. 3–068371, we reverse.

I

Christopher J. Stevens ("Stevens") and Shigeru Tamai ("Tamai") are parties to Interference No. 103,662, declared May 9, 1997. Stevens's involved U.S. Patent No. 5,393,368 ("the '368 patent") was filed February 7, 1994, and issued February 28, 1995. Tamai's involved Application No. 08/196,839 ("the '839 application") was filed February 15, 1994. The '839 application is a continuation-in-part of U.S. Patent Application No. 08/030,183 ("the '183 application"), which was filed March 29, 1993. The notice declaring the interference accorded the '839 application the benefit of the filing date of the '183 application. On the basis of the March 29, 1993 filing date, Tamai was accorded senior party status.

Both parties filed preliminary motions under 37 C.F.R. § 1.633(f), which provides that a party may file a preliminary motion "to be accorded the benefit of the filing date of an earlier filed application."* * *

Stevens' motion was based on several European applications showing a constructive reduction to practice as early as February 10, 1993. Tamai did not oppose the motion, which was granted by the Board.

Tamai's motion was based on Japanese Patent Application No. 3–68371 ("the Japanese '371 application") and PCT Application No. PCT/JP92/00947 ("the PCT '947 application"). Both applications are in Japanese. Tamai filed a translation of the Japanese '371 application with the motion. Stevens opposed the motion, arguing, inter alia, that Tamai had not met its burden of proof because the motion "failed to comply with 37 C.F.R. § 1.637" because "[n]o copies of [the Japanese '371 application] and the PCT '947 application were served with the motion pursuant to 37 C.F.R. § 1.637(f)(2) [and][n]o translation of the PCT '947 application was served with the motion pursuant to 37 C.F.R. § 1.637(f)(2)." In reply, Tamai stated that copies of the Japanese language applications, the Japanese '371 application and the PCT '947 application, while not served with the motion, were in the record. Tamai also submitted an affidavit attesting that the disclosures of the two foreign language applications were substantially the same. Importantly, with neither the original motion nor the reply did Tamai include an English language translation of the PCT '947 application and an affidavit attesting to the accuracy of the translation.

The Board denied Tamai's motion for benefit as directed to the PCT '947 application because "Tamai did not supply a translation of the PCT application." Nonetheless, the Board examined the Japanese '371 application and determined that the Japanese '371 application "is a constructive reduction to practice of the count." Accordingly, the Board entered judgment against Stevens.

Despite prevailing in the interference, Tamai requested reconsideration of that part of the Board's decision denying Tamai's motion for benefit as directed to the PCT '947 application. Tamai's request argued that the translation of the PCT '947 application was in the record because the '183 application was in the record and "the U.S. Patent and Trademark Office identified and accepted the '183 application as a translation of Tamai's foreign language PCT application." According to Tamai, the requirements of Rule 647 that "a translation of the document into English and an affidavit attesting to the accuracy of the translation" be provided, were made inconsequential in light of 37 C.F.R. § 1.639(a).* * *

The Board agreed to reconsider its final decision, but refused to modify it because, "Tamai was required to file a translation of the PCT application along with the motion. This Tamai did not do." Addressing Tamai's argument that the '183 application was the translation of the PCT '947 application, the Board noted that "Tamai did not state that the '183 application is a translation of the PCT application, attaching same, when the motion for benefit was filed." However, by not modifying its judgment, the Board affirmed its judgment in favor of Tamai. Stevens appeals the decision on reconsideration, which is a final decision of the Board. * * *

III

On appeal, Stevens argues that the Board erred in granting Tamai's motion for benefit of the Japanese '371 application. According to Stevens, the statutory limits of 35 U.S.C. § 119(a) preclude Tamai directly claiming the benefit of the Japanese '371 application because that application was filed more than one year before the '183 application. In particular, Stevens asserts that in order to obtain the benefit of the Japanese '371 application, Tamai must obtain the benefit of the intervening PCT '947 application. In Stevens' view, because Tamai failed to prove its claim for priority benefit of the PCT '947 application, and cannot therefore obtain the benefit of the Japanese '371 application, Tamai has failed to prove a constructive reduction to practice of the subject matter corresponding to the count prior to the filing date of the '183 application, March 29, 1993. Based on Stevens' preliminary motion, the Board accorded Stevens an effective filing date of February 10, 1993. Because February 10, 1993 is an earlier effective filing date than March 29, 1993, Stevens argues that he should be awarded judgment in the interference.

Tamai does not argue that his involved application can be accorded the benefit of the Japanese '371 application if he is not accorded the benefit of the PCT '947 application. Rather, Tamai supports the Board's decision in his favor by arguing that the Board erred in not according him the benefit of the PCT '947 application. In particular, Tamai argues that a preliminary motion for benefit is not required for him to be entitled to the benefit of the PCT '947 application, or, alternatively, if a motion for benefit was required, his actions in this case were sufficient to establish entitlement to the benefit of the PCT '947 application.

IV

As a matter of convenience, we first address Stevens' argument. We agree with Stevens: because Tamai failed to prove his entitlement to the benefit of the PCT '947 application, it was error for the Board to accord Tamai the benefit of the Japanese '371 application.

An interference is a proceeding instituted in the United States Patent and Trademark Office, designed to resolve questions of priority and patentability between two or more parties claiming the same patentable invention. See 35 U.S.C. § 135 (2000); 37 C.F.R. § 1.601(i) (2003). To establish priority, parties may rely on earlier filed applications because conception and constructive reduction to practice of the subject matter described in an application occur when the application is filed. See *Hyatt v. Boone*, 146 F.3d 1348, 1352 (Fed.Cir.1998); *Yasuko Kawai v. Metlesics*, 480 F.2d 880, 885–86 (CCPA 1973). If a party is entitled to rely on an earlier filed application and the specification of that application shows a constructive reduction to practice of the count, no further evidence is needed to prove invention as of the filing date of that application. See Hyatt, 146 F.3d at 1352.

A party to an interference seeking to be "accorded the benefit of the filing date of an earlier filed application" under 37 C.F.R. 1.633(f) is seeking to establish an effective filing date. See id. at 1351–52. "The effective filing date of an application is the filing date of an earlier application, benefit of which is accorded to the application under 35 U.S.C. 119, 120, 121, or 365...." 37 C.F.R. § 1.601(g); see also Hyatt, 146 F.3d at 1352 ("When a party to an interference seeks the benefit of an earlier-filed United States patent application, the earlier application must meet the requirements of 35 U.S.C. § 120...."). Section 119(a) of title 35 precludes relying on a foreign application for priority benefit when that application was filed more than one year before the filing of the corresponding U.S. application. *Schmierer v. Newton*, 55 C.C.P.A. 1362, 397 F.2d 1010, 1014–15 (CCPA 1968). Section 119(a) reads:

> (a) An application for patent for an invention filed in this country by any person who has ... filed an application for a patent for the same invention in a foreign country ... shall have the same effect as the same application would have if filed in this country on the date on which the application for patent ... was first filed in such foreign country, if the application in this country is filed within twelve months from the earliest date on which such foreign application was filed....

35 U.S.C. § 119(a) (2000).

In the matter at hand, the Board held that because Tamai did not file with his motion for benefit an English language translation of the PCT '947 application and an affidavit attesting to the accuracy of the translation, Tamai had not proven that he was entitled to be accorded the filing date of the '947 application.

Nonetheless, the Board granted Tamai's involved application the benefit of the Japanese '371 application, which was filed July 31, 1991, more than one year prior to the filing of the '183 application. Because section 119 precludes reliance on a foreign application for priority benefit when that application was filed more than one year before the filing of the corresponding U.S. application, the Board's conclusion was based on an erroneous conclusion of law, and accordingly, constituted an abuse of discretion.

D. THE TRIPS AGREEMENT

AGREEMENT ON TRADE–RELATED ASPECTS OF INTELLECTUAL PROPERTY RIGHTS

Members,

Desiring to reduce distortions and impediments to international trade, and taking into account the need to promote effective and adequate protection of intellectual property rights, and to ensure that measures and procedures to enforce intellectual property rights do not themselves become barriers to legitimate trade;

Recognizing, to this end, the need for new rules and disciplines concerning:

(a) the applicability of the basic principles of GATT 1994 and of relevant international intellectual property agreements or conventions;

(b) the provision of adequate standards and principles concerning the availability, scope and use of trade-related intellectual property rights;

(c) the provision of effective and appropriate means for the enforcement of trade-related intellectual property rights, taking into account differences in national legal systems;

(d) the provision of effective and expeditious procedures for the multilateral prevention and settlement of disputes between governments; and

(e) transitional arrangements aiming at the fullest participation in the results of the negotiations;

Recognizing the need for a multilateral framework of principles, rules and disciplines dealing with international trade in counterfeit goods;

Recognizing that intellectual property rights are private rights;

Recognizing the underlying public policy objectives of national systems for the protection of intellectual property, including developmental and technological objectives;

Recognizing also the special needs of the least-developed country Members in respect of maximum flexibility in the domestic implementation of laws and regulations in order to enable them to create a sound and viable technological base;

Emphasizing the importance of reducing tensions by reaching strengthened commitments to resolve disputes on trade-related intellectual property issues through multilateral procedures;

Desiring to establish a mutually supportive relationship between the WTO and the World Intellectual Property Organization (referred to in this Agreement as "WIPO") as well as other relevant international organizations;

Hereby agree as follows:

PART I

GENERAL PROVISIONS AND BASIC PRINCIPLES

Article 1

Nature and Scope of Obligations

1. Members shall give effect to the provisions of this Agreement. Members may, but shall not be obliged to, implement in their law more extensive protection than is required by this Agreement, provided that such protection does not contravene the provisions of this Agreement. Members shall be free to determine the appropriate method of implementing the provisions of this Agreement within their own legal system and practice.* * *

Article 3

National Treatment

1. Each Member shall accord to the nationals of other Members treatment no less favourable than that it accords to its own nationals with regard to the protection of intellectual property, subject to the exceptions already provided in, respectively, the Paris Convention (1967), the Berne Convention (1971), the Rome Convention or the Treaty on Intellectual Property in Respect of Integrated Circuits.* * *

Article 4

Most–Favoured–Nation Treatment

With regard to the protection of intellectual property, any advantage, favour, privilege or immunity granted by a Member to the nationals of any other country shall be accorded immediately and unconditionally to the nationals of all other Members. Exempted from this obligation are any advantage, favour, privilege or immunity accorded by a Member:

(a) deriving from international agreements on judicial assistance or law enforcement of a general nature and not particularly confined to the protection of intellectual property;

(b) granted in accordance with the provisions of the Berne Convention (1971) or the Rome Convention authorizing that the treatment accorded be a function not of national treatment but of the treatment accorded in another country;

(c) in respect of the rights of performers, producers of phonograms and broadcasting organizations not provided under this Agreement;

(d) deriving from international agreements related to the protection of intellectual property which entered into force prior to the entry into force of the WTO Agreement, provided that such agreements are notified to the Council for TRIPS and do not constitute an arbitrary or unjustifiable discrimination against nationals of other Members.

* * *

Article 6

Exhaustion

For the purposes of dispute settlement under this Agreement, subject to the provisions of Articles 3 and 4 nothing in this Agreement shall be used to address the issue of the exhaustion of intellectual property rights.

Article 7

Objectives

The protection and enforcement of intellectual property rights should contribute to the promotion of technological innovation and to the transfer and dissemination of technology, to the mutual advantage of producers and users of technological knowledge and in a manner conducive to social and economic welfare, and to a balance of rights and obligations.

Article 8

Principles

1. Members may, in formulating or amending their laws and regulations, adopt measures necessary to protect public health and nutrition, and to promote the public interest in sectors of vital importance to their socio-economic and technological development, provided that such measures are consistent with the provisions of this Agreement.

2. Appropriate measures, provided that they are consistent with the provisions of this Agreement, may be needed to prevent the abuse of intellectual property rights by right holders or the resort to practices which unreasonably restrain trade or adversely affect the international transfer of technology.

* * *

SECTION 5: PATENTS

Article 27

Patentable Subject Matter

1. * * *[P]atents shall be available for any inventions, whether products or processes, in all fields of technology, provided that they are new, involve an inventive step and are capable of industrial application. [P]atents shall be available and patent rights enjoyable without discrimination as to the place of invention, the field of technology and whether products are imported or locally produced.

2. Members may exclude from patentability inventions, the prevention within their territory of the commercial exploitation of which is necessary to protect *ordre public* or morality, including to protect human, animal or plant life or health or to avoid serious prejudice to the environment, provided that such exclusion is not made merely because the exploitation is prohibited by their law.

3. Members may also exclude from patentability:

   (a) diagnostic, therapeutic and surgical methods for the treatment of humans or animals;

   (b) plants and animals other than micro-organisms, and essentially biological processes for the production of plants or animals other than non-biological and microbiological processes. However, members shall provide for the protection of plant varieties either by patents or by an effective *sui generis* system or by any combination thereof. The provisions of this subparagraph shall be reviewed four years after the date of entry into force of the WTO Agreement.* * *

Article 28

Rights Conferred

1. A patent shall confer on its owner the following exclusive rights:

   (a) where the subject matter of a patent is a product, to prevent third parties not having the owner's consent from the acts of: making, using, offering for sale, selling, or importing for these purposes that product;

(b) where the subject matter of a patent is a process, to prevent third parties not having the owner's consent from the act of using the process, and from the acts of: using, offering for sale, selling, or importing for these purposes at least the product obtained directly by that process.* * *

Article 30

Exceptions to Rights Conferred

Members may provide limited exceptions to the exclusive rights conferred by a patent, provided that such exceptions do not unreasonably conflict with a normal exploitation of the patent and do not unreasonably prejudice the legitimate interests of the patent owner, taking account of the legitimate interests of third parties.

Article 31

Other Use Without Authorization of the Right Holder

Where the law of a Member allows for other use of the subject matter of a patent without the authorization of the right holder, including use by the government or third parties authorized by the government, the following provisions shall be respected:

(a) authorization of such use shall be considered on its individual merits;

(b) such use may only be permitted if, prior to such use, the proposed user has made efforts to obtain authorization from the right holder on reasonable commercial terms and conditions and that such efforts have not been successful within a reasonable period of time. This requirement may be waived by a Member in the case of a national emergency or other circumstances of extreme urgency or in cases of public non-commercial use. In situations of national emergency or other circumstances of extreme urgency, the right holder shall, nevertheless, be notified as soon as reasonably practicable. In the case of public non-commercial use, where the government or contractor, without making a patent search, knows or has demonstrable grounds to know that a valid patent is or will be used by or for the government, the right holder shall be informed promptly;

(c) the scope and duration of such use shall be limited to the purpose for which it was authorized, and in the case of semi-conductor technology shall only be for public non-commercial use or to remedy a practice determined after judicial or administrative process to be anti-competitive;

(d) such use shall be non-exclusive;

(e) such use shall be non-assignable, except with that part of the enterprise or goodwill which enjoys such use;

(f) any such use shall be authorized predominantly for the supply of the domestic market of the Member authorizing such use;

(g) authorization for such use shall be liable, subject to adequate protection of the legitimate interests of the persons so authorized, to be terminated if and when the circumstances which led to it cease to exist and are unlikely to recur. The competent authority shall have the authority to review, upon motivated request, the continued existence of these circumstances;

(h) the right holder shall be paid adequate remuneration in the circumstances of each case, taking into account the economic value of the authorization;

(i) the legal validity of any decision relating to the authorization of such use shall be subject to judicial review or other independent review by a distinct higher authority in that Member;

(j) any decision relating to the remuneration provided in respect of such use shall be subject to judicial review or other independent review by a distinct higher authority in that Member;

(k) Members are not obliged to apply the conditions set forth in subparagraphs (b) and (f) where such use is permitted to remedy a practice determined after judicial or administrative process to be anti-competitive. The need to correct anti-competitive practices may be taken into account in determining the amount of remuneration in such cases. Competent authorities shall have the authority to refuse termination of authorization if and when the conditions which led to such authorization are likely to recur;

(l) where such use is authorized to permit the exploitation of a patent ("the second patent") which cannot be exploited without infringing another patent ("the first patent"), the following additional conditions shall apply:

    (i) the invention claimed in the second patent shall involve an important technical advance of considerable economic significance in relation to the invention claimed in the first patent;

    (ii) the owner of the first patent shall be entitled to a cross-licence on reasonable terms to use the invention claimed in the second patent; and

(iii) the use authorized in respect of the first patent shall be non-assignable except with the assignment of the second patent.

* * *

Article 33

Term of Protection

The term of protection available shall not end before the expiration of a period of twenty years counted from the filing date.

WTO MINISTERIAL DECLARATION
Adopted on 14 November 2001
WT/MIN(01)/DEC/1
20 November 2001

1.   The multilateral trading system embodied in the World Trade Organization has contributed significantly to economic growth, development and employment throughout the past fifty years. We are determined, particularly in the light of the global economic slowdown, to maintain the process of reform and liberalization of trade policies, thus ensuring that the system plays its full part in promoting recovery, growth and development. We therefore strongly reaffirm the principles and objectives set out in the Marrakesh Agreement Establishing the World Trade Organization, and pledge to reject the use of protectionism.

2.   International trade can play a major role in the promotion of economic development and the alleviation of poverty. We recognize the need for all our peoples to benefit from the increased opportunities and welfare gains that the multilateral trading system generates. The majority of WTO Members are developing countries. We seek to place their needs and interests at the heart of the Work Programme adopted in this Declaration. Recalling the Preamble to the Marrakesh Agreement, we shall continue to make positive efforts designed to ensure that developing countries, and especially the least-developed among them, secure a share in the growth of world trade commensurate with the needs of their economic development. In this context, enhanced market access, balanced rules, and well targeted, sustainably financed technical assistance and capacity-building programmes have important roles to play.

3.   We recognize the particular vulnerability of the least-developed countries and the special structural difficulties they face in the global economy. We are committed to addressing the marginalization of least-developed countries in international trade and to improving their effective participation in the multilateral trading system. We recall the commitments made by Ministers at our

meetings in Marrakesh, Singapore and Geneva, and by the international community at the Third UN Conference on Least–Developed Countries in Brussels, to help least-developed countries secure beneficial and meaningful integration into the multilateral trading system and the global economy. We are determined that the WTO will play its part in building effectively on these commitments under the Work Programme we are establishing.

4.   We stress our commitment to the WTO as the unique forum for global trade rule-making and liberalization, while also recognizing that regional trade agreements can play an important role in promoting the liberalization and expansion of trade and in fostering development.

5.   We are aware that the challenges Members face in a rapidly changing international environment cannot be addressed through measures taken in the trade field alone. We shall continue to work with the Bretton Woods institutions for greater coherence in global economic policy-making.

6.   We strongly reaffirm our commitment to the objective of sustainable development, as stated in the Preamble to the Marrakesh Agreement. We are convinced that the aims of upholding and safeguarding an open and non-discriminatory multilateral trading system, and acting for the protection of the environment and the promotion of sustainable development can and must be mutually supportive. We take note of the efforts by Members to conduct national environmental assessments of trade policies on a voluntary basis. We recognize that under WTO rules no country should be prevented from taking measures for the protection of human, animal or plant life or health, or of the environment at the levels it considers appropriate, subject to the requirement that they are not applied in a manner which would constitute a means of arbitrary or unjustifiable discrimination between countries where the same conditions prevail, or a disguised restriction on international trade, and are otherwise in accordance with the provisions of the WTO Agreements. We welcome the WTOs continued cooperation with UNEP and other inter-governmental environmental organizations. We encourage efforts to promote cooperation between the WTO and relevant international environmental and developmental organizations, especially in the lead-up to the World Summit on Sustainable Development to be held in Johannesburg, South Africa, in September 2002.

7.   We reaffirm the right of Members under the General Agreement on Trade in Services to regulate, and to introduce new regulations on, the supply of services.

8.   We reaffirm our declaration made at the Singapore Ministerial Conference regarding internationally recognized core labour stan-

dards. We take note of work under way in the International Labour Organization (ILO) on the social dimension of globalization.

9.   We note with particular satisfaction that this Conference has completed the WTO accession procedures for China and Chinese Taipei. We also welcome the accession as new Members, since our last Session, of Albania, Croatia, Georgia, Jordan, Lithuania, Moldova and Oman, and note the extensive market-access commitments already made by these countries on accession. These accessions will greatly strengthen the multilateral trading system, as will those of the 28 countries now negotiating their accession. We therefore attach great importance to concluding accession proceedings as quickly as possible. In particular, we are committed to accelerating the accession of least-developed countries.

10.   Recognizing the challenges posed by an expanding WTO membership, we confirm our collective responsibility to ensure internal transparency and the effective participation of all Members. While emphasizing the intergovernmental character of the organization, we are committed to making the WTO's operations more transparent, including through more effective and prompt dissemination of information, and to improve dialogue with the public. We shall therefore at the national and multilateral levels continue to promote a better public understanding of the WTO and to communicate the benefits of a liberal, rules-based multilateral trading system.

11.   In view of these considerations, we hereby agree to undertake the broad and balanced Work Programme set out below. This incorporates both an expanded negotiating agenda and other important decisions and activities necessary to address the challenges facing the multilateral trading system.

WORK PROGRAMME

* * *

TRADE–RELATED ASPECTS OF INTELLECTUAL PROPERTY RIGHTS

17.   We stress the importance we attach to implementation and interpretation of the Agreement on Trade–Related Aspects of Intellectual Property Rights (TRIPS Agreement) in a manner supportive of public health, by promoting both access to existing medicines and research and development into new medicines and, in this connection, are adopting a separate Declaration.

18.   With a view to completing the work started in the Council for Trade–Related Aspects of Intellectual Property Rights (Council for TRIPS) on the implementation of Article 23.4, we agree to negotiate the establishment of a multilateral system of notification and registration of geographical indications for wines and spirits by the

Fifth Session of the Ministerial Conference. We note that issues related to the extension of the protection of geographical indications provided for in Article 23 to products other than wines and spirits will be addressed in the Council for TRIPS pursuant to paragraph 12 of this Declaration.

19. We instruct the Council for TRIPS, in pursuing its work programme including under the review of Article 27.3(b), the review of the implementation of the TRIPS Agreement under Article 71.1 and the work foreseen pursuant to paragraph 12 of this Declaration, to examine, *inter alia*, the relationship between the TRIPS Agreement and the Convention on Biological Diversity, the protection of traditional knowledge and folklore, and other relevant new developments raised by Members pursuant to Article 71.1. In undertaking this work, the TRIPS Council shall be guided by the objectives and principles set out in Articles 7 and 8 of the TRIPS Agreement and shall take fully into account the development dimension.

RELATIONSHIP BETWEEN TRADE AND INVESTMENT

20. Recognizing the case for a multilateral framework to secure transparent, stable and predictable conditions for long-term cross-border investment, particularly foreign direct investment, that will contribute to the expansion of trade, and the need for enhanced technical assistance and capacity-building in this area as referred to in paragraph 21, we agree that negotiations will take place after the Fifth Session of the Ministerial Conference on the basis of a decision to be taken, by explicit consensus, at that Session on modalities of negotiations.

21. We recognize the needs of developing and least-developed countries for enhanced support for technical assistance and capacity building in this area, including policy analysis and development so that they may better evaluate the implications of closer multilateral cooperation for their development policies and objectives, and human and institutional development. To this end, we shall work in cooperation with other relevant intergovernmental organisations, including UNCTAD, and through appropriate regional and bilateral channels, to provide strengthened and adequately resourced assistance to respond to these needs.

22. In the period until the Fifth Session, further work in the Working Group on the Relationship Between Trade and Investment will focus on the clarification of: scope and definition; transparency; non-discrimination; modalities for pre-establishment commitments based on a GATS-type, positive list approach; development provisions; exceptions and balance-of-payments safeguards; consultation

and the settlement of disputes between Members. Any framework should reflect in a balanced manner the interests of home and host countries, and take due account of the development policies and objectives of host governments as well as their right to regulate in the public interest. The special development, trade and financial needs of developing and least-developed countries should be taken into account as an integral part of any framework, which should enable Members to undertake obligations and commitments commensurate with their individual needs and circumstances. Due regard should be paid to other relevant WTO provisions. Account should be taken, as appropriate, of existing bilateral and regional arrangements on investment.

INTERACTION BETWEEN TRADE AND COMPETITION POLICY

23. Recognizing the case for a multilateral framework to enhance the contribution of competition policy to international trade and development, and the need for enhanced technical assistance and capacity-building in this area as referred to in paragraph 24, we agree that negotiations will take place after the Fifth Session of the Ministerial Conference on the basis of a decision to be taken, by explicit consensus, at that Session on modalities of negotiations.

24. We recognize the needs of developing and least-developed countries for enhanced support for technical assistance and capacity building in this area, including policy analysis and development so that they may better evaluate the implications of closer multilateral cooperation for their development policies and objectives, and human and institutional development. To this end, we shall work in cooperation with other relevant intergovernmental organisations, including UNCTAD, and through appropriate regional and bilateral channels, to provide strengthened and adequately resourced assistance to respond to these needs.

25. In the period until the Fifth Session, further work in the Working Group on the Interaction between Trade and Competition Policy will focus on the clarification of: core principles, including transparency, non-discrimination and procedural fairness, and provisions on hardcore cartels; modalities for voluntary cooperation; and support for progressive reinforcement of competition institutions in developing countries through capacity building. Full account shall be taken of the needs of developing and least-developed country participants and appropriate flexibility provided to address them.

CANADA—PATENT PROTECTION OF PHARMACEUTICAL PRODUCTS

Report of the Panel
WT/DS114/R
17 March 2000

VII. FINDINGS

A. MEASURES AT ISSUE

7.1   At issue in this dispute is the conformity of two provisions of Canada's Patent Act with Canada's obligations under the Agreement on Trade–Related Aspects of Intellectual Property Rights ("the TRIPS Agreement"). The two provisions in dispute, Sections 55.2(1) and 55.2(2) of the Patent Act, create exceptions to the exclusive rights of patent owners. Under Article 28.1 of the TRIPS Agreement, patent owners shall have the right to exclude others from making, using, selling, offering for sale or importing the patented product during the term of the patent. According to Article 33 of the TRIPS Agreement, the term of protection available shall not end before the expiration of a period of 20 years counted from the filing date of the application against which the patent was granted. Sections 55.2(1) and 55.2(2) allow third parties to make, use or sell the patented product during the term of the patent without the consent of the patent owner in certain defined circumstances.

(1) SECTION 55.2(1): THE REGULATORY REVIEW EXCEPTION

7.2   Section 55.2(1) provides as follows:

"It is not an infringement of a patent for any person to make, construct, use or sell the patented invention solely for uses reasonably related to the development and submission of information required under any law of Canada, a province or a country other than Canada that regulates the manufacture, construction, use or sale of any product."

Section 55.2(1) is known as the "regulatory review exception". It applies to patented products such as pharmaceuticals whose marketing is subject to government regulation in order to assure their safety or effectiveness. The purpose of the regulatory review exception is to permit potential competitors of the patent owner to obtain government marketing approval during the term of the patent, so that they will have regulatory permission to sell in competition with the patent owner by the date on which the patent expires. Without the regulatory review exception, the patent owner might be able to prevent potential competitors from using the patented product during the term of the patent to comply with testing requirements, so that competitors would have to wait until the patent expires before they could begin the process of obtaining marketing approval. This, in turn, would prevent potential competitors from entering the market for the additional time required to complete the regulatory approval process, in effect extending the patent owner's period of market exclusivity beyond the end of the term of the patent.

* * *

(2) SECTION 55.2(2): THE STOCKPILING EXCEPTION

7.7   Section 55.2(2) of the Patent Act, which is referred to as "the stockpiling exception", reads as follows:

> "It is not an infringement of a patent for any person who makes, constructs, uses or sells a patented invention in accordance with subsection (1) to make, construct or use the invention, during the applicable period provided for by the regulations, for the manufacture and storage of articles intended for sale after the date on which the term of the patent expires."

The provision allows competitors to manufacture and stockpile patented goods during a certain period before the patent expires, but the goods cannot be sold until the patent expires. Without this exception, the patent owner's right to exclude any person from "making" or "using" the patented good would enable the patent owner to prevent all such stockpiling.

7.8   The exception created by Section 55.2(2) does not become effective until implementing regulations are issued. The only regulations issued to date under the stockpiling exception have been regulations making the exception operative with regard to pharmaceutical products. The period during which pharmaceutical products. The period during which pharmaceutical products can be made and stockpiled is six months immediately prior to the expiration of the patent.

7.9   The text of Section 55.2(2) gives permission only to "make, construct or use" the patented product for purposes of stockpiling. In answer to a question from the Panel, however, Canada has taken the position that the exception will be construed also to allow the "sale" of patented ingredients that have been ordered by a producer who is stockpiling the final patented product—for example, with regard to pharmaceuticals, sales by fine chemical producers of active ingredients ordered by the generic producer.

E.   SECTION 55.2(2) (THE STOCKPILING EXCEPTION)

(1) APPLICATION OF ARTICLE 28.1 AND ARTICLE 30 OF THE TRIPS AGREEMENT

* * *

7.19   The TRIPS Agreement contains two provisions authorizing exceptions to the exclusionary patent rights laid down in Article 28—Articles 30 and 31. Of these two, Article 30—the so-called limited exceptions provision—has been invoked by Canada in the present case. It reads as follows:

"Exceptions to Rights Conferred

"Members may provide limited exceptions to the exclusive rights conferred by a patent, provided that such exceptions do not unreasonably conflict with the normal exploitation of the patent and do not unreasonably prejudice the legitimate interests of the patent owner, taking account of the legitimate interests of third parties."

7.20   Both parties agreed upon the basic structure of Article 30. Article 30 establishes three criteria that must be met in order to qualify for an exception: (1) the exception must be "limited"; (2) the exception must not "unreasonably conflict with normal exploitation of the patent"; (3) the exception must not "unreasonably prejudice the legitimate interests of the patent owner, taking account of the legitimate interests of third parties". The three conditions are cumulative, each being a separate and independent requirement that must be satisfied. Failure to comply with any one of the three conditions results in the Article 30 exception being disallowed.

* * *

(c) "Limited Exceptions"

7.27   Canada asserted that the word "limited" should be interpreted according to the conventional dictionary definition, such as "confined within definite limits", or "restricted in scope, extent, amount". Canada argued that the stockpiling exception in Section 55.2(2) is restricted in scope because it has only a limited impact on a patent owner's rights. The stockpiling exception, Canada noted, does not affect the patent owner's right to an exclusive market for "commercial" sales during the patent term, since the product that is manufactured and stockpiled during the final six months of the term cannot be sold in competition with the patent owner until the patent expires. By "commercial sales", Canada clearly meant sales to the ultimate consumer, because it acknowledged that sales of patented ingredients to producers engaged in authorized stockpiling is permitted. Thus, Canada was arguing that an exception is "limited" as long as the exclusive right to sell to the ultimate consumer during the term of the patent is preserved. In addition, Canada also claimed that the exception is further limited by the six-month duration of the exception, and by the fact that it can be used only by persons that have made, constructed or used the invention under Section 55.2(1).

7.28 The EC interpreted the word "limited" to connote a narrow exception, one that could be described by words such as "narrow, small, minor, insignificant or restricted". The EC measured the "limited" quality of the proposed exception by reference to its impact on the exclusionary rights granted to the patent owner under Article 28.1. Applying that measure, the EC contended that the stockpiling exception is not "limited" because it takes away three of the five Article 28.1 rights—the rights to exclude "making", "using" and "importing". The EC argued that the impairment of three out of five basic rights is in itself extensive enough to be considered "not limited". The EC further contended that limitation of the exception to the last six months of the patent term does not constitute a limited impairment of rights when six months is taken as a percentage of the 20–year patent term, and especially not when taken as a percentage of the actual eight to 12–year period of effective market exclusivity enjoyed by most patented pharmaceuticals. In addition, the EC noted, there was no limitation on the quantities that could be produced during this period, nor any limitation on the markets in which such products could be sold. Finally, the EC pointed out that no royalty fees are due for such production, and that the patent holder does not even have a right to be informed of the use of the patent.

* * *

7.30 The Panel agreed with the EC that, as used in this context, the word "limited" has a narrower connotation than the rather broad definitions cited by Canada. Although the word itself can have both broad and narrow definitions, the narrower being indicated by examples such as "a mail train taking only a limited number of passengers", the narrower definition is the more appropriate when the word "limited" is used as part of the phrase "limited exception". The word "exception" by itself connotes a limited derogation, one that does not undercut the body of rules from which it is made. When a treaty uses the term "limited exception", the word "limited" must be given a meaning separate from the limitation implicit in the word "exception" itself. The term "limited exception" must therefore be read to connote a narrow exception—one which makes only a small diminution of the rights in question.

7.31   The Panel agreed with the EC interpretation that "limited" is to be measured by the extent to which the exclusive rights of the patent owner have been curtailed. The full text of Article 30 refers to "limited exceptions to the exclusive rights conferred by a patent". In the absence of other indications, the Panel concluded that it would be justified in reading the text literally, focusing on the extent to which legal rights have been curtailed, rather than the size or extent of the economic impact. In support of this conclusion, the Panel noted that the following two conditions of Article 30 ask more particularly about the economic impact of the exception, and provide two sets of standards by which such impact may be judged. The term "limited exceptions" is the only one of the three conditions in Article 30 under which the extent of the curtailment of rights as such is dealt with.

* * *

F.   SECTION 55.2(1) (THE REGULATORY REVIEW EXCEPTION)

* * *

(a) "Limited Exceptions"

* * *

7.45   In the Panel's view, however, Canada's regulatory review exception is a "limited exception" within the meaning of TRIPS Article 30. It is "limited" because of the narrow scope of its curtailment of Article 28.1 rights. As long as the exception is confined to conduct needed to comply with the requirements of the regulatory approval process, the extent of the acts unauthorized by the right holder that are permitted by it will be small and narrowly bounded. Even though regulatory approval processes may require substantial amounts of test production to demonstrate reliable manufacturing, the patent owner's rights themselves are not impaired any further by the size of such production runs, as long as they are solely for regulatory purposes and no commercial use is made of resulting final products.

7.46   The Panel found no basis for believing that activities seeking product approvals under foreign regulatory procedures would be any less subject to these limitations. There is no a priori basis to assume that the requirements of foreign regulatory procedures will require activities unrelated to legitimate objectives of product quality and safety, nor has the EC provided any evidence to that effect. Nor is there any reason to assume that Canadian law would apply the exception in cases where foreign requirements clearly had no regulatory purpose. Nor, finally, is there any reason to assume that it will be any more difficult to enforce the requirements of Canadian law when Canadian producers claim exceptions under foreign procedures. With regard to the latter point, the Panel concurred with Canada's point that the government is not normally expected to regulate the actual conduct of third parties in such cases. The enforcement of these conditions, as with other enforcement of patent rights, occurs by means of private infringement actions brought by the patent owner. The patent owner merely has to prove that the challenged conduct is inconsistent with the basic patent rights created by national law. Once that initial case is made, the burden will be on the party accused of infringement to prove its defence by establishing that its conduct with respect to foreign regulatory procedures was in compliance with the conditions of Section 55.2(1).

7.47 In reaching this conclusion, the Panel also considered Canada's additional arguments that both the negotiating history of Article 30 of the TRIPS Agreement and the subsequent practices of certain WTO Member governments supported the view that Article 30 was understood to permit regulatory review exceptions similar to Section 55.2(1). The Panel did not accord any weight to either of those arguments, however, because there was no documented evidence of the claimed negotiating understanding, and because the subsequent acts by individual countries did not constitute "practice in the application of the treaty which establishes the agreement of the parties regarding its interpretation" within the meaning of Article 31.3(b) of the Vienna Convention.

7.48 A final objection to the Panel's general conclusion remains to be addressed. Although the point was raised only briefly in the parties' legal arguments, the Panel was compelled to acknowledge that the economic impact of the regulatory review exception could be considerable. According to information supplied by Canada itself, in the case of patented pharmaceutical products approximately three to six-and-a-half years are required for generic drug producers to develop and obtain regulatory approval for their products. If there were no regulatory review exception allowing competitors to apply for regulatory approval during the term of the patent, therefore, the patent owner would be able to extend its period of market exclusivity, de facto, for some part of that three to six-and-half year period, depending on how much, if any, of the development process could be performed during the term of the patent under other exceptions, such as the scientific or experimental use exception. The Panel believed it was necessary to ask whether measures having such a significant impact on the economic interests of patent owners could be called a "limited" exception to patent rights.

7.49 After analysing all three conditions stated in Article 30 of the TRIPS Agreement, the Panel was satisfied that Article 30 does in fact address the issue of economic impact, but only in the other two conditions contained in that Article. As will be seen in the analysis of these other conditions below, the other two conditions deal with the issue of economic impact, according to criteria that relate specifically to that issue. Viewing all three conditions as a whole, it is apparent that the first condition ("limited exception") is neither designed nor intended to address the issue of economic impact directly.

7.50   In sum, the Panel found that the regulatory review exception of Section 55.2(1) is a "limited exception" within the meaning of Article 30 of the TRIPS Agreement.

(b) "Normal Exploitation"

* * *

7.54   The Panel considered that "exploitation" refers to the commercial activity by which patent owners employ their exclusive patent rights to extract economic value from their patent. The term "normal" defines the kind of commercial activity Article 30 seeks to protect. The ordinary meaning of the word "normal" is found in the dictionary definition: "regular, usual, typical, ordinary, conventional". As so defined, the term can be understood to refer either to an empirical conclusion about what is common within a relevant community, or to a normative standard of entitlement. The Panel concluded that the words "normal" was being used in Article 30 in a sense that combined the two meanings.

* * *

7.57   The Panel considered that Canada was on firmer ground, however, in arguing that the additional period of de facto market exclusivity created by using patent rights to preclude submissions for regulatory authorization should not be considered "normal". The additional period of market exclusivity in this situation is not a natural or normal consequence of enforcing patent rights. It is an unintended consequence of the conjunction of the patent laws with product regulatory laws, where the combination of patent rights with the time demands of the regulatory process gives a greater than normal period of market exclusivity to the enforcement of certain patent rights. It is likewise a form of exploitation that most patent owners do not in fact employ. For the vast majority of patented products, there is no marketing regulation of the kind covered by Section 55.2(1), and thus there is no possibility to extend patent exclusivity by delaying the marketing approval process for competitors.

7.58   The Panel could not agree with the EC's assertion that the mere existence of the patent owner's rights to exclude was a sufficient reason, by itself, for treating all gains derived from such rights as flowing from "normal exploitation". In the Panel's view, the EC's argument contained no evidence or analysis addressed to the various meanings of "normal"—neither a demonstration most patent owners extract the value of their patents in the manner barred by Section 55.2(1), nor an argument that the prohibited manner of exploitation was "normal" in the sense of being essential to the achievement of the goals of patent policy. To the contrary, the EC's focus on the exclusionary rights themselves merely restated the concern to protect Article 28 exclusionary rights as such. This is a concern already dealt with by the first condition of Article 30 ("limited exception") and the Panel found the ultimate EC arguments here impossible to distinguish from the arguments it had made under that first condition.

* * *

7.59 In sum, the Panel found that the regulatory review exception of Section 55.2(1) does not conflict with a normal exploitation of patents, within the meaning of the second condition of Article 30 of the TRIPS Agreement. The fact that no conflict has been found makes it unnecessary to consider the question of whether, if a conflict were found, the conflict would be "unreasonable". Accordingly, it is also unnecessary to determine whether or not the final phrase of Article 30, calling for consideration of the legitimate interests of third parties, does or does not apply to the determination of "unreasonable conflict" under the second condition of Article 30.

(c) "Legitimate Interests"

* * *

7.61 The ultimate issue with regard to the regulatory review exception's compliance with the third condition of Article 30 involved similar considerations to those arising under the second condition ("normal exploitation")—the fact that the exception would remove the additional period of de facto market exclusivity that patent owners could achieve if they were permitted to employ their rights to exclude "making" and "using" (and "selling") the patented product during the term of the patent to prevent potential competitors from preparing and/or applying for regulatory approval during the term of the patent. The issue was whether patent owners could claim a "legitimate interest" in the economic benefits that could be derived from such an additional period of de facto market exclusivity and, if so, whether the regulatory review exception "unreasonably prejudiced" that interest.

* * *

7.69 To make sense of the term "legitimate interests" in this context, that term must be defined in the way that it is often used in legal discourse—as a normative claim calling for protection of interests that are "justifiable" in the sense that they are supported by relevant public policies or other social norms. This is the sense of the word that often appears in statements such as "X has no legitimate interest in being able to do Y". We may take as an illustration one of the most widely adopted Article 30–type exceptions in national patent laws—the exception under which use of the patented product for scientific experimentation, during the term of the patent and without consent, is not an infringement. It is often argued that this exception is based on the notion that a key public policy purpose underlying patent laws is to facilitate the dissemination and advancement of technical knowledge and that allowing the patent owner to prevent experimental use during the term of the patent would frustrate part of the purpose of the requirement that the nature of the invention be disclosed to the public. To the contrary, the argument concludes, under the policy of the patent laws, both society and the scientist have a "legitimate interest" in using the patent disclosure to support the advanced of science and technology. While the Panel draws no conclusion about the correctness of any such national exceptions in terms of Article 30 of the TRIPS Agreement, it does adopt the general meaning of the term "legitimate interests" contained in legal analysis of this type.

* * *

7.73   In sum, after consideration of the ordinary meaning of the term "legitimate interests", as it is used in Article 30, the Panel was unable to accept the EC's interpretation of that term as referring to legal interests pursuant to Article 28.1. Accordingly, the Panel was unable the accept the primary EC argument with regard to the third condition of Article 30. It found that the EC argument based solely on the patent owner's legal rights pursuant to Article 28.1, without reference to any more particular normative claims of interest, did not raise a relevant claim of non-compliance with the third condition of Article 30.

* * *

7.80   In the present proceeding, Canada explicitly disputed the legitimacy of the claimed interest. As noted above, Canada appeared to interpret the term "legitimate interests" in accordance with the Panel's view of that term as a widely recognized normative standard. Canada asserted:

> "[N]otwithstanding the private economic advantage that would be obtained by doing so, a patentee can have no legitimate interest deriving from patent law in exercising its exclusive use and enforcement rights within the term of protection to achieve, through exploitation of regulatory re-

view laws, a de facto extension of that term of
protection beyond the prescribed period, thereby
unilaterally altering the bargain between the patentee and society. In this respect, the interests of
a patentee of a pharmaceutical invention can be
no different from those of patentees in other fields
of technology."

7.81   Canada's argument that all fields of technology must be
treated the same implicitly rejected the EC's argument that those
fields of technology affected by marketing approval requirements
should be given certain additional marketing advantages in compensation. Canada was asked by the Panel to explain the distinction
between its decision in Section 55.2(1) to remove the delay in
obtaining marketing approval for competitive producers seeking to
enter the market after the patent expires and its decision not to
correct or compensate for the similar delay encountered by the
patent owner himself. Canada responded that the de facto diminution of the market exclusivity for patent owners was an unavoidable
consequence of the time required to ensure and to demonstrate the
safety and efficacy of the product, whereas the delay imposed on
competitors by use of the patent rights to block product development and initiation of the regulatory review process during the
term of the patent was neither necessary to product safety nor
otherwise an appropriate use of patent rights. Canada's answer
implied a further question as to the extent to which the marketing
delays experienced by patent owners were in fact the result of
government regulatory action, as opposed to the normal consequence of the necessary course of product development for products
of this kind.

7.82   On balance, the Panel concluded that in interest claimed on
behalf of patent owners whose effective period of market exclusivity
had been reduced by delays in marketing approval was neither so
compelling nor so widely recognized that it could be regarded as a
"legitimate interest" within the meaning of Article 30 of the TRIPS
Agreement. Notwithstanding the number of governments that had
responded positively to that claimed interest by granting compensatory patent terms extensions, the issue itself was of relatively
recent standing, and the community of governments was obviously
still divided over the merits of such claims. Moreover, the Panel
believed that it was significant that concerns about regulatory
review exceptions in general, although well known at the time of
the TRIPS negotiations, were apparently not clear enough, or
compelling enough, to make their ways explicitly into the recorded
agenda of the TRIPS negotiations. The Panel believed that Article
30's "legitimate interests" concept should not be used to decide,

through adjudication, a normative policy issue that is still obviously a matter of unresolved political debate.

* * *

7.84   Having reviewed the conformity of Section 55.2(1) with each of the three conditions for an exception under Article 30 of the TRIPS Agreement, the Panel concluded that Section 55.2(1) does satisfy all three conditions of Article 30, and thus is not inconsistent with Canada's obligations under Article 28.1 of the TRIPS Agreement.

* * *

VIII.   CONCLUSIONS

8.1   In light of the findings above, the Panel has concluded as follows:

(1) Section 55.2(1) of Canada's Patent Act is not consistent with Canada's obligations under Article 27.1 and Article 28.1 of the TRIPS Agreement.

(2) Section 55.2(2) of Canada's Patent Act is not consistent with the requirements of Article 28.1 of the TRIPS Agreement.

Accordingly, the Panel recommends that the Dispute Settlement Body request that Canada bring Section 55.2(2) into conformity with Canada's obligations under the TRIPS Agreement.

Notes and Questions

1.   The concept of Paris priority is an important one for global patent practice. The U.S. is unusual in distinguishing between offensive and defensive use of Paris priority. This distinction arises in part because of the limitation under Section 102(e) to applications filed within the United States. Does this distinction work against harmonization of global patent law? Or does it reflect the role for national experimentation in determining such matters as novelty and nonobviousness and the scope of the prior art?

2.   The Patent Cooperation treaty is an important procedural mechanism for streamlining global patent prosecution. Note in the *Stevens* case the implications of the Patent Cooperation Treaty for the use of the PCT application to establish priority. Is the decision in *Stevens* consistent with *Hilmer*? Note that the patent applicant was making offensive use of the foreign application.

3.   The TRIPS Agreement will arise throughout this book. The goal of TRIPS is harmonization of national patent laws. Is there any room for experimentation under TRIPS? IS the Doha Declaration consistent with the international trade and harmonization goals of TRIPS? Does the WTO Dispute Resolution Process provide a fair and adequate means for harmonization? In reading the *Canada Pharmaceutical*

opinion, think about what leeway the TRIPS Agreement provides for countries to provide different scope of patent rights. Is the opinion too lenient?

Chapter 3

PATENTABLE SUBJECT MATTER

A. PATENTABLE SUBJECT MATTER UNDER TRIPS

TRIPS Article 27 contains a general provision that governs the scope of information subject to patent protection, stating, "patents shall be available for any inventions, whether products or processes, in all fields of technology, provided that they are new, involve an inventive step and are capable of industrial application." In addition, subject to certain exclusions, this Article reads, "patents shall be available and patent rights enjoyable without discrimination as to the place of invention, the field of technology and whether products are imported or locally produced." Some highlights are:

- The scope of patentable subject matter is subject to the mandatory "shall," therefore members *must* permit patents to be granted for "any inventions, whether products or processes;"

- Patentable subject matter encompasses "all fields of technology," which prohibits members from excluding certain subject matters (i.e., chemical) from protection. This is underscored by the language "patents shall be available and patent rights enjoyable without discrimination as to ... the field of technology;"

- A member cannot discriminate because the inventive activity occurred on foreign soil or whether the products made under the patent are made elsewhere;

- The TRIPS Agreement states that members may exclude patent protection where the commercial exploitation of an invention within a member's territory must be prevented "to protect ordre public or morality, including to protect human, animal or plant life or health or to avoid serious prejudice to the environment, provided that such exclusion is not made merely because the exploitation is prohibited by their law."

Additionally, TRIPS allows members to exclude from patentability "diagnostic, therapeutic and surgical methods for the treatment of humans or animals," as well as for plants and animals. Do U.S. patentability standards conform to these measures?

B. CHEMICALS AND BIOTECHNOLOGICAL SUBJECT MATTER

Patent protection for pharmaceuticals presents extremely difficult policy choices. As a practical matter, new drugs are expensive to develop. One estimate places these costs between $403 to $802 million to develop a drug to the point of marketing approval. Joseph A. DiMasi, Ronald W. Hansen & Henry G. Grabowski, *The Price of Innovation: New Estimates of Drug Development Costs*, 22 J. Health Econ. 151 (2003). Others dispute this figure, including the consumer advocacy group Public Citizen, which has issued a report that estimates the figure to be much closer to $110 million. Public Citizen, Rx R & D Myths: The Case Against the Drug Industry's R & D "Scare Card" (2001). Moreover, this report observes that the U.S. National Institute of Health, a taxpayer funded agency, spends billions of dollars annually on health care research projects that provide key findings to pharmaceutical companies to guide commercial research. *Id.* at 8. Regardless, even lower estimates demonstrate that drug discovery requires investment. Pharmaceutical companies have maintained that robust patent protection is necessary to recoup these costs and to create new drugs. In the absence of such protection, generic drug makers would undersell—and thereby displace—originators who first undertook the risk and research needed to derive the solution.

Governments that prioritize access to medicine prefer the generic cost competition to ease the strain on public health budgets and lowers prices to insurers and consumers. In contrast, originator companies seek to maintain higher prices against generics by using methods to increase the duration and breadth of patent protection. One of the methods is referred to as "evergreening." A pharmaceutical company engages in evergreening when it files a series of patent applications to cover different attributes of the same product or variations of the initial substance (such as an improvement to the first formulation) to extend patent protection for multiple subsequent terms. At the same time, the originating company markets these improved formulations to doctors and patients. If this strategy is successful, generic drug companies may be required to wait until the last of these patents expire to compete with the originator. Pharmaceutical companies have asserted that these practices are the natural result of incremental innovation. A recent inquiry into the pharmaceutical sector in Europe uncovered some doubts about the practice:

> Incremental research is important as it can lead to significant improvements of existing products, also from the perspective of the patients.... In the course of the sector inquiry generic companies and consumer associations sometimes questioned the actual improvement of certain categories of changes, in particular with respect to their therapeutic benefits.

> The findings of the inquiry suggest that for 40% of the medicines in the sample selected for in depth investigation, which had lost exclusivity between 2000 and 2007, originator companies launched second generation or follow-on medicines. Nearly 60% of the patent related litigation cases between originator and generic companies examined in the context of the inquiry concern medicines that moved from first to second generation products.

> The launch of a second generation product can be a scenario in which an originator company might want to make use of instruments that delay the market entry of generic products corresponding to the first generation product. The companies have an incentive to do so in order to avoid generic exposure for the second generation product.

See COMM'N OF THE EUROPEAN COMMUNITIES, PHARMACEUTICAL SECTOR INQUIRY FINAL REPORT 14–15 (2009).

The following opinion considers patent protection for pharmaceuticals by the Madras High Court in India. The pharmaceutical at issue is Novartis AG's anti-cancer drug Glivec (referred to as "Gleevec" in India). Glivec does not cure cancer; rather the drug halts the disease's progression. Thus, Glivec must be taken continuously for the remainder of a patient's life. *See* Stefan Ecks, *Global Pharmaceutical Markets and Corporate Citizenship: The Case of Novartis' Anti-cancer Drug Glivec*, BIOSOCIETIES, 3, 165–181 (2008). Because the price far exceeds the per capita average income within that nation, one source concluded that, "[a] middle-class family might be able to scrape together the money needed for a year's worth of treatment, but could never afford it for a lifetime." *Id.* at 76. Indeed, Novartis has instituted the Gleevec/Glivec International Patient Assistance Program to provide the drug for patients who cannot afford it.

Novartis first developed the active ingredient in Givec in 1993, at a time when India did not grant patent protection to drug molecules. India's exclusion was founded in the nation's Patent Act of 1970, and was based in part on the view that "such important articles of daily use as medicine ... are vital to the health of the community [and] should be made available to everyone at reasonable prices and that no monopoly should be granted in respect to such articles." N. RAJOGAPALA AYYANGAR, REPORT ON THE REVISION OF THE PATENTS LAW 41 (1959). As a result, India developed expertise reverse engineering and manufacturing pharmaceuticals. As one commentator observed, "[b]y deliberately excluding pharmaceutical products from patent protection for the previous 34 years, India became a world leader in high-quality generic drug manufacturing." Janice M. Mueller, *The Tiger Awakens: The Tumultuous Transformation of India's Patent System and the Rise of Indian Pharmaceutical Innovations*, 68 U. PITT. L. REV. 491, 495 (2006).

After India joined the WTO in 1995, India became obligated to implement TRIPS minimum requirements for patent protection. In 1997, Novartis began filing patent applications worldwide for a second generation Glivec compound, a beta-crystalline form of imatinib mesylate, asserting that this beta version was superior to the first. In 2006, Novatis' application was denied by the Chennai Patent Office under Section 3(d) of the Indian Patents (Amendment) Act of 2005, which states under the title "Inventions Not Patentable":

3. What are not inventions.—The following are not inventions within the meaning of this Act . . . . .

(d) the mere discovery of a new form of a known substance which do not result in the enhancement of the known efficacy of that substance or the mere discovery of any new property or new use for a known substance or the mere use of a known process, machine or apparatus unless such known process results in a new product or employs at least one new reactant.

Explanation: For the purposes of this clause, salts, esters, ethers, polymorphs, metabolites, pure form, particle size, isomers, mixtures of isomers, complexes, combinations and other derivatives of known substance shall be considered to be the same substance, unless they differ significantly in properties with regard to efficacy.

Novartis filed petitions in the Madras High Court, challenging the patent rejection and asserting two arguments. First, Novartis argued that the Patent Act section 3(d) was inconsistent with the Indian Constitution. Second, Novartis asserted that this section was not consistent with TRIPS. The Madras High Court's decision follows.

NOVARTIS AG v. UNION OF INDIA

4 Madras LJ 1153 (2007)

JUSTICE R. BALASUBRAMANIAN

Under Article 27 of TRIPS, all inventions, subject to paragraphs 2 and 3 of that Article, are patentable. Reading Article 27 as a whole, it is argued that the drug invented in the case on hand is patentable....

4. Learned senior counsels on the opposite side would vehemently contend that the amended section is definitely compatible to TRIPS. Even assuming that it is not so, the remedy to have the TRIPS agreement complied with in letter and spirit available to the member countries does not lie before the Indian courts but only before the Dispute Settlement Board, hereinafter referred to as "DSB" created under TRIPS itself.

* * *

13. ... Let us now test the argument advanced before this court by learned Senior Counsels on the validity of the amended section on the touchstone of Article 14 of the Constitution of India. As we understand the amended section, it only declares that the very discovery of a new form of a known substance which does not result in the enhancement of the known efficacy of that substance, will not be treated as an invention. The position therefore is, if the discovery of a new form of a known substance must be treated as an invention, then the Patent applicant should show that the substance so discovered has a better therapeutic effect. Darland's Medical Dictionary defines the expression "efficacy" in the field of Pharmacology as "the ability of a drug to produce the desired therapeutic effect" and "efficacy" is independent of potency of the drug. Dictionary meaning of "Therapeutic", is healing of disease— having a good effect on the body. Going by the meaning for the word "efficacy" and "therapeutic" extracted above, what the patent applicant is expected to show is, how effective the new discovery made would be in healing a disease / having a good effect on the body? In other words, the patent applicant is definitely aware as to what is the "therapeutic effect" of the drug for which he had already got a patent and what is the difference between the therapeutic effect of the patented drug and the drug in respect of which patent is asked for. Therefore it is a simple exercise of, though preceded by research,—we state—for any Patent applicant to place on record what is the therapeutic effect / efficacy of a known substance and what is the enhancement in that known efficacy....

In this case we find that the Explanation creates a deeming fiction of derivatives of a known substance are deemed to be the same substance unless they differ significantly in properties with regard to efficacy. Therefore it is clear from the amended section and the Explanation that in the pharmacology field, if a discovery is made from a known substance, a duty is cast upon the patent applicant to show that the discovery had resulted in the enhancement of a known efficacy of that substance and in deciding whether to grant a Patent or not on such new discovery, the Explanation creates a deeming fiction that all derivatives of a known substance would be deemed to be the same substance unless it differ significantly in properties with regard to efficacy. In our opinion, the amended section and explanation give importance to efficacy. We have already referred to the meaning of "efficacy" as given in Dorland's Medical Dictionary. Scientifically it is possible to show with certainty what are the properties of a "substance". Therefore when the Explanation to the amended section says that any derivatives must differ significantly in properties with regard to efficacy, it only means that the derivatives should contain such properties which are significantly different with regard to efficacy to the substance from which the derivative is made ... As we stated earlier, due to the advanced technology in all fields of science, it is possible to show by giving necessary comparative details based on such science that the discovery of a new form a of known substance had resulted in the enhancement of the known efficacy of the original substance and the derivative so derived will not be the same substance, since the properties of the derivatives differ significantly with regard to efficacy. As rightly contended by learned Additional Solicitor General India and the leaned Senior Counsels and learned counsels for the Pharmaceutical Company opposing the Writ that the writ petitioner is not a novice to the pharmacology field but it, being pharmaceutical giant in the whole of the world, cannot plead that they do not know what is meant by enhancement of a known efficacy and they cannot show that the derivatives differ significantly in properties with regard to efficacy....

15. ... As rightly emphasized by ... learned senior counsel for the petitioners, the statement of objects and reasons for Amending Act 15/2005 emphasises in more than one place that the amendment is in the discharge of India's obligation to TRIPS, which forms part of the "WTO" agreement. Therefore a need has arisen for us to look into the relevant Articles of TRIPS for the limited purpose of what obligations are created under TRIPS, which, India was attempting to discharge by bringing in Amending Act 15/2005. Article 7 of TRIPS provides enough elbow room to a member country in complying with TRIPS obligations by bringing a law in a manner conducive to social and economic welfare and to a balance of rights and obligations. Article 1 of TRIPS enables a member country free to determine the appropriate method of implementing

the provisions of this agreement within their own legal system and practice. But however, any protection which a member country provides, which is more extensive in nature than is required under TRIPS, shall not contravene TRIPS. Article 27 speaks about patentability. Lengthy arguments have been advanced by learned Additional Solicitor General appearing for the Government of India, learned senior counsels and learned counsels appearing for the pharmaceutical companies that India, being a welfare and a developing country, which is pre-dominantly occupied by people below poverty line, it has a constitutional duty to provide good health care to its citizens by giving them easy access to life saving drugs. In so doing, the Union of India would be right, it is argued, to take into account the various factual aspects prevailing in this big country and prevent evergreening by allowing generic medicine to be available in the market. As rightly contended by the learned Additional Solicitor General of India, the Parliamentary debates show that welfare of the people of the country was in the mind of the Parliamentarians when Ordinance 7/2004 was in the House. They also had in mind the International obligations of India arising under TRIPS and under "WTO" agreement. Therefore the validity of the amended section on the touchstone of Article 14 of the Constitution of India must be decided having regard to the object which Amending Act 15/2005 wanted to achieve.

17.   ... It is argued by the learned senior counsels for the petitioners that the Statutory Authority is likely to misuse the discretion vested in it by throwing out the patent application as "not an invention", by relying upon the amended section, when the amended section itself does not contain any guidelines. We have already found that the amended section has in-built protection enabling each of the patent applicant to establish before the patent controller that his discovery had resulted in the enhancement of the known efficacy of that substance and the derivatives are significantly differing in properties with regard to efficacy. Therefore it boils down to only one question namely, could an arbitrary exercise of a discretionary power invalidate an Act? We have a direct answer for this point in favour of the State from a judgment of the Supreme Court reported in 2006 (8) SCC 212 (*M. Nagaraj vs. Union of India*), where, in paragraph No.106, the Supreme Court had held as hereunder:

> "Every discretionary power is not necessarily discriminatory. According to the Constitutional Law of India, by H.M.Seervai, 4th Edn., p.546, equality is not violated by mere conferment of discretionary power. It is violated by arbitrary exercise by those on whom it is conferred. This is the theory of "guided power". This theory is based on the assumption that in the

event of arbitrary exercise by those on whom the power is conferred, would be corrected by the courts.".…

18. … As we have already found, the amended section has in-built measures to guide the Statutory Authority in exercising its power under the Act. We have also found that the amended section does not suffer from the vice of vagueness, ambiguity and arbitrariness. The Statutory Authority would be definitely guided in deciding whether a discovery is an invention or not by the materials to be placed before him by the Patent applicant.…

19. … [W]e have already found, analysing the alleged offending provision that it is not in violation of Article 14 of the Constitution of India. We have borne in mind the object which the Amending Act wanted to achieve namely, to prevent evergreening; to provide easy access to the citizens of this country to life saving drugs and to discharge their Constitutional obligation of providing good health care to it's citizens.… [W]e hold that the amended section is not in violation of Article 14 of the Constitution of India and accordingly, both the writ petitions are dismissed.…

Notes and Questions

1. In the *Novartis* opinion, the High Court declined to decide the question of whether India's Patent Act section 3(d) was in compliance with TRIPS. What reason was provided? As background, TRIPS requires that disagreements concerning compliance with the agreement be resolved under the WTO's dispute settlement procedures incorporated into the Understanding on Dispute Settlement ("DSU"). *See* TRIPS Art. 64 (incorporating GATT's Dispute Settlement Understanding into TRIPS). The DSU provides for a mandatory system to resolve disputes between members, typically nations. A dispute may be subject to consideration before a dispute panel, a Dispute Settlement Board ("DSB"), made up of representatives of all the member states and an Appellate Body, all of whom operate under a series of deadlines. The system is designed to resolve dispute expeditiously and with binding authority on the parties.

According to one source, including a dispute resolution mechanism in the TRIPS Agreement was key for developing nations, some of whom were wary of that industrialized members could otherwise impose unilateral sanctions. As Professor Yu explains:

> By offering a mandatory dispute settlement process, the TRIPs Agreement shields less developed countries from threats of trade sanctions. Indeed, many less developed countries claimed that it would have been pointless for them to join the WTO had the United States been able to continue imposing unilateral sanctions despite their membership. Fortunately, in United States—Sections 301–310 of the Trade Act of 1974, the WTO dispute settlement panel confirmed that a member state could only pursue unilateral

sanctions after it had exhausted all actions permissible under the rules of the international trading body.

See Peter K. Yu, *TRIPS and Its Discontents*, 10 Marq. Intell. Prop. L. Rev. 369, 372–73 (2006) (footnotes omitted). One commentator notes that developed countries have been active in TRIPS matters that have been filed before the DSU to ensure that their interests are represented:

> As for complaints under the TRIPS Agreement, either the United States or EC initiated 21 of the 23 TRIPS complaints brought through January 2003 (15 by the United States and 6 by the EC). Brazil and Canada each initiated one TRIPS complaint, but these were merely symbolic claims that they filed in response to WTO complaints brought by the United States and EC against them. Brazil and Canada never seriously pursued their claims to advance commercial interests, but rather searched for bargaining chips for a potential settlement of the US and EC complaints. As regards TRIPS complaints that resulted in an adopted panel or Appellate Body report, the United States was a party or third party in all seven, and the EC in six of the seven, cases.

Gregory Shaffer, *Recognizing Public Goods in WTO Dispute Settlement: Who Participates? Who Decides?*, 7 J. Int'l Econ. L. 459, 471 (2004).

To date, no disputes challenging India's Patent Act section 3(d) have been filed. If this matter is adjudicated before the WTO, what position might the United States take? What result should the DSB reach?

2. Since the time that the High Court's *Novartis* opinion issued, Novartis pursued prosecution of claims for the improved beta-crystalline imatinib mesylate before the Indian Patent Office. On June 26, 2006, India's Intellectual Property Appellate Board found that Novartis' claims met both the novelty and inventive step requirement. Nonetheless, the Board rejected Novartis' claims based on the failure to meet section 3(d)'s "efficacy" standard, stating:

> ... [W]e have to mention here that the Appellant has never had any object of improving the efficacy for treating cancer in its impugned specification. Had that been there it would have been a startling discovery and definitely would have been prominently found a place in the specification. Rather, it has discovered the new crystalline form with improved thermodynamic stability, improved flow properties and lower hygroscopicity. These physical properties in a drug are important to formulate the active ingredients in solid dosage forms such as capsules, tablets, etc. but has no contribution to actual therapeutic effectiveness of the drug.
>
> ... As we see, the object of amended section 3(d) of the Act is nothing but a requirement of higher standard of inventive step in the law particularly for the drug/pharmaceutical substances. This is also one of the different public interest provisions adopted in the patent law at the pre-grant level, as we see, are also permissible

under the TRIPS Agreement and to accommodate the spirit of the Doha Declaration which gives to the WTO member states including India the right to protect public health and, in particular, to promote access to medicines for all.

According to this decision, how does section 3(d) differ from the inventive step requirement? What attributes of a chemical invention might meet inventive step, but not section 3(d)? How could Novartis' failure to obtain patent protection in India impact the global market for Glivec, assuming that protection is available in other nations?

If so, how? Is the Appellate Board's consideration of the economic conditions within India a valid consideration for determining patentability? Should the U.S. adopt this approach? If so, what other types of economic principles might be considered?

C. THE CONFLICT OVER GENE PATENTING

In the U.S. and Europe, gene patenting is permitting at present so long as all other patentability requirements are met. For example, the U.S. Patent & Trademark Office has taken the position that, "DNA compounds having naturally occurring sequences are eligible for patenting when isolated from their natural state and purified, and when the application meets the statutory criteria for patentability." U.S. PTO Final Guidelines For Determining Utility Of Gene–Related Inventions, 66 FED. REG. 1092, 1093 (Jan. 5, 2001). The agency has issued thousands of gene patents. Nonetheless, case law suggests that patentability standards for gene patents have become more challenging to obtain over the more recent years. *See generally In re Fisher*, 421 F.3d 1365 (Fed. Cir. 2005) (setting utility standards for gene patents); *In re Kubin*, 561 F.3d 1351 (Fed. Cir. 2009) (re-evaluating standards for nonobviousness).

In 1998, the European Parliament and Council of the European Union promulgated Directive 98/44/EC (7/30/98), addressing patenting of genetic and biological material. Article 3 of this Directive states, "[b]iological material which is isolated from its natural environment or produced by means of a technical process may be the subject of an invention even if it previously occurred in nature." In addition, Article 5 states, "[a]n element isolated from the human body or otherwise produced by means of a technical process, including the sequence or partial sequence of a gene, may constitute a patentable invention, even if the structure of that element is identical to that of a natural element." Similar provisions have been adopted by the European Patent Office that govern patentability standards for member nations throughout Europe. *See* Implementing Regulations to the Grant of a European Patent, Rules 26–29 (December 9, 2004).

The preamble to the European Directive specifies that "a mere DNA sequence without indication of a function does not contain any technical information and is therefore not a patentable invention." Additionally, Article 9 of the Directive states that patent protection "on a product containing or consisting of genetic information shall extend to all material ... in which the product in incorporated and in which the genetic information is contained and performs its function." Why do you suppose the European Directive specifies function as a critical element to DNA sequence patentability?

In *Monsanto Technology LLC v. Ceferta BV*, Case C–428/08, 2010 E.C.R. ___ (2010), the Court of Justice of the European Communities relied on these portions of the Directive to narrow protection for claims to a DNA sequence that was used within Monsanto's genetically engineered soy seeds. Unlike soy in its natural state, soy made from seeds containing Monstanto's engineered gene are designed to resist the harmful effects of the insecticide "Round–Up," a product sold by Monstanto. Thus, Monsanto's genetically engineered soy allows farmers to spray Round–Up on their fields without damaging the soy crops, because the soy crops contain a gene that resists any harmful effects. Monsanto asserted infringement against importers of soy meal that had been ground from soy seeds that included Monstanto's patented gene. However, the patent DNA was rendered inert in soy meal, as the Court explained, "the DNA cannot perform its function in soy meal, which is dead material." However, the claimed DNA's function could be restored if isolated from the soy meal and subsequently transferred into living material.

Monsanto's primary claim was directed to the DNA sequence. Nonetheless, the *Monsanto Technology* Court rejected Monsanto's argument that the patent claims could be asserted against the defendant's soy meal. First, the Court maintained that a claim to the DNA sequence could not apply to defendant's soy meal where the DNA failed to perform the function described in Monsanto's patent. Noting that "it should be borne in mind that recital 23 in the preamble to the Directive states that 'a mere DNA sequence without indication of a function does not contain any technical information and is therefore not a patentable invention,'" *Monsanto Technology* stated:

> ... a DNA sequence such as that at issue in the main proceedings is not able to perform its function when it is incorporated in a dead material such as soy meal. Such a sequence does not, therefore, enjoy patent right protection.... Article 9 of the Directive must be interpreted as not conferring patent right protection in circumstances such as those of the case in the main proceedings, in which

the patented product is contained in the soy meal, where it does not perform the function for which it was patented, but did perform that function previously in the soy plant, of which the meal is a processed product, or would possibly again be able to perform that function after it had been extracted from the soy meal and inserted into the cell of a living organism.

Here, the *Monsanto Technology* Court found that the invention's function, which is protection against damage by Round-up, was not present in the accused soy meal. The Court explained, "[s]ince the Directive thus makes the patentability of a DNA sequence subject to indication of the function it performs, it must be regarded as not according any protection to a patented DNA sequence which is not able to perform the specific function for which it was patented." Does the *Monsanto Technology* Court's decision highlight an overlap between patentable subject matter and infringement? What about an overlap between utility and/or industrial applicability?

Beyond this, patents to fundamental components of DNA have raised the issue of patient access to adequate diagnostics and treatment. As one example, in 2001, the European Parliament adopted a resolution directed toward the patentee Myriad Genetics, claiming breast cancer genes BRCA1 and BRCA2. European Parliament Resolution on the Patenting of BRCA1 and BRCA2 ("Breast Cancer") Genes (4/10/2001). Myriad licenses the U.S. versions of these patents to a limited number of genetic laboratories to test for breast cancer screening. Noting that "cheaper and more effective methods of testing for breast cancer genes BRCA1 and BRCA2 exist in the European Union" and that "the existing U.S. patents are already impeding their use," the Parliament observed that:

> . . . the granting of similar patents by the EPO would create a monopoly for the firm in question within the European Union as well, which could seriously impede or even completely prevent the further use of existing cheaper and more effective tests for the breast cancer genes BRCA1 and BRCA2; whereas this development could have an unacceptable detrimental effect on the women concerned and constitute a serious drain on the funds of public health services; whereas moreover it could seriously impede the development of and research into new methods of diagnosis . . . . .

Id. This resolution asked, among other things, that objections be filed against Myriad's EPO breast cancer gene patents. Ultimately, the EPO's Technical Board of Appeal rejected arguments that granting the patents would increase costs to patients and detrimentally impact European diagnosis and research in the field:

The Board accepts that public health care is a sensitive area, however the Board sees no basis in the EPC to distinguish in this respect between inventions concerning different technical fields ... [T]he EPO has not been vested with the task of taking into account the economic effects of the grant of patents in specific areas and restricting the field of patentable subject-matter accordingly. In the Board's opinion the possible conse-quences of exploitation of the patent ... are the result of the exclusionary nature of the rights granted by a patent, that is the right to stop competitors from using the invention.

The objection of [the] Opponent.... reduced to its essence, is that the inevitable consequences of the exploitation of the patent in suit are contrary to "ordre public" or morality. Logically, such an objection applies to the exploitation of any patent, as the nature of the consequences of the exploitation of a patent (which derive from the exclusionary nature of private property rights), are the same for all patents.

In re The University of Utah Research Foundation, Case No. T 1213/05 (9/27/07), available at: http://legal.european-patent-office.org/dg3/biblio/t051213eu1.htm. Ultimately, the EPO's Technical Board allowed a number of Myriad's claims. *In re* The University of Utah Research Foundation, Case No. T 0666/0 (11/13/08), available at http://legal.european-patent-office.org/dg3/biblio/t050666eu1.htm.

In August 2010, Myriad offered to gift an Australian BRCA patent to the people of Australian after a challenge to the patent was filed by, inter alia, an organization called Cancer Voices Aus-tralia, challenging its validity. The Australian challenge followed soon after a U.S. District Court court issued a ruling invalidating certain claims in Myriad's U.S. BRCA patent, a decision that Myriad is appealing to the U.S. Federal Circuit court. See Associa-tion for Molecular Pathology v. United States Patent and Trade-mark Office, 702 F.Supp.2d 181 (S.D.N.Y. 2010). During this same time frame, the Australian Senate undertook an investigation into gene patenting, and is expected to issue a report soon. Why might Myriad allow free use of the patent in Australia, while contesting the validity of the patent in the U.S.?

Other nations bar patent protection for certain types of bio-technological inventions. For example, the Egyptian Patent Act provides that patents shall not be granted for "organs, tissues, live cells, natural biological substances, nuclear acid and genome." Law No. 82/09, art. 2(5), O.J. No. 2 bis (June 2, 2002) (Egypt). Brazil's patent statute provides that any of "[t]he following are not consid-ered to be inventions or utility models:" including "all or part of natural living beings and biological materials found in nature, even if isolated therefrom, including the genome or germoplasm of any natural living being, and the natural biological processes." Brazilian Industrial Property Act, Law No. 9.279, art. 10 IX (1996). As one source explains, such substances are considered unpatentable discoveries rather than inventions. *See* Nuno Pires de Carvalho, *The Problem of Gene Patents*, 3 WASH. U. GLOBAL STUD. L. REV. 701 (2004). Do these approaches conform to TRIPS Article 27, which provides that patents must be available for "any inventions"?

D. SOFTWARE

Patents for inventions implemented in computers are controversial. One prominent example derives from Article 52 of the European Patent Convention, which states:

> (1) European patents shall be granted for any inventions, in all fields of technology, provided that they are new, involve an inventive step and are susceptible of industrial application.

> (2) The following in particular shall not be regarded as inventions within the meaning of paragraph 1:

>> (a) discoveries, scientific theories and mathematical methods;

>> (b) aesthetic creations;

>> (c) schemes, rules and methods for performing mental acts, playing games or doing business, and programs for computers;

> (3) Paragraph 2 shall exclude the patentability of the subject-matter or activities referred to therein only to the extent to which a European patent application or European patent relates to such subject-matter or activities as such.

These three sections impact software patentability. Despite the broad definition of patentable subject matter in Article 52(1), the limitations of Article 52(2) expressly carve out "programs for computers" from protection. Additionally, subsection (3) states that the limitations set forth in subsection (2) relate to the software patents "as such." What is a computer program "as such"? Read together, these sections have been interpreted to allow protection for claims that have a technical character. *See* Guidelines for Examination in the European Patent Office, Part IV–4 (April 2009). Generally, software is not deemed to have a technical character *per se*, rather:

> ... a computer program claimed by itself is not excluded from patentability if the program, when running on a computer or loaded into a computer, brings about, or is

capable of bringing about, a technical effect which goes beyond the "normal" physical interactions between the program(software) and the computer (hardware) on which it is run.

IBM/Computer programs, [2000] E.P.O.R. 219. The EPO has provided some general guidance for how the requirement for a further technical effect should be applied:

Such further technical effect might be the more secure operation of the brake of a car or train. A further technical effect might also be a faster communication between two mobile phones with improved quality of voice transmission. However, such claims are only allowed by the EPO if they are based on a new and inventive technical process that may be carried out by a computer program.

How should claims be analyzed where there is a mix of technical and non-technical features? Consider a claim for a computer program for an Internet auction. Does the fact that in-person auctions have long been considered non-technical mean that the claim does not have a further technical effect? Should the existence of hardware in the claim, such as a client computer, a central server or monitor, save the claim? Additionally, could there be a legal distinction between a claim to a "computer program" and "a method of operating a computer program," where both fundamentally address the same subject matter? *See generally* HITACHI/Auction method [2004] E.P.O.R. 55 (finding that a claim to an Internet auction met the patentable subject matter requirement, but failed inventive step for the failure to make a technical contribution to the art).

Coupled with these issues was the question of whether the prior art should play any role in determining patentable subject matter. In *Aerotel/Macrossan*, [2006] EWCA Civ. 1371, the the court required that the further technical effect also constitute a contribution to the prior art In other words, the claim was compared to the prior art, and if this contribution constituted subject matter excluded by Article 52(2), then patentable subject matter failed. Consider how the following case dealt with these issues.

DUNS LICENSING ASSOCIATES/ESTIMATING SALES ACTIVITY (T154/04)

Technical Board of Appeal
[2007] E.P.O.R. 38

... The appellant's submissions may be summarised as follows:

The invention provided a system and a method suitable for estimating sales or product distribution at a non-reporting sales outlet, based on sample sales data from reporting outlets, more accurately than achieved by previous systems and methods. ...

The technical problem to be solved was to find a more accurate technique for estimating sales activity at a given outlet using a data-processing system to process data representing sales activity at further outlets even although sales activity was a discontinuous function of location.

Document D1, the closest prior art, only disclosed that each store had an in-store device which detected, interpreted, processed, and stored data on a real-time basis. The technical solution of the present invention was to measure the distances between the various sales outlets, to formulate the weighting factor using that distance information for each of the plurality of sales outlets under consideration and the characteristics of the sales outlet and then to process this data to produce the desired estimate. There was no mention in the prior art, of using sales data at one store to estimate sales data at another non-reporting store on the basis of the geographic distances between the stores. The invention, therefore, was clearly novel and inventive over the prior art. . . .

Case law related to patentability of inventions

. . . [T]he issue raised boils down to the application of Arts 52, 54, and 56 EPC in the context of subject matter and activities excluded from patentability under Art. 52(2) EPC.

The constant jurisprudence of the Boards of Appeal as far as it is relevant to the present case may be summarised succinctly in the following principles:

(A) Article 52(1) EPC sets out four requirements to be fulfilled by a patentable invention: there must be an invention, and if there is an invention, it must satisfy the requirements of novelty, inventive step, and industrial applicability.

(B) Having technical character is an implicit requisite of an "invention" within the meaning of Art. 52(1) EPC (requirement of "technicality").

(C) Article 52(2) EPC does not exclude from patentability any subject matter or activity having technical character, even if it is related to the items listed in this provision since these items are only excluded "as such" (Art. 52(3) EPC).

(D) The four requirements invention, novelty, inventive step, and susceptibility of industrial application are essentially separate and independent criteria of patentability, which may give rise to concurrent objections. Novelty, in particular, is not a requisite of an invention within the meaning of Art. 52(1) EPC, but a separate requirement of patentability. . . .

Article 52(1) EPC expresses the fundamental maxim of the general entitlement to patent protection for any inventions in all technical fields. Any limitation to the general entitlement to patent protection is thus not a matter of judicial discretion, but must have a clear legal basis in the European Patent Convention.

The application of Art. 52(1) EPC presents a problem of construction as there was no legal or commonly accepted definition of the term "invention" at the time of conclusion of the Convention in 1973. Moreover, the EPO has not developed any such explicit definition ever since, for good reasons. The second paragraph of Art. 52 EPC is merely a negative, non-exhaustive list of what should not be regarded as an invention within the meaning of Art. 52(1) EPC. It was the clear intention of the contracting states that this list of "excluded" subject matter should not be given a too broad scope of application, as follows from the legislative history of Art. 52 (2) EPC, then Art. 50, amended on initiative of the German delegation with the reasoning:

> "This could lead to the erroneous conclusion that a broad interpretation should be given to items not limited in this way in paragraph 2." (see the Historical Documentation (Travaux préparatoires) relating to the European Patent Convention, Munich 1999, document M/11 of March 1973, Vol.35E, No.21 and document M/PR/I, Vol. 42E, No. 42).

> Paragraph 3 of the present Art. 52 EPC was introduced as a bar to such a broad interpretation of Art. 52(2) EPC. By referring explicitly to the "patentability of the subject-matter or activities", paragraph 3 actually enshrined the entitlement to patent protection for the non-inventions enumerated in para.2—albeit restricting the entitlement by excluding patentability "to the extent to which the European patent application or European patent relates to such subject matter or activities as such".

The intention of Art. 52(3) EPC was clearly to ensure that anything which was a patentable invention before under conventional patentability criteria should remain patentable under the European Patent Convention. That no paradigm shift was intended may also be seen from the fact that, e.g. Switzerland as a contracting state has considered it unnecessary ("überflüssig") to include the contents of Art. 52(2) and (3) EPC in the national regulations when harmonising them with the EPC.

As expressed in the VICOM decision T208/84 (above), Reasons No.16, "decisive [for the invention to be patentable] is what technical contribution the invention as defined in the claim when considered as a whole makes to the known art". This principle is referring to the patentable invention, i.e. an invention meeting all the patentability criteria of the Convention. VICOM thus does not postulate that the technical contribution to the prior art is the actual criterion to be applied for deciding on the requirement of invention.

Taking into account object and purpose of the patentability requirements and the legal practice in the contracting states of the EPO, the boards of appeal considered the technical character of the invention to be the general criterion embodied in paras 2 and 3 of Art. 52 EPC. By having technical character, any product, method etc., even if formally relating to the list enumerated in para. 2, is not excluded from patentability under paras 2 and 3 of Art. 52 EPC.

It was indeed always common ground that creations in engineering and technology were entitled to patent protection under the European Patent Convention. As the Board judged in T930/05, this criterion is reflected by the internal logic of Art. 52(1) and (2) EPC. The mere fact that the Art. 52(2) list of items not to be regarded as inventions is non-exhaustive ("in particular") is indicative of the existence of an exclusion criterion common to all those items and allowing for additions to the list that were thought possible. The enumeration of typical non-inventions in Art. 52(2) EPC covers subjects whose common feature is a substantial lack of technical character. The formulation of the law ultimately derives from the classical notion of invention adopted, which distinguishes between practical scientific applications and intellectual achievements in general. The connection of the notions of invention and technical character of the invention arises immediately, because the list of exclusions in Art. 52(2) EPC, with its reference to Art. 52(1) EPC, must be viewed as a negative definition of the notion of invention. This connection is also inherent in other provisions of the EPC, such as Arts 18 and 56 and 27(1) and 29(1) EPC, which clearly express this underlying principle of patent law.

* * *

The "technical effect approach" endorsed by Jacob L.J. in the *Aerotel/Macrossan* judgement seems to be rooted in this second ordinary meaning of the term invention, a practice which might be understandable "given the shape of the old law", but which is not consistent with a good-faith interpretation of the European Patent Convention in accordance with Art. 31 of the Vienna Convention on the Law of Treaties of 1969.

Actually, any reference to the prior art in the context of Art. 52(2) and (3) EPC would lead to insurmountable difficulties; the prior art, the "state of the art" in the terminology of the Convention, is a complex concept finely tuned by a combination of provisions, Arts

54 to 56 EPC, and depending on the filing and priority dates of the application or patent as well as on the patentability requirement involved. There is, however, no rule whatsoever defining the prior art which should be applied in the context of Art. 52(2) EPC. It is simply inconceivable that the contracting states missed such an important point in the conclusion of the Convention. Hence, there are convincing reasons why the "contribution" or "technical effect" approach should be abandoned, which the boards did some ten years ago.

The "technical effect approach (with the rider)" applied in the *Aerotel/Macrossan* judgement is irreconcilable with the European Patent Convention also for the further reason that it presupposes that "novel and inventive purely excluded matter does not count as a 'technical contribution' " (*Aerotel/Macrossan*). This has no basis in the Convention and contravenes conventional patentability criteria; referring e.g. to mathematical methods and to discoveries, the Enlarged Board of Appeal said in decision G2/88 (above), Reasons No. 8:

> "[...], as was recognised in Decision T208/84 [...] (dealing there with a mathematical method rather than a discovery, but the same principle applies), the fact that the idea or concept underlying the claimed subject-matter resides in a discovery does not necessarily mean that the claimed subject-matter is a discovery 'as such' ".

In fact, a non-technical feature may interact with technical elements so as to produce a technical effect, e.g. by its application for the technical solution of a technical. If this is true for some purely excluded matter, for example the intellectual exercise cited in the Opinion, then—to the extent it contributes to the technical effect— it must count as a contribution to the technical character....

* * *

Claim 1 of the main request defines a method for estimating sales activity of a product at a (non-reporting) sales outlet. The estimated sales activity is calculated essentially by correlating sales activities at reporting sales outlets according to the respective distance between the non-reporting sales outlet and the respective reporting sales outlet. Such a method is not an invention within the meaning of Art. 52(1) to (3) EPC.

Creating information about sales activities or other types of business data using mathematical and statistical methods to evaluate data gathered from the respective business environment is a business research activity, which like other research methods does not serve to solve a technical problem relevant to any technical field.

The Board judges that in analogy to schemes, rules, and methods of doing business, methods of business research are excluded "as such" from patentability under Art. 52(2)(c) and (3) EPC.

Interacting with and exploiting information about the physical word belongs to the very nature of any business-related activity. Accepting such features as sufficient for establishing patentability would render the exclusion of business methods under Art. 52(2)(c) EPC meaningless. Therefore, the Board judges that gathering and evaluating data as part of a business research method, even if the data relates to physical parameters or geographic information as in the present case, do not convey technical character to a business research method if such steps do not contribute to the technical solution of a technical problem.

Determining sales data and geographical distances between outlets and using this data to estimate sales at specific outlets by means of the statistical method claimed and disclosed in the application do not solve any technical problem in a technical field. The definitions in claim 1 do not imply the use of any technical system or means. The term "database", in particular, may be construed to designate any collection of data so that claim 1 encompasses methods which may be performed without using any technical means at all.

The method of claim 1 is hence excluded from patentability under Art. 52(1), (2)(c) and (3) EPC.

* * *

Requirement of inventive step.

The contribution to the prior art is the use of the known system for performing a new market analysis different from the statistical calculations disclosed in document D1 and hence requiring the implementation of a new algorithm for processing the sales data and creating the desired information about the non-reporting sales outlets. This, however, does not imply the use of any new technical means. The contribution to the prior art is therefore limited to the implementation of the new algorithm.

For the reasons given above, this new algorithm and the method of estimating sales activity at a non-reporting outlet are part of a business research method and do not contribute to the solution of any technical problem. They have thus to be ignored in assessing inventive step. The only technical aspect of the claimed system, namely to use a processor to implement the non-technical method and the corresponding algorithm, is an obvious consequence of using computer systems for market analysis like in document D1. Hence, the main request and the auxiliary requests 1 to 3 are not allowable for lack of inventive step (Art. 56 EPC)....

COMPUTER PROGRAM EXCLUSION/G 3/08

Enlarged Board of Appeal
[2010] E.P.O.R. ___

7.2.1 ... The European Patent Organisation is an international, intergovernmental organisation, modelled on a modern state order and based on the separation of powers principle, which the sovereign contracting states have entrusted with the exercise of some of their national powers in the field of patents. Thus the EPC assigns executive power to the Office to grant patents and to its President to manage the Office in organisational respects, while to the Administrative Council it assigns limited legislative powers restricted to lower-ranking rules, along with financial and supervisory powers.

Finally, the Boards of Appeal, which in their decisions are bound only by the EPC, are assigned the role of an independent judiciary in this patent system, even if for the present, pursuant to Article 4(2) EPC and to EPC Part 1 Chapter III, they are not an independent organ of the Organisation but structurally integrated departments of the Office under Article 15 EPC. . . .

7.2.3 Another essential element of a democratic legal order is the principle that a public authority is bound by law and justice. This is supplemented by the principle of uniform application of the law. Both principles are designed to ensure predictability of jurisdiction and hence legal certainty by preventing arbitrariness. Those subject to the law, in the case of the EPC the parties to proceedings before the Office, but also the public, must be able to expect that the Office as patent granting authority and consequently the Boards of Appeal will settle cases of the same nature in the same way and will apply comprehensible arguments and methods to justify any substantive differences in such decisions. For the stated reasons, these principles also constitute essential precepts for administration and jurisdiction in the European patent system as codified in the EPC. Ensuring compliance with them is ultimately the task of the Boards of Appeal, including the Enlarged Board, the latter though only in the context of referrals by the Boards of Appeal and the President under Article 112(1) EPC and concerning petitions for review.

7.2.4 In keeping with these principles, Article 112 EPC-like corresponding provisions in the legal orders of the Contracting States— defines the conditions in which legal uniformity within the European patent system may be established by means of a referral to the Enlarged Board of Appeal. It requires the Boards or the President to deem the referral necessary in order to ensure uniform application of the law or if points of law of fundamental importance arise, and a further admissibility criterion for a referral by the President is that two Boards of Appeal must have given different decisions on the question referred.

Hence the Enlarged Board does not rule on abstract points of law, but only ever on real issues arising from the cited differing decisions, as well as on specific legal questions adduced in the referral. It is to be noticed that the President is not a party in a referral procedure because she or he can not be adversely affected by answers given by the Enlarged Board.

7.2.5   Thus it is clear that the interpretation of the EPC is primarily the responsibility of the Boards of Appeal. As a rule they have interpretative supremacy with regard to the EPC because their decisions are subject to review only under the narrowly defined conditions of Article 112(1) and 112a(2) EPC. It is only when these apply that the Enlarged Board has the last word. The fact that the Enlarged Board takes action only on a referral from the Boards of Appeal or the President (with the exception of petitions for review under Article 112a EPC, which however concern procedural matters and have a very narrow scope) and thus does not constitute a further instance ranking above the Boards of Appeal within the EPC judicial system is a clear indication of the extent of its significance for legal uniformity.

* * *

10.   Question 1 "Can a computer program only be excluded as a computer program as such if it is explicitly claimed as a computer program?"

Admissibility

10.1   The first step is interpretation of the question. On the face of it all that is asked is whether one has to use the actual words "computer program". If the question is interpreted in this fashion it is easily answered; a claim utilising a synonym for "computer program", such as "a sequence of computer-executable instructions" or "an executable software module" perhaps, would clearly not avoid exclusion from patentability if the equivalent claim to a computer program did not. However the alleged divergence identified in the referral does not simply relate to the form of words chosen. Moreover the "Background" to Question 1 includes the following:

"In this field, claim formulations along the following lines are common:

- methods

- systems (i.e. computer systems)

- computer-implemented methods

- computer programs

- computer program products, storing a computer program.

However the substance of these claims, i.e. the underlying method to be performed by a computer, is often identical". The discussion also refers to "the function of the computer program (does the claimed program have technical character) rather than the manner in which it is claimed (e.g. as a computer program, a computer program product or a computer-implemented method)."

Thus it would seem that the first reference to a "computer program" in the question is in fact intended to encompass claims to various matters which involve a computer program without necessarily literally being one, and that the question to which the referral is seeking an answer is something along the lines of: If a particular claim to a computer program ("1. A program for a computer comprising instructions to carry out steps x, y, z,") is excluded from patentability by Article 52(2) EPC, are any of the following (or anything else) automatically excluded under the same article? "2. A computer system loaded with the program of claim 1." "3. A method of operating a computer comprising executing the program of claim 1." "4. A computer program product storing the program of claim 1."

10.2 The only "divergence" in the case law identified by the referral with respect to this question is between the decisions in cases T 1173/97, IBM (OJ EPO 1999, 609) and T 424/03, Microsoft, dated 23 February 2006. It is argued in the referral that according to T 424/03 only a claim of the form "computer program for method x" could possibly be excluded from patentability as a computer program as such, whereas claims of the form "computer implemented method x" or "computer program product storing executable code for method x" would not be excluded (irrespective of the nature of the method x). T 1173/97 is said however to place the emphasis on the function of the computer program rather than on the manner in which it is claimed, for example as a computer program product or a computer-implemented method.

T 1173/97 concerned an application where the examining division had come to the conclusion that there was an invention and was prepared to grant a patent including claims of the types which had been accepted at least since T 208/84, VICOM (OJ EPO 1987, 14), namely for a method of operating a computer and for a computer adapted to carry out the method (i.e. a computer loaded with an appropriate program)....

10.2.2 The Board ... did comment on the question whether claiming the program on a medium could overcome exclusion: "Furthermore, the Board is of the opinion that with regard to the exclusions under Article 52(2) and (3) EPC, it does not make any difference whether a computer program is claimed by itself or as a record on a carrier. . . . ''

* * *

10.5   T 1173/97 also drew the consequence from its abandonment of the "contribution approach" that, "Determining the technical contribution an invention achieves with respect to the prior art is therefore more appropriate for the purpose of examining novelty and inventive step than for deciding on possible exclusion under Article 52(2) and (3).''

10.6   For readers unfamiliar with the jargon, an analogy may help to understand the distinction between the "contribution approach" and the approach adopted by the Board in T 1173/97. Note, however, that what follows is intended to be merely illustrative, not definitive. Suppose a patent application claims a cup carrying a certain picture (e.g. a company logo). We assume that no effect beyond information, "brand awareness" or aesthetic pleasure is ascribed to the picture. According to the "contribution approach", cups are known, so that the "contribution to the art" is only in a field excluded from patentability by Article 52(2) EPC and the application may be refused under this provision, i.e. the European patent application is considered to relate to (cf. Article 52(3) EPC) an aesthetic creation, a presentation of information or possibly even a method for doing business "as such".

According to the approach laid down by T 1173/97, for the purposes of Article 52(2) EPC the claimed subject matter has to be considered without regard to the prior art. According to this view a claim to a cup is clearly not excluded from patentability by Article 52(2) EPC. Whether or not the claim also includes the feature that the cup has a certain picture on it is irrelevant. This approach, at least as formulated in e.g. T 258/03, Hitachi and T 424/03, has been characterised in some of the amicus curiae briefs as the "any hardware" or "any technical means" approach.

10.7   Over a series of decisions the Boards of Appeal explored this consequence of abandoning the contribution approach. . . .   T 424/03, Microsoft, finally extended the reasoning applied in T 258/03 to come to the conclusion that a claim to a program ("computer executable instructions" in the claim in question) on a computer-readable medium also necessarily avoids exclusion from patentability under Article 52(2) EPC (see Catchword 2 and Reasons, point 5.3, "The subject matter of claim 5 has technical character since it relates to a computer-readable medium, i.e. a technical product involving a carrier (see decision T 258/03—Auction method/Hitachi . . .)''). This statement is quite unequivocal and stands alone as a reason for the claim not to be excluded under Article 52(2) EPC.

10.7.1 The decision in T 424/03 did go on to note that the particular program involved had the potential of achieving a further technical effect when run and thus also contributed to the technical character of the claimed subject-matter. This fact however was not necessary to the conclusion that the claimed subject-matter avoided exclusion, since according to the reasoning of T 258/03 any technical means claimed was sufficient to overcome the exclusion of Article 52(2) EPC. The question whether the program itself caused a "further technical effect" when run, and would therefore also qualify as technical means, only assumed importance for the question of inventive step—in parallel to these decisions the Board had been developing an approach to the appraisal of inventive step taking into account the fact that some of the features of a claim might, considered alone, fall under the exclusions of Article 52(2) EPC (see T 154/04, Duns). For this approach it is important which features contribute to the technical character of the claimed subject-matter, since only such features are taken into account for the assessment of inventive step. In the particular case of T 424/03, both the computer-readable medium and the program itself were features which gave the subject-matter of the particular claim as a whole a technical character, and were both therefore to be taken into account for the assessment of its inventive step.

10.7.2 Thus finally the Board had arrived at a conclusion which clearly contradicted the position (or rather one of the positions) taken in T 1173/97. T 1173/97 declared, "Furthermore, the Board is of the opinion that with regard to the exclusions under Article 52(2) and (3) EPC, it does not make any difference whether a computer program is claimed by itself or as a record on a carrier ...,", whereas T 424/03 stated, "The subject-matter of claim 5 has technical character since it relates to a computerreadable medium, i.e. a technical product involving a carrier (see decision T 258/03–Auction method/Hitachi ...)".

10.8 Thus there was a difference between the positions taken in T 1173/97 and T 424/03 on this point. It is still however necessary to decide whether this difference constitutes a divergence allowing a question to be referred by the President on the point. The considerations to be taken into account have been discussed in points 5 to 7 above.

10.8.1 Although both these cases were decided by Board 3.5.01 as an organisational unit, the compositions of the Board were completely different, so that a referral on the basis of these two decisions is not excluded. However there are factors which suggest that the difference should be treated as a development of the case law. . . .

10.8.4 T 1173/97 declares that a claim to a computer program is not excluded from patentability if the program, when run, shows a "further technical effect", i.e. a technical effect going beyond those effects which occur inevitably when any program is run. It further states that this "further technical effect" need not be new and there should be no comparison with the prior art when making the judgement whether there is such a "further technical effect". It cannot have been intended that there be no comparison with the prior art for computer programs, but that there should be for other claimed subject-matters. So it may be concluded that the judgement whether some subject matter is excluded under Articles 52(2) and (3) EPC from patentability is, according to T 1173/97, always to be decided without regard to the prior art.

10.8.5 Following this principle, a claim to a particular kind of computer-readable medium memory with certain special properties, e.g. a Blu–Ray disk, is evidently not excluded from patentability by Articles 52(2) and (3) EPC, whether or not it is new at the relevant date. But applying the principle consistently, the claim does not have to be a special kind of memory—"A computer-readable data storage medium," specifying no further details, has the "technical effects" of being computer-readable and of being capable of storing data. And since there is no entry in the list of Article 52(2) EPC relating to computer-readable media as such there is no requirement for a "further" effect going beyond the basic properties of such a computer readable storage medium. In short, according to the logic of T 1173/97 the following claim is not excluded from patentability by Articles 52(2) and (3) EPC: "A computer-readable storage medium."

10.8.6 In the case law of the Boards of Appeal there has never been any suggestion that narrowing a claim can bring it under the exclusions of Articles 52(2) and (3) EPC, which would require weighting of features or a decision as to which features define the "essence" of the invention, in contrast to e.g. the Bundespatentgericht, where such a weighing up of features has at some times been used. Thus according to Boards of Appeal case law, since the claim, "A computer-readable storage medium," is not excluded from patentability by Articles 52(2) and (3) EPC, neither is a claim, "A computer-readable storage medium storing computer program X," (cf. "A cup decorated with picture X").

10.8.7 It might be argued that whereas "A Blu–Ray disk with program X written on it," would escape the exclusion of Article 52(2) EPC, "A computer-readable storage medium with program X written on it," should not. The only basis for such an argument which the Enlarged Board can envisage would be that the feature "computer-readable storage medium" loses its technical nature because it is too generic or "functionally defined". There is however no case law known to the Enlarged Board that would support this view.

10.8.8 Thus the position taken in T 424/03 that a claim to a program on a computer-readable storage medium is necessarily not excluded from patentability by the provisions of Articles 52(2) and (3) EPC is in fact a consequence of the principles laid out in T 1173/97; the contrary position taken in that decision is inconsistent with its own premises. It would appear that the Board in that case did adopt an implicit "essence of the invention" position ("[T]he hardware is not part of the invention.... Furthermore, it is clear that if, for instance, the computer program product comprises a computer-readable medium on which the program is stored, this medium only constitutes the physical support on which the program is saved, and thus constitutes hardware.") But as explained above there is no support for such an approach in the general case law of the Boards of Appeal.

The arguments above apply with equal force to claims which "mention" a computer.

10.9 Returning to the direct question of admissibility of the referred question it is further noted that there was a period of approximately seven years between the issuance of the two decisions, a period which, although not very long in legal terms, is nonetheless compatible with the notion of development of the case law.

* * *

10.13 The present position of the case law is thus that a claim in the area of computer programs can avoid exclusion under Articles 52(2)(c) and (3) EPC merely by explicitly mentioning the use of a computer or a computer-readable storage medium. But no exposition of this position would be complete without the remark that it is also quite clear from the case law of the Boards of Appeal since T 1173/97 that if a claim to program X falls under the exclusion of Articles 52(2) and (3) EPC, a claim which specifies no more than "Program X on a computer-readable storage medium," or "A method of operating a computer according to program X," will always still fail to be patentable for lack of an inventive step under Articles 52(1) and 56 EPC. Merely the EPC article applied is different. While the Enlarged Board is aware that this rejection for lack of an inventive step rather than exclusion under Article 52(2) EPC is in some way distasteful to many people, it is the approach which has been consistently developed since T 1173/97 and since no divergences from that development have been identified in the referral we consider it not to be the function of the Enlarged Board in this Opinion to overturn it, for the reasons given above....

Notes and Questions

1. Under *Duns Licensing* and *Computer Related Exclusions/G 3/08*, how would the EPO analyze patentable subject matter to a claim to a "computer program," compared to one for "a method of operating a computer program?" How about a claim to a computer program that creates the capability for an Internet auction site, where auctions are well known in the art at the time of invention? Compare these to how one would analyze these claims under the U.S. Supreme Court's *Bilski v. Kappos*, 130 S.Ct. 3218 (2010). Is the result the same under each legal test?

2. *Computer Related Exclusions/G 3/08* was considered by the European Patent Office's Enlarged Board of Appeal on referral from the EPO's President. *See* President's Reference/ Computer Program Exclusion, [2009] E.P.O.R. 9. According to the President's Reference, the question addressed by the Enlarged Court of Appeal has implications for innovation within the software industry:

> In the field of computer technology, innovation frequently lies in the particular method performed by a computer program while executed by conventional hardware. Consequently, the exclusion of computer programs as such under art. 52(2) and (3) EPC should be of key importance in this field. However, if one were to follow the reasoning of T424/03, overcoming the exclusion of programs for computers would become a formality, merely requiring formulation of the claim as a computer implemented method or as a computer program product.

How does the determination of the Enlarged Board of Appeals impact the software industry? Does *Computer Related Exclusions/G 3/08* make a distinction that can be easily circumvented by a prosecuting attorney's word choice, given that software must operate within a hardware environment in all cases? Does the opinion place more pressure on the inventive step requirement to sift out unpatentable inventions? Is this consistent with the approach taken in the U.S.?

3. The key concept to distinguish patent eligible subject matter from ineligible subject matter under Japanese patent law is the utilization or application of a law of nature. Japanese patent law defines a statutory invention as the highly advanced creation of technical ideas that utilize a law of nature. The statute requires highly advanced technical ideas to distinguish the subject matter of the patent from that of the utility model, which is a type of petite patent that requires only a low level of nonobviousness or inventive step. When applying the definition of statutory invention to computer software related inventions, the JPO has been using a test similar to the machine prong of the Federal Circuit's Bilski machine-or transformation test, requiring that a system or method for processing information using software be implemented with a particular machine. (JPO Examination Guidelines) A system or

method meets this requirement if the input of software into a computer results in cooperation between software and hardware resources to provide a machine or method for a specific use. Since the USPTO has interpreted *Bilski v. Kappos,* 130 S.Ct. 3218 (2010) to endorse the machine-or-transformation test as an important factor by incorporating the test in its patent eligibility examination guidelines, the examination practices at the JPO and the USPTO are in line with respect to the requirements established by the machine prong of the test.

It is not clear whether the JPO has also adopted the transformation prong of the Bilski test. Japanese Patent Law provides three categories of inventions: a product, a process, and a process for producing. The second category does not require producing or transforming an article as long as the process utilizes a law of nature. The IP High Court found a statutory invention regarding a claim for a method for finding words in a bilingual dictionary. Judgment of the IP High Court, August 26, 2008 Case No. 2008 (gyo-ke) 10001. This method helps a non-English speaker, such as a native Japanese speaker, to find an English word in the dictionary by utilizing a unique phonetic index multi-element matrix. The matrix includes rows consisting of four elements of a particular English word: (1) a consonant in the word, (2) the vocal accent and consonants (phonetic symbols), (3) spelling, and (4) translation. Columns consist of English words in alphabetical order. The claim does not require a computer or machine to use the method because Japanese people generally recognize consonants in English words more easily than vowels, and Japanese users can find the same combination of consonants in the matrix and look up the word in the dictionary. Reversing a rejection of JPO Board, the court held that the claimed method constitutes a statutory invention because it solves a technical problem (finding an English word in the dictionary) by using a matrix that uses a law of nature (the ability for a Japanese person to recognize consonants better than vowels). Is this method patent eligible under U.S. Patent Law?

E. PATENTABILITY EXCLUSION: OBJECTIONS ON MORAL GROUNDS

The United States Patent Act contains no express authorization to withhold patent protection for lack of moral utility, although our courts and the United States Patent and Trademark Office have recognized that protection for an invention may be denied if "injurious to the well-being, good policy, or sound morals of society." *Lowell v. Lewis,* 15 F. Cas. 1018, 1019 (C.C.D. Mass. 1817) (No. 8568). The TRIPS Agreement expressly authorizes members to withhold patent protection on these grounds. Article 27 states in pertinent part:

Members may exclude from patentability inventions, the prevention within their territory of the commercial exploitation of which is necessary to protect *ordre public* or morality, including to protect human, animal or plant life or health or to avoid serious prejudice to the environment, provided that such exclusion is not made merely because the exploitation is prohibited by their law.

An entity that is not formally a TRIPS member, the EPO, has promulgated standards to assess policy limits to patentable subject matter. Article 53(a) of the EPC provides that European patents will not be granted for "inventions the publication or exploitation of which would be contrary to 'ordre public' or morality...."

Like the U.S., the EPO supports the patentability of living things, including animals. In *HARVARD/Transgenic animal* (T–315/03), [2005] E.P.O.R. 31, the EPO found that certain claims to a transgenic mouse are patentable, and recognizing that "the law is clear: there is no excluded or excepted category of 'animals in general.' " However, ethical concerns have been raised for particular inventions when "living things" include human or human-derived material. Additionally, Rule 28 of the EPC provides the following specific exclusions from patentability of biotechnological inventions:

(a) processes for cloning human beings;

(b) processes for modifying the germ line genetic identity of human beings;

(c) uses of human embryos for industrial or commercial purposes;

(d) processes for modifying the genetic identity of animals which are likely to cause them suffering without any substantial medical benefit to man or animal, and also animals resulting from such processes.

An invention that falls within the enumerated categories of Rule 28 of the EPC is deemed unpatentable. However, those categories are not exhaustive. If a biotechnological invention does not fall within one of these categories, the patent claim must be assessed under Article 53 of the EPC. *See HARVARD/Transgenic animal* (T–315/03), *supra*. Provisions corresponding to both Article 53 and Rule 28 of the EPC are stated in Article 6 of the European Parliament and Council Directive 98/44, Legal Protection of Biotechnological Inventions, 1998 O.J. (L 213) 13.

Several of these authorities are considered in the following decision, in which the Opposition Division of the European Patent Office (the "OD") considered the patentability of claims directed to a modified animal, a immunocompromised mouse implanted with human tissue. Various opponents objected to the patentability of the claimed animal-human chimera. In this excerpt of the OD's opinion, one of the opponents (referred to as "OII" in the opinion), objected on the grounds that the invention violated morality.

STANFORD/MODIFIED ANIMAL

European Patent Office (Opposition Division)

[2002] E.P.O.R. 2

YEATS, BURKHARDT, AND GROSSKOPF

European patent no. 0322240 is based on European patent application no. 88312222.8 filed on December 22, 1988 and claiming the priority of US 137173 from December 23, 1987.

Mention of grant of the patent was published in the European Patent Bulletin 1995/09 of March 1, 1995. . . .

OII argued that it was intrinsically unethical and against the general moral principles of Western society to grant patents on life. Animals were not to be placed on the same level as industrial products or inaminate objects. Patenting animals would extend a monopoly into daily life areas. It would cause an undesirable dependency in the medical research area, increasing the cost of medicines and experimental animals, and was against the interests of farmers and consumers. OII requested the OD to carry out the so-called "balancing act" . . . *i.e.* to weigh up the suffering of the claimed animals against the benefit conferred on humankind by the invention, when considering whether the animals were patentable under Article 53(a) EPC. Although OII acknowledged that the animals of the opposed patent were associated with a potential medical benefit, he contended that this was outweighed by the fact that the invention was patented and that this would hamper further research in this field. Moreover, the preparation of the chimeras of the patent in suit was ethically unacceptable, as was the use of human foetal cells and tissue from a child as sources for xenografts. Xenotransplants were furthermore ecologically risky since they could result in the generation of new pathological viruses.

As already set out above, the OD notes that according to Article 4.2 of E.U. Directive 98/44 and the corresponding Rule 23c EPC, animals are patentable if the technical feasibility of the invention is not confined to a particular animal variety, provided that if the animals result from a genetic modification that is likely to cause them suffering, the invention confers a substantial medical benefit on man or animal (Art. 6.2 of the Directive, Rule 23d EPC). OII's argument that the patenting of animals is regarded as intrinsically unethical in Western society cannot therefore be followed.

The OD has furthermore weighed up the potential medical benefits of the present invention against the possible suffering of the animals. Although it is true, as P has pointed out, that the animals of the opposed patent are not genetically modified, so that, strictly speaking Rule 23d(d) EPC does not apply, the OD is nevertheless of the opinion that the spirit of the rule requires a "balancing act" test for all patents concerning animals, whether genetically modified or not.

In the case of the present animals, all parties agree that there are enormous medical benefits associated with the invention. The patent exemplifies immunocompromised mice implanted with human hematopoietic tissue. The resulting chimeric animal is useful as a source for human hematopoietic cells, and as an animal model for human hematopoiesis. As such, the animals provide the only available animal model for HIV–I infection and can be used to test potential anti-AIDS therapies before human trials are undertaken. The claimed invention further offers the promise of providing human cells and organs for transplant in the future, an undoubtedly worthy aim when the acute shortage of available organs is taken into account. The hypothetical potential risks associated with xenotransplantation cited by OII are not considered to be a ground for denying patentability on ethical grounds. First, it would be unjustified to deny a patent under Article 53(a) EPC merely on the basis of possible, rather than conclusively documented hazards. Secondly, the EPO is not vested with carrying out the task of monitoring and estimating such risks; this is rather a matter for the numerous regulatory authorities charged with regulating research and medical practice (T356/93, above). The field of xenotransplantation is subject to a tight regulation and careful cost-benefit assessment, and will certainly continue to be so in the future.

As P has asserted, the grant of a patent does not mean that anything will be put into practice. The primary purpose of a patent is to protect a party's invention in the form of intellectual property, not to regulate research; the legal framework for carrying out an invention is defined by national laws.

As for the alleged negative effects of patenting the present invention on research and the cost of medicines, even were the OD to agree with OII that patenting the present invention would hinder research, which it does not, this argument is immaterial since the EPO has not been vested with the task of taking into account the economic effects of the grant of patents in specific areas and of restricting the field of patentable subject-matter accordingly. The standard to apply for an exclusion under Article 53(a) EPC is whether the publication or exploitation of the invention is contrary to ordre public or morality.

Finally, OII has argued that it is ethically unacceptable to create animal human chimeras such as those of the opposed patent, and in doing so to take cells and tissue from aborted foetuses or children aged below three years of age as a source of human tissues. In this regard it is undeniable that the production of chimeric animals containing human organs grown from human cells isolated from aborted foetuses or deceased persons, whether children or adults, instinctively appears distasteful, if not immoral, to many people at first glance. On the other hand, the medical benefits conferred by the invention are not in dispute among the parties to the present proceedings (see above), and the use of donated human material for research is widely accepted provided consent was given, which there is no reason to doubt in the present case. The P has emphasised that no objection to the practice of the invention have been raised by any regulatory authorities. OII dwelt on the fact that the claim of the patent in suit include in their scope a large number of theoretically possible embodiments, of which some might be considered particularly unacceptable. On this issue the OD points out that the practice of each individual embodiment of every invention in the medical field is subject to approval by the appropriate regulatory bodies in the Contracting States; in consequence, it is possible for every state to authorise only those embodiments deemed acceptable in that state.

The OD agrees with the P that as long as a claimed invention has a legitimate use, it cannot be the role of the EPO to act as moral censor and invoke the provisions of Article 53(a) EPC to refuse on ethical grounds to grant a patent on legal research and directed to an invention indisputably associated with medical benefits. The technology underlying the present invention is undoubtedly controversial and the subject of intensive discussion in the media and among members of the public. However, there is at present no consensus in Europe society about the desirability or otherwise of this technology, and public opinion is still being formed on this and related matters. It would be presumptuous for the EPO to interfere in this public debate. The provisions of Article 53(a) EPC are intended to exclude from patentability not subject-matter that is controversial, but rather that kind of extreme subject-matter (*e.g.* letter-bombs and anti-personnel mines) which would be regarded by the public as so abhorrent that the grant of a patent would be inconceivable. The present invention does not in the estimation of the OD fall under this category.

In conclusions, the opposed patent is considered to meet the requirements of Article 53(a) EPC.

Notes and Questions

1. In *Howard Florey/Relaxin*, [1995] E.P.O.R. 541, the EPO's Opposition Division explained that Article 53(a) is not commonly invoked:

Article 53(a) EPC is likely to be invoked only in rare and extreme cases, for example that of a letter bomb. In addition, some general guidance is given as to when such a case might arise: A fair test to apply is to consider whether it is probable that the public in general would regard the invention as so abhorrent that the grant of patent rights would be inconceivable. If it is clear that this is the case, objection should be raised under Article 53(a); otherwise not. Article 53(a) constitutes an exception to the general principle, set out in Article 52(1) EPC, that patents shall be granted for inventions which are industrially applicable, novel and inventive.

The *Relaxin* opinion considered the patentability a claim directed to DNA derived from tissue obtained from pregnant women.

[T]he patenting of the DNA would indeed be abhorrent to the overwhelming majority of the public if it were true that the invention involved the patenting of human life, an abuse of pregnant women, a return to slavery and the piecemeal sale of women to industry. However, the Opposition Division emphatically rejects these arguments.

With regard to the isolation of mRNA from tissue taken from pregnant women, the proprietor stated that the women who donated tissue consented to do so within the framework of necessary gynaecological operations. There is no reason to perceive this as immoral. Indeed, human tissue or other material, such as blood, bone, and so on, has been widely used for many years as a source for useful products, often proteins but now also RNA or DNA, which are unavailable elsewhere.

Additionally, *Relaxin* rejected the argument that patenting DNA was objectionable because it was akin to patenting human life, observing that "DNA is not 'life,' but a chemical substance which carries genetic information and can be used as an intermediate in the production of proteins which may be medically useful."

2. Compare the recent decision of the EPO's Enlarged Board of Appeal in *WARF/Stem Cells*, [2009] E.P.O.R. 15, which considered the patentability of an invention which, as of the filing date, could be prepared exclusively by a method which necessarily involved the destruction of the human embryos. Although such destruction was not part of the claim, the *Stem Cells* opinion determined that patentability was barred by Rule 28 of the EPC, *supra*, which excludes from patentability "uses of human embryos for industrial or commercial purposes." The *Stem Cells* Board explained that Article 28(c) expressly prevented such claims and refused to balance the benefits of the invention to humanity against the prejudice to the embryo, stating "there is no room for manoeuvre." Can the *Stanford/Modified Animal*, *Howard Florey/Relaxin* and *WARF/Stem Cells* decisions be harmonized?

3. The United States Patent and Trademark Office has rejected an application for a biotechnological invention on moral utility grounds. *See* Final Office Action on U.S. Patent Application No. 08/993,564

(Aug. 11, 2004). The application sought protection for a chimeric embryo that incorporated both human and non-human cells. The rejection stated that the U.S. Patent "Office does not agree that humans are patentable subject matter." *Id.*, at 22. Additionally, the rejection found that the application lacked any practical utility based on the view that toxicology studies would not produce sufficiently usable data applicable to either humans or non-humans, given that the claim was not directed to either. Can *Stanford/Modified Animal* be distinguished from the U.S.P.T.O's treatment of this issue?

F. PATENTABILITY EXCLUSION: DIAGNOSTIC AND SURGICAL METHODS

The field of diagnostic, therapeutic and surgical methods for the treatment of humans or animals represents another potential exclusion from patentability. TRIPS Article 27(3)(a) permits—but does not require—WTO members to exclude patent protection for these subject matters. Patenting medical methods raise ethical issues about patient access to innovative procedures, the encouragement an unencumbered flow of information about new methods within the profession and freedom from limitations on the practice of scientific knowledge by a threat of injunctions or royalty payments. *See, e.g.*, AMERICAN MEDICAL ASSOCIATION, REPORT OF THE COUNCIL ON ETHICAL AND JUDICIAL AFFAIRS, 2 (3/1/07) (medical organization expressing concerns about the "physician's ethical responsibility to contribute to and share scientific knowledge"); *Eli Lilly and Company's Application* (1975) RPC 438 (Eng.) (noting that "the reasons for such an exclusion appear to us to be based in ethics rather than logic....."). Are these concerns less acute in nations where compulsory licensing systems are existent and consumer health care costs are controlled or subsidized?

Most nations vary patent protection in the medical field to some degree. As one example, the United Kingdom's Patent Act provides that patents will not be granted for either "a method of treatment of the human or animal body by surgery or therapy," or "a method of diagnosis practised on the human or animal body." Patents Act, 1977, c. 37, § 4 (Eng.). Japan's Patent Examination Guidelines state that "[m]ethods of surgery, therapy or diagnosis of humans have been termed 'medical activity' and are normally practiced by medical doctors," and therefore do not satisfy the "industrially applicable" requirement of Japan's Patent Act. THE EXAMINATION GUIDELINES FOR PATENT AND UTILITY MODEL, sec. 2.1.1 (Oct. 2009) (Japan). These Guidelines note that "[m]ethods for contraception or delivery are included in "methods of surgery, therapy or diagnosis of humans."

Other nations issue patents for medical and diagnostic procedures, but exclude medical professionals from the legal definition of infringement. For example, in the U.S., a medical practitioner and related health care entities are exempt from liability under theories of direct infringement and active inducement. *See* 35 U.S.C. § 287(c). Why do you suppose that this limitation did not extend to the doctrine of contributory infringement? Similarly, Brazil's patent statute provides that the right to exclude does not apply "to the preparation of a medicine in accordance with a medical prescription for individual cases, carried out by a qualified professional, as well as to the medicine so prepared." Industrial Property Law No. 9.279, art. 43 (5/14/96 as amended by Law 10.196 of 2/14/01) (Brazil). Do you find Brazil's broader or narrower than U.S. law? Do you prefer an approach that bars patents for medical procedures entirely, or one that excludes certain parties and activities from infringement?

Some nations allow the right to exclude to extend to medical treatments. For example, *Bristol–Myers Squibb Co. v. F. H. Faulding & Co. Ltd.*, [2000] FCA 316, the Federal Court of Australia determined that patent directed to a method of administering an anti-cancer drug met that nation's patentability requirement. In addition to the lack of statutory support for any applicable exclusion in Australia's patent statute, the court explained a concern with:

> ... what seems to us to be the insurmountable problem, from a public policy viewpoint, of drawing a logical distinction which would justify allowing patentability for a product for treating the human body, but deny patentability for a method of treatment.... This seems particularly the case where, as here, the claim is for an invention for the administration of a product.

Id. (citation omitted). Although *Faulding* invalidated the patent on the basis of novelty, there are now two Australian decisions indicating in dicta that medical procedures may be patentable subject matter in that nation. *See also, Anaesthetic Supplies Pty. Ltd. v. Rescare Ltd.* (1994) 50 FCR 1.

Where the exception is accepted, how broadly is it applied? Consider a recent decision of the European Enlarged Board of Appeal, which considered the European Patent Convention Article 53(c), which states, "methods for treatment of the human or animal body by surgery or therapy and diagnostic methods practised on the human or animal body; this provision shall not apply to products, in particular substances or compositions, for use in any of these methods." *See* EUROPEAN PATENT CONVENTION art. 53. The claim at issue concerned a cardiac imaging, whereby a doctor could view the real-time condition of a patient's heart enhanced by the use of a substance known as "^{129}XE" that was inhaled or injected into the patient. *Medi–Physics/Treatment by Surgery* (G/107) [2010] E.P.O.R. 25. According to the opinion, this method could be used to help a physician made the decision about whether to conduct surgery, to provide feedback during surgery or to examine cardiac effects during drug therapy.

The decision noted that, to the extent that the claims at issue concerned invasive work that required professional medical expertise and entailed a health risk, they were excluded from patent protection under the EPC. With respect to claims directed to the use of the method solely for diagnostic purposes, the Enlarged Board explained:

> Article 53(c) EPO prohibits the patenting of surgical methods and not the patenting of any methods which can be used in the context of carrying out a surgical method. . . . the fact that one of the possible and described uses of the imaging method is the use by a surgeon during a surgical intervention allowing the surgeon to decide on the course of action to be taken in the intervention by taking note of the immediately produced image data, does not render that imaging method excluded from patentability.

Why might the Enlarged Board of Appeals wish to construe this limitation narrowly? How narrowly does this rule apply? For example, how might the administration of a vaccine by means of an injection be considered under EPC Art. 53(c)?

Chapter 4

INDUSTRIAL APPLICABILITY

A. DEFINITIONS OF INDUSTRY AND APPLICABILITY

Outside the United States, the requirement comparable to utility under § 101 is industrial applicability. TRIPS Article 27, Paragraph 1 requires an invention to be capable of industrial application. EPC Article 57 adopts a broad definition for meeting the requirement, i.e. if an invention can be made or used in any kind of industry, including agriculture. To what extent, do EPC member states harmonize their industrial applicability requirements under their national laws?

Regarding biotechnological inventions, the EU Biotechnology Directive (98/44/EC) states that DNA sequences must have an indication of their function in order to be patented. Reflecting this requirement, the EPO Boards interpret Article 57 to require that the function of DNA sequences must be reasonably credible. This statement sounds very similar to the specific, substantial and credible test for utility at the Federal Circuit and the USPTO. However, the counsel for Human Genome Science in the following case suggests that the U.S. utility requirement is more stringent than the European industrial applicability test. Moreover, even when applying the same test, it is often difficult for the EPO and national courts to reach the same conclusion because of the fact specific nature of the industrial applicability question.

The following case raises anew the question of when a newly isolated compound that exists in nature and is isolated by a method involving an inventive step may be patented. Is it sufficient that the new compound is one that will be the subject of an active research program, or alternatively, must patentability be postponed until more is known about the compound. If it is the latter, then what level of certainty regarding this additional knowledge must be shown? The case itself is an appeal from a finding that followed a decision, T 0018/09, by one of the European Patent Office's Boards of Appeal to allow the following independent claims in European Patent 939,804 over a claim that they lacked industrial applicability, a finding that differed from that of the English trial court:

1. An isolated nucleic acid molecule comprising a polynucleotide sequence encoding a Neutrokine-α polypeptide wherein said polynucleotide sequence is elected from the group consisting of:

(a) a polynucleotide sequence encoding the full length Neutrokine-α polypeptide having the amino sequence of residues 1 to 285 of SEQ ID NO:2; and

(b) a polynucleotide sequence encoding the extracellular domain of the eutrokine-á polypeptide having the amino acid sequence of residues 73 to 285 of SEQ ID NO:2.

6. A recombinant vector containing an isolated nucleic acid molecule consisting of a polynucleotide sequence encoding a Neutrokine-α polypeptide wherein said polynucleotide sequence is selected from the group consisting of:

(a) a polynucleotide sequence encoding the full length Neutrokine-α polypeptide having the amino sequence of residues 1 to 285 of SEQ ID NO:2; and (b) a polynucleotide sequence encoding the extracellular domain of the Neutrokine-α polypeptide having the amino acid sequence of residues 73 to 285 of SEQ ID NO:2

13. An isolated antibody or portion thereof that binds specifically to

(g) the full length Neutrokine-α polypeptide (amino acid sequence of residues 1 to 285 of SEQ ID NO: 2); or

(h) the extracellular domain of the Neutrokine-α polypeptide (amino acid sequence of residues 73 to 285 of SEQ ID NO: 2).

These claims are simply directed to the genes coding for the protein Neutrokine-α, vectors containing such genes, and most importantly antibodies to Neutrokine-α such as antibodies actually shown to be useful to treat a particular disease such as the antibodies claimed in U.S. Pat. No. 7,317,089. This protein has had other names besides Neutrokine-α in the literature, but it is now officially known as TNFSF13b.

ELI LILLY & CO. v. HUMAN GENOME SCIENCES INC.

Court of Appeal, Civil Division

[2010] EWCA Civ 33, 9 February 2010

LORD JUSTICE JACOB:

1. Kitchin J held ([2008] EWHC 1903 (Pat), 31st July 2008) that HGS's EP (UK) 0,939,804 was invalid and could not be saved by some proffered amendments. HGS appeals. At the time of his decision the Opposition Division ("OD") of the European Patent Office ("EPO") had also held the Patent invalid.

2. Since the Judge's decision things have moved on. In particular on 21st October 2009, the Technical Board of Appeal ("TBA") of the EPO allowed HGS's appeal based on some more restricted claims. It gave its reasons on 1st December 2009, doing so as part of an accelerated proceeding in co-operative effort with this court (see [1–4] of its reasons).

3. The case is basically about the patentability or otherwise of a protein called by HGS Neutrokine-α, antibodies to it and the polynucleotide sequence encoding for it. HGS were the first to discover its existence, doing so by "bioinformatics" (see more below). Others independently made the same discovery shortly thereafter, each discoverer giving it a different name. That is not very surprising given the very fast accumulation of genetic code information coupled with improvements in computing power and other techniques.

[Appellant challenged Mr. Justice Kitchin's finding that the claims lacked industrial applicability. Before giving reasons for the dismissal of the appeal against this finding, Justice Jacob explained the co-operation between the EPO and national courts, and compared the natures of a first instance decision and appeal in England and Wales in contrast to the nature of proceedings in the EPO, focusing the scope and procedure for admitting new arguments and evidence.]

The status of EPO and especially TBA decisions on questions of law in National (and especially UK) proceedings.

The Broad Context of the Invention

42. From the beginning of the genetic engineering revolution (starting around 1980) until the early 90s, scientists created genetically engineered versions of proteins that were already known. The basic, so-called "wet-lab" technique went as follows: the protein of interest was identified and isolated. Some

amino-acid sequence data was obtained. The corresponding nucleic acid sequence(s) encoding for the identified sequence could then be deduced. Probes using that sequence or those sequences (generally the latter owing to redundancy) were made and used to clone the actual gene from a library. The cloned gene could then be inserted into a host cell used to express the required protein.

44. By the early to mid–90s another way of doing research became possible—research using "bioinformatics". By then major projects to obtain the full genetic code—the genomes—of living things and particularly the genome of humans were producing results. Large amounts of nucleotide sequence data from the human genome were becoming available as techniques (and computer power) improved.

45. Now just having large amounts of such data tells you nothing in itself. You do not know what the reading frame is. Nor can you tell introns (junk) from sequence data encoding for actual bodily proteins. More has to be done to identify a sequence (excluding introns) encoding for a real protein. It is in that context that expressed sequence tags ("ESTs") started to be identified. ESTs are part of a cDNA clone, but not the full length sequence encoding the entire protein. Knowing the sequence of an EST does not get you all that far. You still do not know what the full-length sequence is, and you do not even know what the reading frame is to deduce the partial amino-acid sequence for which the EST encodes.

46. As techniques improved and amounts of data became more substantial it became possible to do better than ESTs. It was possible to identify from published sequence data full length nucleotide sequences for proteins. Once that is done you can deduce the amino acid sequence of the protein encoded. And you should be able to make it (the details of how do not matter). But, unlike the days of wet-lab techniques (where you knew it at the outset), you do not know what function the protein has.

47. Even at that stage, however, it is more than reasonable to suppose that it has some biological function—after all the body is carrying the gene for it. One can say in general terms that if there is a disease or condition involving a deficiency of the protein then it may be treatable with it. Or if there is a disease or condition caused by overproduction of the protein it may be treatable with an antibody to the protein. So in a very general sense one can say there is probably an application for the protein or its antibodies. As will be seen, however, that is not good enough to make the protein or its antibodies patenta-

ble. You have to say something more about their proposed use than they will probably be useful in medicine, though that is very likely to be so. The question in general is how much more you need to say and how reliable what you say needs to be.

48. Without *in vitro* and ultimately *in vivo* assays, you cannot definitely know what the protein you have discovered actually does. However even before that stage it may, in the case of some proteins, be possible to make an informed guess. This can be done by seeing how closely the amino-acid sequence of your newly identified protein resembles the amino-acid sequence of a known protein or "family" of proteins. You look for homology between your protein and the known protein or family of proteins. If there is some degree of homology and you know or can predict reasonably well what the known family member(s) do then you can hazard a guess that your unknown one does something like it or them.

49. Of course how likely it is that your guess will turn out to be true depends on a host of factors, for instance how homologous your protein sequence is to the other protein sequence(s), how specific the action of the known protein or family of proteins is known to be and how specific your surmise as to its function is. No doubt other factors also come into play. Depending on all the circumstances the "guess" can range from that which is no more than a "shot in the dark"—something which can be fairly described as wholly speculative—to a firm prediction which is almost surely right.

Susceptible of Industrial Application?

The Legislation: Art. 57 and the Biotech Directive

* * *

51. An invention is only patentable if it is "susceptible of industrial application" (EPC Art.52(1)). Art. 57 of the EPC says:

> An invention shall be considered as susceptible of industrial application if it can be made or used in any kind of industry, including agriculture.

So if an invention does not comply with that requirement it not a patentable invention and the patent for it may (which in context means "must") be revoked (s.72(1) of the Patents Act 1977).

54. Whilst no-one suggests that the Biotech Directive (99/44EC) altered the meaning of the EPC (it could hardly do so, given that the EPC is a free-standing international treaty whose signatories do not include Member States of the EU), it is

common ground that it throws some light on the interpretation of Art. 57.

55. Article 5 provides:

> "1. The human body, at the various stages of its formation and development, and the simple discovery of one of its elements, including the sequence or partial sequence of a gene, cannot constitute patentable inventions.
>
> 2. An element isolated from the human body or otherwise produced by means of a technical process, including the sequence or partial sequence of a gene, may constitute a patentable invention, even if the structure of that element is identical to that of a natural element.
>
> 3. The industrial application of a sequence or partial sequence of a gene must be disclosed in the patent application."

56. Art. 5.3 is a key provision. Recitals 22 to 24 put its meaning in context:

22. Whereas the industrial application of a sequence or partial sequence [of a gene] must be disclosed in the patent application as filed;

23. Whereas a mere DNA sequence without indication of a function does not contain any technical information and is therefore not a patentable invention;

24. Whereas, in order to comply with the industrial application criterion it is necessary in cases where a sequence or partial sequence of a gene is used to produce a protein or part of a protein, to specify which protein or part of a protein is produced or what function it performs.

57. The upshot, stated broadly, is that you can patent an isolated gene sequence but only if you disclose the industrial application of the protein for which it encodes. However clever and inventive you may have been in discovering a gene sequence, you cannot have a patent for it or for the protein for which it encodes if you do not disclose how it can be used.

* * *

The EPO Case Law on Art. 57

65. This view is consistent with the important case-law of the TBAs. The decision of the TBA concerning the patent in suit does not purport to lay down any new principles. For these it is necessary to go to the main cases involving DNA sequences and proteins discovered by bioinformatics. These are *Max–Planck* T 0870/04 (May 2005) *Johns Hopkins* T 1329/04 (June 2005) *Genentech* T 0604/04 (March 2006), *ZymoGenetics* T

0898/05 (July 2006), *Bayer* T 1452/06 (May 2007) and *Schering* T 1165/06 (July 2007). It is not necessary or useful to refer to any others. Nor to the meagre English case-law on the subject.

66. I take them in turn. *Max–Planck* was an *ex parte* appeal from a refusal to grant by the examining division. The applicants had identified what they called a "BDP1 polypeptide". They sought to justify a claim to it on the basis that it could be made and used as a tool for research. That was rejected. It is now settled that the "research tool" justification for a new polypeptide or the nucleotide sequence encoding for it is not enough to satisfy the Art. 57 test. As the Board said:

> In the board's judgment, although the present application describes a product (a polypeptide), means and methods for making it, and its prospective use thereof for basic science activities, it identifies no practical way of exploiting it in at least one field of industrial activity. In this respect, it is considered that a vague and speculative indication of possible objectives that might or might not be achievable by carrying out further research with the tool as described is not sufficient for fulfillment of the requirement of industrial applicability. The purpose of granting a patent is not to reserve an unexplored field of research for an applicant.

67. That last sentence is full of importance. If you allow patenting of chemicals whose use you do not really know you will subvert the patent system and be likely to stultify research by others rather than encourage it. A merely "vague and speculative indication of possible objectives" is not enough.

68. The present case indeed provides an example of the danger of what can happen if patenting too far upstream is allowed. Both sides (HGS in collaboration with GlaxoSmithKline) are conducting clinical trials but each is trying a different antibody to Neutrokine-α and for different conditions. As a matter of interest the HGS trials are for the treatment of lupus, one of the few diseases not mentioned in the patent. If the patent were valid, the valuable research and development work done by Lilly into a field apparently not researched (and certainly not taken through to clinical trial) by HGS would potentially be rendered futile. The patent system would not be working as it should. It would be operating to prevent research, not to encourage it.

69. It is also important to note an earlier paragraph of *Max Planck*, for the Boards still regard it as good law:

> In cases where a substance, naturally occurring in the human body, is identified, and possibly also structurally

characterised and made available through some method, but either its function is not known or it is complex and incompletely understood, and no disease or condition has yet been identified as being attributable to an excess or deficiency of the substance, and no other practical use is suggested for the substance, then industrial applicability cannot be acknowledged. While the jurisprudence has tended to be generous to applicants, there must be a borderline between what can be accepted, and what can only be categorized as an interesting research result which per se does not yet allow a practical industrial application to be identified. Even though research results may be a scientific achievement of considerable merit, they are not necessarily an invention which can be applied industrially.

70. So the question here is which side of the borderline the case lies—a question of degree turning on the facts and not a pure question of law.

* * *

79. The next case is *Genentech,* an opposition appeal as opposed to one *ex parte.* I take the facts from the Board's summary:

In summary, the patent in suit identifies applications for the claimed polypeptides which may ultimately lead to some profitable use. It provides a structural characterisation which enables their assignment to the category of receptors which bind members of the PF4A family of chemokines and, insofar, indicates what their function might be. Yet, in the absence of any characterisation of their ligands, this function remains at best incompletely understood.

80. The Board then referred to *Max Planck* and specifically quotes [6] cited above. That is why I said earlier that it is still regarded as good law.

81. The Board then held that the Patent alone did not provide enough information to comply with Art. 57, though if one added to it the common general knowledge of the skilled man, there was enough. It said:

The board agrees with the criteria defined in T 870/04 and observes that, taken in isolation, the technical data provided in respect of the polypeptides of Figures 4 and 5 fall somewhat short of fulfilling them insofar as, as already above mentioned, there is no evidence available as to which ligands these polypeptides bind to. Yet, of course, each case has to be considered on its own merit (see e.g. T 338/00 of 6 November 2002) and it is important here to take into account the common general knowledge at the priority date as well as the then prevalent attitude of the person skilled in the art as it may be inferred from the documents illustrating this common general knowledge.

82. The Board's reference to each case being considered on its own merits is of course not only right but important. It shows that one cannot jog from the facts of one case to the facts of another. What matters is the applicable legal principle, not the detailed facts of a particular case.

* * *

101. Finally I turn to *Schering*, another *ex parte* case. The application was to patent a protein called "IL (interleukin)–17". The Board dealt with Art. 57 briefly, the main question being obviousness. As regards Art. 57 it said:

> The board is convinced that the requirements of Article 57 EPC are fulfilled. The sequence information provided in the application with respect to the presence in IL–174 of the characteristic cysteine spacing of the IL–17 cytokine family makes it plausible that this polypeptide may belong to this family and have biological activities similar to those of the other family members known at the filing date, in particular CTLA–8. This is confirmed by post-published evidence filed by the appellant.

102. It is clear from these authorities that discovering a nucleotide sequence encoding for a human protein and being able to show that the protein concerned has some common homology with known proteins (i.e. is a member of a family) may satisfy Art.57. But whether it does or not is case dependent and in particular depends upon how well established the functions of the other members of the family are. To say "my new protein is similar to a known family of proteins" is not all that helpful in indicating a possible use if the function of that family is itself poorly understood at best.

103. Kitchin J reviewed these and other authorities and drew from them a series of propositions which he set out at [226] which I set out here...

> (i) The notion of industry must be construed broadly. It includes all manufacturing, extracting and processing activities of enterprises that are carried out continuously, independently and for commercial gain.

> (ii) However, it need not necessarily be conducted for profit and a product which is shown to be useful to cure a rare or orphan disease may be considered capable of indus-

trial application even if it is not intended for use in any trade at all.

(iii) The capability of industrial exploitation must be derivable by the skilled person from the description read with the benefit of the common general knowledge.

(iv) The description, so read, must disclose a practical way of exploiting the invention in at least one field of industrial activity.

(v) More recently, this has been re-formulated as an enquiry as to whether there is a sound and concrete basis for recognising that the contribution could lead to practical application in industry. Nevertheless, there remains a need to disclose in definite technical terms the purpose of the invention and how it can be used to solve a given technical problem. Moreover, there must be a real prospect of exploitation which is derivable directly from the specification, if not already obvious from the nature of the invention or the background art.

(vi) Conversely, the requirement will not be satisfied if what is described is merely an interesting research result that might yield a yet to be identified industrial application. A speculative indication of possible objectives that might or might not be achievable by carrying out research is not sufficient. Similarly, it should not be left to the skilled reader to find out how to exploit the invention by carrying out a research programme.

(vii) It follows that the purpose of granting a patent is not to reserve an unexplored field of research for the applicant, nor to give the patentee unjustified control over others who are actively investigating in that area and who might eventually find ways actually to exploit it.

(viii) If a substance is disclosed and its function is essential for human health then the identification of the substance having that function will immediately suggest a practical application. If, on the other hand, the function of that substance is not known or is incompletely understood, and no disease has been identified which is attributable to an excess or a deficiency of it, and no other practical use is suggested for it, then the requirement of industrial applicability is not satisfied. This will be so even though the disclosure may be a scientific achievement of considerable merit.

(xi) Using the claimed invention to find out more about its own activities is not in itself an industrial application.

(x) Finally, it is no bar to patentability that the invention has been found by homology studies using bioinformatics techniques although this may have a bearing on how the skilled person would understand the disclosure.

The Patent in suit

* * *

117. The key claims of the Patent as now settled by the TBA are in part to nucleic acid sequences encoding for Neutrokine-α or important parts of it and for Neutrokine-α or important parts of it.

118. The Judge drew these important conclusions:

> Overall, the Patent contains extravagant and sometimes contradictory claims. By way of illustration, it suggests in paragraph [0123] that Neutrokine-α inhibits immune cell function and in paragraph [0143] that antagonists of Neutrokine-α also inhibit immune cell function. There is nothing by way of experimental evidence to support the claims made and I accept Professor Saklatvala's evidence that the idea that Neutrokine-α and antagonists to Neutrokine-α could be used to treat the extraordinary range of diseases identified was fanciful. He found it hard to believe that anyone could seriously suggest on the basis of no experimental data at all that that Neutrokine-α was the answer to so many conditions, from treating cancer to treating worms. In my judgment the skilled person would come to the conclusion that the inventors had no idea as to the activity of Neutrokine-α when drafting the Patent. It teaches the skilled person nothing useful about its activity other than that Neutrokine-α is another member of the TNF ligand superfamily.

> In this case I am quite satisfied that the skilled person would consider the Patent does not of itself identify any industrial application other than by way of speculation. As is apparent from my review in paragraphs [100]–[134] of this judgment, it contains an astonishing range of diseases and conditions which Neutrokine-α and antibodies to Neutrokine-α may be used to diagnose and treat and there is no data of any kind to support the claims made. The skilled person would consider it totally far-fetched that Neutrokine-α could be used in relation to them all and, as I have found, would be driven to the conclusion that the authors had no clear idea what the activities of the protein were and so included every possibility. To have included

such a range of applications was no better than to have included none at all.

But that is not the end of the matter because the disclosure must be considered in the light of the common general knowledge which I have considered in paragraphs [34]–[77] of this judgment. The skilled person would have known that TNF was involved as a primary mediator in immune regulation and the inflammatory response and had an involvement in a wide range of diseases as septic shock, rheumatoid arthritis, inflammatory bowel disease, tissue rejection, HIV infection, and some adverse drug reactions. He would have known that all the members of the TNF ligand superfamily identified hitherto were expressed by T cells and played a role in the regulation of T cell proliferation and T cell mediated responses. Further, as Professor Saklatvala accepted, the skilled person would anticipate that the activities of Neutrokine-α might relate to T cells and, in particular, be expressed on T cells and be a co-stimulant of B cell production; that it might play a role in the immune response and in the control of tumours and malignant disease; that it might have an effect on B cell proliferation; and that it would have the same roles, to some degree, as those described in the Gruss paper.

On the other hand, the skilled person would have also known that the members of the family had pleiotropic actions; that some of those activities were unique to particular TNF ligands and others were shared by some or all the other TNF ligands and that no disease had been identified in which they were all involved. Moreover, as explained in the Maini publication, the therapeutic application of TNF-a monoclonal antibody for the treatment of rheumatoid arthritis was believed to operate by interrupting the cytokine cascade and by controlling the recruitment and trafficking of blood cells to the joint—a rather specific activity.

Does that common general knowledge, taken as a whole, disclose a practical way of exploiting Neutrokine-α? Or does it provide a sound and concrete basis for recognising that Neutrokine-α could lead to practical application in industry? In my judgment it does not. The fact that Neutrokine-α might be expected to play a role in regulating the activities of B cells and T cells and play an unspecified role in regulating the immune and inflammatory response did not reveal how it could be used to solve any particular problem. Neither the Patent nor the common general knowledge identified any disease or condition which Neutrokine-α could be used to diagnose or treat. Its functions were, at best, a matter of expectation and then at far too high a level of generality to constitute a sound or concrete basis for anything except a research project.

119. So the Judge addressed the crucial question: is it enough to make the invention "susceptible of industrial application" to tell the skilled reader that Neutrokine-α is "structurally similar to TNF and related cytokines and is believed to have similar biological effects and activities"? That depends on what was known about the biological effects and activities of the known members of the superfamily. Each of the postulated uses of Neutrokine-α or its antagonists was possible in the sense that one could not rule that out as a matter of science based on what was known about other superfamily members. So in one sense each was "plausible", even though all of them collectively were not and indeed some contradicted others so both could not be true. But that is miles away from being able to say that any particular use was plausible in the sense of being taken, by the reader, to be reasonably so. In reality one was faced with a research program to see which, if any, of the possible uses of the Neutrokine-α or its antagonists was real.

132. Now it is true that it was known that all members of the superfamily were expressed by activated T cells, that they all played a role in the regulation of T cell proliferation and T cell mediated immune responses and that some of the ligands played a role in the regulation of B-cell proliferation and antibody secretion and some took part in T cell dependent regulation of B cells. But it by no means follows that any member of the superfamily has a practical use or that the skilled reader would envisage such a use (other than as a speculation) on being told that a new member of the superfamily had been found. You would have to investigate each of them to find out. It is not impossible they would have such a use of some sort, but no more. It is all too speculative to say, on the basis of the information in the patent and common general knowledge that a newly found member of the superfamily is "capable of industrial application." That view is surely reinforced by the fact that only TNF-a had found any use and that was rather specialised, as I have already noted.

133. The Judge thought his conclusion as to the speculative nature of the claims in the patent was confirmed by the subsequent history of investigations by both HGS and others, particularly into B cells and T cells. He set out the detail (which was not challenged) at [141–175]. His summary is as follows:

[176] The papers and work to which I have referred represent only a very small fraction of the work carried out on Neutrokine-α. Nevertheless, I believe the following general conclusions can be drawn from them and the expert evidence. From 1999 it became increasingly clear that Neutrokine-α is expressed by peripheral blood leukocytes, and in the spleen and lymph nodes. From that time it also became apparent that Neutrokine-α plays a significant and particular role in the proliferation and differentiation of B cells. Subsequently it has also been shown to play a part in the regulation of T cell proliferation and activation. As the activities of Neutrokine-α have gradually been elucidated, and particularly those relating to B cells, it has become increasingly recognised as a potential therapeutic target for diseases that are specifically associated with altered B cell function. Notable amongst these are autoimmune diseases such as rheumatoid arthritis and SLE and B cell malignancies such as lymphoma. Neutrokine-α has now been shown to have an important role in the development of autoimmune disease and B cell cancers; but, at the same time, much of its biology remains unclear and is the subject of continuing study by many different research centres. In my judgment the nature and extent of all this research work, the limited conclusions ultimately drawn and the amount of work that remains to be done point strongly to the conclusion that the therapeutic and diagnostic applications suggested in the Patent were indeed speculative.

136. Accordingly based on the evidence before him, I conclude that the Judge's decision about Art. 57 cannot be faulted and the appeal falls to be dismissed.

137. Although the Judge and the TBA asked the same key question and identified the same "kernel" the real difference is that the Judge found on the facts before him that the "kernel" did not provide any basis for supposing that the invention was susceptible of industrial application whereas on the facts before it the Board thought there was.

158. For the above reasons I have come to the clear conclusion that the Judge was right to hold that the invention failed to comply with Art. 57.

Notes and Questions

1. *Eli Lilly* highlights some of the challenges in determining when to apply for patent protection for a biotechnological invention under a first-to-file system that lacks a grace period, such as the one created by

the European Patent Convention (EPC). To secure priority in a competitive research environment, applicants want to file an application with the patent office as early as possible. However, researchers may also want to publish their works early for both scientific priority and recognition. Due to the lack of a grace period under the EPC, researchers must file an application before publication. Since it is unpredictable how the EPO and courts in EPC member states would view the state of art and the general knowledge of a skilled person at the priority date, it is difficult for applicants to decide how much experimentation is required to identify a credible protein function before filing. It is even more challenging to decide the timing for securing patents in major markets if patent offices and courts apply different industrial applicability standards. What strategies should you adopt for drafting applications to minimize the likelihood of a finding of a lack of industrial applicability?

2. Why did Judge Kitchin and the EPO TBA reach opposite conclusions regarding industrial applicability? Did the differences in procedure between the two forums affect their conclusions? If so, would it be possible for EPC member states and other WIPO member states to accomplish harmonization without harmonizing procedures in their patent offices and national courts?

3. *Eli Lilly* made it clear that under the EPC it is necessary to decide the industrial applicability requirement by taking into account the common general knowledge of a skilled person in the art of invention at the time of priority. In contrast, the US patent system follows the first-to-invent system, and thus inventors must establish a specific utility at the time of invention. *Brenner v. Manson*, 383 U.S. 519 (1966). However, utility is frequently disputed based on whether the disclosure included enough information to support a specific, substantive, and credible utility. When utility is determined in the context of the quality of disclosure, US courts take account of the state of art as of the priority date.

4. In *In re Fisher*, 421 F.3d 1365 (Fed. Cir. 2005), Judge Rader disagreed with Judges Michel and Bryson as to whether ESTs have specific and substantial utility as a research tool.

> In simple terms, ESTs are research tools. Admittedly ESTs have use only in a research setting. However, the value and utility of research tools generally is beyond question, even though limited to a laboratory setting. See U.S. Pat. & Trademark Off., Manual of Patent Examining Procedure (MPEP) § 2107.01 at 2100–33 (8th ed. 2001, rev. Feb. 2003) ("Many research tools such as gas chromatographs, screening assays, and nucleotide sequencing techniques have a clear, specific and unquestionable utility (e.g., they are useful in analyzing compounds)."). Thus, if the claimed ESTs qualify as research tools, then they have a "specific" and "substantial" utility sufficient for § 101...

Do research tools meet the industrial applicability standard under EPC and UK patent law?

Chapter 5

PRIORITY, NOVELTY AND INVENTIVE STEP

A. PRIORITY AND NOVELTY

The United States is the only country which follows the first-to-invent principle. To facilitate collaboration among patent offices, WTO member states are urging the U.S. to adopt a first-to-file system to harmonize the conditions for obtaining a patent. Since 2003, the U.S. Congress has been looking to pass a bill to adopt a first-inventor-to-file system that would be perfectly in line with the first-to-file principle with a one-year grace period.

FIRST–TO–FILE v. FIRST–TO–INVENT

Toshiko Takenaka, The Novelty and Priority Provision under the United States First-to-File Principle: Comparative Law Perspective Toshiko Takenaka ed, Patent Law and Theory (2008)

The Simple Structure of First-to-File Novelty and Priority

1. Novelty. Novelty provisions of major first-to-file countries, namely those of the European Patent Convention (EPC) and Japanese Patent Law (JPL), have a simple and short definition of prior artany form of disclosure gives rise to the prior art, regardless of the actor of such disclosure. For example, the EPC provides the following definition of novelty:

(1) An invention shall be considered to be new if it does not form part of the state of art.

(2) The state of the art shall be held to comprise everything made available to the public by means of a written or oral description, by use, or in any other way, before the date of filing of the European patent application.

The novelty definition of Japanese Patent Law is similar to the EPC definition, except the Japanese definition also lists items that constitute the prior art, including information available via the Internet. Unlike the United States, neither the European nor Japanese provisions distinguish the definition of prior art by actors and thus do not have separate provisions for the inventor's and others' actions. Terms used to define the prior art are given ordinary meaning. The simple, key concept to make information give rise to prior art is public accessibility. Under the European and Japanese novelty approaches, any information made publicly available in any form of publication anywhere in the world, as of the date of application, constitutes prior art. In other words, European and Japanese novelty does not discriminate disclosures by form or the place of disclosure.

Although technically not available as of the application date of the subject matter under examination, first-to-file countries also view subject matter described in an application pending in their own patent office as prior art, provided that the application is later published through an eighteen-month publication, thus becoming publicly available. This is because the subject will soon become publicly available, and has already become available at least to the patent office. Both the EPC and JPL adopted the "whole contents" approach, making the whole contents of European and Japanese applications the prior art as of the filing date. With respect to applications claiming priority right under the Paris Convention, the whole contents of applications become the prior art as of the priority date.

As an exception to this simple novelty principle, most first-to-file countries provide a grace period provision. A commentator of a first-to-file country defines grace period as a specific period of time prior to the filing of a patent application by the inventor or his or her successor in title, during which time disclosures of an invention do not forfeit a right to patent the invention. Under the first-to-file system, grace period provisions are provided as an exception to the principle that novelty is determined as of the application date. Because grace periods are an exception and not a rule, conditions that allow one to take advantage of the grace period are very restrictive. Among those countries that provide a grace period, the majority, 57%, adopted a six-month period and only 30% adopted a one-year grace period. To limit the scope of subject matter that can take advantage of the exception, the vast majority of countries have adopted a disclosure-specific grace period, in which only certain categories of disclosure are qualified to take advantage of a grace period. The most common disclosure-qualified categories include: experimental use, disclosure by an applicant, disclosure by a third party, abuse of right, display at an international exhibition, and presentation at a scientific meeting. Further, applicants cannot take advantage of the system unless they invoke the grace period at the date of application and submit evidence of the claimed subject matter.

One extreme example of the first-to-file grace period is the system under the EPC. The scope of disclosure that can take advantage of the EPC grace period is very limited and applicants must meet procedural requirements to invoke the system. In contrast, the scope of the Japanese grace period is more generous than that of the European system and includes a broad range of inventors' activities to take advantage of the system including a presentation at a science meeting and a publication in document. Under the Japanese system, an applicant can take advantage of the grace period with not only subject matter that is identical to the subject matter disclosed prior to the date of application, but also obvious subject matter.

2. *Priority*. The priority provisions of major first-to-file countries are predicated on a simple rule, a patent should be granted to the first applicant. For example, EPC Article 60, Paragraph 2 provides:

> If two or more persons have made an invention independently of each other, the right to the European patent shall belong to the person whose European patent application has the earliest date of filing; however, this provision shall apply only if this first application has been published under Article 93 and shall only have effect in respect of the Contracting States designated in that application as published.

Because priority is granted based on the date an applicant files an application to be examined by the European Patent Office (EPO), a procedure to decide the priority among more than one application is unnecessary as long as the date is clear. When more than two applicants file applications for the same invention on the same date, the EPO gives patents to both applicants. The Japanese rule is very similar to the European rule, except for the rule to handle more than one application with the same application date. JPL requires applicants who filed for the same invention on the same date to negotiate for an agreement to identify one applicant who will obtain the patent. If applicants cannot reach an agreement, the Japan Patent Office (JPO) refuses to give a patent to either party. This practice avoids an expensive proceeding to award the priority among applicants who filed their applications on the same day.

This rule also applies to determination of priority during the grace period. Under the grace period provisions of first-to-file countries, if a third party files prior to the date of application by the inventor who disclosed the same invention during the grace period, the inventor's application is rejected for being the second to file. If the third party's date of application is after the inventor's date of disclosure, the disclosure destroys the novelty of the third party application and thus a patent is granted to neither party.

Notes and Questions

1. On its face, the current § 102 novelty and priority provisions under the U.S. first-to-invent system are very different from the novelty and priority provisions of first-to-file systems. The first provision defining novelty in § 102(a) sets forth a determination of novelty as of the invention date, and § 102(g) provides a rule that determines priority based on the date of the first to invent rather than the first to file. Are these differences in fact real? Would adoption of the first-inventor-to-file system bring major changes to the U.S. patent system? In the above article, Prof. Takenaka argues that the current U.S. patent system already follows the first-to-file principle with limited exceptions.

2. Many first-to-file countries provide inventors with a 6–month or 12–month grace period for allowing them to make their inventions known to the public before filing for a patent. However, EPC member states do not provide a grace period for such disclosures. Why do these countries refuse to give a grace period? How does a lack of grace period affect the technology transfer activities at European universities and research institutions? For an academic discussion of grace periods in EU member states, see Joseph Straus, *Grace Period and the European and International Patent Law—Analysis of Key Legal and Socio–Economic Aspects*, 20 IIC Studies (2001).

INVENTORSHIP AND OWNERSHIP

An applicant must be the true inventor, or a person who legally succeeded him or her in title, to prevail in a priority contest in the United States. Thus, no separate procedure is needed to weed out those who did not invent the subject matter or who did not legally succeed the inventor in title. While a first-to-file system can readily determine priority between two actual inventors based on their respective filing times, a procedure is necessary to determine whether one of the applicants unlawfully misappropriated the invention. In the European patent system, EPC Article 61 provides such a procedure. However, since EPC member states have not harmonized their rules for inventorship and ownership determination, entitlement to European patent rights depends on governing national law. The following opinion excerpt shows the complexity of priority contest procedures at the EPO when a derivation from the second-to-file inventor apparently bars the true inventor from obtaining a European patent. In the following case, the thief had filed for a European patent and allowed it to be published by the EPO. The thief then abandoned its application, but the published application apparently served as prior art against the European application filed by the true inventor after the inventor learned of the misappropriation.

LATCHWAYS

Opinion of the Enlarged Board of Appeal, June 13, 1994
G 3/92, 1994 OJ EPO 607

1.   The referred question specifically concerns the interpretation of Article 61(1) EPC, which governs the procedural rights of a person who has been adjudged to be entitled to the grant of a European patent, as against the actual applicant in respect of a European patent application. However, Article 61 EPC is part of a system of legal process which is provided under the EPC for determining the right to a European patent application when this is in dispute, and for implementing such a determination. The terms of Article 61 EPC have to be interpreted in this context and in the light of the object and purpose of this system. It is accordingly necessary to consider in the first place the nature of this system and the place of Article 61 EPC within it, before considering the detailed wording of Article 61 EPC and the Rules which are intended to implement it.

2.   According to Article 60(1) EPC, the right to a European patent shall belong to the inventor or his successor in title. Consequently, as a matter of law, only the inventor (or his successor in title) is entitled to apply to the EPO for the grant of a European patent and, subject to examination of the application for conformity with the patentability and other requirements of the EPC, to be granted a European patent for his invention. However, Article 58 EPC provides that a European patent application may be filed by any legal or natural person and Article 60(3) EPC provides that "For the purposes of proceedings before the EPO, the applicant shall be deemed to be entitled to exercise the right to a European patent". Consequently, as a matter of fact, a European patent application may actually be filed in respect of potentially inventive subject-matter by a person other than the inventor of such subject-matter or his successor in title, contrary to the legal right of the latter, and before the latter has himself filed a European patent application in respect of such subject-matter.

3.   Under the European patent system, the EPO has no power to determine a dispute as to whether or not a particular applicant is legally entitled to apply for and be granted a European patent in respect of the subject-matter of a particular application. Determination of questions of entitlement to the right to the grant of a European patent prior to grant is governed by the "Protocol on Jurisdiction and the Recognition of Decisions in respect of the Right to the grant of a European Patent" (the "Protocol on Recognition"), which is an integral part of the EPC. This Protocol

gives the courts of the Contracting States jurisdiction to decide claims to entitlement to the right to the grant of a European patent, provides a system for determining which national court shall decide such claims in individual cases, and requires the mutual recognition of decisions in respect of such claims, within the Contracting States to the EPC.

* * *

5.1 According to Article 61(1) EPC, the lawful applicant (being "a person referred to in Article 60(1) EPC other than the applicant") may, within the three-month time limit following such a final decision by the appropriate national court and "provided that the European patent has not yet been granted", with reference to the unlawful applicant's earlier application,

"(a) prosecute the application as his own application in place of the applicant,

(b) file a new European patent application in respect of the same invention, or

(c) request that the application be refused."

[The Enlarged Board in a split decision held that the abandoned application had not been granted and hence that the lawful applicant can file a new application by claiming the benefit of the earlier application even if the earlier unlawful application is no longer pending at EPO as of the filing date of the new application.]

Notes and Questions

1. To what extent are the remedies for true inventors and owners at the EPO similar to interference procedures in the United States? How does the role of inventorship differ between first-to-invent and the first-to-file systems?

2. In the majority of first-to-file systems, inventors are the original owners of a patent right. However, there are some countries such as France that give original ownership to the employers of inventors. (French Intellectual Property Code, Art. L. 611–7, Para. 1). Other countries such as Germany require payment of reasonable remuneration for the transfer of ownership from the employee-inventor. (German Employee Invention Act, Sec. 9) No international agreements provide any rule for determining inventorship or ownership. What kind of problems do you anticipate if the rules for inventorship and ownership differ from one country to another for patent procurement and enforcement?

3. Japanese Patent Law requires all owners of the right to a patent to jointly file an application. Although these owners can independently practice their invention, they need permission from other owners for

granting a license or transferring their ownership share. Why does the Japanese patent system limit the power of owners in this way?

ANTICIPATION AND INHERENCY

Novelty is a fundamental requirement in all patent systems. Compared with 35 USC § 102, novelty provisions in major first-to-file countries are less complex. For example, both the EPC and Japanese patent law provide a short definition of prior art—any form of disclosure that has been made available to the public before the priority date, regardless of the actors or place of disclosure. Additionally, the content of a pending unpublished patent application constitutes prior art if the patent application is published after the priority date. (EPC Art. 54 (1), JPL Art. 29–2) However, such unpublished applications may be used only for anticipation.

MERRELL DOW PHARMACEUTICALS INC. v. H.N. NORTON & CO. LTD.

House of Lords
[1996] R.P.C. 76

Lord Hoffmann

1. The Patent in Suit

Merrell Dow Pharmaceuticals Inc is a U.S. company with a U.K. subsidiary. I shall call them both "Merrell Dow". About 25 years ago Merrell Dow discovered an anti-histamine drug called terfenadine. It is used by people who suffer from hay fever and similar allergies and has the advantage that, unlike some other anti-histamines, it does not have the side-effect of making one drowsy. In 1972 Merrell Dow obtained a patent for terfenadine in the United Kingdom. After a period of extension under the Patents Act 1977, it finally expired in December 1992. Other pharmaceutical companies then started to make and market terfenadine.

In these proceedings Merrell Dow claim that their monopoly in terfenadine continues by virtue of a later patent which still has another 5 years to run. It was obtained in the following circumstances. After they had patented terfenadine, they did some research into the way it worked. They found that it passed through the stomach to be absorbed in the small intestine and was then 99.5% metabolized in the liver. This was why it had no side-effects. They analyzed the chemical composition of the acid metabolite formed in the liver. Its chemical name is 4–[4–(4–hydroxydiphenyl-methyl-l-piperidinyl)-l-hydroxybutyl]—dimethylbenzeneacetic acid, but I shall call it the acid metabolite. No one had identified it before. So they patented the acid metabolite as claim 24 of a patent granted in 1980 for a number of related anti-histamine products. This is the patent in suit.

The Claim for Infringement

A patent for a product is infringed by anyone who makes the product without the consent of the proprietor: see section 60(*l*)(a) of the Act of 1977. Merrell Dow's research, which they made public at a symposium in Strasbourg in January 1982, showed that one cannot swallow terfenadine without shortly afterwards making the acid metabolite in one's liver. This is claimed to be an act falling within section 60(1)(a). It is not however alleged to be an infringement, because section 60(5)*(a)* exempts any act "done privately and for purposes which are not commercial." Nevertheless, say Merrell Dow, another pharmaceutical company cannot supply terfenadine to the public without infringing under section 60(2):

> "Subject to the following provisions of this section, a person (other than the proprietor of the patent) also infringes a patent for an invention if, while the patent is in force and without the consent of the proprietor, he supplies or offers to supply in the United Kingdom a person other than a licensee or other person entitled to work the invention with any of means, relating to an essential element of the invention, for putting the invention into effect when he knows, or it is obvious to a reasonable person in the circumstances, that those means are suitable for putting, and are intended to put, the invention into effect in the United Kingdom."

Merrell Dow say that supplying terfenadine commercially is an infringement under this subsection because it involves knowingly supplying consumers with the means, relating to an essential element for the making of the acid metabolite, for putting the invention into effect. So they retain their monopoly in marketing terfenadine until the metabolite patent expires in the year 2000. Indeed, the monopoly is stronger than it was under the terfenadine patent during its last four years of extension under the Patents Act 1977 because it is not subject to licences of right.

3.   The Proceedings

Merrell Dow has commenced two actions for infringement against other pharmaceutical companies. This appeal come before your Lordships' House in consequence of motions to strike them out as disclosing no cause of action. The motions were heard by Aldous J., who was invited to decide as a matter of law (under RSC Ord 14A) that on the undisputed facts which I have stated, the patent was invalid. Several grounds were put forward but I need trouble your Lordships with only one, namely, that so far as the claim to the acid metabolite includes its manufacture by the action of terfenadine in the human body, the patent was invalid because the invention was not new. It was on this ground that Aldous J. dismissed the actions and his decision was affirmed by the Court of Appeal. Your Lordships decided in the first instance to hear argument on this point alone. The hearing was then adjourned. Since I understand your Lordships to be of the opinion that the Court of Appeal and Aldous J. were right and the other points have not been argued, I shall say nothing about them.

5. The Invention

Before coming to the question of whether the invention was new, one must first be clear about what it was. Claim 24 of the patent in suit was to the acid metabolite as a product. The scope of the monopoly conferred by a product claim is defined by section 60(*l*)(a), which provides that where the invention is a product, a person infringes the patent if, without the consent of the proprietor, he "makes, disposes of, offers to dispose of, uses or imports the product or keeps it whether for disposal or otherwise." For this purpose it does not matter how the product is made or what form it takes. The monopoly covers every method of manufacture and every form which comes within the description in the claim. So claim 24 includes the making of the acid metabolite in one's liver just as much as making it by synthetic process; in the body as well as in isolation. Nor does it matter whether or not the infringer knows that he is making, using etc. the patented product. Liability is absolute.

The corollary of this principle is that the novelty of the invention must be co-extensive with the monopoly. If there is any method of manufacture or form of the product which is part of the state of the art, then to that extent the invention is not new. As the Enlarged Board of Appeal of the EPO said in its *Decision G02/88 MOBIL/Friction reducing additive* [1990] EPOR 73, 83:

> "It is generally accepted as a principle underlying the EPC that a patent which claims a physical entity *per se,* confers absolute protection upon such physical entity; that is, wherever it exists and whatever its context. . . . It follows that if it can be shown that such physical entity (that is, a compound) is already in the state of the art (for example in the context of a particular activity), then a claim to the physical entity *per se* lacks novelty."

In this case, the respondents would have no objection to a claim to the synthesisation of the acid metabolite or to the product in isolation. The only respect in which they say it is not new is when made by terfenadine as part of the human body. It may be possible for Merrell Dow to amend the specification to exclude manufacture in this manner and form. In ordering the patent to be revoked, Aldous J. granted a stay pending an application to amend. Your Lordships need not therefore be concerned with the fact that a good deal of the ground covered by the patent is admittedly new. The argument may proceed as if the invention were confined to making the acid metabolite in the manner and form which the respondents challenge. In the rest of this judgment, when I speak of "the invention," I shall therefore mean the making of the acid metabolite within the human body by the ingestion of terfenadine.

Mr. Thorley Q.C., who appeared for Merrell Dow, realistically acknowledged that a U.K. patent lawyer's intuitive response to his claim was likely to be one of incredulity. A patent is granted for a new invention. But in 1980 there was nothing new about terfenadine. Full information about its chemical composition and method of use had been published in its patent specification in 1972. Participants in clinical trials had actually been taking the drug. Making and using terfenadine was therefore part of the state of the art. What did the acid metabolite patent teach the person who was using terfenadine? It gave him some information about how the product worked in terms of chemical reactions within the body. But it did not enable him to do anything which he had not been doing before.

Why, therefore, should the later patent confer a right to stop people from doing what they had done before? Ever since the power of the Crown to grant monopolies was curbed by Parliament and the courts at the beginning of the seventeenth century, it has been a fundamental principle of U.K. patent law that the Crown could not grant a patent which would enable the patentee to stop another trader from doing what he had done before. In this case it so happens that Merrell Dow held both the terfenadine patent and the acid metabolite patent. So the problem did not emerge until the first patent had expired. But the argument would have been exactly the same if someone else had discovered and patented the acid metabolite. If Mr. Thorley is right, he would have been entitled to stop Merrell Dow selling terfenadine.

Other extraordinary consequences were discussed in argument. Someone discovers an interesting-looking chemical and patents it. It is later discovered that this chemical is made in a temporary and unstable form during the cooking of a well-known dish according to a recipe in Elizabeth David. Can the patentee bring infringement proceedings against anyone who uses the recipe on a commercial scale? Examples to reinforce one's initial incredulity could be multiplied.

Mr. Thorley meets these arguments head-on. He says that the 1977 Act overturned the previous principles of U.K. patent law. It was passed, as its long title said, to introduce a new law of patents. Under the EPC, it is no longer the case that a patent cannot enable the patentee to stop someone doing what he has done before. Under the definition of the state of the art in section 2(2), it is not enough that something should have been done before. It requires that information about what was being done should have been made available to the public. In this case, Mr. Thorley says that no information about the acid metabolite had been made available to the public before the priority date of the later patent. Parliament, says Mr. Thorley, was aware that this change of principle might produce hardships and anomalies. It provided to some extent for such cases in section 64 of the 1977 Act. This gives a person who, before the priority date, was doing or making effective and serious preparations to do an act which would have been an infringement if the patent was in force, a personal right to continue doing that act. But the section is narrowly drawn. It has no application in this case because none of the defendants were marketing terfenadine before the priority date of the acid metabolite patent. Nevertheless, Mr. Thorley says that the very existence of section 64 shows that Parliament recognised that the effect of the new law was that people might find themselves unable to go on doing what they or someone else had done before.

These are serious arguments which cannot be dismissed simply on the grounds that they produce results which seem contrary to common sense. I must therefore invite your Lordships to look more closely at the grounds upon which the respondents say that, although the acid metabolite as a chemical compound had not previously been identified, its manufacture in the body by the ingestion of terfenadine was nevertheless part of the state of the art.

Two Kinds of Anticipation?

An anticipation is the traditional English term for that part of the state of the art which is inconsistent with the invention being new. The word is not used in the 1977 Act but is nevertheless convenient. In this case, Mr. Floyd Q.C., who appeared for H. N. Norton & Co. Ltd., the respondents in the first appeal, said that the invention had been anticipated in two ways. First, he said it had been *used* before the priority date. According to the paragraph 5 of the Joint Statement of Facts and Issues put before your Lordships, "Terfenadine was made available to and used by volunteers in clinical trials in 1977/1978." They had made the acid metabolite in their livers and experienced its anti-histamine effects. Secondly, Mr. Floyd said before the priority date the invention had been *disclosed* in the specification of the terfenadine patent. That was a publicly available document which told one how to make terfenadine and that it should be taken for its anti-histamine effect. The inevitable result of following those instructions was to make the acid metabolite. I shall call these two arguments anticipation by use and anticipation by disclosure.

[Lord Hoffmann compared the novelty provisions in the pre 1979 Patent Act and current Patent Act and concluded that the use of a product makes the invention part of the state of the art only if such use makes available the necessary information of the product. Thus, he refused to find anticipation for the metabolite acid by use only because the acid was created in human body.]

Anticipation by disclosure

I turn therefore to the ground upon which the respondents succeeded before Aldous J. and the Court of Appeal, namely that the disclosure in the terfenadine specification had made the invention part of the state of the art. This is different from the argument on anticipation by use because it relies not upon the mere use of the product by members of the public but upon the communication of information. The question is whether the specification conveyed sufficient information to enable the skilled reader to work the invention.

Mr. Thorley says that no one can know about something which he does not know exists. It follows that if he does not know that the product exists, he cannot know how to work an invention for making that product in any form. The prior art contained in the terfenadine specification gave no indication that it would have the effect of creating the acid metabolite in the human body. Therefore it did not contain sufficient information to enable the skilled reader to make the substance in that or any other form. It did not make the acid metabolite available to the public.

* * *

My Lords, I think that on this point the Patents Act 1977 is perfectly clear. Section 2(2) does not purport to confine the state of the art about products to knowledge of their chemical composition. It is the *invention* which must be new and which must therefore not be part of the state of the art. It is therefore part of the state of the art if the information which has been disclosed enables the public to know the product under a description sufficient to work the invention.

For most of the purposes of a product claim, knowledge of its chemical composition will be necessary to enable the public to work the invention. It is something they will need to know in order to be able to make it. So in *Decision GO1/92 Availability to the Public* [1993] EPOR 241 the President of the EPO referred to the Enlarged Board of Appeal the question of the circumstances in which making a product available to the public would count as making available its chemical composition. The Board answered that the composition or internal structure of a product become part of the state of the art if it is possible for a skilled person to discover it and reproduce it without undue burden. Mr. Thorley took this case to mean that in no context can a product be part of the state of the art unless its chemical composition is readily discoverable. But that is not what the case says. The Board was asked about the circumstances in which the chemical composition of a product becomes part of the state of the art. It was not asked about the circumstances in which knowing its chemical composition was necessary for the purpose of treating the product as part of the state of the art.

Other decisions of the EPO seem to me to make it clear that, at least for some purposes, products need not be known under their chemical description in order to be part of the state of the art. In *Decision T12/81 BAYER/Diastereomers* [1979–85] EPOR Vol. B. 308, 312, the Technical Board of Appeal said:

" . . . [T]he concept of novelty must not be given such a narrow interpretation that only what has already been described in the same terms is prejudicial to it. The purpose of Art. 54(1) EPC is to prevent the state of the art being patented again. Art. 54(2) EPC defines the state of the art as comprising everything made available to the public before the date of filing in any way, including by written description. There are many ways of describing a substance in chemistry and this is usually done by giving its precise scientific designation. But the latter is not always available on the date of filing . . . [It] is the practice of a number of patent offices to accept the process parameter, in the form of a product-by-process claim, for closer characterisation of inventions relating to chemical substances. To the Board's knowledge this is also the practice at the European Patent Office. If inventions relating to chemical substances defined by claims of this kind are patented, it necessarily follows that the resulting patent documents, once they enter the state of the art, will be prejudicial to the novelty of applications claiming the same substance although in a different and perhaps more closely defined form."

In other words, if the recipe which inevitably produces the substance is part of the state of the art, so is the substance as made by that recipe. *Decision T303/86 CPC/Flavour Concentrates* [1989] 2 EPOR 95 was a case about actual recipes for cooking. The application was to patent a process for making flavour concentrates from vegetable or animal substances by extraction with fat solvents under pressure in the presence of water. The claim specified certain parameters for the ratio between the vapour pressure of the water in the meat or vegetables and the vapour pressure of the free water.

Opposition was based upon two cook-book recipes for pressure-frying chickens and making stews which in non-technical terms disclosed processes having the same effect. The Technical Board of Appeal said (at p. 98):

"It is sufficient to destroy the novelty of the claimed process that this process and the known process are identical with respect to starting material and reaction conditions since processes identical in these features must inevitably yield identical products."

Furthermore, it did not matter that the cook did not realise that he was not only frying a chicken, but also making a "flavour concentrate" in the surplus oil. It was enough, as the Board said, that "some flavour of the fried chicken is extracted into the oil during the frying process even if this is not the desired result of that process."

Mr. Thorley said that *CPC/Flavour Concentrates* can be explained on the ground that the flavour concentrates as made according to the cooking recipes could have been analysed and chemically identified. Perhaps they could. But this was not the ground for the Board's decision. It proceeded on the basis that for the purpose of being part of the state of the art, a process for making flavour concentrates was sufficiently described by a recipe for cooking food which did not expressly refer to the flavour concentrates but would inevitably have the effect of making them.

In this case, knowledge of the acid metabolite was in my view made available to the public by the terfenadine specification under the description "a part of the chemical reaction in the human body produced by the ingestion of terfenadine and having an anti-histamine effect." Was this description sufficient to make the product part of the state of the art? For many purposes, obviously not. It would not enable anyone to work the invention in the form of isolating or synthesising the acid metabolite. But for the purpose of working the invention by making the acid metabolite in the body by ingesting terfenadine, I think it plainly was. It enabled the public to work the invention by making the acid metabolite in their livers. The fact that they would not have been able to describe the chemical reaction in these terms does mean that they were not working the invention. Whether or not a person is working a product invention is an objective fact independent of what he knows or thinks about what he is doing. (The position may be different when the invention is a use for a product; in such a case, a person may only be working the invention when he is using it for the patented purpose: see the discussion of the *MOBIL* case in the next section). The Amazonian Indian who treats himself with powdered bark for fever is using quinine, even if he thinks that the reason why the treatment is effective is that the tree is favoured by the Gods. The teachings of his traditional medicine contain enough information to enable him to do exactly what a scientist in the forest would have done if he wanted to treat a fever but had no supplies of quinine sulphate. The volunteers in the clinical trials who took terfenadine were doing exactly what they would have done if they had attended Merrell Dow's Strasbourg symposium and decided to try making the acid metabolite in their livers by ingesting terfenadine.

It may be helpful at this point to highlight the similarities and the distinctions between the case for anticipation by use, which I have rejected, and the case for anticipation by disclosure, which I have accepted. In both cases no one was aware that the acid metabolite was being made. In the case of anticipation by use, however, the acts relied upon conveyed no information which would have enabled anyone work the invention, i.e. to make the acid metabolite. The anticipation in this form relies solely upon the fact that the acid metabolite was made, as the anticipation in *Bristol–Myers Co. (Johnson's) Application* [1975] R.P.C. 127 relied solely upon the fact that ampicillin trihydrate had been made and sold to the public. It disavows any reliance upon extraneous information, such as the formula for making terfenadine and the instructions to take it for its anti-histamine effect. Anticipation by disclosure, on the other hand, relies upon the communication to the public of information which enables it to do an act having the inevitable consequence of making the acid metabolite. The terfenadine specification teaches that the ingestion of terfenadine will produce a chemical reaction in the body and for the purposes of working the invention in this form, this is a sufficient description of the making of the acid metabolite. Under that description the acid metabolite was part of the state of the art.

The MOBIL Case

Mr. Thorley claimed support from the decision of the Enlarged Board of Appeal, to which I have already referred, in *Decision G02/88 MOBIL/Friction reducing additive* [1990] EPOR 73. Mobil had attempted to patent a substance for use as a friction reducing additive in lubricating oil. This was opposed by Chevron, who were able to show that the substance was already known and in use for inhibiting rust-formation in ferrous metal. There was no dispute that this put an end to the product claim, which would have entitled Mobil to a monopoly of the product for every possible use. But Mobil then applied to amend the application to restrict it to the *use* of the substance for reducing friction, saying that its usefulness for this purpose had not been previously appreciated. The Technical Board of Appeal, hearing an appeal by Mobil from a successful opposition by Chevron, referred three questions to the Enlarged Board of Appeal, of which the third was:

"Is a claim to the use of a compound for a particular non-medical purpose novel for the purpose of Art 54 EPC, having regard to a prior publication which discloses the use of that compound for a different non-medical purpose, so that the only novel feature in the claim is the purpose for which the compound is used?"

(The reference to "non-medical" purpose is because patents for a second use of medical products give rise to certain special problems under the EPC. It can for present purposes be ignored.)

The Enlarged Board accepted Chevron's submission that while using an old substance in a new way to achieve a new purpose might be novel, the use of an old substance in an old way to achieve a new purpose would not. In the latter case, the only difference would lie in the mind of the user: he would be doing the same thing with the same substance but with a different purpose in mind. One might expect this to lead to the conclusion that if the additive was the same and it was being used in the same way (e.g. by pouring it into the engine) then an attempt to patent its use as a friction reducer when it was previously thought only to inhibit rust should fail.

The Board went on to say, however, that a claim for the use of an old compound in an old way for a new purpose (B) could be interpreted to include "the function of achieving purpose B (because this is the technical result)." In such case, the fact that the substance achieved that purpose would be an objective "functional technical feature" of the invention, not residing only in the mind of the user. Thus the fact that the substance *did* reduce friction was a new technical feature which, if novel, could constitute a patentable invention.

I think it is fair to say that, in the United Kingdom at least, this aspect of the Board's decision has been criticised on the ground that a patent for an old product used in an old way for a new purpose makes it difficult to apply the traditional U.K. doctrine of infringement. Liability for infringement is, as I have said, absolute. It depends upon whether the act in question falls within the claims and pays no attention to the alleged infringer's state of mind. But this doctrine may be difficult to apply to a patent for the use of a known substance in a known way for a new purpose. How does one tell whether the person putting the additive into his engine is legitimately using it to inhibit rust or infringing by using it to reduce friction? In this appeal, however, we are not concerned with this aspect of the case. The part upon which Mr. Thorley relies is the decision that the claimed technical feature, i.e. the friction reducing quality, was novel even though it was 'inherent' in the substance. The Board said, in a passage which I have already quoted:

> "... under Article 54(2) EPC the question to be decided is what has been 'made available' to the public: the question is not what may have been 'inherent' in what was made available (by a prior written description, or in what has previously been used (prior use), for example). Under the EPC, a hidden or secret use, because it has not been made available to the public, is not a ground of objection to [the] validity of a European patent."

My Lords, I do not think that this principle is in issue in this appeal. I have accepted it fully in the discussion of anticipation by use, in which the above passage has already been quoted. It was applied by the Technical Board of Appeal to the facts of *MOBIL/Friction reducing additive* when that case went back to the Technical Board of Appeal after the decision in principle by the Enlarged Board: see [1990] EPOR 514. The Technical Board decided that so far as friction reduction had been an inevitable concomitant of the use of the additive for other purposes, it was a case of uninformative use like *Bristol–Myers Co. (Johnson's) Application* [1975] R.P.C. 127. Or to put the same thing in another way, a description of the product by its chemical composition or as "something in the lubricating oil which inhibits rust formation" or any other of the descriptions under which it was previously known would not enable anyone to use it *for the purpose* of reducing friction, even though this would be the inevitable consequence of doing so. It did not therefore prevent the invention in the form sanctioned by the Enlarged Board from being novel.

But the argument in this appeal for anticipation by disclosure involves no "doctrine of inherency." It does not claim that the acid metabolite must be deemed to have been made available by the teachings of the terfenadine patent even though all information about it remained hidden. It claims instead that the acid metabolite was sufficiently disclosed under the description "an anti-histamine chemical reaction in the human body which occurs after taking terfenadine." The respondents say that for the purposes of the particular invention in issue, the specification contained sufficient information about the acid metabolite to make it part of the state of the art. For the reasons I have given, I think it did. I would therefore dismiss the appeal.

Notes and Questions

1. § 102 (a) and (b) exclude a foreign knowledge from the prior art unless the knowledge is in a written form, either as a printed publica-

tion or patent. This geographical limitation was introduced under the Patent Act of 1836, and it may be outdated. Prof. Bagley argues that this geographical limitation facilitates biopiracy. Margo Bagley, *Patently Unconstitutional: The Geographical Limitation on Prior Art in a Small World*, 87 Minn. L. Rev. 679. Do you agree with her? Is there any provision in § 102 to bar an applicant from patenting an invention derived from information obtained abroad?

2.   What would be the result if House of Lords did not find anticipation by inherent disclosure? What kind of claims would the patentee have had against generic drug companies had the patent on the metabolite acids been found to be valid? The Federal Circuit also found anticipation for a previously unknown product if the compound is later discovered to be a metabolite of a compound which has been known to the public. *Schering Corp. v. Geneva Pharms., Inc.*, 339 F.3d 1373 (Fed. Cir. 2003). Are you surprised that Mr. Justice Jacob (as he then was) permitted the patentee on October 1, 1996 to add the words "other than formed by metabolism Terfenadine in vivo" to the claims so as to permit the thus amended claims to define over the prior art after the decision of the House of Lords? Do you think a patent system should allow claim amendment after a final holding of invalidity by the country's highest court?

3.   EPC member states codified the rule in *Mobil* through the 2000 EPC revision. EPC Art. 54(4) expressly endorses the novelty of a known substance if the substance is limited by a specific new use which has not been available to the public even if such use is inherent in the substance. Moreover, the so called Swiss-type claim format is no longer available for the protection of new uses of an old substance as it is no longer necessary, *Dosage Regime/Abbott Respiratory*, G2/08, Opinion of the Enlarged Board of Appeal.

* * *

The Federal Circuit has ruled that a reference must be enabling to anticipate the claimed invention. *Schering Corp. v. Geneva Pharms., Inc.*, 339 F.3d 1373 (Fed. Cir. 2003) However, the degree of disclosure necessary for meeting the enablement requirement for anticipation is not exactly the same as that of the enablement requirement under § 112 para. 1. In *In re Schoenwald*, 964 F.2d 1122 (Fed. Cir. 1992), the court clarified that a reference does not need to disclose a particular utility to be anticipatory of a claim to an old compound. The UK House of Lords also distinguishes the enablement for anticipation from the enablement for sufficient disclosure. However, courts often confuse these distinct requirements in examining the disclosure of a reference for anticipation. The House of Lords took up these requirements in the context of an unpublished application available only for use as an anticipation reference.

SYNTHON B.V. v. SMITHKLINE BEECHAM PLC

House of Lords

[2005] UKHL 59

Lord Hoffmann

The invention

Paroxetine is a compound used to treat depression and related disorders. It has for some time been marketed in the form of its hydrochloride hemihydrate salt under the name Paxil or Seroxat. These proceedings arise out of the more or less simultaneous discovery in about 1997 by the appellants Synthon BV, a Dutch pharmaceutical company, and the respondents, Smithkline Beecham plc ("SB"), a UK pharmaceutical company, that a different paroxetine salt, paroxetine methanesulfonate ("PMS"), has properties which make it more suitable for pharmaceutical use. It is more stable, less hygroscopic and much more soluble, so that it can be prepared in higher concentrations.

The Synthon disclosure

On 10 June 1997 Synthon filed an international application under the Patent Cooperation Treaty for a patent which claimed a broad class of sulfonic acid salts including PMS. This was published on 17 December 1998. The specification said that a known useful salt of paroxetine was the hydrochloride in various forms but that each of them had, to a greater or lesser extent, disadvantages for safe handling and formulation. The object of the invention was to provide a compound with improved characteristics. It then set out, by reference to a formula with a number of variables, a class of compounds which were said to exhibit good stability and high solubility. These included PMS.

The specification, as is customary in patents for chemical compounds, then narrowed its focus to a preferred group within the class which was said to exhibit a very high degree of solubility and then, by way of illustration, to a particular compound in that group. That compound was PMS, which features in the first example of the preparation of a salt of paroxetine suitable for pharmaceutical use. Under the heading "Example 1", the specification describes how to make PMS in crystalline form.

The notion of crystalline form may require some explanation. The same substance may exist in different solid forms, depending upon the arrangement of its molecules. In crystalline form the molecules arrange themselves in an organised pattern called a lattice which gives the crystal a distinctive shape. On the other hand, in an amorphous form or an oil, the molecules are randomly distributed and the substance has no particular shape. Some substances have only one crystalline form. They are called monomorphic. But others have a variety of patterns into which the molecules may arrange themselves. They are polymorphic. Different crystalline forms can be distinguished by a number of conventional tests. Infra-red radiation (IR) will result in a spectrum of readings of absorbance which are characteristic of that particular crystal. X-ray diffraction (XRD) will likewise give a characteristic series of readings. The IR and XRD readings are the crystal's fingerprint. Some compounds form one or more types of crystals which include, as part of their crystalline structure, molecules of the solvent from which the crystal has been precipitated. They are called solvates or, if the solvent is water, hydrates.

Example 1 teaches how to make PMS from a solution of paroxetine, prepared in accordance with a procedure disclosed in a previous US patent, by adding methane sulphonic acid. This is the standard method of producing a salt by adding an acid to a base. In the example, crystallisation is obtained by the use of a seeding crystal which induces precipitation of crystals from the solution. This is said to produce a 99.5% yield of crystals having a 98% purity. The characteristics of the crystals are described in Table 1, giving their melting point (142o to 144oC), DSC (differential scanning calorimetry) curve, IR spectrum and NMR (nuclear magnetic resonance) readings which map the hydrogen and carbon atoms in the structure of the crystal. A note after Table 1 draws attention to the fact that "the compounds of the invention are crystalline, with defined melting points, DSC curves and IR spectra" but that they may be polymorphic and exist in other crystalline forms. The crystals of the acid addition salts with organic sulphonic acids, like PMS, are "substantially free of bound organic solvents", that is to say, they are not solvates, but some "may contain crystallisation water and also unbound water, that is to say water which is other than water of crystallisation." The particular example in Table1, however, is said to be a crystal of 98% purity and therefore not a hydrate.

Example 1, as I have said, requires a seeding crystal to start the process of crystallisation and is preceded by a description of how such a seeding crystal had been obtained. It involved dissolving paroxetine in hot ethanol, adding methanesulfonic acid, cooling and then freezing the mixture and evaporating it to reduce it to an oil. After being left for a month, a waxy solid was obtained, part of which was dissolved in EtOAc and the rest used to precipitate crystals from the solution in a freezer.

The SB patent

After Synthon had filed its application but before it was published, SB filed a document dated 6 October 1998 which gave it
priority for a UK patent application filed on 23 April 1999. The
patent was published on 10 May 2000 as UK Patent No 2 336 364.
SB, like Synthon, appears at first to have thought that PMS was a
novel compound. The SB specification began by saying that it had
been surprisingly discovered. The title of the patent is "Paroxetine
Salt". But during the course of prosecution, it appeared that there
was prior art in which PMS had been identified as one of many
paroxetine salts suitable for a method of treatment patented in the
United States. SB therefore confined its claim to a particular form
of crystalline PMS. It is described in claim 1, upon which other
claims are dependent:

"Paroxetine methanesulfonate in crystalline form having inter
alia the following characteristic IR peaks: 1603, 1513, 1194,
1045, 946, 830, 776, 601, 554, and 539 4cm–1.; and/or the
following characteristic XRD peaks: 8.3, 10.5, 15.6, 16.3, 17.7,
18.2, 19.8, 20.4, 21.5, 22.0, 22.4, 23.8, 24.4, 25.0, 25.3, 25.8,
26.6, 30.0, 30.2, and 31.6 0.2 degrees 2 theta."

It will be seen that the claim identified a particular crystalline
form by reference to its IR and XRD peaks. If, as the specification
said was possible, PMS turned out to be polymorphic, no other
forms of crystal were claimed. And it is of particular importance to
notice that the IR peaks in claim 1 are different from those in Table
1 of the Synthon application. A person skilled in the art, reading
both documents, would think that they identified different polymorphs.

Although the specification does not spell out the advantages of
PMS or sulfonate salts in general in the way that the Synthon
application does, the specification makes it clear that the inventive
step was the discovery of the sulfonate salt of paroxetine as an
alternative to the hydrochloride salt.

11.   The specification suggests a variety of solvents which may be
used for dissolving paroxetine before mixing it with commercially
available methanesulfonic acid and goes on to say that "the salt
may be isolated in solid form by conventional means from a
solution thereof obtained as above." Examples of non-crystalline
and crystalline solids are given. As for the crystalline form, the
specification says:

"A crystalline salt may be prepared by various methods such as
directly crystallising the material from a solvent in which the
product has limited solubility or by triturating for example
with ethers such as diethyl ether or otherwise crystallising a
non-crystalline salt. A number of solvents may be used for the
crystallisation process including those that are useful industri-

ally; eg paroxetine methanesulfonate may be crystallised from a relatively crude feedstock such as is commonly produced during the final stage of the chemical synthesis of paroxetine."

A number of other alternative methods are then given over the following pages. But there is no suggestion that any of them involved an inventive step. They are all described as involving commonly used solvents and conventional methods (eg "vigorous stirring is particularly useful").

The proceedings

On 7 March 2001 Synthon commenced proceedings to have the SB patent revoked on the ground that the crystalline form of PMS described in claim 1 was not new. Section 1(1)(a) of the Patents Act 1977 provides that a patent may be granted only for an invention which is new. Section 2(1) provides that an invention shall be taken to be new if it does not form part of the state of the art. Section 2(2) and (3) define the state of the art:

"(2) The state of the art in the case of an invention shall be taken to comprise all matter (whether a product, a process, information about either, or anything else) which has at any time before the priority date of that invention been made available to the public (whether in the United Kingdom or elsewhere) by written or oral description, by use or in any other way.

(3) The state of the art in the case of an invention to which an application for a patent or a patent relates shall be taken also to comprise matter contained in an application for another patent which was published on or after the priority date of that invention, if the following conditions are satisfied, that is to say—

(a) that matter was contained in the application for that other patent both as filed and as published; and

(b) the priority date of that matter is earlier than that of the invention."

Synthon do not rely on section 2(2). They accept that the crystalline form of PMS identified in claim 1 of the patent in suit had not been "made available to the public", whether by description or in any other way, before the priority date. They rely on section 2(3), claiming that the invention in claim 1 was disclosed by their own patent application.

In order to make good their case, Synthon had to satisfy the judge on two points. The first was that their application disclosed the invention which had been patented as claim 1. I shall call this requirement "disclosure". The second was that an ordinary skilled

man would be able to perform the disclosed invention if he attempted to do so by using the disclosed matter and common general
knowledge. I shall call this requirement "enablement". If both
these requirements are satisfied, the invention is not new. I shall
later have to discuss the law on disclosure and enablement and the
relationship between them in some detail, but for the moment that
is enough to explain the course which the proceedings took before
the judge.

For the purposes of disclosure, Synthon relied upon the fact
that their application disclosed the existence of PMS in crystalline
form. An immediate difficulty, however, was that the differences in
the IR spectra suggested that it was not the same crystalline form
as was claimed in the patent. Synthon nevertheless pressed on with
experiments designed to show that they also satisfied the requirement of enablement. That means, as I have said, that the ordinary
skilled man would be able to perform the invention. Synthon,
however, left nothing to chance and engaged Sir Jack Baldwin FRS,
Waynflete Professor of Chemistry in the University of Oxford and
one of the foremost organic chemists in the world, together with Dr
Robert Adlington, whom Professor Baldwin described as the best
practical organic chemist he had ever worked with, to conduct the
experiments. They were given in a sealed bottle a sample of the
mixture of paroxetine dissolved in ethanol mixed with methanesulfonic acid mixed with ethanol described in the Synthon application
as having been used to make seeding crystals and asked to reproduce the experiment. The result was a complete failure. The method failed to produce any crystals at all. Eventually, after a good deal
of skilled manipulation of a kind not described by Synthon's application, Professor Baldwin and Dr Adlington produced some crystals. These turned out not to have the IR spectrum predicted by
Synthon in Table 1. Instead, they had the spectrum described in
the patent in suit.

Faced with these results Synthon had to retreat and regroup.
When it came to the trial, they advanced new arguments. First,
they called evidence to show that the IR spectrum in Table 1 of
their application was the result of a mistaken reading in their own
laboratory. They submitted that the totality of the evidence, including the IR readings of the crystals obtained by Professor Baldwin,
showed that PMS was monomorphic. Any PMS crystal would have
the characteristics described in the patent in suit. The judge
accepted this submission. He therefore found that a disclosure of a
crystalline form of PMS necessarily meant that it would be the
form described in the patent, even though a person who had read
the patent and set out to make the form described in the application might have thought he was making something different.

Secondly, Synthon put forward a new argument on enablement. They said that although the method described in the application did not produce seeding crystals, that did not mean that the ordinary skilled man would not be able to crystallise PMS. The trouble with the described method turned out to be that it had used an unsuitable solvent. Ethanol produced a reaction which inhibited crystallisation. But the ordinary skilled man, if not confined to a particular solvent, would try another. Crystallisation was an art rather than an exact science and commonly involved some routine trial and error before results were achieved. For these propositions, Synthon relied mainly upon the evidence of SB's own expert, Dr Ward. They also relied, as evidence of what would have been thought within the abilities of the ordinary skilled man, upon the terms of SB's own specification, which described the process of crystallisation as conventional and capable of being effected with a variety of solvents and in a number of different ways. They abandoned reliance upon any particular method disclosed by their application and relied upon it only for the information it contained about the chemistry of PMS which the skilled man might find useful in choosing solvents and methods of crystallisation.

Jacob J accepted this argument as well. He found that the reader of the application, seeking to crystallise PMS, would be able to overcome any problems within a reasonable time. The crystals he made would then inevitably be the crystals described in the patent in suit. The judge therefore held that the matter contained in the application did disclose the existence of the very product which was the subject of the SB patent and that the making of that product was enabled. The patent was therefore invalid.

The law

Before I discuss what the Court of Appeal made of these findings, I must say something about the law. I have said that there are two requirements for anticipation: prior disclosure and enablement.

(a) Disclosure

The concept of what I have called disclosure has been explained in two judgments of unquestionable authority. [Lord Hoffmann cited statements from the two judgments]...

If I may summarise the effect of these two well-known statements, the matter relied upon as prior art must disclose subject-matter which, if performed, would necessarily result in an infringement of the patent. That may be because the prior art discloses the same invention. In that case there will be no question that performance of the earlier invention would infringe and usually it will be apparent to someone who is aware of both the prior art and the patent that it will do so. But patent infringement does not require that one should be aware that one is infringing: "whether or not a person is working [an] . . . invention is an objective fact independent of what he knows or thinks about what he is doing": *Merrell Dow Pharmaceuticals Inc v. H N Norton & Co Ltd* [1996] RPC 76, 90. It follows that, whether or not it would be apparent to anyone at the time, whenever subject-matter described in the prior disclosure is capable of being performed and is such that, if performed, it must result in the patent being infringed, the disclosure condition is satisfied. The flag has been planted, even though the author or maker of the prior art was not aware that he was doing so.

* * *

Although it is sometimes said that there are two forms of anticipatory disclosure: a disclosure of the patented invention itself and a disclosure of an invention which, if performed, would necessarily infringe the patented invention (see, for example, Laddie J in *Inhale Therapeutic Systems Inc v. Quadrant Healthcare Plc* [2002] RPC 21 at para 43) they are both aspects of a single principle, namely that anticipation requires prior disclosure of subject-matter which, when performed, must necessarily infringe the patented invention.

If performance of an invention disclosed by the prior art would not infringe the patent but the prior art would make it obvious to a skilled person how he might make adaptations which resulted in an infringing invention, then the patent may be invalid for lack of an inventive step but not for lack of novelty. In the present case, the Synthon application is deemed to form part of the state of the art for the purposes of novelty (section 2(3)) but not for the purpose of obviousness (section 3). As Synthon rely solely upon section 2(3) matter as prior art, they do not rely and cannot succeed on obviousness.

(b) Enablement

Enablement means that the ordinary skilled person would have been able to perform the invention which satisfies the requirement of disclosure. This requirement applies whether the disclosure is in matter which forms part of the state of the art by virtue of section 2(2) or, as in this case, section 2(3). The latter point was settled by the decision of this House in *Asahi Kasei Kogyo KK's Application* [1991] RPC 485.

Asahi's case was decided on the assumed facts that there had been a prior disclosure of the same invention (a particular polypeptide) but that neither the disclosed information nor common general knowledge would have enabled the skilled man to make it. The House therefore did not have to consider the test for deciding what degree of knowledge, skill and perseverance the skilled man was assumed to have. But the concept of enablement is used in other contexts in the law of patents (see *Biogen Inc v. Medeva Plc* [1997] RPC 1, 47) and in particular as a ground for the revocation of a patent under section 72(1)(c): "the specification of the patent does not disclose the invention clearly enough and completely enough for it to be performed by a person skilled in the art". The question of what will satisfy this test has been discussed in a number of cases. For example, in *Valensi v. British Radio Corporation* [1973] RPC 337, 377 Buckley LJ said:

> "The hypothetical addressee is not a person of exceptional skill and knowledge, that he is not to be expected to exercise any invention nor any prolonged research, inquiry or experiment. He must, however, be prepared to display a reasonable degree of skill and common knowledge of the art in making trials and to correct *obvious* errors in the specification if a means of correcting them can readily be found."

There is also a valuable and more extended discussion in the judgment of Lloyd LJ in *Mentor Corporation v. Hollister Incorporated* [1993] RPC 7. In the present case the Court of Appeal was reluctant to say that the test of enablement of a prior disclosure for the purpose of anticipation was the same as the test of enablement of the patent itself for the purpose of sufficiency. But I can think of no reason why there should be any difference and the Technical Board of Appeal has more than once held that the tests are the same: see *ICI/Pyridine Herbicides* [1986] 5 EPOR 232, para 2; *COLLABORATIVE/Preprorennin* [1990] EPOR 361, para 15. In my opinion, therefore, the authorities on section 72(1)(c) are equally applicable to enablement for the purposes of sections 2(2) and (3). There may however be differences in the application of this test to the facts; for example, because in the case of sufficiency the skilled person is attempting to perform a claimed invention and has that goal in mind, whereas in the case of prior art the subject-matter may have disclosed the invention but not identified it as such. But no such question arises in this case, in which the application plainly identified crystalline PMS as an embodiment of the invention.

(c) Keeping the concepts distinct

It is very important to keep in mind that disclosure and enablement are distinct concepts, each of which has to be satisfied and each of which has its own rules.

* * *

Likewise, the role of the person skilled in the art is different in relation to disclosure and enablement. In the case of disclosure, when the matter relied upon as prior art consists (as in this case) of a written description, the skilled person is taken to be trying to understand what the author of the description meant. His common general knowledge forms the background to an exercise in construction of the kind recently discussed by this House in *Kirin–Amgen Inc v. Hoechst Marion Roussel Ltd* [2005] RPC 9. And of course the patent itself must be construed on similar principles. But once the meanings of the prior disclosure and the patent have been determined, the disclosure is either of an invention which, if performed, would infringe the patent, or it is not. The person skilled in the art has no further part to play. For the purpose of enablement, however, the question is no longer what the skilled person would think the disclosure meant but whether he would be able to work the invention which the court has held it to disclose.

There is also a danger of confusion in a case like *Merrell Dow Pharmaceuticals Inc v. H N Norton & Co Ltd* [1996] RPC 76, in which the subject-matter disclosed in the prior art is not the same as the claimed invention but will, if performed, necessarily infringe. To satisfy the requirement of disclosure, it must be shown that there will necessarily be infringement of the patented invention. But the invention which must be enabled is the one disclosed by the prior art. It makes no sense to inquire as to whether the prior disclosure enables the skilled person to perform the patented invention, since ex hypothesi in such a case the skilled person will not even realise that he is doing so. Thus in *Merrell Dow* the question of enablement turned on whether the disclosure enabled the skilled man to make terfenadine and feed it to hay-fever sufferers, not on whether it enabled him to make the acid metabolite.

Applying the law to the facts

(a) *Disclosure*

Did the Synthon application disclose an invention which, if performed, would infringe the SB patent? Because it covered a class of chemicals defined by reference to a formula, it disclosed a myriad of compounds, each of which may be regarded as an invention. But that does not matter if one of those inventions was the crystalline PMS claimed in the patent.

There seems to me no doubt that the application disclosed the existence of PMS crystals of 98% purity and claimed that they could be made. Whether in fact they could be made is the question of enablement which I shall come to in a moment. But their existence and their advantages for pharmaceutical use were clearly disclosed in the application. And on the basis of the judge's finding of monomorphism, a PMS crystal of 98% purity must necessarily have all the characteristics of the crystals claimed in the patent, including the IR and XRD spectra.

Does it matter that the disclosure attributed to PMS crystals an IR spectrum which, on the judge's findings, was wrong? In my opinion it does not. Of course if the crystals were polymorphic, it would be necessary to specify an IR spectrum or some other way of distinguishing between them. The skilled person, having made his crystals, might find that they infringed the patent or they did not, depending upon which kind he had made. If there had been more than one polymorph, he would not have infringed if he had made the one disclosed by the application. But when the crystals are monomorphic, the IR spectrum is a superfluous part of the description. It may be that the skilled person, having successfully made what the application describes, namely PMS crystals of 98% purity, would be puzzled, perhaps even disconcerted, to find that their IR spectrum turned out to be different from what he had been led to believe. But he would have made the crystals and they would necessarily infringe the patent.

In some contexts one might say that the IR spectrum in the application was a *falsa demonstratio* which did not prevent the described compound, upon the true construction of the application, from being simply pure crystalline PMS, in the way one might conclude, from various details and circumstantial evidence that a witness was describing a particular motor car, even though his reading of the number plate was inaccurate. That is a perfectly legitimate way of approaching the question. But it is, I think, more easily answered if one remembers the general principle that anticipation requires a prior disclosure which, if performed, would infringe the patent. The subject-matter described was crystalline PMS and a skilled person who performed that invention, though he might, if he had read the patent, think that he was not going to infringe it, would inevitably do so.

(b) Enablement

Once one has decided that the disclosure in the application was crystalline PMS and that the IR spectrum was superfluous and irrelevant, the question of enablement is whether the skilled person would have been able to make crystalline PMS. If he did, he would necessarily have made the product claimed in the patent. There is no dispute that the disclosure enabled him to make PMS. The issue is whether he would have been able to get it to crystallise. That is a question of fact, involving the application of the standards laid down in cases like *Mentor Corporation v. Hollister Incorporated* [1993] RPC 7 to the evidence of the nature of the problem, the assistance provided by the disclosure itself and the extent of common general knowledge. Synthon, as I have said, got off to a bad start by specifying, in their main example, a solvent which proved unsuitable for crystallisation. Nevertheless, the judge found that the skilled man would have tried some other solvent from the range mentioned in the application or forming part of his common general knowledge and would have been able to make PMS crystals within a reasonable time. This is a finding of fact by a very experienced judge with which an appellate court should be reluctant to interfere: compare *Biogen Inc v. Medeva Plc* [1997] RPC 1, 45.

The Court of Appeal

The Court of Appeal (Aldous, Sedley and Rix LJJ), in a judgment given by Aldous LJ, reversed the judge's decision. As will appear, I have not found it easy to understand the judgment; I shall have to look at some passages in detail, but the main source of my difficulty is that, with great respect to Aldous LJ, who is an acknowledged master of patent law, the questions of disclosure and enablement are so intermingled that it is often difficult to say which of them he is talking about.

After referring to some of the authorities, Aldous LJ said:

"The dispute between the parties essentially involves a dispute of fact, namely what is explicitly and implicitly disclosed in the application. Thereafter, the court has to decide whether that disclosure is sufficient to make the invention of the patent available."

If that means that there are two questions: first, did the application disclose, explicitly or implicitly, an invention which would, if performed, infringe the patent and secondly, was that invention enabled, then of course I would agree. After setting out the arguments of the parties and saying that clear guidance could be obtained from the *General Tire* and *UNION CARBIDE* cases (to which I have referred above) the judge went on:

"There are no clear and unmistakeable directions to make PMS as claimed in claim 1 of the patent as required by the *General Tire* case. The general teaching of the application does not mention PMS. It is one of a number of compounds described by reference to formulae. The only specific reference is in example 1. That describes a different form. It follows that the skilled person would not expect to produce the PMS claimed in claim 1 by carrying out the general teaching of the application. If he attempted to carry out example 1, he would fail to obtain crystalline PMS. He would therefore not know that there was only one form of crystalline PMS and that was not the form described in the application."

I find this passage particularly confusing. What are the "clear and unmistakeable directions to make PMS as claimed in claim 1"? Is this disclosure (ie identifying crystalline PMS as a desirable compound) or does it refer to enablement? If it refers to enablement, does it mean that the disclosure itself must enable? That cannot be right because, as I have said, the disclosure may consist entirely of putting a compound on the market and enablement may be found in the ordinary skilled man's ability to analyse and reproduce it. Likewise, if the problem is crystallisation, the enablement may be found in the armoury of the ordinary skilled man with little, if any, assistance from the disclosure. Then, why does it matter that it is one of a number of compounds identified in the invention and that it is mentioned at a certain point in the application? The question is whether it is disclosed. To say that the application discloses a different form begs the question because there is no different form. Disclosure of crystalline PMS was disclosure of the patented product. The fact that the skilled man, surveying the result of his labours, would have thought he had made a product different from that described in the application seems to me irrelevant.

* * *

The main reasons for the Court of Appeal's rejection of the judge's finding of fact appear from para 56 of the judgment of Aldous LJ:

"The crucial question was not whether the skilled addressee would expect success, but whether the application made available PMS as claimed. There was no attempt to ask Mr. Ward whether there were directions in the application which, if followed, would produce the claimed form of PMS. No doubt that was because the answer would have been 'No'. Once it had been established that example 1 did not disclose a successful route to PMS as claimed in the patent, the skilled addressee might have adopted obvious modifications. But such an approach is not permissible when considering novelty."

This passage again suggests to me a serious confusion between disclosure and enablement. The evidence of Mr. Ward was relied upon solely for the purpose of proving enablement. But the reference at the end to "obvious modifications" being impermissible is a reference to the requirement that the prior art must have planted the flag on the patented invention, which is a principle of disclosure. On that question Mr. Ward's evidence about making crystals could have nothing to contribute.

Paragraph 56 again leaves me in doubt about whether the Court of Appeal thought that the prior art did not disclose the invention or whether it did so but was not enabled. If it was the former, then, as I have said, I think that they were wrong. If it was the latter, then I do not think that they have offered adequate reasons for disturbing the judge's finding of fact. I would therefore allow the appeal and restore the decision of Jacob J.

Notes and Questions

1. Japanese Patent Law adopts a more liberal view when an unpublished application is used for anticipation. Toshiko Takenaka, *The Substantial identity Rule Under the Japanese Novelty Standard*, 9 UCLA Pac. Basin L. J. 220 (1991). Why does the Japanese system relax the standard only for unpublished applications?

2. In a landmark opinion by the German Federal Court (Tenth Senate), the chamber that makes final decisions for Germany on all issues of patent law, narrowly construed the disclosure of a genus of chemical compounds when it held that a specific compound chosen from the genus was not anticipated by the disclosure of the genus. Olanzapine, Judgment of BGH, Dec. 16, 2008, 2009 GRUR 382. Many inventions are made by selecting a subset of amino acid sequences from a DNA sequence, by defining a specific and limited numerical range for operating a known process, or by choosing a specific compound from a large genus of compounds. These selection inventions must overcome both anticipation and obviousness attacks to be patentable. These requirements are distinct but courts often intermingle the enablement requirement of anticipation and obviousness.

When rejecting the claim, the German Federal Patent Court cited a reference that disclosed some compounds of a general formula that contained olanzapine, as well as methods that a person skilled in the art could use to create the drug. However, it did not expressly discuss olanzapine itself. The Patent Court held that a person skilled in the art of invention could start from a general formula and make olanzapine by using his or her general knowledge, finding that the claims for olanzapine were anticipated. The Tenth Senate found error in the Patent Court's analysis because it took into account the ability of a skilled person using their general knowledge to conceive of olanzapine. For claims relating to a species compound to be rejected, the species compound must clearly and expressly be derived from the disclosure of a general formula that contains the species compound. In supporting the rule, the Court examined EPO case law and the corresponding UK cases and concluded that its rule was in line with the anticipation rules in these jurisdictions. It distinguished this case where the exercise of skill and general knowledge was necessary to reach the claimed subject matter from cases where the claimed subject matter was immediately and clearly evident to a skilled person from a prior disclosure. In the court's view, it is appropriate to reject claims for lack of novelty only in the latter cases. Other important jurisdictions have also reached the same conclusion, *see Eli Lilly & Co. v. Zenith Goldline Pharms., Inc.*, 471 F.3d 1369 (Fed. Cir. 2006); *Dr. Reddy's Laboratories v. Eli Lilly & Co.* [2009] EWCA Civ 1362 (U.K. Court of Appeal, 2009).

3. Should a different test apply to selection inventions for anticipation? Prof. Adelman proposes multiple factors for deciding the novelty

of selection inventions. 1 Martin J. Adelman, *Patent Law Perspectives*, § 2.2[4] at n.67 (2d ed. 1996). Among these factors, the Federal Circuit emphasizes the presence of an unknown property to prevent anticipation by a genus disclosure. *In re Kalm*, 378 F.2d 959 (CCPA 1967). How does this test differ from the nonobviousness test?

B. INVENTIVE STEP

Inventive step is a requirement comparable to nonobviousness under 35 U.S.C. § 103. This concept, as established under the EPC, is based on German jurisprudence dealing with the concept of inventive height or level (*Erfindingshöhe*). Under the German patent system, there were two competing tests for patentability that went beyond novelty: advance in the art and nonobviousness. The latter test was the one eventually included in the EPC. Section 56 adopts a definition of inventive step that is very similar to that of nonobviousness under 35 U.S.C. § 103, where an invention shall be considered as involving an inventive step if, having regard to the state of the art, it is not obvious to a person skilled in the art. Hanns Ullrich, *Standards of Patentability for European Inventions*, 1 IIC Studies (1977).

Many Asian countries, including Japan, South Korea, and China, have adopted the same concept of patentability in their patent systems, and the patent offices in these countries determine inventive step in a way similar to the problem-solution approach.

PROBLEM SOLUTION APPROACH

The EPO examined its first application on June 1, 1978. These original examiners were selected from the patent offices of the seven original member states, each of which had previously used different patentability standards. The EPO adopted the so-called "problem-solution approach" in order to develop uniform examination standards for determining inventive step. The first excerpt is an EPO Technical Board of Appeal case showing the application of the problem-solution approach.

However, courts in the EPC member states do not necessary follow the problem-solution approach for determining inventive step. The second and third excerpts from the U.K. Court of Appeal and the German Federal Court compare their own approach with the problem-solution approach.

BASF/METAL REFINING

[1979–1985] E.P.O.R. B354 (EPO (Technical Bd. App.) 1983)

European patent application No. 79 101 414.5 ... filed on 9 May 1979 ..., claiming priority from the German prior application of 11 May 1978, was refused by the decision of the Examining Division of the European Patent Office dated 17 February 1981, on the basis of the eight claims as filed ... Claim 1 is worded as follows: Method for treating melts of pig-iron and steel or steel alloys in a converter, crucible or other vessel, characterised in that the entire oxidising (for carbon elimination) and treatment process is carried out using carbonic acid (Kohlensäure—The German term is traditionally used also to denote carbon dioxide) in one vessel on a continuous basis until the finished steel is produced....

When assessing inventive step for this method, it is not a question of the subjective achievement of the inventor, so that the case history of the invention presented at the oral proceedings is irrelevant. It is rather the objective achievement which has to be assessed. As in the case of novelty, inventive step is an objective concept. Objectivity in the assessment of inventive step is achieved by starting out from the objectively prevailing state of the art, in the light of which the problem is determined which the invention addresses and solves from an objective point of view ..., and consideration is given to the question of the obviousness of the disclosed solution to this problem as seen by the man skilled in the art and having those capabilities which can be objectively expected of him. This also avoids the retrospective approach which inadmissibly makes use of knowledge of the invention....

If this yardstick is applied to the present case, the inventive step must be considered from the point of view of a practitioner in the steel sector who was already familiar with the publications cited in the lower instance and with the oxygen-blowing process which ... was introduced into technology thirty years ago. The marked overheating of the melt during the oxidising is regarded as a disadvantage in this method, since the converter lining is thereby damaged, leading to the steel melt becoming contaminated with particles from the lining.... A proposed solution to avoid these disadvantages is already described in DD–A–103 266. In order, among other things, to increase the cooling effect of the gases and thus increase the durability of the converter lining ..., the pig-iron melt is here oxidised with a pulsating oxygen jet surrounded by a blanketing medium, especially steam (Claims 1 to 10), and the steel melt is subsequently scavenged by introducing an inert or low-reactivity pulsating gas jet with surrounding blanketing medium to reduce undesirable gas inclusions (Claim 14). Nitrogen, argon, carbon dioxide or flue gas are used as the scavenging gas (Claim 15).

In the search for a further solution to the known problem the appellant set himself the dual task of both (a) avoiding an overheating of the melt which necessarily leads to a reduction in the service life of the converter lining and to contamination of the melt with converter particles and (b) preventing the formation of red iron-oxide smoke during the oxidising process, in order thereby to dispense with the need for costly filtering equipment. The problem thus defined was determined from an objective point of view on the basis of the result aimed at and actually attained by the invention.

To solve this problem the application proposes essentially the use of carbonic acid as oxidising and scavenging agent.

The skilled practitioner seeking a new solution to this problem in the prior art was aware of the fact that pig-iron melts cool off when oxidises with carbon dioxide (see DE–C–934 772, Claim 1 and page 2, lines 24/25 and 81/82). The cooling off is a result of the endothermic reaction of the carbon contained in the pig-iron with the carbon dioxide oxidising agent to form carbon monoxide ... The use of carbon dioxide as an oxidising agent therefore presented itself from the point of view of the skilled practitioner as a solution to sub-problem (a).

FR–A–1 058 181 was able to provide the required suggestion for solving sub-problem (b). This publication imparts the teaching that the formation of the feared red iron-oxide smoke in the treatment of pig-iron melts with oxygen can be significantly reduced by adding to the oxygen blowing gas a compound which undergoes an endothermic reaction through dissociation or reduction (Résumé 1), e.g. carbon dioxide (Résumé 2b). On the basis of this teaching it was to be expected that—with a view to solving sub-problem (a)—switching over to carbon dioxide as oxidising agent would lead to complete suppression of the red smoke. Moreover, the close connection between the two sub-problems is already clear from the above-mentioned FR–A–.

If these teachings from the prior art are combined, a man skilled in the art could expect the dual problem posed to be solvable by using carbon dioxide as the oxidising agent. In addition it was clear that—unlike the single-stage process as in the above-mentioned DE–C– and FR–A for which patent applications were filed in 1938 and 1951 respectively—the stringent requirements as to the purity of steel at the date of priority (11 May 1978), particularly with regard to undesirable gas inclusions, could only be met by additional subsequent scavenging of the steel melt with a scavenging gas, as exemplified in the above-mentioned DD–A–103 266. Since the solution of the overall problem posed demanded the use of carbon dioxide for the oxidising, it was obvious, for reasons of simplifying the process, to use the same inexpensive gas as a scavenging gas as well.

Once the development of a method for refining pig-iron by oxidising and subsequent scavenging of the melt by means of carbon dioxide as oxidising and scavenging agent in a single converter became obvious, determination of the amounts of carbon dioxide required for this was purely a matter of routine experimentation. . . .

The appellant, on the other hand, takes the view that by combining these publications a man skilled in the art would not have arrived at the claimed method without inventive effort, because he would have only taken into consideration those embodiments which were particularly emphasised therein. . . . [T]he Board does not share the appellant's view that only those embodiments described as being preferred in a citation are to be considered when assessing the inventive step. In fact, when examining for inventive step, the state of the art must be assessed from the point of view of the man skilled in the art at the time of priority relevant for the application. Consequently all previously published embodiments must be taken into consideration which offered a suggestion to the skilled practitioner for solving the problem addressed, even where the embodiments were not particularly emphasised. It is therefore not a matter of what was regarded as advantageous at that time in the publications constituting the prior art. . . .

The appellant sees the fact that the steel industry has passed by the method as applied for, despite the significant economic contribution it makes to solving the environmental problems in this field, as an indication of the presence of inventive step. . . . Where any such indications are present, the overall picture of the state of the art and consideration of all significant factors may indeed show that inventive step is involved, without however leading to the compelling conclusion that inventive step must generally follow from this situation. The considerable technical effect here claimed provides no basis for the presence of inventive step, if only because it is not surprising, but was on the contrary certainly to be expected in view of the problem facing the skilled practitioner.

The fact that the steel industry has passed by the method as applied for becomes understandable if the question is considered as to whether and when the appellant's method met an urgent need. The appellant has himself stated that the oxygen-blowing process was rational and economically attractive when introduced into technology thirty years ago, but that the advent and especially the tightening of environmental laws over the last few years have raised investment costs for dust-removal and filtering equipment by about 25%, leading to an increase in the price of steel by 5 to 10 DM/t. In the view of the Board this indicates that over a long period of time there was no motive for breaking away from the oxygen-blowing process which had been successfully introduced and more-over involved expensive plant of long service life, and that the need for the appellant's method which from the present-day point of view is environmentally innocuous arose relatively shortly before the date of priority of the present application. A process developed in the light of a need which arose relatively shortly before the application cannot be regarded as involving inventive step if this need could be readily met by an obvious combination of teachings from the prior art. . . .

ACTAVIS UK LIMITED v. NOVARTIS AG

High Court of Justice Court of Appeal (Civil Division)
[2010] EWCA Civ 82

Before: The Rt Hon Lord Justice Jacob
The Rt Hon Lord Justice Lloyd and
The Rt Hon Lord Justice Stanley Burnton

Lord Justice Jacob:

The Patent and its background

3. The Patent, whose priority date is October 1996, is for a sustained release formulation of fluvastatin. In 1996 fluvastatin was a well-known statin available in an immediate release formulation consisting of capsules containing 20 or 40 mg of the sodium salt. By that date there was a strong and well-known school of thought in favour of a dosage regime consisting of a 40 mg capsule to be taken twice a day.

4. Also at the priority date there was extensive knowledge of sustained release formulations generally. The Patent puts it this way under the heading "background art":

> [0002] In recent years there has been a large increase in the development and use of sustained-release tablets which are designed to release the drug slowly after ingestion. With these types of dosage forms, the clinical utility of drugs can be improved by means of improved therapeutic effects, reduced incidence of adverse effects and simplified dosing regimens.

> Mr. Meade suggested that this paragraph should be read as specific to the invention and was saying that the invention would lead to improved therapeutic effects, reduced adverse effects and simplified dosing regimens. But

it is clear that it is no more than a general background statement about the increasing use of sustained release drugs and the reasons therefore. It is saying you may or may not get improved therapy (for one or other or both reasons) and you will (obviously) get a simplified dosing regime. That was common general knowledge.

5. The Patent then explains that by "sustained release" is meant a release which takes typically more than 3 and less than 30 hours. It then points out that there are several different known types of sustained release formulation and describes three types: use of an insoluble matrix, an eroding matrix, and release through a semipermeable membrane. Just before it describes these it says:

    > [0004]. . . . The actual approach taken for a given drug depends inter alia on the physical chemical properties of the drug. One of these is the solubility of the drug, which has a major impact on the pharmaceutical formulation strategy. A high solubility of the drug substance may induce problems, as discussed further below.

6. The Patent later returns to high solubility and the problems it may cause:

    > [0008] As mentioned above, the drug release from sustained release formulations is related to the drug solubility. The higher the water solubility of the drug, the faster the drug release and the shorter the duration of drug delivery. A fast release of the drug might mean that the desired rate and duration can not be obtained and that the beneficial effects of sustained release administration are lost. Thus, a special challenge is met when trying to formulate water soluble substances for sustained release formulations. One way to try to solve this problem would be to include large amounts of slow release excipients in the formulation. However, this approach has drawbacks such as increased costs and increased size of the formulation. Increased physical size of the dosage form may present problems for some patients, since the tablet will be more difficult to swallow. Another possibility is to use a less water soluble salt. However, such a change requires a more extensive development work and may also lead to bioavailability problems due to incomplete dissolution.

7. This is all perfectly general, still under the general heading "Background, sustained release formulations."

8. The Patent then goes on to discuss statins generally and then fluvastatin, which it acknowledges is known. It then suggests that its solubility is so great that one would expect problems in creating a sustained release formulation:

    [0012] Fluvastatin is a water soluble drug. For example, the solubility of the sodium salt of fluvastatin in water extends to more than 50 g/l. Biopharmaceutical requirements of a sustained release product of this water soluble drug would then at first sight impose formulation problems as discussed above.

    The Patent then explains why, in relation to each of the types of sustained release formulation, high solubility causes problems.

9. The Patent then says what problem the invention is aimed at:

    [0015] Consequently, there is a need for pharmaceutical formulations of HMG–CoA reductase inhibitors which avoid the above mentioned drawbacks and are possible to prepare, e.g., without including large amounts of slow release excipients or the use of highly advanced techniques. Preferably, the production costs of the formulations should be low.

    Clearly in context the "need" referred to is a need for slow-release formulations, not merely any kind of formulation. That is the problem the invention of the Patent seeks to overcome

10. The clear message of all this is simple: there is a need for a sustained release formulation of fluvastatin but its solubility is so high that there is at least a perception that any of the conventional methods would not work.

11. The Patent now moves on to "Disclosure of the invention". The first paragraph under this heading sets out what the inventors claim to have discovered and the second the consequential invention:

    [0017] It has surprisingly been found that sustained-release compositions, comprising fluvastatin as a water soluble salt, exhibit particularly favorable release characteristics such as unexpectedly long duration and slow rate of drug release. In the present context, the term "water soluble" should be understood as a solubility of more than 30 mg/ml in water at +37°C.

    [0018] Consequently, the present invention provides a pharmaceutical composition for sustained release comprising a water soluble salt, preferably the sodium salt, of fluvastatin as an active ingredient. The sustained-release fluvastatin compositions for which these favorable properties are obtained are selected from the group comprising matrix formulations, diffusion-controlled membrane coated formulations; and combinations thereof.

12. This is saying that, contrary to what the skilled person would have thought from its high solubility, you can in fact make sustained release formulations of fluvastatin by using any of the three conventional techniques already acknowledged.

13. After some detail which does not matter the Patent says this, and only this, about the utility of the invention:

> [0027] The pharmaceutical formulations according to the invention are useful for lowering the blood cholesterol level in animals, in particular mammals, e.g. humans. They are therefore useful as hypercholesterolemic and anti-atherosclerotic agents

14. The Patent presents some data which shows that fluvastatin is released more slowly from a sustained release formulation than two other, less soluble drugs. This is done "to exemplify the unexpectedly favorable properties of fluvastatin in matrix and membrane coated formulations."

15. It is worth noting that there is no comparison with a drug which has such a high solubility that it cannot put into a sustained release form.

16. Examples of sustained release formulations are given (nothing turns on these) and then the Patent comes to its claims. Although there were lurking in the background some arguments about other claims, the only claim which really matters is claim 1, as permitted to be amended by Warren J:

> A sustained release pharmaceutical composition comprising a water soluble salt of fluvastatin as active ingredient and being selected from the group consisting of matrix formulations, diffusion-controlled membrane coated formulations and combinations thereof, wherein the sustained release formulation releases the active ingredient over more than 3 hours.

Obviousness: the Law

17. The statutory question is beguilingly simple and is set out in the European Patent Convention, enacted by the Patents Act 1977. The Convention says:

Art 52 Patentable Inventions

(1) European patents shall be granted for any inventions which are susceptible of industrial application, which are new and which involve an inventive step.

Art 56 Inventive Step

An invention shall be considered as involving an inventive step if, having regard to the state of the art, it is not obvious to a person skilled in the art.

So at bottom the question is simply whether the invention is obvious. Any paraphrase or other test is only an aid to answering the statutory question.

18.   In our courts we have found a structure helpful to approach—not answer—the question. In its latest refinement (see *Pozzoli v. BDMO* [2007] FSR 37) it runs as follows:

(1) (a) Identify the notional "person skilled in the art"

(b) Identify the relevant common general knowledge of that person;

(2) Identify the inventive concept of the claim in question or if that cannot readily be done, construe it;

(3) Identify what, if any, differences exist between the matter cited as forming part of the "state of the art" and the inventive concept of the claim or the claim as construed;

(4) Viewed without any knowledge of the alleged invention as claimed, do those differences constitute steps which would have been obvious to the person skilled in the art or do they require any degree of invention?

Obvious for the purposes of step 4 means technically rather than commercially obvious.

19.   I would only add an extra word about step 2—identifying the inventive concept. It originally comes from Oliver LJ's formulation of the approach in *Windsurfing v. Tabur Marine* [1985] RPC 59 at 73. Strictly, the only thing that matters is what is claimed—as Lord Hoffmann said in *Conor v. Angiotech* [2009] UKHL 49, [2008] RPC 716 at [19]:

the patentee is entitled to have the question of obviousness determined by reference to his claim and not to some vague paraphrase based upon the extent of his disclosure in the description.

20. The "inventive concept" can be a distraction or helpful. It is a distraction almost as soon as there is an argument as to what it is. It is helpful when the parties are agreed as to what it is. In this case, for instance, although the claim has a numerical limitation defining what is meant by "sustained release", as a practical matter both sides proceeded on the basis that it was for a sustained release formulation of fluvastatin.

21. The first three steps merely orientate the tribunal properly. Step 4 is the key, statutory step.

22. I am conscious that some appear to think that this structured process is something peculiarly British. I do not think it is. It merely makes explicit that which is implicit in all other approaches. No one would dispute for instance, that obviousness must be considered through the eyes of the skilled man (steps 1(a) and (b)). Nor that you have to identify the target of alleged obviousness (step 2). Nor that you have to identify the differences between the target and the prior art (step 3).

23. As to step (4), all it does is to pose the question. It does not attempt to provide any structure for answering it. Depending on the facts, various approaches may assist.

24. One, for instance, is "obvious to try". The limits of that approach were discussed in *Conor* by Lords Hoffmann and Walker. Lord Hoffmann said this:

> [42] In the Court of Appeal, Jacob LJ dealt comprehensively with the question of when an invention could be considered obvious on the ground that it was obvious to try. He correctly summarised the authorities, starting with the judgment of Diplock LJ in *Johns–Manville Corporation's Patent* [1967] RPC 479, by saying that the notion of something being obvious to try was useful only in a case in which there was a fair expectation of success. How much of an expectation would be needed depended upon the particular facts of the case.

25. Another approach, often used in the EPO both for examination and opposition is the "problem and solution approach" ("PSA"). It is conveniently described in the EPO's Guidelines for Substantive Examination:

11.7   *Problem-and-solution approach*

In practice, in order to assess inventive step in an objective and predictable manner, the examiner should normally apply the so-called "problem-and-solution approach".

In the problem-and-solution approach, there are three main stages:

(i) determining the "closest prior art",

(ii) establishing the "objective technical problem" to be solved, and

(iii) considering whether or not the claimed invention, starting from the closest prior art and the objective technical problem, would have been obvious to the skilled person.

26.   I have a few comments about the PSA. First, and most important, is to emphasise that no-one suggests or has ever suggested that it is the only way to go about considering obviousness. The Guidelines say no more than that the examiner should "normally" apply it. That makes sense for an examining office which needs a common structured approach. When it comes to a national court making a full multifactorial assessment of all relevant factors (which may include so-called "secondary indicia" such as commercial success, especially if there has been a long-felt want) it may perhaps be used less often—particularly where there is significant room for argument about what the "objective technical problem" is. In this case, however, as will be seen, I think the approach is indeed useful.

27.   My second comment is about stage 1—identify the closest piece of prior art. It is not related to the remaining steps. It is about where they start from. Generally it is an immensely practical way of dealing with the fact that practitioners before the Office seem to think they can improve opposition attacks by the citation of a very large number of pieces of prior art. Currently there is nothing in the procedural rules (for instance a fee or costs sanction) to prevent this. Nor, in many cases, have practitioners themselves developed a culture of identifying their best piece or pieces (perhaps 2 or 3 maximum) of prior art. What is the Office to do when faced with a profligate number of citations? Laboriously consider the question of obviousness over each, one by one? Even though there may be fifty or more? That would be intolerable besides leading to even worse delays than there are now. So step 1 is essentially Office protective. It is an attempt to identify

the best obviousness attack. The logic is simple: if that succeeds it does not matter if there are other attacks which might also succeed. And if it fails, other, weaker attacks would also do so.

28. So step 1 is a useful tool when there are many citations. It can have its difficulties—for instance deciding which piece of prior art is the closest can lead to something of a satellite dispute. You could argue, for instance, about whether you use a mechanical approach of just identifying which citation has the highest number of elements corresponding to elements in the claim, or use a more holistic approach of asking which is conceptually or technically closest.

29. It will be noticed that there is nothing like PSA step 1 in the *Pozzoli/Windsurfing* approach. The reason is essentially this: that practitioners before the English Patents Court have learned to confine themselves to their best cases, especially by the time of trial. English patent judges are simply not faced with profligate citations. And indeed if a party attempted to indulge in profligate citation it would be likely to find that when the case-management stage of the case was reached, it would be made to identify its best case, or few best cases. Moreover wasteful conduct, which would generally include profligate citation of prior art, is likely be met with adverse costs orders.

30. I turn to the next step—establishing the "objective technical problem." The Guidelines say this:

> In the context of the problem-and-solution approach, the technical problem means the aim and task of modifying or adapting the closest prior art to provide the technical effects that the invention provides over the closest prior art. The technical problem thus defined is often referred to as the **"objective technical problem"**.
>
> The objective technical problem derived in this way may not be what the applicant presented as "the problem" in his application. The later may require reformulation, since the objective technical problem is based on objectively established facts, in particular appearing in the prior art revealed in the course of the proceedings, which may be different from the prior art of which the applicant was actually aware at the time the application was filed. In particular, the prior art cited in the search report may put the invention in an

entirely different perspective from that apparent from reading the application only.

31. There is recognition here of that fact that in many cases the patentee did not start from the closest piece of prior art identified by step 1. He may have thought he was solving some larger or different problem. He may not have known of this piece of prior art.

32. The "reformulation" referred to thus involves the court or tribunal artificially creating a problem supposed to be solved by the invention. It is perhaps here that there can be real difficulties: for so much may depend on that reformulation however objectively one attempts the reformulation.

33. The Guidelines grapple with those difficulties:

It is noted that the objective technical problem must be so formulated as not to contain pointers to the technical solution, since including part of a technical solution offered by an invention in the statement of the problem must, when the state of the art is assessed in terms of that problem, necessarily result in an ex post facto view being taken on inventive activity (T 229/85, OJ 6/1987, 237).

The expression "technical problem" should be interpreted broadly; it does not necessarily imply that the technical solution is a technical improvement over the prior art. Thus the problem could be simply to seek an alternative to a known device or process providing the same or similar effects or which is more cost-effective.

34. For myself, I think the re-formulation—which really means retrospective construction—of a problem is perhaps the weakest part of the PSA. It will be noted that with the *Pozzoli/Windsurfing* approach, once one has finished the orienting step 3, the question is simply left open: is the invention obvious? There is no attempt to force the question into a problem/solution.

35. Moreover the PSA does not really cope well with cases where the invention involves perceiving that there is a problem, or in appreciating that a known problem, perhaps "put up with" for years, can be solved. Take for instance the "Anywayup Cup" case, *Haberman v. Jackel International* [1999] FSR 683. The invention was a baby's drinker cup fitted with a known kind of valve to prevent it leaking. Babies drinker cups had been known for years. Parents all over the world had put up with the fact that if

they were dropped they leaked. No-one had thought to solve the problem. So when the patentee had the technically trivial idea of putting in a valve, there was an immediate success. The invention was held non-obvious, a conclusion with which most parents would agree. Yet fitting reasoning to uphold the patent into a PSA approach would not really work. For by identifying the problem as leakage and suggesting it can be solved, one is halfway to the answer—put in a valve.

36.   Another aspect of obviousness which is not readily answered by the PSA is illustrated by the 5¼ inch plate paradox. This runs like this. Suppose the patent claim is for a plate of diameter 5¼ inches. And suppose no-one can find a plate of that particular diameter in the prior art. Then (a) it is novel and (b) it is non-obvious for there is no particular reason to choose that diameter. The conclusion, that the plate is patentable, is so absurd that it cannot be so.

37.   What then is the answer to the paradox? It is this: the 5¼ inch limitation is purely arbitrary and non-technical. It solves no problem and advances the art not at all. It is not inventive. And although "inventive step" is defined as being one which is not obvious, one must always remember the purpose of that definition—to define what is inventive. That which is not inventive by any criteria is not made so by the definition. Trivial limitations, such as specifying the plate diameter, or painting a known machine blue for no technical reason are treated as obvious because they are not inventive.

38.   The PSA does not assist in providing an answer to the paradox. This is for the simple reason that there is no problem and so no solution to it.

39.   Having said that the PSA has its limitations I hasten to add this: the PSA is apt to work very well when there is no need to reformulate the problem. This, as will be seen, is such a case. And it also generally works where, although there needs to be a reformulation, the reformulation is not controversial.

40.   The last step of the PSA, asking whether the invention is obvious starting from the closest prior art and the objective technical problem corresponds to *Pozzoli/Windsurfing* step 4, though the latter is not limited to any "objective technical problem". As I have said it leaves the question unconstrained by any necessary requirement to identify a problem.

41.   That is because in the end obviousness is a multifactorial question. Kitchin J put thus in a manner approved by Lord Hoffmann at [42] in *Conor*:

> The question of obviousness must be considered on the facts of each case. The court must consider the weight to be attached to any particular factor in the light of all the relevant circumstances. These may include such matters as the motive to find a solution to the problem the patent addresses, the number and extent of the possible avenues of research, the effort involved in pursuing them and the expectation of success. (*Generics v. Lundbeck* [2007] RPC 32 at [72]).

42.   Finally I should say a word about what is sometimes called the could/would point. For it was part of Mr. Meade's submissions that even though it was conceded that the idea of a slow-release formulation of fluvastatin would occur to the skilled person, that was not enough to make a claim to it obvious. It was necessary to show that skilled person would implement it.

43.   The argument went on in this way: since in practice implementation would involve quite a lot of trouble and expense by way of trials going right through to clinical trials, it was not shown that the idea, although conceptually obvious, would be followed through: it was not shown that the skilled person would actually make a sustained release form.

44.   In support of his "would" argument Mr. Meade relied upon the Guidelines and two TBA cases, *s-triazines/CSI-RO* T632/91 and *Xanthin ketals/Beecham–Wuelfing* T116/90.

45.   The Guidelines say this:

> *Could-would approach*
>
> In the third stage the question to be answered is whether there is any teaching in the prior art as a whole that **would** (not simply could, but would) have prompted the skilled person, faced with the objective technical problem, to modify or adapt the closest prior art while taking account of that teaching, thereby arriving at something falling within the terms of the claims, and thus achieving what the invention achieves (see IV, 11.4).
>
> In other words, the point is not whether the skilled person could have arrived at the invention by adapting or modifying the closest prior art, but whether he

would have done so because the prior art incited him to do so in the hope of solving the objective technical problem or in expectation of some improvement or advantage (see T 2/83, OJ 6/1984, 265). This must have been the case for the skilled person before the filing or priority date valid for the claim under examination.

46. I do not read this as involving a requirement that the notional skilled person would actually physically implement the idea. What the passage is saying, sensibly enough, is that it not enough the skilled man could have arrived at the invention from the prior art, it must be shown that he would have done. Whether he would actually press ahead and implement the idea depends on a host of other, commercial considerations.

47. That that must be so seems to me to be self-evident. A requirement that an idea can only be held obvious upon proof that it would actually be implemented would make many self-evident ideas non-obvious. For many obvious ideas may not be worth implementing commercially.

* * *

The Judgment under Appeal

51. The Judge analysed the evidence in detail, for which I am very grateful. Because of that it is unnecessary to go over it all again. Before going to the Judge's conclusions, it is worth noting that Actavis put its case higher than it needed to. It advanced a case that a sustained release form of fluvastatin would be expected not only to be a more convenient formulation for patient compliance but would be likely to have significant medical advantages, namely improved therapeutic effect and fewer side effects. Hence, the argument ran, there was a strong motive to create a sustained release form and a strong expectation that all three types of benefit would be obtained, the two medical and the convenience.

52. On the facts the Judge rejected the "medical advantage" motivation as having a significant enough expectation of success. But he did accept the "more convenient" advantage point. His detailed summary of the position, which is unchallenged, reads as follows:

> [312] In the light of the totality of the evidence, the essentials of which I have discussed above, I reach the following conclusions:

a. The skilled team is to be seen as engaged upon the task of formulating fluvastatin for use in humans for the treatment of hypercholesterolemia. There is no suggestion that the team would be formulating the drug for the treatment of different animals or for the treatment of any other condition.

b. Part of the common general knowledge of the team includes the fact that an immediate release formulation was already available. That formulation could be taken at a dose of up to 40 mg once a day and up to 80 mg per day in two doses.

c. Whether or not the team was expressly directed to consider formulating fluvastatin in a sustained release dosage form, it would at least consider such a formulation as a possible way forward and not dismiss it out of hand.

d. The skilled team would seek to identify the benefits (or incentives) and problems (or disincentives) of a sustained release formulation.

e. The team would regard improved patient compliance as a benefit which would certainly be obtained if a satisfactory formulation of an 80 mg dose could be successfully achieved.

f. The team would be concerned about clinical efficacy. It would be uncertain about whether improvement could be achieved. It could not be ruled out. But it certainly could not be said with any confidence that any improvement would be achieved, nor that there was a strong expectation that it would be achieved.

g. The team would also be concerned with side-effects. Again, it would be unable to predict with anything approaching certainty that any reduction in the risk of side-effects would be achieved, but there would be some hope of reduced risks of hepatotoxicity (on a population basis as explained above) and a reasonable expectation of improvements in myopathy. However, neither of these was seen as serious problems with fluvastatin at the priority date.

h. The team would have, as a result of common general knowledge and secondary common general knowledge, an expectation of being able to develop an 80 mg sustained release formulation which released over at least 3 hours *in vivo* and would be confident that it would have some clinical efficacy. But it would have no confidence that it would achieve better, or even the same, efficacy as the existing maximum dosage of 2 x 40 mg daily immediate release. It would expect, but could not be certain, that this would not produce a greater risk of side-effects than the existing maximum dosage.

i. It would have been rational, from a technical perspective, for the team to have produced a sustained release formulation for 80 mg once daily dosage with a view to improved patient compliance, anticipated reduction in side-effects and possible improved efficacy. But in the light of the uncertainties, such a course might well be seen as commercially unjustifiable; but that would be a matter for the decision of commercial people not of the skilled team.

j. The team, if it were asked to do so, would be confident of producing a sustained release formulation of fluvastatin at various doses which had the release characteristics *in vitro* described in the Patent. It would be confident that such a formulation could be taken by humans and would have some therapeutic effect albeit perhaps of lesser efficacy than the equivalent dosage taken in immediate release form as a single dose (up to 40 mg daily) or two doses (up to 80 mg daily). There would, however, be no reason for producing such a formulation for its own sake if it were thought impossible or highly unlikely that such a formulation would have, or would lead to a product which would have, improved efficacy and/or reduced side-effects.

53. I should also set out a further finding:

[320] The Patent claims that, surprisingly, fluvastatin sodium exhibits particularly favourable release characteristics. The evidence, however, shows that the high absolute solubility of a drug is a problem only at very high and very low levels. The evidence also shows that the high (but not very high) solubility of fluvastatin would not have been seen as a serious problem at least *in vitro*; it would only have been seen as limiting the

available technology for producing a sustained release formulation releasing *in vitro* over a period of 3 hours or more.

54. So the whole basis for the invention as set out in the Patent was destroyed. The Patent says the skilled man would think the solubility of fluvastatin was so high that the skilled man would think a sustained release form could not be made. But that was not so. The skilled man would not think that, based on his common general knowledge alone. The problem presented in the Patent was illusory (Lloyd LJ's happy choice of word)—it was in reality a non-problem because fluvastatin is not so highly soluble that the skilled person would expect it to be impossible or difficult to make a sustained release form.

55. I will be more specific about this. Combining finding (c) and (h) first sentence leads to this: that the skilled person would consider a sustained release formulation and would expect (contrary to what the Patent says) that he could develop a formulation within claim 1 which had some clinical efficacy. Finding (j) is to the same effect ("confident that such a formulation could be taken by humans and would have some therapeutic effect albeit perhaps of lesser efficacy...."). Later the Judge put the same findings this way:

    > [321] ... the skilled team (including clinician) would be confident that some level of dose could be given in sustained release form which it would also be confident (i) would have some efficacy (perhaps not as good as the existing immediate release formulations) and (ii) would not produce unacceptable side-effects.

56. Mr. Meade had to accept that the basis of the invention as presented by the patentee would not in reality have been seen as a problem by the skilled person. So he pointed to the PSA, submitting that this clearly allowed for a reformulation of the problem. It would be good enough to support the Patent if there was another problem in the way. That problem, he suggested was this: that the skilled person would not have a sufficient expectation of success to make it worthwhile trying to make a sustained release formulation. This case should be considered on an "obvious to try" basis. And because of an insufficient expectation of success Actavis should fail.

58. The Judge went along with this approach, but only up to a point. For after his summary of the facts he went on to conclude that the invention was not obvious on the basis

of a notional project to develop a sustained release formulation which had a fair expectation of success. By "success" he meant a formulation which had improved therapeutic effects or fewer side effects as compared with immediate release formulations.

59. Having got this far the judge went on to consider the case on the basis of the 5¼ inch plate paradox. At this point he held that there was no motivation to produce a sustained release form and said this:

> [323] In my judgment, this absence of motivation does not prevent claim 1 from being technically obvious. The skilled team would, for reasons already given, not reject a sustained release formulation out of hand. Even though its focus will be on the end result of an 80 mg once daily formulation having improved efficacy and less serious side effects, coupled with better patient compliance, the concept of sustained release will be present. It does not need a commercial boss to ask the question "Can you make a formulation [within claim 1]" for the skilled formulator to appreciate its technical obviousness any more than it needs a commercial boss to ask a similar question of the plate designer for that designer to appreciate the technical obviousness of the odd-sized plate. I conclude that claim 1 is obvious over the common general knowledge.

I am not sure why the judge at this point said there was no motivation. After all finding (i) had indicated a technical motivation—patient compliance at the very least. Moreover, the Patent itself said there was a motive—see [a] above I think he must have meant commercial motivation—but the absence of that is not enough to defeat an obviousness attack.

60. Because of the way the Judge dealt with the matter, Mr. Meade appealed in respect of the "technically obvious" finding and Mr. Wyand challenged the decision that apart from that point the invention was not obvious. I have to say I do not think that the two-bite approach is actually a convenient way to deal with obviousness. It is, after all, a multi-factorial assessment. The thing to do is to identify all the relevant factors, orientate oneself à la *Pozzoli* and then decide whether the invention is obvious.

61. I start with Mr. Wyand's challenge. He submitted that the Judge had made an error in assessing what was meant by "success" in terms of the Patent. It was not improved clinical efficacy or the same efficacy with fewer side ef-

fects. It was simply a sustained release formulation which one would expect to work. Moreover if one wanted a motive, there was one—improved patient compliance. Whether it was worth actually developing such a formulation (there would be costs of testing and compliance with regulatory requirements) was irrelevant. As the Patent said at [15] there was a need for a slow release formulation which it was possible to prepare.

62. I accept that submission. Once the obstacle put forward in the Patent against being able to make a sustained formulation was shown to be illusory, then a sustained release formulation is obvious. You might get better efficacy or fewer side effects, but you would certainly get better compliance. In *Pozzoli* terms the only difference between the prior art and the claim is the idea of making a sustained release formulation. For that there was a technical motivation and no difficulty, real or apparent.

63. The PSA gives the same answer. What is the objective problem? Why that which the patentee himself stated—to produce a sustained release form of fluvastatin. Was the solution obvious? Yes, any of the standard methods for such formulations would clearly work: there is no reason why they would not.

64. There is no need and it would be wrong to re-formulate the problem as suggested by Mr. Meade. This is not a case where some prior art unknown to the patentee has turned up. Nor is it right to reformulate the problem as one of looking for better medical effects when that was not the problem as seen by the patentee or to reformulate the solution as having found such effects when the patentee has not promised any.

65. In the latter respect this case is quite unlike the case, relied upon by Mr. Meade, about a sustained release form of oxycodone recently considered by this court, *Napp v. Ratiopharm* [2009] EWCA Civ 252, [2009] RPC 539. Oxycodone was, until the patent, known as a minor weak opiod generally administered, to the extent that it was administered at all, as a co-drug. The slow-release form transformed it, as the patent said, into a serious alternative to morphine—something that was wholly unexpected. Of course the invention was non-obvious.

66. The upshot is that I would uphold the decision of the Judge. Unlike him, however, I do not think the case was finely balanced. Once the basis of the Patent was proved illusory there was nothing left to save it.

Notes and Questions

1. Lord Justice Jacob views the first step of identifying the closest prior art in the problem solution approach as difficult to apply and useless in British courts. German judges who are members of the Tenth Senate view the step as dangerous because it may subject the inventive step analysis to hindsight bias. In examining obviousness of selecting olanzapine from a general formula including 1,452 compounds, the German Federal Court refused to follow the problem-solution approach stating:

> "Because the examination of the inventive step must always be based on the closest art, the step to select the starting compound cannot be disregard[ed]. Such compound can be the 4'—(N-methyl-piperazinyl) compounds described by the Chakrabarti reference or even one specific compound from a general formula this reference. In fact, there was a no closest prior art. One can decide which prior art reference is the closest to the invention and how the inventor could have begun his invention to conceive the solution only if he uses hindsight. The selection of the starting point is justified by the fact that a skilled person always makes efforts to find a better solution than one in the prior art." Olanzapine, Judgment of BGH, Dec. 16, 2008, 2009 GRUR 382.

2. What are the differences between the approach taken in the United States to determine obviousness and the problem-solution approach used in *Jackel* to determine inventive step? What are the differences between the EPO approach and the British approach? Is the British approach to inventive step more helpful than the EPO approach in mitigating concerns over hindsight bias?

3. JPO's approach is similar to the problem-solution approach, but does not require a step of reformulating an objective problem:

> "After finding of a claimed invention and one or more cited inventions, one cited invention most suitable for the reasoning is selected. And comparison of the claimed invention with a cited invention is made, and the identicalness and the difference in matters defining the inventions are clarified. Then, the reasoning for lacking an inventive step of the claimed invention is attempted on the basis of the contents of the selected invention, other cited inventions (including well-known or commonly used art) and the common general knowledge. The reasoning can be made from various and extensive aspects. For example, the examiner evaluates whether a claimed invention falls under a selection of an optimal material, a workshop modification of design, a mere juxtaposition of features on the basis of cited inventions, or whether the contents of cited inventions disclose a cause or a motivation for a person skilled in the art to arrive at the claimed invention. If advantageous effects of the claimed invention over a cited invention can be clearly found in the description in the specification,

etc., it is taken into consideration as facts to support to affirmatively infer the involvement of an inventive step." Japan Patent Office, Examination Guidelines Part II, Chapter II 2.2.4

SECONDARY CONSIDERATIONS

The EPO gives much less weight to non-technical factors than U.S. courts. Such factors include technical prejudice, unexpected effects, long-felt needs, and commercial success. EPO Examination Guidelines Part C, Chapter IV, 11.10. The evidence of secondary considerations is merely auxiliary to the technical assessment of the invention as evaluated from the perspective of a skilled person in the art of the invention. Such evidence has a significant value only in cases where the presence of inventive step is unclear from the technical assessment. The following excerpt indicates how difficult it is for an applicant to rely on evidence of secondary considerations to establish inventive step in the EPO. In the following case, an EPO Technical Board of Appeal refused to take evidence of secondary considerations into account when determining whether the use of pyrazolopyrimidinones for the treatment of impotence (Viagra) was patentable. The board concluded that because Viagra itself had already been patented as an anti-hypertensive drug, Pfizer had protection under the all uses doctrine for Viagra itself.

T 1212/01

Opinion of the Technical Board of Appeal, February 3, 2005

Technical prejudice

5.1   The following represents a good working definition of a technical prejudice and how such a prejudice is to be established:

"According to the case law of the boards of appeal (see T 119/82 (OJ 1984, 217) and T 48/86), inventiveness can sometimes be established by demonstrating that a known prejudice, i.e. a widely held but incorrect opinion of a technical fact, has been overcome. In such cases, the burden is on the patentee (or patent applicant) to demonstrate, for example by reference to suitable technical literature, that the alleged prejudice really existed (T 60/82, T 631/89, T 695/90). A prejudice in any particular field relates to an opinion or preconceived idea widely or universally held by experts in that field. The existence of such prejudice is normally demonstrated by reference to the literature or to encyclopedias published before the priority date. The prejudice must have existed at the priority date, any prejudice which might have developed later is of no concern in the judgment of inventive step (T 341/94, T 531/95 and T 452/96).

Generally speaking, prejudice **cannot** be demonstrated by a statement in a single patent specification, since the technical information in a patent specification or scientific article might be based on special premises or on the personal view of the author. However, this principle does not apply to explanations in a standard work or textbook representing common expert knowledge in the field concerned (T 19/81 (OJ 1982, 51), T 104/83, T 321/87,T 392/88, T 601/88, T 519/89, T 453/92, T 900/95)."("Case Law etc", op cit, page 134; emphasis as in the original.)

* * *

Commercial success and scientific awards

6.1 Commercial success and similar arguments can only ever be secondary *indicia* of inventiveness, which are usually only of importance in cases where an objective evaluation of the prior art has not provided a clear answer. In such cases, secondary *indicia* may show that an inventive step is involved (see generally, "Case Law etc", *op cit*, pages 133 to 134, paragraph 7.1 and pages 136 to 137, paragraph 7.5). Since in the present case the claimed subject-matter merely follows plainly and logically from the prior art, secondary *indicia* cannot assist in the assessment of inventive step.

However, since the parties' arguments in this area were developed at some length, particularly during the oral proceedings, the Board considers it appropriate to make certain observations.

6.2 The principal difficulties faced by the appellants' arguments in this area lie with the nature of their evidence (summarised in paragraph VI (9) and (10) above). To establish commercial success as an *indicia* of inventive step requires two evidentiary steps—first, to show that there has been commercial success and, second, to show that such success results from the claimed invention and not from one or more other causes.

6.3 That Viagra, the brand name of sildenafil citrate, has been the subject of various awards and praise in various journals has been shown by the press releases and press cuttings filed as document (D101). While the press releases are those of the appellants themselves, and the press articles may well have been prompted by such releases, there is no objection *per se* to such use of a party's own material provided, as the Board accepts is the case here, the content is correct—after allowing for the almost usual self-congratulation found in such announcements, there can be no doubt that the prizes referred to were awarded and the laudatory articles were published.

6.4 Indeed, the respondents did not challenge the existence of such "prizes and praises". They did however question exactly what such "prizes and praises" related to and the Board shares that scepticism. The prizes would be significant if awarded by persons who understand patent law for the unobvious nature of the technical contribution to the art made by the claimed invention. If however the prizes were awarded for the product's life-enhancing nature, or for the appellants' high standard of research, or for a high level of sales, then, for all that any of those reasons might well be prize-worthy, the prizes can have no significance in the context of inventive step. The evidence does not establish that the "prizes and praises" resulted from the claimed inventive step. To take one example, the appellants' own documents—their press release and "Pfizer World Café" newsletter both of 27 November 2000 (both in document (D101)—respectively describe the Prix Galien, awarded in 2000 to Viagra, as: "the highest accolade for research and development in the biomedical industry" and as recognition of "the dedicated teamwork that underpins pharmaceutical innovation . . . also a tribute to how the drug has revolutionized the treatment of erectile dysfunction, not only by offering the first oral therapy, but by bringing this sensitive topic into the open, making it easier for patients to seek medical advice."

Thus the appellants themselves ascribe that prize to no fewer than four reasons—research and development effort, corporate teamwork, the first oral therapy for erectile dysfunction, and making advice on that condition easier to obtain. Only the third of those reasons comes anywhere near the nature of the invention—if the appellants claim three other reasons for such a prize, how can the Board accept it was in fact awarded for the technical nature of the alleged invention?

6.5 Similarly, the laudatory comments on Viagra in scientific review articles offer an ambiguity, or even multiplicity, of reasons for their praise. Thus, while document (D113) says (page 1689, third paragraph) "The licensing of the first extremely effective oral therapy sildenafil citrate (Viagra®) must be regarded as a major breakthrough in the treatment of erectile dysfunction." the whole paragraph reads:

> "As knowledge of the pharmacology and physiology of the erectile process has advance, new pharmacological approaches to treatment have emerged. The licensing of the first extremely effective oral therapy sildenafil citrate (Viagra®) must be regarded as a major breakthrough in the treatment of erectile dysfunction.

It will open the door for future research and development of huge potential."

So, according to this review article, while sildenafil was a "major breakthrough", it was one of a number of emerging approaches to treatment, and at least one reason for being a breakthrough was the further research it would induce. While the article does explain the drug's mechanism, its "breakthrough" status is not ascribed solely or even primarily to the claimed invention. The same can be said of the other such documents relied on. Thus the statement in document (D114) (page 759, second paragraph, last sentence) "To most sufferers a tablet treatment must have seemed too good to be true." is preceded by the following:

> "The popular interest in Viagra (sildenafil) is not solely the result of media hype and the drug's association with sex: the demand for treatment has been enormous. Since its launch in the United States in March it has become the fastest selling drug ever. The demand is being met by prescription in the United States and globally through the internet and on the street, which in Europe precedes its licensing for prescription by doctors. The level of demand was predictable, given a prevalence of erectile dysfunction of over 50% in men aged 50–70, and the unacceptability, poor effectiveness, or unavailability of existing treatments, such as implants, intracavernosal injection, intraurethral pellets, vacuum devices, and sex therapy. To most sufferers a tablet treatment must have seemed too good to be true."

Thus, while they clearly acknowledge the commercial success of Viagra, the introductory paragraphs of this document also tells the reader that success is at least partly due to media hype, to an association with sex, and to the drawbacks of prior art products. The epithet "revolutionary" applied to the approval of Viagra in document (D115) (page 233, second column) is immediately preceded by the use of "breakthrough" for a previous development:

> "The introduction of intracavernous injection therapy in 1982 was a **major breakthrough** in the pharmacologic treatment of erectile dysfunction. In 1998, the approval of oral phosphodiesterase type 5 inhibitor by the US Food and Drug Administration marked another **revolutionary** event in combating erectile dysfunction." (emphasis added) The comment relied on in document (D116) (page 60, last sentence):

>> "The recent advent of safe and effective oral therapy has greatly increased the number of patients seeking treatment and has significantly altered the medical management of the disorder" (the "therapy" being identified by footnotes as the appellants' product) in fact ascribes Viagra's success to subsequent medicosocial events rather than to the claimed invention. All the documents just referred to supply some description of the mechanism employed in the appellants' product as sold and all make clear that, as

the first such product capable of oral administration, it has significant advantages. However, as demonstrated above, these documents also offer a variety of reasons for Viagra's success and none of them ascribes that success, either exclusively or even primarily, to the nature of the claimed invention.

6.6   Similarly, the appellants relied on the notoriety acquired by Viagra and the respondents did not deny this. The Board can add that evidence of such notoriety is almost unnecessary—Viagra as a product is so wellknown to the public (indeed, for a pharmaceutical product quite remarkably well-known beyond its users) that the Board would if asked have taken judicial notice of such notoriety. But again there is no evidence that such notoriety resulted from the exact nature of the claimed invention—it might equally possibly have resulted from massive advertising and/or public relations campaigns. The press articles relied on by the appellants do not, unlike, the specialist reviews considered above, all contain a description of the drug mechanism but those that do also fail to ascribe Viagra's success even primarily to that. Indeed, almost as one might expect, the less specialist press offers further reasons, less closely related to the product's content, for its success—for example, a large pent-up demand created by widespread publicity (SCRIP, 1 May 1998, page 20), the appellants' preparation of large-scale manufacture while the product was still being tested (Business Week, 11 May 1998, page 97), and Viagra's role as a "life-enhancing" drug (*ibid*, cover and Pharma Business, March/April 2000, page 60 *et seq*).

6.7   Similar observations can be made in relation to the remaining category of such "success" evidence—volume of sales (see paragraph VI (10) above). While, as mentioned below, there is no real comparative data, there is little doubt that the early sales of Viagra were very substantial. However, there is no evidence to demonstrate whether the level of sales was due to the technical advance claimed for the product or to advertising or other publicity, or any of the other reasons already mentioned, or indeed yet others. Moreover, in the case of the appellants' sales evidence, there are two further problems. First, the information supplied was simply provided in written arguments filed by the appellants' representatives. It is of course the role of representatives to present the evidence of others and not to give evidence themselves. Second, when presenting evidence of commercial success in the form of sales figures (whether by market share or money value or units sold or, in the case of pharmaceuticals, prescriptions written or dispensed) the figure for one year is of little if any value, however high that figure may be. Only some comparison can make such evidence meaningful and the comparison must be such as to show at least a *prima facie* case of success—such as a comparison between sales of prior art products and patented products, or between the patentee's sales before and after manufacture in accordance with the invention. A prudent patentee will also provide parallel information relating to advertising and similar expenditure to anticipate the argument that such activities could explain the growth in sales. All such information is typically available from each year's auditing process and, if filed with an appropriate certificate from the patentee's auditors, is likely to be conclusive in itself (there will of course still remain the need to prove a nexus between success and the invention).

6.8 To summarise, the appellants' case on commercial success consists of a considerable volume of their press releases, specialist and general press articles, and sales data all of which suggests (rightly) that Viagra has been successful. However, rather than actually link that success to the claimed invention, the appellants simply argue that such a link must exist. Yet, as the previous paragraphs show, even a cursory examination of the evidence does not bear this out. The requirement for a demonstrated nexus between the facts relied on and the claimed inventive step is missing. That Viagra has been successful is beyond question: whether that success has anything to do with the patent in suit is a question which remains unanswered. There is therefore no relevant conclusion which can be drawn as to the alleged secondary *indicia*, let alone any conclusion which could play a role in the assessment of inventive step.

Notes and Questions

1. The EPC member states also give some weight to evidence of secondary considerations when evaluating inventive step, however this may vary from one state to another. The following statement by Justice Jacob in the excerpt from *Nichia Corporation v. Argos Limited* [2007] EWCA Civ. 741 explains why such evidence is relevant in UK courts:

> For many years the evidence of the inventor and the efforts (or absence of them) of the objector has been held admissible. Sometimes it is the patentee who prays this in aid, sometimes the objector. Why is this so? I think the answer lies in the ultimate (Windsurfing/Pozzoli step 4) question: is there an inventive step? The question involves a value judgment which takes into account a variety of factors. Some are purely technical, others not. That is why, for instance, an apparently simple technical step may be held inventive where it can be shown to have led to commercial success—and all the more so if there was a long-felt want. Again the age of the prior art may matter. "If it was so obvious, why was it not done before?" is a powerful question for the patentee to ask

when the cited art is old, and more so when it is old and well-known . . .

Now one of the factors which is relevant in the overall assessment is what people in the art were doing at the time—the history. To form a proper view of this, in theory the thing to do would be to make a world survey—for it is not only what the patentee, and his opponent, but also what all others in the field were doing and thinking which would inform the court as to what the notional skilled man would readily perceive having regard to his own knowledge and any particular piece of cited prior art.

Laddie J put it well in Pfizer:

"This does not mean that evidence from those in the art at the relevant time is irrelevant. It is not. As I have said, it may help the court to assess the possible lines of analysis and deductions that the notional addressee might follow. Furthermore, sometimes it may be very persuasive. If it can be shown that a number of ordinary workers in the relevant field at the relevant time who were looking for the same goal and had the same prior art, missed what has been patented then that may be telling evidence of non-obviousness. This is particularly the case where the commercial benefits of the development would have been apparent and a long time had passed between the publication of the prior art and the priority date of the patent. Hence, the impact and interrelationship between the familiar concepts of long felt want and commercial success. Likewise evidence that ordinary men in the art and working from the same prior art at the relevant time independently came to the same development may be some evidence that the notional skilled man would have done likewise.

A world survey is of course impossible. But one can at least see what the patentee and the defendant were doing at the time, in cases where both were conducting research at the relevant time. It is difficult to suppose that this is wholly irrelevant even though it is only a part of the picture. Thus, for instance, disclosure by a defendant who was a major player in the art at the time showing that it recognised, and struggled unsuccessfully with, the problem solved by the patent can sometimes play a significant role in the assessment of obviousness. The Mölnlycke case, [1994] RPC 49, is an example: disclosure showed one of the leading companies in the field of disposable nappies, P & G, struggled for years over the problem and its concern when it learned of the patentee's success in solving it. The trial Judge, Morritt J, had particular regard to these matters, see p.88 ("The concern of P & G to find a workable multiple taping system is apparent from the documents disclosed on discovery"). Likewise he took into account P & G's reaction when it learned of the patented product, p.89 ("Thus allowing for a measure of exaggeration I think the bi-weeklies [P & G disclosed documents] constitute a valuable pointer to whether the arrangement disclosed in the patent in suit was obvious"))."

2. The JPO and Japanese courts also give some weight to evidence of secondary considerations. To show the existence of an inventive step that relies on the technical effects of the claimed invention, the effect must be so remarkable in comparison to the closest prior art that a person skilled in the art of the invention could not have foreseen the result. JPO Examination Guidelines Part 11: Chapter 2, 2.5. Such an effect must be included in the specification as originally filed. Although evidence of commercial success has very limited value, the JPO and Japanese courts may take such evidence into account to overcome the conclusion of a technical assessment:

> "The idea of using the gas residue from an oil refinery, such as is claimed in the petitioner's invention, is completely different from the cited invention, and it is not something that a person skilled in the art could easily accomplish. It is clear that this invention is very economically beneficial in that it allows for the exhaust petroleum residue from refineries to be efficiently turned into low-cost raw materials. The claimed invention can be highly valued for its effectiveness, and we do not find that a person regularly skilled in the art could have easily made this invention based on the cited invention." Judgment of Tokyo High Court, Dec. 9, 1992.

Chapter 6

DISCLOSURE REQUIREMENTS

A. ENABLEMENT

TRIPS Article 29 establishes disclosure requirements that require enablement disclosure, but make disclosure of the best mode optional. Consequently, the majority of TRIPS member states only require disclosure of the enablement requirement in a specification. For example:

EPC Article 83: Disclosure of the Invention

> The European patent application shall disclose the invention in a manner sufficiently clear and complete for it to be carried out by a person skilled in the art.

JPL Article 36

> (4) The statement of the detailed explanation of the invention as provided in item (iii) of the preceding Paragraph shall comply with each of the following items:
>
> > (i) in accordance with the relevant Ordinance of the Ministry of Economy, Trade and Industry, the statement shall be clear and sufficient as to enable any person ordinarily skilled in the art to which the invention pertains to work the invention

A written description is not provided elsewhere in TRIPS. However, both the EPC and the JPL set forth a requirement comparable to the written description requirement under 35 USC § 112¶ 1 as a requirement for claim drafting:

EPC Article 84: Claims

> The Claims shall be defined the matter for which protection is sought. They shall be clear and concise and be supported by the description.

JPL Article 36

> (6) The statement of the scope of claims as provided in paragraph (2) shall comply with each of the following items:
>
> > (i) the invention for which a patent is sought must be described in the detailed explanation of the invention

However, as Federal Circuit struggled to distinguish the enablement requirement and written description requirement under 35 USC § 112¶ 1, the EPO Boards of Appeals and the EPC member states face a challenge in setting different roles for the two requirements. Unlike the United States, Article 84 is only grounds for rejection during prosecution at EPO. Because of this it is neither grounds for opposition at the EPO nor grounds for invalidation. The EPO and its member states use Article 83 to reject claims that are not enabled by the disclosure of any operable claim, as well as claims that have undue breadth the scope that are not fully supported by disclosure of the specification.

IN RE BAYER SCHERING PHARMA A.G.

Opinion of the Technical Board of Appeal, February 3, 2009
T 1063/06, 2009 OJ EPO 516

Summary of facts and submissions

* * *

IV. In oral proceedings before the board on 3 February 2009 the appellant filed two auxiliary requests, each comprising two claims. In claim 1 of auxiliary request 1, a passage was added at the end of claim 1 as per the main request, setting out a further functional feature of the compounds to be used. It thus read as follows:

> "1. Use of compounds, which are also capable of stimulating the soluble guanylate cyclase independently of the heme group in the enzyme, for the manufacture of medicaments for the treatment of cardiovascular disorders such as angina pectoris, ischemia and cardiac insufficiency, the compounds selected stimulating both the heme-containing and the heme-free soluble guanylate cyclase in *in vitro* tests."

Claim 1 of auxiliary request 3 differed from claim 1 as per the main request by expanding on the word "also" to indicate that the compounds stimulated the soluble guanylate cyclase "both dependently on and independently of" the heme group in the enzyme. It thus read as follows:

> "1. Use of compounds, which are capable of stimulating the soluble guanylate cyclase both dependently on and indepen-

dently of the heme group in the enzyme, for the manufacture of medicaments for the treatment of cardiovascular disorders such as angina pectoris, ischemia and cardiac insufficiency."

* * *

Reasons for the decision

1. The appeal is admissible.

Main request
Formulation of the claim

2. Claim 1 concerns the use of compounds for the manufacture of medicaments to treat an illness (in this case cardiovascular diseases). However, the compounds used therein are defined in terms not of their chemical structure, their composition or other verifiable parameters, as chemical products usually are (T 248/85, OJ EPO 1986, 261, Reasons 3), but solely of their specific capability to stimulate the soluble guanylate cyclase independently of the heme group in the enzyme, which the skilled person can establish only by means of the screening method set out in the description as a new kind of research tool.

This type of functional definition of the chemical compounds to be used is directed not only to the compounds actually found according to general formula I of the application in suit, but also to any compound not yet structurally defined on the priority or filing date of the application in suit and found only by means of the screening method set out in the description as a new kind of research tool. Such a formulation of a claim thus constitutes a "reach-through" claim, i.e. a claim which is also directed to future inventions based on the one now being disclosed.

3. Citing T 68/85 (*loc. cit.*), the appellant argued that a formulation of a claim in which the compounds to be used are defined in purely functional terms was allowable.

3.1 However, applicants cannot simply define a technical feature in a claim as they wish; they must define their invention for which protection is sought in the objectively most precise form possible (see T 68/85, *loc. cit.*, Reasons 8.4.2). The characterisation of chemical compounds in a claim in non-structural, purely functional terms (in this case in terms of a specific capability) is therefore allowable only in those exceptional cases in which the invention cannot be defined more precisely in any other way without simultaneously unduly limiting its technical contribution to the art (T 68/85 *loc. cit.*, Reasons 8.4.1 and 8.4.2).

3.2 Since however patent protection is limited to applicant's actual contribution to the art, i.e. their actual invention, it is both reasonable and indeed imperative to limit the claims' subject-matter to the invention actually disclosed in the application, which at least does not include the use of chemical compounds not yet structurally defined on its priority date and to be found only in the future using the new kind of research tool set out in the description. This follows from the principle that inventions for which patents are granted under the European Patent Convention must make a contribution to the state of the art, i.e. provide a technical solution to a problem arising from the state of the art. Patent protection under the EPC is not designed for the purpose of reserving an unexplored field of research for a particular applicant, but to protect factual results of successful research as a reward for making concrete technical results available to the public.

3.3 The appellant objected that, at the time it made the invention, only such compounds were known which stimulated the soluble guanylate cyclase either by releasing NO or by interacting directly with the enzyme's heme group. The invention, for the first time, had found compounds capable of activating the soluble guanylate cyclase independently of the heme group in the enzyme by means of a new mechanism of action. The screening method set out in the description as a new kind of research tool could detect compounds which showed this heme-independent mechanism of action. Medically, this was a very important contribution to the art, so a very broad claim formulation extending to chemical compounds not yet found and disclosed was justified to reward that contribution adequately and prevent circumvention by third parties. But the claims as filed are directed neither to the screening method for detecting the chemical compounds nor to any other research tool *per se* for detecting that they possess the desired capability, but merely to the use of chemical substances. The appellant's objection therefore fails to address the actual subject-matter of the claims on file. And the "circumvention by third parties" referred to relates rather to future inventions which are by definition not yet disclosed in the application in suit and therefore not part of its actual contribution to the state of the art. The inventor is entitled only to the protection of its actual contribution. Therefore, the appellant's argument must fail.

Nor can the appellant successfully rely on the EPO's Guidelines for Examination to support its right to a functional definition of chemical compounds before the board. It may be left open whether or not the appellant's contentions with respect to the contents of the Guidelines are correct, because the Guidelines are issued by the President of the European Patent Office and have no normative binding effect on the boards of appeal (T 162/82, OJ EPO 1987, 533, Reasons 9). Under Article 23(3) EPC, in exercising their judicial powers, the members of the boards are not bound by any instructions, including the Guidelines, but only by the European Patent Convention.

4. The board therefore concludes that in the present case it is indeed reasonable to require the appellant-applicant to replace the chemical compounds' functional definition with the invention actually disclosed in its application, i.e. to limit itself to its actual contribution to the state of the art.

Sufficiency of disclosure (Article 83 EPC)

5. It is the established jurisprudence of the boards of appeal that the requirement of sufficiency of disclosure is only met if the invention as defined in the independent claims can be performed by a skilled person within the entire scope claimed without undue burden, using common general knowledge and having regard to further information given in the application (see T 409/91, OJ EPO 1994, 653, Reasons 3.5; T 435/91, OJ EPO 1995, 188, Reasons 2.2.1).

That principle applies to any invention irrespective of the way the claims are defined, be it by way of a structural or a functional feature. The peculiarity of the functional definition of a technical feature resides in the fact that it is defined by means of its effect. That mode of definition comprises an indefinite and innumerable host of possible alternatives of diverse structure, which is acceptable as long as all these alternatives achieve the desired result and are available to the skilled person. This reflects the general principle in law whereby the protection sought must match the technical contribution made by the disclosed invention to the state of the art. Therefore, it has to be established whether or not the application in suit discloses a technical concept fit for generalisation which makes available to the skilled person the host of variants encompassed by the functional definition of a technical feature as claimed.

5.1 In the present case, the invention seeks to "develop medicaments to treat cardiovascular disorders or other disorders treatable in organisms by influencing the cGMP signal path" (application in suit, page 4, lines 1 to 3).

The means provided to achieve this as indicated in claim 1 is to use compounds which are also capable of stimulating the soluble guanylate cyclase independently of the heme group in the enzyme. A technical feature of the subject-matter of the invention is therefore defined in the claim in purely functional terms because the chemical compounds to be used are characterised solely by indicating their capability, i.e. to stimulate the soluble guanylate cyclase independently of the heme group in the enzyme. This functional formulation in claim 1 therefore encompasses all chemical compounds possessing the aforementioned capability; it thus covers a priori every conceivable chemical compound of whatever structure, including every conceivable organochemical family in organic chemistry, where applicable with the most diverse functional or reactive groups, organometallic compounds, their salts, etc. Since the claim contains no structural limitation, not even with regard to the claimed compounds, it encompasses an indefinite and innumerable host of alternatives, which is acceptable as long as all these alternatives possess the desired capability to stimulate the soluble guanylate cyclase independently of the heme group in the enzyme.

5.2   However, at the time of filing of the application in suit, the only compounds known as guanylate cyclase stimulants were those which stimulate the enzyme either by direct interaction with the heme group or by heme-dependent interaction (see also the application in suit, page 3, lines 27 to 30). Thus not all conceivable compounds possess the capability of stimulating the soluble guanylate cyclase independently of the heme group in the enzyme as required by the claim, and it is up to the skilled person to pick from this indefinite and innumerable host of alternatives the suitable ones.

In order to pick from that host the skilled person cannot draw on his common knowledge to identify from the host of possible alternatives those suitable chemical compounds which, along with the compounds of general formula (I) exemplified in the application in suit, are also covered by the functional definition in the claim, because the application in suit (page 1, lines 5 and 6) discloses that the invention is based on a "new mechanism of action". In selecting the chemical compounds possessing the necessary capability, all he has to rely on is the information provided in the application in suit. In the absence of any selection rule in the application in suit, not even in the form of a structure-activity relationship on the basis of which he could identify from the outset suitable compound classes, the skilled person must resort to trial-and-error experimentation on arbitrarily selected chemical compounds using the screening method cited in the application in suit to identify within the host of possible alternative compounds those which stimulate the soluble guanylate cyclase independently of the heme group in the enzyme. Nor does he have any information at his disposal in the application in suit leading necessarily and directly towards success through the evaluation of initial failures. Nor would the simple structural identification of one suitable compound class of general formula (I) in the application in suit be of any help to the skilled person. To find all the suitable alternatives, he would therefore have to test every conceivable chemical compound for the claimed capability; this represents for the skilled person an invitation to perform a research programme and thus an undue burden (see T 435/91, *loc. cit.*

Reasons 2.2.1, last paragraph, and T 1151/04, not published in OJ EPO, Reasons 3.1.2).

5.3 Moreover, the fact that claim 1 is formulated as a "reach-through claim" would cast doubt on the sufficiency of the invention's disclosure throughout the entire area claimed, since this open-ended formulation, as stated above in point 2, is also directed to future inventions based on the present one, i.e. inventions not yet made by the priority date of the application in suit.

5.4 The appellant submitted that the skilled person merely had to apply the screening method which was disclosed in the application in suit and which provided sufficient information as to its implementation to the various chemical compounds in order to identify them. Since the screening method was very easy and quick to implement, the effort involved was reasonable, so the invention could be carried out in its entirety.

However, the fact that the application in suit contains enough information to implement the screening method described is only a necessary requirement for its performability, but the indication of the method alone is not sufficient to carry out the subject-matter of the claim within the entire area claimed because it only shows the skilled person the presence or absence of the claimed capability, but in the absence of any selection rule provides no guidance as to how to purposively select suitable chemical compounds.

5.5 The appellant submitted with reference to T 216/96 (*loc. cit.*) that a purely functional definition of the chemical compounds to be used was allowable. Claim 13 in the cited decision referred to a kit, for the detection of specific nucleic acid sequences, containing each of two primers defined in terms not of their chemical structure, but merely of the nucleic acid sequence (also not structurally defined) to be detected, and regarded as sufficiently disclosed because the manufacture of a primer was described in an example. As some examples of compounds were also given in the application in suit, here too a purely functional definition of chemical compounds was allowable and not exceptionable for insufficient disclosure.

However, the primers claimed in the cited decision do not constitute an innumerable host of alternatives from which the skilled person has to pick the suitable ones but rather a finite number, which have already been narrowed down to a single chemical family by reference to their function of primer, and are also defined by the nucleic acid sequence, which is to be determined, as being its complementary sequence in accordance with the lock-and-key principle. That is why the basis for the decision in T 216/96 (*loc. cit.*) is different, and consequently the conclusions reached in that case do not apply here either. The board therefore does not concur with this argument on the part of the appellant.

6. For these reasons, the board concludes that, since the chemical compounds to be used are characterised in functional terms only, the skilled person cannot carry out the claimed invention within the entire scope claimed without undue burden, so the requirements of Article 83 EPC are not met.

Auxiliary requests 1 and 3
Amendments (Article 123(2) EPC)

7. Claim 1 of auxiliary request 1 differs from claim 1 of the main request only by the additional wording "the compounds selected stimulate both the heme-containing and the heme-free soluble guanylate cyclase in *in vitro* tests" at the end of the claim (see point IV, supra). A basis for this amendment is to be found on page 4, lines 15 to 17, of the application as filed. Reference is made to *"in vitro* tests" on pages 64 to 65 of the application as filed.

Claim 1 of auxiliary request 3 differs from claim 1 of the main request in stipulating, vis-à-vis the original version, that the compounds to be used are capable of stimulating, both dependently on and independently of the heme group (see point IV, *supra*). The basis for this resides in the application as filed on page 4, lines 15 to 17. The amendments to claim 1 of the auxiliary requests are therefore allowable within the meaning of Article 123(2) EPC.

Sufficiency of disclosure (Article 83 EPC)

8. In claim 1 of both auxiliary requests, the chemical compounds to be used are still characterised exclusively in functional terms and not by structural definitions. The functional definition of the compounds to be used, which was already objected to in respect of the main request, i.e. that they should be capable of stimulating the soluble guanylate cyclase independently of the heme group in the enzyme, is still present in claim 1 of both auxiliary requests. The indication of an additional capability in auxiliary request 3, i.e. that the compounds stimulate the soluble guanylate cyclase "both dependently on and independently of" the heme group in the enzyme, does not contribute to meeting the objection in respect of the functional definition comprised in the main request. Introducing in auxiliary request 1 a further functional definition of the compounds to be used, i.e. the further capability to stimulate in *in vitro* tests both the heme-containing and the heme-free soluble guanylate cyclase, also does not contribute to meeting the objection raised against the main request with respect to sufficiency of disclosure. Introducing further required capabilities in the form of an additional functional feature renders it even more difficult for the skilled person to find suitable chemical compounds, i.e. compounds possessing all these capabilities.

9. Consequently, the considerations and conclusions in respect of the main request also apply to the two auxiliary requests, i.e. that,

because the chemical compounds to be used are characterised in terms of the same functional feature as in the main request, the skilled person cannot carry out the claimed invention within the entire scope claimed without undue burden, so the requirements of Article 83 EPC are not fulfilled.

Order
For these reasons it is decided that:
The appeal is dismissed.

GENERICS LIMITED v. H. LUNDBECH A/S
House of Lords
[2009] UKHL 12

Lord Walker of Gestingthorpe

Introduction

9. The scientific background to this appeal and the essential features of the patent in suit are set out fully in the first-instance judgment of Kitchin J [2007] RPC 729, paras 8–25 and 26–35 respectively. The same material is covered more briefly at the beginning of the judgment of my noble and learned friend Lord Hoffmann when sitting in the Court of Appeal [2008] RPC 19, paras 1–5. I gratefully adopt Lord Hoffmann's summary:

"1. Citalopram is one of a class of anti-depressant drugs known as selective serotonin reuptake inhibitors ('SSRIs') which inhibit reuptake of the neurotransmitter serotonin by nerve cells and thereby promote neural transmission. This is claimed to alleviate the symptoms of depression, although the mechanism is far from clear and the claim remains controversial: see Kirsch et al, Initial Severity and Antidepressant Benefits (2008) 5 P LoS Medicine 260–268. Nevertheless, the SSRIs have had huge commercial success. Citalopram is sold in the United Kingdom under the brand name Cipramil and other SSRIs are fluoxetine (sold as Prozac) and paroxetine (Seroxat). The patent for Citalopram was held by the Danish company H Lundbeck A/S ('Lundbeck') but expired several years ago. Since then it has been sold in its generic form by a number of manufacturers.

2. Citalopram is a racemate, consisting of equal numbers of two molecules called enantiomers, which are made up of the same atoms and have much the same physical properties, but differ in the three-dimensional shape in which the atoms are bonded together. Such molecules are called chiral (from X [epsilon] [iota] [rho], a hand) because, like a pair of hands, they are mirror images which cannot be completely supraimposed

on each other. They are conventionally designated (+) and (-). It has been well known for many years that, despite their similarities, the two enantiomers may bind to different proteins and produce different biological effects. The most notorious example was thalidomide, which consisted of a (+) enantiomer which was effective to prevent morning sickness in pregnant women and, unknown to the consumers, a (-) enantiomer which was teratogenic and caused severe birth defects.

3. The resolution of a racemate by separation into its enantiomers is not a straightforward matter. Because they have the same boiling point, they cannot be separated by conventional fractional distillation. For similar reasons, fractional crystallisation may not work. There are indirect methods of coming at the problem and Lundbeck began to try to find one of them from about 1980. It seems to have involved a good deal of trial and error and they were not successful until 1987.

4. When they had resolved the racemate, Lundbeck found that the reuptake inhibitory effect was caused entirely by the (+) enantiomer, which is called escitalopram. In 1989 they applied for the patent in suit, EP (UK) 0, 347, 066, with a priority date of 14 June 1988. The drug has been marketed with success under the brand name Cipralex. More recent research has shown that the (-) enantiomer actually slows down the inhibitory effect, so that the (+) enantiomer works better without it.

5. The patent is entitled 'New enantiomers and their isolation.' Three claims are in issue:

 (a) Claim 1, to the enantiomer itself: "(+)-1-(3-dimenthylaminopropyl)-1-(4'-fluorophenyl)-1,3-dihydroisobenzofuran-5-carbonitrile . . . and non-toxic addition salts thereof."

 (b) Claim 3, to a 'pharmaceutical composition in unit dosage form comprising, [as] an active ingredient, a compound as defined in claim1.'

 (c) Claim 6, to 'a method', (which I shall describe later) 'for the preparation of a compound as defined in claim 1.' "

10. It will be apparent that claims 1 and 3 in the patent are to products (a chemical compound and a pharmaceutical preparation with that compound as its active ingredient); claim 6 is to a process. The distinction between product claims and process claims, especially in relation to the appropriate test for sufficiency, is at the heart of this appeal. The sufficiency of the claims is now the only issue in the appeal. Initially the appellants (all companies which make or market generic forms of citalopram) attacked claims 1 and 3 as lacking novelty (because of the disclosure of the racemate in

the patent which the respondent, Lundbeck, holds for citalopram); they attacked claims 1, 3 and 6 as invalidated by obviousness; and they attacked claims 1 and 3 as invalidated by insufficiency, in that they claimed the (+) enantiomer in general terms (that is, however it was produced) but disclosed only two methods of producing it.

12. The distinction between product claims and process claims is assumed, rather than spelled out, in the Patents Act 1977 (which notoriously does not define "invention", but in section 1 lays down various inclusionary or exclusionary conditions for patentable inventions). The distinction is implicit in section 60 (1) (meaning of infringement), which defines infringement primarily by reference to these terms:

> "(a) where the invention is a product, he makes [etc] the product . . .
>
> (b) where the invention is a process, he uses the process [etc] . . .
>
> (c) where the invention is a process, he disposes of [etc] any product obtained directly by means of that process . . ."

13. The distinction is however not always straightforward. Although there is a requirement that an application for a patent should be limited so as to "relate to one invention only or to a group of inventions so linked as to form a general inventive concept" (EPC Art 82; compare Patents Act 1977 section 14(5)(d) which has "single inventive concept"), it is commonplace (as in the patent in suit) for the claims to be a mixture of product claims and process claims.

14. The appellants' case, reduced to its simplest form, is that the Court of Appeal's decision is an unwarranted departure from *Biogen*, and infringes the general legal principle (stated by the Technical Board of Appeal in para 3.3 of its decision in *Fuel Oils/EXXON* (T 409/91) [1994] OJEPO 653,—*"Exxon"*—by way of explanation of "support" in Art 84 of the EPC),

> "that the extent of the patent monopoly, as defined by the claims, should correspond to the *technical contribution* to the art in order for it to be supported, or justified."

Lord Hoffmann cited this passage in *Biogen*, at p.49, and again in his judgment in the Court of Appeal in this case, para 35. The respondent's case, again in its simplest form, is that the relevant claims are claims to a product, not a process, and that (as Lord Hoffmann put it in para 36 of his judgment in the Court of Appeal):

> "When a product claim satisfies the requirements of section 1 of the 1977 Act, the technical contribution to the art is the

product and not the process by which it was made, even if that process was the only inventive step."

Sufficiency

15.   I shall have more to say about product claims, but I must now address sufficiency. The three commonest grounds for attacking the validity of a patent are (a) lack of novelty (that is, the invention does not go beyond the state of the art); (b) obviousness (that is, that there is an advance in the state of the art, but it is an obvious advance lacking any inventive step); and (c) insufficiency. Insufficiency is less easily summarised because it is generally used (though the terminology is not always uniform) to link two concepts, drawn from EPC Articles 83 and 84:

> "83.   Disclosure of the Invention
>
> The European patent application must disclose the invention in a manner sufficiently clear and complete for it to be carried out by a person skilled in the art.
>
> 84.   The Claims
>
> The claims shall define the matter for which protection is sought. They shall be clear and concise and be supported by the description."

16.   The word "sufficiently" in Article 83 echoes the primary requirement of sufficiency which is expressed in almost identical words in section 14(3) of the Patents Act 1977:

> "The specification of an application shall disclose the invention in a manner which is clear enough and complete enough for the invention to be performed by a person skilled in the art."
>
> Article 84 is reproduced in section 14(5)(c):
>
> "The claim or claims shall—
>
>   . . .
>
> (c) be supported by the description."

The significance of the reference to the "person skilled in the art", and this notional technician's approach to the task of performing an invention, have often been described by the court. There are helpful passages in the judgment of Aldous J in *Mentor Corp v. Hollister Inc* [1991] FSR 557, 562 and in the judgment of Lloyd LJ in the same case [1993] RPC 7, 10–13.

* * *

20.   Section 14(3) and (5)(c) operate together, as EPC Articles 83 and 84 operate together, to spell out the need for an "enabling disclosure", which is central to the law of patents: see Lord Oliver in *Asahi* at pp. 531–532, and Lord Hoffmann in *Biogen* at pp. 46–51

and in *Kirin–Amgen Inc v. Hoechst Marion Roussel Ltd* [2005] RPC 169 (*"Kirin–Amgen"*) at paras 102–116. The disclosure must be such as to enable the invention to be performed (that is, to be carried out if it is a process, or to be made if it is a product) to the full extent of the claims. The question whether there is sufficient enabling disclosure often interacts with a question of construction as to the extent of the claims. For instance in *American Home Products Corp v. Novartis Pharmaceuticals UK Ltd* [2001] RPC 159 (*"American Home Products"*) the disclosure would have been insufficient if the claims had extended, not merely to rapamycin (a known antifungal antibiotic which proved effective as an immunosuppressant) but also to derivatives of rapamycin. The Court of Appeal held that the claims should be narrowly construed, and on that basis there was sufficient enabling disclosure.

21.   The main thrust of the appellants' case is that Lundbeck made only a limited technical contribution to the resolution of citalopram, because it fully disclosed only one method of producing the (+) enantiomer, that is by the route of resolution of the diol intermediate. Therefore, it is said, the *Exxon* principle invalidates claims 1 and 3 because (although expressed as ordinary product claims) they are really in the nature of product-by-process claims, and should have been limited to escitalopram as produced by the diol intermediate method. In considering this argument I find it necessary to return to some fairly basic points of patent law—commonplace to the specialist in this field, but not necessarily obvious to the non-specialist.

Product claims

22.   Judges have often observed that the wide abstract terms in which patent law is expressed must always be related to the facts of the particular case. That is especially true in relation to the sufficiency of a product claim, since the term "product" covers such an extremely wide variety. A product may be as simple as a baby's disposable diaper (see *Mölnlycke AB v. Procter & Gamble Ltd* [1992] FSR 549—*"Mölnlycke"*) or a corkscrew (see *Hallen Co v. Brabantia (UK) Ltd* [1991] RPC 195) or as complex as an "heavier-than-air flying machine" referred to by Lord Hoffmann in *Biogen*, or a class of microscopic organisms, produced by recombinant DNA technology, such as was considered by this House in *Biogen* and *Kirin–Amgen*. Where the product is manufactured the specification is likely to include drawings as well as a verbal description, but the drawings are almost always described as an example (or embodiment). Otherwise (in the absence from United Kingdom patent law of a doctrine of equivalents—see *Kirin–Amgen* [2005] RPC 169, paras 36 ff) competitors would probably be able, by some small variation in design, to exploit the inventive concept without in-

fringement. For similar reasons (especially in the field of chemical compounds) patent applications are likely to seek to obtain protection, not for a single compound, but for a class of compounds, and sometimes an almost unimaginably large class (see for instance *Pharmacia Corp v. Merck & Co Inc* [2002] RPC 41, where claim 1 is set out, in an accessible form, in para 11; Arden LJ recorded, in para 150, that it comprised "literally trillions" of formulae).

* * *

The claims in Biogen and in the patent in suit

26. That is in my opinion the fundamental reason why *Biogen* does not provide a direct answer to this appeal (although it is certainly material to the issue of "technical contribution"). The invention set out in claim 1 of the patent in suit in *Biogen* was one with a very large number of possible embodiments. As Lord Hoffmann put it in his opinion in *Biogen* (p 40, emphasis supplied):

> "The claim is to a product, a molecule identified partly by the way in which it has been made ('recombinant DNA') and partly by what it does (the words following 'characterised by'). It generalises what Professor Murray had done in two ways. First, as to the results he had achieved. He had made a particular form of recombinant plasmid (pBR322 with fragments of Dane particle DNA) which had transformed *E coli* and, he said, caused it to express the genes of HBcAg and HBsAg. The claim was for any recombinant DNA molecule which expressed the genes of any HBV antigen in any host cell. Secondly, there was generalisation of the method which he had used. He had made his DNA molecule from a standard pBR322 plasmid and large fragments from Dane particle DNA, chosen simply on the basis that they should be large. This was a technique imposed upon him by lack of information about the coding sequences. Thereafter, he employed conventional means to express the DNA in a conventional bacterial host. The claim was for any method of making a DNA molecule which would achieve the necessary expression."

27. Where classes of compounds are claimed, difficult interlocking problems as to construction and sufficiency may arise (as in *American Home Products*). They do not arise in this case. The fact that claim 1 is to a single chemical compound is what makes the present appeal unusual (and, I venture to say, relatively straightforward, once the issues of lack of novelty and obviousness are out of the way, as they are in your Lordships' House).

28. In describing the issues before the House as relatively straightforward I do not in any way disparage the lengthy written and oral submissions which have been addressed to your Lordships.

Those submissions have been of great assistance. But as the argument in the appeal has progressed I have formed the view that the appellants can succeed only if they persuade your Lordships that there is a general principle in EPC Article 84 and section 14(5)(c) of the Patents Act 1977 that requires a product claim to a single chemical compound to be restricted to the invention's technical contribution to the art, and that that means the inventive concept (in this case the diol intermediate process).

Technical contribution

29.   During the oral argument before your Lordships there was some discussion of whether "inventive concept" means the same as "technical contribution to the art." Neither expression is a statutory term of art. Lord Hoffmann used both expressions several times in his opinion in *Biogen*, the former mostly in section 10 (headed "Inventive Step") and the latter mostly in section 12 ("Support for the Claims"). Mr Thorley QC submitted in his reply that the two expressions (as used in Lord Hoffmann's opinion) are synonymous.

30.   I do not think that this is quite right. The expressions are certainly connected, but I do not think it is helpful (either in considering Lord Hoffmann's opinion, or generally) to treat them as having precisely the same meaning. "Inventive concept" is concerned with the *identification* of the core (or kernel, or essence) of the invention—the idea or principle, of more or less general application (see *Kirin–Amgen* [2005] RPC 169 paras 112–113) which entitles the inventor's achievement to be called inventive. The invention's technical contribution to the art is concerned with the *evaluation* of its inventive concept—how far forward has it carried the state of the art? The inventive concept and the technical contribution may command equal respect but that will not always be the case.

31.   *Biogen* itself is, I think, a good illustration of this. Before your Lordships Lord Hoffmann's opinion in *Biogen* has been subjected to closer and more searching scrutiny by the House than any that I can recall, with the possible exception of the House's scrutiny in *Deutsche Morgan Grenfell v. Inland Revenue Commissioners* [2007] 1 AC 558 of the speech of Lord Goff of Chieveley in *Kleinwort Benson Ltd. v. Lincoln City Council* [1999] 2 AC 349. If I may respectfully say so, Lord Hoffmann's opinion in *Biogen* is a *tour de force*. I have frequently commended it to bar students as an example of how a great judge can suffuse even the most technical subject with intellectual excitement. But its vivid and powerful language must be read in the context of the facts and issues in that case.

32. *Biogen* was a difficult and complicated case—much more complicated than the present appeal before the House The first-instance hearing occupied two working weeks and the hearing in the Court of Appeal took even longer. It is noteworthy that despite the much-quoted passage in Lord Hoffmann's opinion (at p 45) counselling caution in an appellate court's review of a trial judge's evaluation of the facts, Lord Hoffmann did differ from Aldous J in his identification of the inventive concept, and (at pp 45–46) he differed from the Court of Appeal (and agreed with Aldous J) on the issue of obviousness for the very reason that the Court of Appeal had unquestioningly accepted the judge's view of the inventive concept. The better view was that the inventive concept was (p 45, emphasis supplied):

> "The idea of trying to express unsequenced eukaryotic DNA in a prokaryotic [non-mammalian] host."

32. This was a striking achievement by Professor Murray (Lord Hoffmann, at p 52, called it "a brilliant Napoleonic victory") which stole a march on researchers who were taking the more systematic route of sequencing the genome. But in terms of its technical contribution to the art it was not of lasting strategic importance because within a few months of Professor Murray's achievement the genome had been sequenced. As Lord Hoffmann put it (p 52):

> "Professor Murray invented a way of working with the genome in the dark. But he did not switch on the light and once the light was on his method was no longer needed. Nor, once they could use vectors for mammalian cells, would they be concerned with the same problem of introns which had so exercised those skilled in the art in 1978. Of course there might be other problems, but Biogen 1 did not teach how to solve them. The respondents Medeva who use restriction enzymes based on knowledge of the HBV genome and mammalian host cells, owe nothing to Professor Murray's invention."

> In short, the invention's technical contribution to the art was not (except as a matter of history) something of lasting importance; and the patent was insufficient (p 53) to sustain a claim to every method of using recombinant DNA technology to produce HBV antigens.

34. *Biogen* is therefore an example of a brilliant inventive concept which did not however make a significant permanent contribution to the art, because of the pace at which the state of the art was advancing. Pharmaceutical research is a highly competitive activity, backed by huge resources, and there will always be winners and losers. Jacob LJ (at para 57) was rightly not moved by the thought that Professor Bogeso might be getting "more than he deserved". Had he spent seven years isolating the enantiomers and found that

both were equally effective and non-toxic his invention would, at least in commercial terms, have made no significant technical contribution to the art. Neither Lundbeck nor any of its competitors would have wanted to manufacture escitalopram. But the inventive concept would have been no different. The technical contribution was, as the Court of Appeal recognised (paras 36 and 59) the isolated enantiomer now called escitalopram, but it would on this hypothesis have proved no more useful than the unresolved racemate citalopram.

Exxon

35.   My noble and learned friends Lord Mance and Lord Neuberger of Abbotsbury (whose opinions I have had the advantage of reading in draft) both draw attention to the importance of UK patent law aligning itself, so far as possible, with the jurisprudence of the EPO (and especially decisions of its Enlarged Boards of Appeal). National courts may reach different conclusions as to the evaluation of the evidence in the light of the relevant principles, but the principles themselves should be the same, stemming as they do from the EPC. There is no decision of an Enlarged Board of Appeal directly in point on the subject of technical contribution. The most relevant decision of a Technical Board of Appeal is *Exxon,* decided in 1993.

36.   The claimed invention was in the field of additives for fuel oils to prevent the oil filter in a diesel engine being clogged at low temperatures by the formation of very small ice crystals. It was an area in which much research had already been undertaken. The appellant made a main request and an auxiliary request, both of which failed on grounds related to EPC Articles 83 and 84. After the passage quoted at para 19 the Technical Board of Appeal continued (para 3.3):

> "This means that the definitions in the claims should essentially correspond to the scope of the invention as disclosed in the description. In other words, as was stated in decision T 26/81 (OJ EPO 1982, 211, point 4 of the reasons), the claims should not extend to subject-matter which, after reading the description, would still not be at the disposal of the person skilled in the art."

37.   The Board also stated (para 3.5):

> "Although the requirements of Article 83 and Article 84 are directed to different parts of the patent application, since Article 83 relates to the disclosure of the invention, whilst Article 84 deals with the definition of the invention by the claims, the underlying purpose of the requirement of support by the description, insofar as its substantive aspect is concerned, and of the requirement of sufficient disclosure is the

same, namely to ensure that the patent monopoly should be justified by the actual technical contribution to the art. Thus a claim may well be supported by the description in the sense that it corresponds to it, but still encompass subject-matter which is not sufficiently disclosed within the meaning of Article 83 EPC as it cannot be performed without undue burden, or vice versa."

38. These statements of principle appear to me to support the views that I have expressed. But for present purposes the most significant part of the decision in *Exxon* is in the later part of para 3.5:

"In the Board's judgment, this case differs from those where a class of chemical compounds is claimed and only one method of preparing them is necessary to enable a skilled person to carry out the invention, ie to prepare all compounds of the claimed class. Rather, the present case is comparable to cases where a group of chemical compounds is claimed, and not all of the claimed compounds can be prepared by the methods disclosed in the description or being part of the common general knowledge (see eg T 206/83, OJ EPO 1987, 5). In the latter case, it was not held sufficient for the purpose of Article 83 EPC to disclose a method of obtaining only some members of the claimed class of chemical compositions."

That statement could hardly be clearer. Claim 1 in the patent in suit is to a single chemical composition.

39. Your Lordships were referred to other decisions of Technical Boards of Appeal of the EPO that are in line with the decision in *Exxon*. But it is not necessary to multiply statements of essentially the same point.

40. For these reasons, which I understand to be essentially the same as those of Lord Mance and Lord Neuberger, I would dismiss this appeal.

Notes and Questions

1. The Federal Circuit, in its en banc *Ariad* opinion, found that the written description requirement is distinct and separate from the enablement requirement, and attempted to set boundaries for compliance with these two requirements:

"This inquiry, as we have long held, is a question of fact. Thus, we have recognized that determining whether a patent complies with the written description requirement will necessarily vary depending on the context. Specifically, the level of detail required to satisfy the written description requirement varies depending on the nature and scope of the claims and on the complexity and predictability of the relevant technology. *Id*. For generic claims, we have set forth a number of factors for evaluating the adequacy of the disclosure, including "the existing knowledge in the particular field, the extent and content of the prior art, the maturity of the science or technology, [and] the predictability of the aspect at issue."

"Perhaps there is little difference in some fields between describing an invention and enabling one to make and use it, but that is not always true of certain inventions, including chemical and chemical-like inventions. Thus, although written description and enablement often rise and fall together, requiring a written description of the invention plays a vital role in curtailing claims that do not require undue experimentation to make and use, and thus satisfy enablement, but that have not been invented, and thus cannot be described. For example, a propyl or butyl compound may be made by a process analogous to a disclosed methyl compound, but, in the absence of a statement that the inventor invented propyl and butyl compounds, such compounds have not been described and are not entitled to a patent."

Judge Linn disagreed and criticized the majority:

"It is inconsistent to say that on its filing date, a patent does not show that the inventor "possessed" subject matter that the claims actually encompass and the specification fully enables. Doing so perpetuates an unnecessary tension between the claims and the written description as the definition of a patented invention."

Lord Oliver's statement that "if that which is contained in the description of the specification does not enable the claim to be established, it cannot be said to 'support' it" from the *Generics* opinion supports Judge Linn's above argument. In the *Bayer Schering* opinion, EPO Technical Board of Appeals rejection of a claim for lack of enablement regarding the subject matter is analogous to the example cited by the *Ariad* majority. The inventor never made some of the compounds that fell within the scope of the claim, except for the written description of these compounds, even though they can be made easily by using the methods disclosed in the specification. Why did the Federal Circuit refuse to apply the enablement requirement for a claim that encompassed subject matter that the inventor never made, even though it was relatively easy to make? If an invention is not enabled through operable embodiment, an invention is not always described.

2. In the *Bayer Schering* opinion, the subject matter is defined by reach-through claims that define the claim by function instead of structure. However, the EPC does not include any provision comparable to 35 USC § 112¶ 6. The scope of reach-through claims includes any structure or compound that produces the function recited in the claim, and because of this the scope of product-by-process in EPC member states is broader than that of product-by-process claims in the United States. The scope of European patents in product-by-process

format extends to products which are identical to those made by the process recited in the claim regardless of how the products are made. *Kirin–Amgen Inc. v. Hoechst Marion*, House of Lords Oct. 21, 2004, [2004] UKHL 46. This rule is a stark contrast to the rule adopted by the en banc Federal Circuit decision in *Abbott Labs. v. Sandoz, Inc.*, 566 F.3d 1282 (Fed. Cir. 2009). In this decision, the majority of the court decided that the scope of product-by-process claims should be limited to products that were made by the process recited in the claim.

3.   In the *Bayer Schering* and *Generics* opinions, analyses by the EPO Board and the UK House of Lords focus on the concept of technical contribution. The EPO Board and Lord Gestingthorpe emphasized determination of technical contribution based on disclosures in the specification. Is this technical contribution test similar to the possession as shown in the disclosure test emphasized by Judge Michel in *Ariad?*

4.   A claim with undue breath, such as the reach-through claim in *Bayer Sharing*, might have been found valid had the case been litigated in Germany. The Federal Supreme Court of Germany made it clear that the undue breadth of a claim itself is not necessarily grounds for invalidity. (Blasenfreie Gummibahn I/II, Judgment of BGH, Sept 24, 2004, Sept. 3, 2003, 2004GRUR 47, 268). Once a patent has been issued, German courts are very reluctant to restrictively interpret claims as long as the whole scope of claim can produce the advantage of the invention. ((Mehrgangnabe,. Judgment of BGH, Feb. 12, 2008, 2008 GRUR 779). However, this broad interpretation makes German patents more susceptible to inventive step challenges because more references in different technological fields are available as analogous art. (Schussfaedentransport, Judgment of BGH, Dec. 12, 2006, 2007GRUR 309) In essence, only the prior art limits German patents to fairly reward pioneer inventors reflecting the scale of contribution to the state of art.

B.   WRITTEN DESCRIPTION REQUIREMENT

Japan follows an approach similar to the one endorsed by the *en banc* Federal Circuit in *Ariad*. JPL Art. 36, Para. 6, Item 1 requires that a claimed invention be included in the written description of the specification, providing a distinct requirement from the enablement requirement. As shown in the following except, the Intellectual Property High Court of Japan attempts to distinguish the scope of these two requirements by focusing on their respective purposes. The corresponding patent applications filed at the USPTO and the EPO were issued as US 7,151,103 and EP 1,446,122.

IN RE BOEHRINGER INGELHEIM PHARMA

Judgment of the IP High Court of Japan, January 22, 2010
Hanrei Jihô [Hanji] 2073–105

JUDGES IIMURA, OSUGA, & SAIKI

[The plaintiff-applicant filed an application that included a claim for the use of flibanserin to treat sexual disorders. A JPO examiner rejected the claim due to a failure to meet the written description requirement. The JPO Board of Appeals affirmed the rejection. The applicant filed an appeal with the IP High Court, arguing that the JPO misinterpreted Japanese Patent Law Article 36 Paragraph 6 Item 1, which establishes the written description requirement.]

Holding of the Court

This Court found that the JPO Board of Appeals erroneously found that the claim in this application failed to meet the requirements of Article 36, Paragraph 6, Item 1, explaining that the specification must include pharmacological data or its equivalent for a medication claim to meet the requirement that "the statement of the scope of claims . . . shall comply with that the invention for which a patent is sought must be stated in the detailed explanation of the invention" under the said provision.

The reasoning of the court is as follows:

1. The Relationship Between Article 36, Paragraph 4, Item 1 and Article 36, Paragraph 6, Item 1:

> (1) The purpose of provisions Article 36, Paragraph 4, Item 1 and Article 36, Paragraph 6, Item 1
>
> Article 36 establishes the required information to be included in the application when an applicant files for a patent. However, within this article a sharp distinction is drawn between the following provisions: Paragraph 4, Item 1 requires a detailed explanation of the invention for the specifications included in the application, while Paragraph 6, Item 1 sets requirements for the claims included in the application.
>
> In other words, Article 36, Paragraph 4, Item 1, requires "a detailed explanation of the invention," that includes the "necessary data to allow a person ordinarily skilled in the art who may try to understand the invention to understand the relevant technical problems and how to solve them, and be able to understand the technical significance of the invention." (Ordinance for Enforcement of the Pat-

ent Act Article 24–2) The invention should be "described clearly and sufficiently to enable a person ordinarily skilled in the relevant art to practice the described invention." The purpose of this provision is to create a patent system that grants a monopoly right for a set period of time to inventors who publically disclose their invention as compensation for that disclosure. However, the purpose of this system that rewards inventors for disclosing their invention, as well as the structure of its technical ideas, is lost if a monopoly right is given to an inventor without disclosure of information necessary to understand the technical problems, solutions to those problems, and technical significance of the invention, as well as sufficient information to practice the invention. The "detailed description of the invention" requirement for patent specifications given above is intended to satisfy this purpose.

In contrast, Article 36, Paragraph 6, Item 1 requires that the "claim" include "a detailed description of the invention for which a patent is sought." This provision was created in light of Article 68, which protects the right of a patentee to have an exclusive right to commercially practice the patented invention, and Article 70, Paragraph 1 that establishes that the technical scope of a patented invention must be based on the description of the claim included in the application. If the scope of "claim" exceeds the scope of technical information described and disclosed in the "detailed explanation of the invention," a grant of an exclusive right to such claims conflicts with the purpose of a patent system where an exclusive right is granted only to the extent of the scope of disclosure because a patent is granted as compensation for that disclosure. Thus, Article 36, Paragraph 6, Item 3 does not allow the inclusion of claims that exceed the scope of disclosure. For example, if the "embodiments" description only allows for a limited and narrow understanding of the technical aspects of the invention, while the "claims" description goes beyond the technical description encompassing a much wider technical scope, the claims will be in conflict with Article 36, Paragraph 6, Item 1, and should not be allowed.

Simply put, Article 36, Paragraph 6, Item 1 is intended to eliminate the issuance of overly-broad monopoly rights in situations where the "claims" are different in scope from the "detailed description of the invention."

(2) Examination of Requirements under Article 36, Paragraph 6, Item 1

To determine whether the requirements under Article 36, Paragraph 6, Item 1 has been met, in other words, whether the written description of the "claims" includes a "detailed explanation of the invention" for which the applicant is seeking a patent, it is necessary to understand the technical information disclosed in "the detailed explanation of the invention." In addition, since Article 36, Paragraph 6, Item 1 has two purposes: (1) to make sure that monopoly rights are not granted too widely in relation to the scope of the "detailed specifications of the invention and (2) to provide a requirement for the claims to be met, it is necessary to adopt a method suitable for fully understanding the detailed explanations of the invention in order to determine the compliance with the requirement with respect to the two purposes of the above provision. On the other hand, because Article 36, Paragraph 4, Item 1 independently provides the requirement that the "detailed description of the invention" must include the "information necessary to understand the problem the invention seeks to solve, the method for solving that problem, and the information necessary for understanding the technical significance of that problem," as well as a "clear and sufficient description for putting (the invention) into practice," the failure to meet these requirements creates grounds independently for rejection of the application, rejection, and a patent granted to under the application has inherent grounds of invalidation (Patent Law, Article 123, Paragraph 1, Item 4) regardless of whether the description of claims meets Article 36, Paragraph 6, Item 1. Examining whether a claim meets the requirements of Article 36, Paragraph 6, Item 1 may lead to examining the description of the application twice regarding exactly the same requirement if a method suitable examining the requirement of Article 36, Paragraph 4, Item 1 is adopted for the examination of the requirement under Article 36, Paragraph 6, Item 1 without taking into account the purpose of the provision that is to prevent the granting of an exclusive right that is too wide relative to the scope of technical information disclosed in the detailed explanation of the invention. Adding Paragraph 4, Item 1 under Article 36 as a separate requirement for a condition to grant a patent would become meaningless if a finding of a failure to meet the requirement under Article 36, Paragraph 4, Item 1 regarding the description of the detailed explanation of the invention necessarily results in a finding of failure to meet the requirement under Article 36, Paragraph 6, Item 1 regarding claims that is accompanied with the explanation.

Accordingly, claims are examined through a comparison between the scope of claims and the scope of the description in the detailed explanation of the invention only to determine a question whether the former scope exceeds the latter scope. The requirement under Article 36, Paragraph 6, Item 1 should not be interpreted in the same manner for examining the requirement under Article 36, Paragraph 4, Item 1 unless there are exceptional circumstance such as a case where claims under the examination are drafted in a special manner and it is necessary to examine such claims in the same manner as examining the requirement under Article 36, Paragraph 4, Item 1 to avoid a result conflicting with the purpose of the patent system.

2. Reasons Given by Board of Appeal

The Board of Appeal found that the application failed to meet the requirements of Article 36, Paragraph 6, Item 1 citing a failure of the "detailed explanation of the invention" to include a description of the pharmacological data or its equivalent to establish the utility of flibanserin compounds for the treatment of sexual disorders as the grounds of invalidity. The decision of the board is as follows:

(1) "When examining a claim for the novel use of a medicine, it is generally difficult to predict the usefulness of a particular pharmaceutical compound by looking only at its active ingredients and chemical structures. Even when information such as effective dosage, method of administration, and information on manufacture is included in the detailed explanation of the invention that does not necessarily give sufficient information for a person with ordinary skill in the art of the invention to predict whether the compound is in fact effective for the asserted new use. Accordingly, it is necessary that the utility of the asserted use be established by pharmacological data or its equivalent in the detailed explanation of the invention. Unless the detailed explanation of the invention includes such data, a claim directed to a new use of the pharmaceutical compound fails to meet the requirement under Article 36, Paragraph 6, Item 1." (Citation omitted)

(2) "The invention described in Claim 1 is "directed to the use of flibanserin optionally in the form of pharmacologically acceptable acid addition salts thereof or the preparation of a medicament for the treatment of disorders of sexual desire." In applying the above rule, Claim 1 does not include a description

of how to use optionally in form of the pharmacologically acceptable acid addition salts thereof (hereunder, flibanserin and its derivatives) as a medicament for treating sexual disorders.

The detailed explanation of the invention in the application explains the invention in the following excerpt: "In studies of male and female patients suffering from sexual dysfunction it has been found that flibanserin, in form of pharmacologically acceptable acid addition salts, displays sexual desire enhancing properties. Accordingly, the instant invention relates to the use of flibanserin, optionally in form of the pharmacologically acceptable acid addition salts, for the manufacture of medication to treat sexual desire disorders."

Based on these descriptions, this is an application for the invention of a new pharmaceutical use of flibanserin and its derivatives for manufacturing medication for sexual disorder treatment. The invention resulted from a finding of a new pharmacological use in flibanserin and its derivatives regarding their sexual desire enhancing properties. The invention described in this application constitutes an invention as described in the detailed explanation of the invention only where the detailed explanation of the invention includes <u>pharmacological data or its equivalent to establish the utility of flibanserin and its derivatives</u> as medication for the treatment of sexual disorders and thus <u>the utility of the patent is established by such data.</u>

Applying this rule to examine the specifications in this application, <u>the detailed explanation of the invention does not include any pharmacological data or its equivalent to establish the use of flibanserin and its derivatives</u> as medication for the treatment of sexual disorders. ... <u>Description in (a) through (f) in the detailed explanation of the invention is not equivalent to pharmacological data to establish the use of flibanserin and its derivatives as medication for the treatment of sexual disorders. Accordingly, the detailed explanation of the invention does not include pharmacological data or its equivalent to establish the utility of the use of a chemical compound as a medicament.</u> ... In conclusion, this application fails to meet the requirements of Patent Law Article 36, Paragraph 6, Item 1." (Citation omitted)

3. Review of Reasons Given by the Board of Appeal:

(1) The Board of Appeal did not compare the scope of "claims" and "the detailed explanation of the invention" to determine whether the scope of the former exceeds the scope of the latter, and instead the Board's decision relied solely on its finding that "the detailed explanation of the invention" in the specification did not include pharmacological data or its equivalent to establish the utility of flibanserin and its derivatives

as a medicament for the treatment of sexual disorders as grounds for rejecting the application under Article 36, Paragraph 6, Item 1. However, the board failed to explain why the lack of a description regarding pharmacological data or its equivalent to establish the effectiveness of flibanserin and its derivatives constitutes a failure to meet the requirements of Article 36, Paragraph 6, Item 1.

    a. The Board of Appeal gave the following reasoning for its decision: "When examining a claim for the use of a pharmaceutical compound, it is generally difficult to predict the usefulness of that compound from the identification of the active ingredients and chemical structures alone, and including information regarding effective dosage, method of administration, and the data necessary for manufacture in the detailed explanation of the invention does not necessarily give sufficient information for an ordinarily skilled person in the art of the invention to predict whether the compound in fact includes the asserted utility. When filing a patent for an invention, it is necessary to back up an assertion of utility with pharmaceutical data or its equivalent in the detailed description of the invention for such a description to fulfill its purpose." One can't deny that Article 36, Paragraph 4, Item 1 is at times applied in light of the purpose of the provision when determining whether its requirements have been satisfied.

Article 36, Paragraph 4, Item 1 requires an applicant to describe in the detailed explanation of the invention in light of the view that to obtain an exclusive right, an applicant must provide information necessary for a third party to understand the technical problem to be solved by the invention, its solution, and technical significance, thereby providing clear and sufficient information for practicing the invention. Under the Japanese patent system, which allows patenting the new use of a pharmaceutical product, it is often reasonable to require information to establish the utility of claimed use in "the detailed explanation of the invention," and data showing the relationship between the medication and its use is most appropriate way of showing such information. Failure to include such data often results in insufficient evidence to meet the requirement that the invention must be clearly and sufficiently described in the detailed explanation of the invention.

In examining the requirement for satisfying Article 36, Paragraph 6, Item 1, the Board of Appeal stated: "it is necessary that the utility of the asserted use must be established by pharmacological data or its equivalent in the detailed explanation of the invention." This statement is inappropriate because a disclosure of pharmacological data or its equivalent is not essential for meeting Article 36, Paragraph 6, Item 1 unless there are some sort of exceptional circumstances. As discussed above, Article 36, Paragraph 6, Item 1 requires a comparison between the scope of claims and the scope of the detailed explanation of the invention because the purpose of the provision is to prevent patents with claims that exceed the scope of the detailed explanation of the invention. An examination of the detailed explanation of the invention should follow in a manner necessary and reasonable to determine whether the subject matter of the "claims" is described in "the detailed explanation of the invention" in light of the purpose of the requirement under Article 36, Paragraph 6, Item 1. Accordingly, it is sufficient for an examiner to examine technical information described and disclosed through embodiments and other data in "the detailed explanation of the invention" as it is described unless there are exceptional circumstances.

In short, the rule in the Board of Appeal's decision that Article 36, Paragraph 6, Item 1 is not met unless "the utility of the asserted use is established by pharmacological data or its equivalent" is not always applicable, and using that as the only reason for rejecting the patent is improper in cases where there are no special circumstances to be considered.

b.   The Board of Appeal examined the description of the detailed explanation of the invention and concluded that this application does not meet the requirement under Article 36, Paragraph 6, Item 1, stating that "the description in the detailed explanation of the invention in the specification of this application does not include pharmacological data or its equivalent to establish the utility of use as a medication." However, the Board did not compare the scope of technical information in the detailed explanation of the invention with the scope of claims. Instead, it examined only the description of the detailed explanation of the invention with respect to a question whether it includes "pharmacological data or its equivalent" and concluded that this application fails to meet the requirement under Article 36, Paragraph 6, Item 1 because of the lack of such data. The Board made an error in finding a failure to meet the requirement under Article 36, Paragraph 6, Item 1 without giving any reason why the scope of claims of this application exceeds the scope of technical information disclosed in the detailed explanation of the invention. In this case, there is no exceptional circumstance where the claim under the examination is drafted in a special format that would require this court to find a violation of the requirement under Article 36, Paragraph 6, Item 1 to avoid hindering industrial development.

c. Defendant (Japan Patent Office) cites a decision of Grand Panel of the IP High Court in which the Court found a violation of the requirement under Pre-revision Patent Law Article 36, Paragraph 5, Item 1(Article 36, Paragraph 6, Item 1 under the current Patent Law) regarding a claim directed to subject matter that includes a range limitation defined by an equation of multiple technical variables (parameters) representing technical aspects. Defendant alleges that if the rule adopted by the Grand Panel applies to a claim for a new use of a pharmaceutical compound, it is necessary to include "a description of pharmacological data or its equivalent" in the detailed explanation of the invention to meet the requirements of Article 36, Paragraph 6, Item 1.

This court is unable to follow the assertion of the Defendant for the following reasons. As was stated previously, the Grand Panel Decision relates to an examination of a claim directed to subject matter that includes a range limitation defined by an equation of multiple technical variables (parameters) representing technical aspects to determine whether the claim meets the requirements of Article 36, Paragraph 5, Item 1, Patent Law which was revised with the enactment of Law No. 116 of 1994 (Article 36 Paragraph 6, Item 1 under current law) finding a violation of the requirement. The decision includes a section entitled "a comparison of subject matter described in the detailed invention and subject matter described in the claim." In the section, the Grand Panel examined the description of embodiments in "the detailed explanation of the invention," concluding that "the description does not include sufficient information with specific examples to convince an ordinarily skilled person in the art of invention to believe that the asserted advantage (performance) can be produced throughout the range defined by the equation." The Grand Panel also held that because the scope of subject matter disclosed in the detailed explanation of the invention cannot expand or be generalized to the scope of the claim under examination, expanding and generalizing the former scope to the latter scope of the claim to meet the support requirement for the specification conflicts with the patent policy of a grant of patent in exchange of the disclosure of an invention. Therefore, such expansion should not be allowed.

In summary, the IP High Court Grand Panel decision relates to (1) a dispute on the scope of a claim directed to subject matter defined by multiple parameters; and (2) compared the description of "the claim" with the disclosed "detailed explanation of the invention" to determine whether the scope of the claim exceeds the scope of technical information described and disclosed in "the detailed explanation of the invention." In contrast, this case does not involve any dispute on the scope of a claim drafted in a special format which requires interpretation of the claim to clarify the technical scope and does not involve a comparison of the description of a claim with the description of "the detailed explanation of the invention" to find the scope of the exceeds the scope of the description. Therefore, the facts in this case are distinguishable from those in the Grand Panel decision. It is an error for the Defendant to assert that an application of the rule in the Grand Panel decision to the examination of subject matter for use as medication results in the requirement of describing "pharmacological data and its equivalents" for meeting the requirement under Article 36, Paragraph 6 Item 1 because of the different facts between this case and the Grand Panel decision. In conclusion, this Court rejects the Defendant's finding of a violation of the requirement under Article 36, Paragraph 6 Item 1 regarding a claim directed to a new use of a pharmaceutical compound because of a failure to include a description of pharmacological data and its equivalents, relying on this Court's Grand Panel decision.

d.　Because the Board of Appeals applied the rule that a description of "pharmacological data or its equivalent" is always necessary to meet the requirement under Article 36, Paragraph 6 Item 1, it erroneously rejected the claim under examination for a violation of the requirement under Article 36, Paragraph 6 Item 1, only relying on the fact that "a description of pharmacological data and its equivalents is not included."

(2) [After examining the description of the claim under examination and the description of the detailed explanation of the invention, the Court concluded that the scope of the former description does not exceed the scope of latter description.]

4.　In conclusion, the Board of Appeal erroneously found the description of claims of this application failed to meet the requirement under Article 36, Paragraph 6 Item 1. This Court finds a ground for reversal asserted by Plaintiff. The decision of the Board of Appeal should be reversed.

Notes and Questions

1.   In Japan, jurisdiction over patent infringement cases is limited to the Tokyo and Osaka District courts, where special divisions hear patent and software copyright cases. The Japanese IP High Court has exclusive jurisdiction over appeals from the Tokyo and Osaka District courts and decisions issued by the Japan Patent Office Board of Appeals. When an appeal from the district courts reaches the IP High Court, a three-judge panel decides the case. The Grand Panel was created alongside the IP High Court in 2005 to handle very complex and important issues unique to technology related IP cases. The Grand Panel consists of the presiding judges from all four divisions, including the President of the IP High Court and a senior judge who is assigned to draft the decision for the original panel. In theory, any judicial precedent that is not from the Supreme Court, including decisions from the IP High Court Grand Panel, is not binding on Japanese judges because Japan is a civil law country. However, in practice precedent plays a very important role in IP cases. What kind of role does Grand Panel precedent play in *Boehringer?*

2.   Is the requirement established by Article 36, Paragraph 6, Item 1 the same as the written description requirement under 35 USC § 112? How is the requirement established by Article 36, Paragraph 6, Item 1 distinguished from the enablement requirement under 35 USC § 112? How would the Federal Circuit decide the *Boehringer* case?

Chapter 7

INFRINGEMENT

A. LITIGATION PROCEDURE

TRIPS Article 41 requires member states to ensure that IP enforcement procedures are available under their laws to allow for effective action against any act of infringement of intellectual property rights. Enforcement procedures are to be to be fair and equitable, and the reasons behind a decision on the merits of a case shall preferably be given in writing.

In Germany, an accused infringer is not allowed to raise a defense of patent invalidity because the Federal Patent Court has exclusive jurisdiction over validity. This is in stark contrast to U.S. practice where patent validity was raised mainly as a defense in patent litigation until the introduction of ex-parte reexamination in 1980. Until recently Japan, South Korea, Taiwan and China have largely followed the German approach. However, the lack of jurisdiction over validity forces courts to adopt an obscure claim interpretation method to prevent the enforcement of a patent against an accused product or method that is in the prior art. In the *Kilby* decision, which was issued in the year 2000, the Supreme Court of Japan gave lower courts the power to deny enforcement when the asserted patent is obviously invalid. This power was codified by a patent law revision in 2004. Taiwan recently followed Japan's example, and now an accused infringer can challenge the validity of a patent in infringement litigation.

No WTO member states other than the United States use juries in patent litigation. In those countries judges interpret patent claims and apply claims to the accused product or process when determining infringement. WTO TRIPS Article 43 allows courts in WTO member states to secure access to evidence to establish infringement when a party has presented reasonably available evidence sufficient to support its claims and has specified evidence relevant to the substantiation of its claims that is controlled by the opposing party. However, access to evidence to establish infringement and damages is much more limited in these countries than it is in the United States.

B. EXTENT OF PATENT PROTECTION

TRIPS Article 28 defines which rights of the patentee are protected under the law. However, TRIPS does not include any provision for determining what constitutes a patented invention. However, European countries have adopted a uniform principle that is widely used in Asian countries.

EUROPE

KIRIN AMGEN INC. v. HOECHST MARION ROUSSEL LTD.

House of Lords
[2004] UKHL 46, October 21, 2004

The proceedings

Extent of protection: the statutory provisions

18.   Until the Patents Act 1977, which gave effect to the European Patent Convention ("EPC") there was nothing in any UK statute about the extent of protection conferred by a patent. It was governed by the common law, the terms of the royal grant and general principles of construction. It was these principles which Lord Diplock expounded in the leading case of *Catnic Components Ltd v. Hill & Smith Ltd* [1982] RPC 183, which concerned a patent granted before 1977. But the EPC and the Act deal expressly with the matter in some detail. Article 84 specifies the role of the claims in an application to the European Patent Office for a European patent:

> "The claims shall define the matter for which protection is sought. They shall be clear and concise and be supported by the description."

19.   For present purposes, the most important provision is article 69 of the EPC, which applies to infringement proceedings in the domestic courts of all Contracting States:

> "The extent of the protection conferred by a European patent or a European patent application shall be determined by the terms of the claims. Nevertheless, the description and drawings shall be used to interpret the claims."

20.   In stating unequivocally that the extent of protection shall be "determined" (in German, "*bestimmt*") by the "terms of the

claims" (*den Inhalt der Patentansprüche*) the Convention followed what had long been the law in the United Kingdom. During the course of the 18th and 19th centuries, practice and common law had come to distinguish between the part of the specification in which the patentee discharged his duty to disclose the best way of performing the invention and the section which delimited the scope of the monopoly which he claimed: see Fletcher–Moulton LJ in *British United Shoe Machinery Co Ltd v. A. Fussell & Sons Ltd* (1908) 25 RPC 631, 650. The best-known statement of the status of the claims in UK law is by Lord Russell of Killowen in *Electric and Musical Industries Ltd v. Lissen Ltd* (1938) 56 RPC 23, 39:

> "The function of the claims is to define clearly and with precision the monopoly claimed, so that others may know the exact boundary of the area within which they will be trespassers. Their primary object is to limit and not to extend the monopoly. What is not claimed is disclaimed. The claims must undoubtedly be read as part of the entire document and not as a separate document; but the forbidden field must be found in the language of the claims and not elsewhere."

21.   The need to set clear limits upon the monopoly is not only, as Lord Russell emphasised, in the interests of others who need to know the area "within which they will be trespassers" but also in the interests of the patentee, who needs to be able to make it clear that he lays no claim to prior art or insufficiently enabled products or processes which would invalidate the patent.

22.   In Germany, however, the practice before 1977 in infringement proceedings (validity is determined by a different court) was commonly to treat the claims as a point of departure ("*Ausgangspunkt*") in determining the extent of protection, for which the criterion was the inventive achievement ("*erfinderische Leistung*") disclosed by the specification as a whole. Likewise in the Netherlands, Professor Jan Brinkhof, former Vice–President of the Hague Court of Appeals, has written that the role of the claims before 1977 was "extremely modest": see *Is there a European Doctrine of Equivalence?* (2002) 33 IIC 911, 915. What mattered was the "essence of the invention" or what we would call the inventive concept.

The Protocol

23.   Although the EPC thus adopted the United Kingdom principle of using the claims to determine the extent of protection, the Contracting States were unwilling to accept what were understood to be the principles of construction which United Kingdom courts applied in deciding what the claims meant. These principles, which I shall explain in greater detail in a moment, were perceived as having sometimes resulted in claims being given an unduly narrow

and literal construction. The Contracting Parties wanted to make it clear that legal technicalities of this kind should be rejected. On the other hand, it was accepted that countries which had previously looked to the "essence of the invention" rather than the actual terms of the claims should not carry on exactly as before under the guise of giving the claims a generous interpretation.

24. This compromise was given effect by the "Protocol on the Interpretation of Article 69":

> "Article 69 should not be interpreted in the sense that the extent of the protection conferred by a European patent is to be understood as that defined by the strict, literal meaning of the wording used in the claims, the description and drawings being employed only for the purpose of resolving an ambiguity found in the claims. Neither should it be interpreted in the sense that the claims serve only as a guideline and that the actual protection conferred may extend to what, from a consideration of the description and drawings by a person skilled in the art, the patentee has contemplated. On the contrary, it is to be interpreted as defining a position between these extremes which combines a fair protection for the patentee with a reasonable degree of certainty for third parties."

25. It is often said, on the basis of the words "a position between these extremes", that the Protocol represents a compromise between two different approaches to the interpretation of claims. But that is not quite accurate. It is a protocol on the interpretation of article 69, not a protocol on the interpretation of claims. The first sentence does deal with interpretation of the claims and, to understand it, one needs to know something about the rules which English courts used to apply, or impose on themselves, when construing not merely patents but documents in general. The second sentence does not deal with the interpretation of claims. Instead, it makes it clear that one cannot go beyond the claims to what, on the basis of the specification as a whole, it appears that "the patentee has contemplated". But the last sentence indicates that, in determining the extent of protection according to the content of the claims but avoiding literalism, the courts of the Contracting States should combine "a fair protection for the patentee with a reasonable degree of certainty for third parties."

26. Both article 69 and the Protocol are given effect in United Kingdom law, in relation to infringement, by sections 60 and 125 of the Act. Section 60 provides that a person infringes a patent if he does various things in the United Kingdom "in relation to the invention" without the consent of the proprietor of the patent. Section 125 defines the extent of "the invention":

"(1) For the purpose of this Act an invention for a patent for which an application has been made or for which a patent has been granted shall, unless the context otherwise requires, be taken to be that specified in a claim of the specification of the application or patent, as the case may be, as interpreted by the description and any drawings contained in that specification, and the extent of the protection conferred by a patent or application for a patent shall be determined accordingly.

(3) The Protocol on the Interpretation of Article 69 of the European Patent Convention (which Article contains a provision corresponding to subsection (1) above) shall, as for the time being in force, apply for the purposes of subsection (1) above as it applies for the purposes of that Article."

The English rules of construction

27.   As I indicated a moment ago, it is impossible to understand what the first sentence of the Protocol was intending to prohibit without knowing what used to be the principles applied (at any rate in theory) by an English court construing a legal document. These required the words and grammar of a sentence to be given their "natural and ordinary meaning", that is to say, the meanings assigned to the words by a dictionary and to the syntax by a grammar. This meaning was to be adopted regardless of the context or background against which the words were used, unless they were "ambiguous", that is to say, capable of having more than one meaning. As Lord Porter said in *Electric & Musical Industries Ltd v. Lissen Ltd* (1938) 56 RPC 23, 57:

> "If the Claims have a plain meaning *in themselves* [emphasis supplied], then advantage cannot be taken of the language used in the body of the Specification to make them mean something different."

28.   On the other hand, if the language of the claim "in itself" was ambiguous, capable of having more than one meaning, the court could have regard to the context provided by the specification and drawings. If that was insufficient to resolve the ambiguity, the court could have regard to the background, or what was called the "extrinsic evidence" of facts which an intended reader would reasonably have expected to have been within the knowledge of the author when he wrote the document.

29.   These rules, if remorselessly applied, meant that unless the court could find some ambiguity in the language, it might be obliged to construe the document in a sense which a reasonable reader, aware of its context and background, would not have thought the author intended. Such a rule, adopted in the interests of certainty at an early stage in the development of English law,

was capable of causing considerable injustice and occasionally did so. The fact that it did not do so more often was because judges were generally astute to find the necessary "ambiguity" which enabled them to interpret the document in its proper context. Indeed, the attempt to treat the words of the claim as having meanings "in themselves" and without regard to the context in which or the purpose for which they were used was always a highly artificial exercise.

30.   It seems to me clear that the Protocol, with its reference to "resolving an ambiguity", was intended to reject these artificial English rules for the construction of patent claims. As it happens, though, by the time the Protocol was signed, the English courts had already begun to abandon them, not only for patent claims, but for commercial documents generally. The speeches of Lord Wilberforce in *Prenn v. Simmonds* [1971] 1 WLR 1381 and *Reardon Smith Line Ltd. v. Yngvar Hansen–Tangen* [1976] 1 WLR 989 are milestones along this road. It came to be recognised that the author of a document such as a contract or patent specification is using language to make a communication for a practical *purpose* and that a rule of construction which gives his language a meaning different from the way it would have been understood by the people to whom it was actually addressed is liable to defeat his intentions. It is against that background that one must read the well known passage in the speech of Lord Diplock in *Catnic Components Ltd v. Hill & Smith Ltd* [1982] RPC 183, 243 when he said that the new approach should also be applied to the construction of patent claims:

> "A patent specification should be given a purposive construction rather than a purely literal one derived from applying to it the kind of meticulous verbal analysis in which lawyers are too often tempted by their training to indulge."

31.   This was all of a piece with Lord Diplock's approach a few years later in *The Antaios* [1985] AC 191, 201 to the construction of a charterparty:

> "I take this opportunity of re-stating that if detailed semantic and syntactical analysis of words in a commercial contract is going to lead to a conclusion that flouts business commonsense, it must be made to yield to business commonsense."

32.   Construction, whether of a patent or any other document, is of course not directly concerned with what the author meant to say. There is no window into the mind of the patentee or the author of any other document. Construction is objective in the sense that it is concerned with what a reasonable person to whom the utterance was addressed would have understood the author to be using the words to mean. Notice, however, that it is not, as is sometimes said,

"the meaning of the words the author used", but rather what the notional addressee would have understood the *author* to mean by using those words. The meaning of words is a matter of convention, governed by rules, which can be found in dictionaries and grammars. What the author would have been understood to mean by using those words is not simply a matter of rules. It is highly sensitive to the context of and background to the particular utterance. It depends not only upon the words the author has chosen but also upon the identity of the audience he is taken to have been addressing and the knowledge and assumptions which one attributes to that audience. I have discussed these questions at some length in *Mannai Investment Co Ltd v. Eagle Star Life Assurance Co Ltd* [1997] AC 749 and *Investors Compensation Scheme Ltd v. West Bromwich Building Society* [1998] 1 WLR 896.

33.   In the case of a patent specification, the notional addressee is the person skilled in the art. He (or, I say once and for all, she) comes to a reading of the specification with common general knowledge of the art. And he reads the specification on the assumption that its purpose is to both to describe and to demarcate an invention—a practical idea which the patentee has had for a new product or process—and not to be a textbook in mathematics or chemistry or a shopping list of chemicals or hardware. It is this insight which lies at the heart of "purposive construction". If Lord Diplock did not invent the expression, he certainly gave it wide currency in the law. But there is, I think, a tendency to regard it as a vague description of some kind of divination which mysteriously penetrates beneath the language of the specification. Lord Diplock was in my opinion being much more specific and his intention was to point out that a person may be taken to mean something different when he uses words for one purpose from what he would be taken to mean if he was using them for another. The example in the *Catnic* case was the difference between what a person would reasonably be taken to mean by using the word "vertical" in a mathematical theorem and by using it in a claimed definition of a lintel for use in the building trade. The only point on which I would question the otherwise admirable summary of the law on infringement in the judgment of Jacob LJ in *Rockwater Ltd v. Technip France SA* (unreported) [2004] EWCA Civ 381, at paragraph 41, is when he says in sub-paragraph (e) that to be "fair to the patentee" one must use "the widest purpose consistent with his teaching". This, as it seems to me, is to confuse the *purpose* of the utterance with what it would be understood to *mean*. The purpose of a patent specification, as I have said, is no more nor less than to communicate the idea of an invention. An appreciation of that purpose is part of the material which one uses to ascertain the meaning. But purpose and meaning are different. If, when speaking of the widest

purpose, Jacob LJ meant the widest meaning, I would respectfully disagree. There is no presumption about the width of the claims. A patent may, for one reason or another, claim less than it teaches or enables.

34. "Purposive construction" does not mean that one is extending or going beyond the definition of the technical matter for which the patentee seeks protection in the claims. The question is always what the person skilled in the art would have understood the patentee to be using the language of the claim to mean. And for this purpose, the language he has chosen is usually of critical importance. The conventions of word meaning and syntax enable us to express our meanings with great accuracy and subtlety and the skilled man will ordinarily assume that the patentee has chosen his language accordingly. As a number of judges have pointed out, the specification is a unilateral document in words of the patentee's own choosing. Furthermore, the words will usually have been chosen upon skilled advice. The specification is not a document *inter rusticos* for which broad allowances must be made. On the other hand, it must be recognised that the patentee is trying to describe something which, at any rate in his opinion, is new; which has not existed before and of which there may be no generally accepted definition. There will be occasions upon which it will be obvious to the skilled man that the patentee must in some respect have departed from conventional use of language or included in his description of the invention some element which he did not mean to be essential. But one would not expect that to happen very often.

35. One of the reasons why it will be unusual for the notional skilled man to conclude, after construing the claim purposively in the context of the specification and drawings, that the patentee must nevertheless have meant something different from what he appears to have meant, is that there are necessarily gaps in our knowledge of the background which led him to express himself in that particular way. The courts of the United Kingdom, the Netherlands and Germany certainly discourage, if they do not actually prohibit, use of the patent office file in aid of construction. There are good reasons: the meaning of the patent should not change according to whether or not the person skilled in the art has access to the file and in any case life is too short for the limited assistance which it can provide. It is however frequently impossible to know without access, not merely to the file but to the private thoughts of the patentee and his advisors as well, what the reason was for some apparently inexplicable limitation in the extent of the monopoly claimed. One possible explanation is that it does not represent what the patentee really meant to say. But another is that he did mean it, for reasons of his own; such as wanting to avoid arguments with the examiners over enablement or prior art and have his patent

granted as soon as possible. This feature of the practical life of a patent agent reduces the scope for a conclusion that the patentee could not have meant what the words appear to be saying. It has been suggested that in the absence of any explanation for a restriction in the extent of protection claimed, it should be presumed that there was some good reason between the patentee and the patent office. I do not think that it is sensible to have presumptions about what people must be taken to have meant but a conclusion that they have departed from conventional usage obviously needs some rational basis.

The doctrine of equivalents

36.   At the time when the rules about natural and ordinary meanings were more or less rigidly applied, the United Kingdom and American courts showed understandable anxiety about applying a construction which allowed someone to avoid infringement by making an "immaterial variation" in the invention as described in the claims. In England, this led to the development of a doctrine of infringement by use of the "pith and marrow" of the invention (a phrase invented by Lord Cairns in *Clark v. Adie* (1877) 2 App Cas 315, 320) as opposed to a "textual infringement". The pith and marrow doctrine was always a bit vague ("necessary to prevent sharp practice" said Lord Reid in *C Van Der Lely NV v. Bamfords Ltd* [1963] RPC 61, 77) and it was unclear whether the courts regarded it as a principle of construction or an extension of protection outside the claims.

37.   In the United States, where a similar principle is called the "doctrine of equivalents", it is frankly acknowledged that it allows the patentee to extend his monopoly beyond the claims. In the leading case of *Graver Tank & Manufacturing Co Inc v. Linde Air Products Company* 339 US 605, 607 (1950), Jackson J said that the American courts had recognised?

> "that to permit imitation of a patented invention which does not copy every literal detail would be to convert the protection of the patent grant into a hollow and useless thing. Such a limitation would leave room for—indeed encourage—the unscrupulous copyist to make unimportant and insubstantial changes and substitutions in the patent which, though adding nothing, would be enough to take the copied matter outside the claim, and hence outside the reach of law."

38.   In similar vein, Learned Hand J (a great patent lawyer) said that the purpose of the doctrine of equivalents was "to temper unsparing logic and prevent an infringer from stealing the benefit of the invention": *Royal Typewriter Co v. Remington Rand Inc* (CA2nd Conn) 168 F2nd 691, 692. The effect of the doctrine is thus to extend protection to something outside the claims which per-

forms substantially the same function in substantially the same way to obtain the same result.

39. However, once the monopoly had been allowed to escape from the terms of the claims, it is not easy to know where its limits should be drawn. In *Warner–Jenkinson Co v. Hilton Davis Chemical Co* 520 US 17, 28–29 (1997) the United States Supreme Court expressed some anxiety that the doctrine of equivalents had "taken on a life of its own, unbounded by the patent claims." It seems to me, however, that once the doctrine is allowed to go beyond the claims, a life of its own is exactly what it is bound to have. The American courts have restricted the scope of the doctrine by what is called prosecution history or file wrapper estoppel, by which equivalence cannot be claimed for integers restricting the monopoly which have been included by amendment during the prosecution of the application in the patent office. The patentee is estopped against the world (who need not have known of or relied upon the amendment) from denying that he intended to surrender that part of the monopoly. File wrapper estoppel means that the true scope of patent protection often cannot be established without an expensive investigation of the patent office file. Furthermore, the difficulties involved in deciding exactly what part of the claim should be taken to have been withdrawn by an amendment drove the Federal Court of Appeals in *Festo Corporation v. Shoketsu Kinzoku Kogyo Kabushiki Co Ltd* 234 F3rd 558 (2000) to declare that the law was arbitrary and unworkable. Lourie J said:

> "The only settled expectation currently existing is the expectation that clever attorneys can argue infringement outside the scope of the claims all the way through this Court of Appeals."

40. In order to restore some certainty, the Court of Appeals laid down a rule that any amendment for reasons of patent validity was an absolute bar to any extension of the monopoly outside the literal meaning of the amended text. But the Supreme Court reversed this retreat to literalism on the ground that the cure was worse than the disease: see *Festo Corporation v. Shoketsu Kinzoku Kogyo Kabushiki Co Ltd* (28 May 2002) US Supreme Court.

41. There is often discussion about whether we have a European doctrine of equivalents and, if not, whether we should. It seems to me that both the doctrine of equivalents in the United States and the pith and marrow doctrine in the United Kingdom were born of despair. The courts felt unable to escape from interpretations which "unsparing logic" appeared to require and which prevented them from according the patentee the full extent of the monopoly which the person skilled in the art would reasonably have thought he was claiming. The background was the tendency to literalism which then characterised the approach of the courts to the interpretation

of documents generally and the fact that patents are likely to attract the skills of lawyers seeking to exploit literalism to find loopholes in the monopoly they create. (Similar skills are devoted to revenue statutes).

42. If literalism stands in the way of construing patent claims so as to give fair protection to the patentee, there are two things that you can do. One is to adhere to literalism in construing the claims and evolve a doctrine which supplements the claims by extending protection to equivalents. That is what the Americans have done. The other is to abandon literalism. That is what the House of Lords did in the *Catnic* case, where Lord Diplock said (at [1982] RPC 183, 242:

> "Both parties to this appeal have tended to treat 'textual infringement' and infringement of the 'pith and marrow' of an invention as if they were separate causes of action, the existence of the former to be determined as a matter of construction only and of the latter upon some broader principle of colourable evasion. There is, in my view, no such dichotomy; there is but a single cause of action and to treat it otherwise ... is liable to lead to confusion."

43. The solution, said Lord Diplock, was to adopt a principle of construction which actually gave effect to what the person skilled in the art would have understood the patentee to be claiming.

44. Since the *Catnic* case we have article 69 which, as it seems to me, firmly shuts the door on any doctrine which extends protection outside the claims. I cannot say that I am sorry because the *Festo* litigation suggests, with all respect to the courts of the United States, that American patent litigants pay dearly for results which are no more just or predictable than could be achieved by simply reading the claims.

Is Catnic consistent with the Protocol?

45. In *Improver Corp v. Remington Consumer Products Ltd* [1989] RPC 69 the Court of Appeal said that Lord Diplock's speech in *Catnic* advocated the same approach to construction as is required by the Protocol. (See also *Southco Inc v. Dzus Fastener Europe Ltd* [1992] RPC 299.) But in *PLG Research Ltd v. Ardon International Ltd* [1995] RPC 287, 309 Millett LJ said:

> "Lord Diplock was expounding the common law approach to the construction of a patent. This has been replaced by the approach laid down by the Protocol. If the two approaches are the same, reference to Lord Diplock's formulation is unnecessary, while if they are different it is dangerous."

46. This echoes, perhaps consciously, the famous justification said to have been given by the Caliph Omar for burning the library of

Alexandria: "If these writings of the Greeks agree with the Book of God, they are useless and need not be preserved: if they disagree, they are pernicious and ought to be destroyed"—a story which Gibbon dismissed as Christian propaganda. But I think that the Protocol can suffer no harm from a little explanation and I entirely agree with the masterly judgment of Aldous J in *Assidoman Multipack Ltd v. The Mead Corporation* [1995] RPC 321, in which he explains why the *Catnic* approach accords with the Protocol.

47. The Protocol, as I have said, is a Protocol for the construction of article 69 and does not expressly lay down any principle for the construction of claims. It does say what principle should *not* be followed, namely the old English literalism, but otherwise it says only that one should not go outside the claims. It does however say that the object is to combine a fair protection for the patentee with a reasonable degree of certainty for third parties. How is this to be achieved? The claims must be construed in a way which attempts, so far as is possible in an imperfect world, not to disappoint the reasonable expectations of either side. What principle of interpretation would give fair protection to the patentee? Surely, a principle which would give him the full extent of the monopoly which the person skilled in the art would think he was intending to claim. And what principle would provide a reasonable degree of protection for third parties? Surely again, a principle which would not give the patentee more than the full extent of the monopoly which the person skilled in the art would think that he was intending to claim. Indeed, any other principle would also be unfair to the patentee, because it would unreasonably expose the patent to claims of invalidity on grounds of anticipation or insufficiency.

48. The *Catnic* principle of construction is therefore in my opinion precisely in accordance with the Protocol. It is intended to give the patentee the full extent, but not more than the full extent, of the monopoly which a reasonable person skilled in the art, reading the claims in context, would think he was intending to claim. Of course it is easy to say this and sometimes more difficult to apply it in practice, although the difficulty should not be exaggerated. The vast majority of patent specifications are perfectly clear about the extent of the monopoly they claim. Disputes over them never come to court. In borderline cases, however, it does happen that an interpretation which strikes one person as fair and reasonable will strike another as unfair to the patentee or unreasonable for third parties. That degree of uncertainty is inherent in any rule which involves the construction of any document. It afflicts the whole of the law of contract, to say nothing of legislation. In principle it is without remedy, although I shall consider in a moment whether uncertainty can be alleviated by guidelines or a "structured" approach to construction.

Equivalents as a guide to construction

49. Although article 69 prevents equivalence from extending protection outside the claims, there is no reason why it cannot be an important part of the background of facts known to the skilled man which would affect what he understood the claims to mean. That is no more than common sense. It is also expressly provided by the new article 2 added to the Protocol by the Munich Act revising the EPC, dated 29 November 2000 (but which has not yet come into force):

> "For the purpose of determining the extent of protection conferred by a European patent, due account shall be taken of any element which is equivalent to an element specified in the claims."

50. In the *Catnic* case [1982] RPC 183, 243 Lord Diplock offered some observations on the relevance of equivalence to the question of construction:

> "The question in each case is: whether persons with practical knowledge and experience of the kind of work in which the invention was intended to be used, would understand that strict compliance with a particular descriptive word or phrase appearing in a claim was intended by the patentee to be an essential requirement of the invention so that *any* variant would fall outside the monopoly claimed, even though it could have no material effect upon the way the invention worked.
>
> The question, of course, does not arise where the variant would in fact have a material effect upon the way the invention worked. Nor does it arise unless at the date of publication of the specification it would be obvious to the informed reader that this was so. Where it is not obvious, in the light of then-existing knowledge, the reader is entitled to assume that the patentee thought at the time of the specification that he had good reason for limiting his monopoly so strictly and had intended to do so, even though subsequent work by him or others in the field of the invention might show the limitation to have been unnecessary. It is to be answered in the negative only when it would be apparent to any reader skilled in the art that a particular descriptive word or phrase used in a claim cannot have been intended by a patentee, who was also skilled in the art, to exclude minor variants which, to the knowledge of both him and the readers to whom the patent was addressed, could have no material effect upon the way in which the invention worked."

51. In *Improver Corporation v. Remington Consumer Products Ltd* [1990] FSR 181, 189 I tried to summarise this guidance:

"If the issue was whether a feature embodied in an alleged infringement which fell outside the primary, literal or a contextual meaning of a descriptive word or phrase in the claim ("a variant") was nevertheless within its language as properly interpreted, the court should ask itself the following three questions:

(1) Does the variant have a material effect upon the way the invention works? If yes, the variant is outside the claim. If no?

(2) Would this (ie that the variant had no material effect) have been obvious at the date of publication of the patent to a reader skilled in the art? If no, the variant is outside the claim. If yes?

(3) Would the reader skilled in the art nevertheless have understood from the language of the claim that the patentee intended that strict compliance with the primary meaning was an essential requirement of the invention? If yes, the variant is outside the claim.

On the other hand, a negative answer to the last question would lead to the conclusion that the patentee was intending the word or phrase to have not a literal but a figurative meaning (the figure being a form of synecdoche or metonymy) denoting a class of things which include the variant and the literal meaning, the latter being perhaps the most perfect, best-known or striking example of the class."

52. These questions, which the Court of Appeal in *Wheatly v. Drillsafe Ltd* [2001] RPC 133, 142 dubbed "the Protocol questions" have been used by English courts for the past fifteen years as a framework for deciding whether equivalents fall within the scope of the claims. On the whole, the judges appear to have been comfortable with the results, although some of the cases have exposed the limitations of the method. When speaking of the "*Catnic* principle" it is important to distinguish between, on the one hand, the principle of purposive construction which I have said gives effect to the requirements of the Protocol, and on the other hand, the guidelines for applying that principle to equivalents, which are encapsulated in the Protocol questions. The former is the bedrock of patent construction, universally applicable. The latter are only guidelines, more useful in some cases than in others. I am bound to say that the cases show a tendency for counsel to treat the Protocol questions as legal rules rather than guides which will in appropriate cases help to decide what the skilled man would have understood the patentee to mean. The limits to the value of the guidelines are perhaps most clearly illustrated by the present case and therefore, instead of discussing the principles in the abstract as I

have been doing so far, I shall make my comments by reference to the facts of the case.

The judge's construction of the claims

53.   It will be recalled that claim 1 is to a DNA sequence, selected from the sequences set out in Table VI or related sequences, for securing the expression of EPO in a "host cell". The chief question of construction is whether the person skilled in the art would understand "host cell" to mean a cell which is host to the DNA sequence which coded for EPO. The alternative, put forward by Amgen, is that it can include a sequence which is endogenous to the cell, like the human EPO gene which expresses GA–EPO, as long as the cell is host to some exogenous DNA. In the TKT process, it is host to the control sequence and other machinery introduced by homologous recombination.

54.   On this question, the judge had the advantage of hearing the evidence of a number of witnesses who were highly skilled in the art. They all said that they would have understood claim 1 to be referring to a DNA sequence coding for EPO which had been isolated or synthesised and was suitable for expression in a host cell. In other words, the claim was to a sequence coding for EPO which was exogenous to the cell in which expression took place. The judge summed up his conclusions in paragraph 215:

> "I am of the view that a cell is not a 'host cell' unless it is host to exogenous DNA encoding for EPO or its analogue. Such a conclusion is based in part on the teaching of the [patent in suit]. The terms 'host' and 'host cell' are used consistently to describe cells which have been transfected with exogenous or foreign DNA (ie DNA from outside that particular cell) which encodes EPO, with a view to securing expression of EPO in those host cells. That was accepted by [Amgen's expert] Dr Brenner. The examples contained in the [patent in suit] are all concerned with EPO-encoding DNA which has been isolated outside the cell and inserted into the cell to which it is foreign. Indeed, at the relevant time, the routine method of production of a recombinant protein was by cloning the gene encoding the protein and the introduction of that clone into a self-replicating organism by transfection or transformation. There was no knowledge of the technique of 'switching on' an endogenous encoding sequence by transfecting the cell with exogenous DNA sequences as including an artificial promoter."

55.   Besides these general considerations, the judge relied upon other indications in the language of the specification. The words "for use in securing expression ... of a polypeptide" suggested the DNA which coded for that polypeptide rather than a control sequence which promoted expression of endogenous DNA. That was

supported by paragraph (b) of claim 1, which extended the claim to sequences which were not in Table VI but which hybridised under stringent conditions to "the protein coding regions" of Table VI.

56.   Furthermore, the specification appears anxious to point out that the invention covers the use of mammalian cells which already have an EPO gene of their own:

> "It will be understood that expression of, eg, monkey origin DNA in monkey host cells in culture and human host cells in culture, actually constitute instances of 'exogenous' DNA expression inasmuch as the EPO DNA whose high level expression is sought would not have its origins in the genome of the host."

57.   That certainly suggests that the patentee regarded it as essential to his invention that the DNA of which high level expression was sought should not have its origin in the genome of the host cell. That would clearly exclude the DNA sequence which expresses GA–EPO, which forms part of the genome of the host cell.

* * *

The decision of the Court of Appeal

76.   I agree with the Court of Appeal on construction for a number of reasons. First, I think that the judge's construction pays no attention to the claims. It does not even use them as "guidelines" but goes straight to Table VI and declares that to be the invention. Secondly, I think that the Court of Appeal was right in saying that Table VI could not have been the invention. Standing alone, it was a "discovery ... as such" within the meaning of section 1(2) of the Act: see *Genentech Inc's Patent* [1989] RPC 147, per Purchas LJ at p 204 and per Dillon LJ at p 237. On the other hand, as Whitford J said in the *Genentech* case ([1987] RPC 553, 566):

> "It is trite law that you cannot patent a discovery, but if on the basis of that discovery you can tell people how it can be usefully employed, then a patentable invention may result. This in my view would be the case, even though once you have made the discovery, the way in which it can be usefully employed is obvious enough."

77.   In such a case, while it may be true to say, as the Court of Appeal did ([2003] RPC 31, 62) that Table VI lay "at the heart of the invention", it was not the invention. An invention is a practical product or process, not information about the natural world. That seems to me to accord with the social contract between the state and the inventor which underlies patent law. The state gives the inventor a monopoly in return for an immediate disclosure of all the information necessary to enable performance of the invention. That disclosure is not only to enable other people to perform the

invention after the patent has expired. If that were all, the inventor might as well be allowed to keep it secret during the life of the patent. It is also to enable anyone to make immediate use of the information for any purpose which does not infringe the claims. The specifications of valid and subsisting patents are an important source of information for further research, as is abundantly shown by a reading of the sources cited in the specification for the patent in suit. Of course a patentee may in some cases be able to frame his claim to a product or process so broadly that in practice it will be impossible to use the information he has disclosed, even to develop important improvements, in a way which does not infringe. But it cannot be right to give him a monopoly of the use of the information as such.

New technology

78.   The effect of the construction for which Amgen contends is that claim 1 should be read as including any DNA sequence, whether exogenous or endogenous, which expresses EPO in consequence of the application to the cell of any form of DNA recombinant technology. It would have been easy to draft such a claim. Whether the specification would have been sufficient to support it, in the sense of enabling expression by any form of DNA recombinant technology, is another matter to which I shall return when I deal with validity. But the person skilled in the art (who must, in my opinion, be assumed to know the basic principles of patentability) might well have thought that the claims were restricted to existing technology because of doubts about sufficiency rather than lack of foresight about possible developments. Amgen would have been well aware in 1983 that recombinant technology was developing rapidly and that artificial homologous recombination had been achieved in bacterial and yeast cells and that its use in mammalian cells was regarded as a desirable goal.

79.   Amgen submit that although homologous recombination was a known phenomenon in 1983, its use to achieve "gene activation" was unknown. The method of manufacture by DNA recombinant technology referred to in the claim was the only one known at the priority date. At the time, it was in practice equivalent to a general claim for manufacture by recombinant DNA technology. It should therefore be construed as such. Amgen say that if the claims cannot be construed in terms sufficiently general to include methods unknown at the priority date, the value of a patent would be destroyed as soon as some new technology for achieving the same result was invented.

80.   I do not dispute that a claim may, upon its proper construction, cover products or processes which involve the use of technology unknown at the time the claim was drafted. The question is

whether the person skilled in the art would understand the description in a way which was sufficiently general to include the new technology. There is no difficulty in principle about construing general terms to include embodiments which were unknown at the time the document was written. One frequently does that in construing legislation, for example, by construing "carriage" in a 19th century statute to include a motor car. In such cases it is particularly important not to be too literal. It may be clear from the language, context and background that the patentee intended to refer in general terms to, for example, every way of achieving a certain result, even though he has used language which is in some respects inappropriate in relation to a new way of achieving that result: compare *Regina (Quintavalle) v. Secretary of State for Health* [2003] 2 AC 687. In the present case, however, I agree with the Court of Appeal (and with the judge, before he came to apply the Protocol questions) that the man skilled in the art would not have understood the claim as sufficiently general to include gene activation. He would have understood it to be limited to the expression of an exogenous DNA sequence which coded for EPO.

85.   For these reasons I would hold that TKT did not infringe any of the claims and dismiss Amgen's appeal.

CUTTING BLADE I (SCHNEIDMESSER I)

Federal Supreme Court of Germany
IIC 2002 873, March 12, 2002

From the Facts:

The plaintiff is the holder of an exclusive license to German patent 3719721 filed on June 12, 1987 (patent at issue), and has lodged an action against the defendant for infringement of patent
. . .

The defendant is the successor in title of E. GmbH. E. supplied appropriate cutting blades to a French undertaking that had purchased a rotation cutting machine from the plaintiff, an action regarded by the plaintiff as an infringement of the patent at issue. The appeal court ordered the defendant as petitioned to cease and desist and render accounts, and held that it was obliged to pay damages and reasonable compensation. The defendants appeal was dismissed. The defendants appeal on the law is directed against this decision.

From the Opinion:

The appeal on the law is admissible, but is dismissed. The appeal court rightly concluded that the contested cutting blades were embraced by the extent of protection of the patent at issue and that the defendant was obliged to cease and desist, pay damages, compensate and render accounts with respect to their manufacture and distribution (Secs. 14, 137(1) and (2), 33(1) Patent Act; Sec. 242 Civil Code).

I. The patent at issue concerns a cutting blade for rotating cutter systems for paper. Such blades, according to the findings of the appeal court, interact with a counter-blade to cut a block out of individual overlapping products. They consist of a round base piece with a cutting edge at right angles to the axis of rotation with a conical bearing surface fitted with a number of blades.

In a cutting blade of this kind known from German disclosure document 3536989, the conical bearing surface faces the cutting level in the form of the front surface of the base piece. If the cutting surfaces of the (non-adjustable) blades located in openings in the bearing surface are worn, they can be sharpened, but this results in a corresponding reduction of the cutting blade diameter.

In conformity with the details in the patent specification at issue, the appeal court worded the technical problem as being to increase the useful life of such cutting blades while simultaneously ensuring that the effective radius of the cutting surfaces can remain unchanged even after any sharpening, and broke down the solution in the invention according to maintained patent claim 1 into features as follows:

1. The invention concerns a cutting blade interacting with a counter-blade for rotation cutting systems for paper, in particular multi-layer individual paper products in block form.

2. The cutting blade is fitted with a round essentially conical base piece.

3. The base piece has a bearing surface with a conical cutting level at right angles to the axis of rotation and bearing blades or the like.

4. The blades

    a) are arranged on the truncated conical rear surface of the base piece and form an angle of 10° to 22°, preferably 16°, with the cutting level,

    b) are located in a variety of cutting positions aligned along the cutting level in longitudinal openings on the base piece, in which they can be adjusted and fixed,

    c) with their longitudinal axis forming an acute angle to the radius of the base piece, the angle being between 9° and 12°,

    d) when seen from above, are rectangular, and

    e) form the cutting surface in a tooth form. . . .

II. Nor has any objection been raised against the appeal courts correct finding that the cutting blade manufactured and sold by E. corresponded literally with patent claim 1 of the patent at issue with the exception of feature 4c). . . .

3. The conclusion of the appeal court can only be partly upheld.

a) Pursuant to Sec. 14 of the Patent Act and the identical provision of Art. 69 (1) of the EPC, the extent of protection of the patent is determined by the terms of the patent claims, with the description and drawings being used to interpret the claims. According to the principles developed by this Court, the interpretation of the patent claims serves not only to remedy any ambiguities but also to explain the technical terms used therein and to clarify the meaning and scope of the invention described (Federal Supreme Court decisions, 98 BGHZ 12, 18 *et seq.* [18 **IIC** 795 (1987)]—*Formstein*; 105 BGHZ 1, 10[22 **IIC** 249 (1991)]—*Ionanalyse*; 125 BGHZ 303, 309 *et seq.* [26 **IIC** 261 (1995)]—*Zerlegvorrichtungfür Baumstämme*). This must be based on the vantage point of the person skilled in the art, whose interpretation determines the definition of the contents of the patent claims including the concepts used, and is also decisive for the determination of the extent going beyond the wording of the protection based on the patent claims. In the examination of the question whether the invention protected by the patent has been used, it is therefore first necessary to use this interpretation to determine the contents of the patent claims, *i.e.*, the meaning attached to the wording of the claim by the person skilled in the art.

If the contested embodiment uses the essential meaning of a patent claim determined in this way, use has been made of the invention under protection. In the case of a realization that departs from the essential meaning of the patent claims, there may be a use if the person skilled in the art could combine considerations based on the essential meaning of the invention protected in the claims with his specialist knowledge in order to find the modified means used in the contested embodiment as having the same effect for the solution of the problem underlying the invention [citations omitted]. In this process, the requirement of legal certainty, which enjoys the same importance as the reasonable protection of the inventive achievement, requires that the semantic content of the patent claims to be determined by interpretation forms not only the starting point but also the decisive basis for the determination of the extent of protection; this determination must be based on the patent claims [citations omitted]. Thus, if an embodiment departing from the essential meaning of the patent claim is to be included within the extent of protection, it is not sufficient that (1.) it solves the problem underlying the invention with modified but objectively equivalent means and (2.) that the person skilled in the art is able to use his specialist knowledge to identify the modified means as having the same effect. Just as the same effect cannot be found without focusing on the patent claim, (3.) the considerations that the person skilled in the art must apply must in addition be focused on the essential meaning of the technical teaching protected in the patent claim in such a way that the person skilled in the art regards the different embodiment with its modified means as being equivalent to the solution in question.

There is no occasion to depart from these principles. They agree with the Protocol on the Interpretation of Art. 69 (1) of the EPC [citation omitted], which according to the established case law of this Court [citations omitted] is also to be used to interpret Sec. 14 of the Patent Act. According to Art. 2, No. 1, of the Munich Amendment Act to the European Patent Convention dated November 29, 2002, Art. 2 of the Revised Protocol on Interpretation expressly lays down for the future that, for the purpose of determining the extent of protection of the European patent, due account shall be taken of such elements that are equivalent to the elements specified in the patent claims.

b) The principles for the determination of the extent of protection are also to be applied if the patent claim contains figures or measurements. Such details participate in the binding nature of the patent claim as the decisive basis for the determination of the extent of protection. The inclusion of figures or measurements in the claim makes it clear that they are intended to participate in and hence also limit the determination of the subject matter of the patent [citations omitted]. Consequently, such details must not be regarded as less binding, merely exemplary statements of the protected technical teaching, as was held to be possible in the case law concerning the legal situation in Germany before entry into effect of Art. 69 of the EPC and the corresponding amendment of national law [citations omitted].

c) Like any element of a patent claim, figures and dimensions are fundamentally capable of interpretation. As elsewhere, the decisive factor is how the person skilled in the art understands such details in the overall context of the patent claim, with the description and drawings also being

used here to elucidate this context. Account must be taken
of the fact that figures and measurements, if only because
of their objective substance, a factor that also contributes
to the interpretation by the person skilled in the art, are
not uniform but can, in a variety of forms, designate
constellations of facts with entirely different contents.

d) These facts alone prevent the person skilled in the art
always attaching a constant fixed meaning to details of
figures, measurements or ranges. However, such details
will as a rule be ascribed a greater clarity and freedom
from ambiguity than would be the case for a verbal description of the element of the teaching in the invention.
For figures are as such unambiguous, while linguistic
formulations of general terms constitute a certain degree
of abstraction from the object designated by them. In
addition, such terms, if used in a patent specification, need
not necessarily be used in the meaning attached to them
by general technical linguistic use, and in this way the
patent specification can form its own dictionary'' [citations
omitted]. From the point of view of the specialist reader,
concretized features can, through the details of figures and
measurements, be made to mean that the objective
achievement to be reached by the invention is to be defined more narrowly and where appropriate more closely
than would be the case for a mere verbal definition. Since
it is the applicants responsibility to ensure that everything
for which he requests protection is set out in the patent
claims [citations omitted], the reader of the patent specification is entitled to assume that this requirement has also
been satisfied through the inclusion of figures in the
wording of the patent claims. This is all the more the case
since the applicant, when specifying the figures, has a
particular reason to identify the effect of the wording of
the claim on the limits of the patent protection requested.

Accordingly, a considerably stricter assessment is appropriate than was the practice under the legal situation in
Germany before 1978 [citation omitted]. An unambiguous
specification of figures fundamentally determines and limits the subject matter of protection exhaustively; figures
above the maximum or below the minimum are as a rule
not to be ascribed to the subject matter of patent protection.

On the other hand, this does not prevent the person
skilled in the art regarding certain vagueness, for instance
comprising the usual tolerances, as being compatible with
the essential technical meaning of figures. Thus the House

of Lords in the *Catnic* decision (1982 R.P.C. 163 [12 **IIC** 699 (1981)]), which, however, concerned the legal situation in the United Kingdom before European harmonization, held that where a feature concerned a right angle, deviations of 6° and 8° from the right angle were compatible with an assumption of the use of the protected teaching. In such a case, the decisive factor cannot as a matter of principle be whether the claim refers to a right angle or of 90°. The decisive factor is, on the contrary, the essential meaning of the patent claim, which is to be determined with the assistance of the description and the drawings. In a different context, the same angle can be regarded by the person skilled in the art as a figure to be complied with exactly. This also applies as a matter of principle to ranges of figures with limit values. An interpretation that a value must be complied with exactly will above all correspond with the notions of the person skilled in the art if he realizes that this is a "critical" value. Accordingly, the construction of specific figures or measurements in the patent claim is a question of the experts understanding in the individual case, and a matter to be assessed by the trial judge.

d) As with the determination of the essential technical meaning of a patent claim, it is also the case for the determination of an extent of protection going beyond such meaning that figures or measurements contained in the claim limit the protected object to the values given. In the course of the determination of the extent of protection, an abstraction must not be made from the essential meaning of the figures and dimensions. For the question whether the person skilled in the art can identify an embodiment with figures deviating from those in the claim as being an equivalent solution as a result of considerations based on the essential meaning of the invention described in the claim must, on the contrary, be examined in the light of the restriction imposed by the figures on the objective achievement to be obtained according to the invention. The same effect as the content of the patent claim can only be ascribed to such embodiments that can be identified by the person skilled in the art as achieving not merely the effect of a feature—limited by the figures in the claim—of the invention but also precisely the effect that the numeric restriction of this feature is intended to achieve according to the claim and according to the understanding of the person skilled in the art. If this condition is not satisfied, an embodiment that is otherwise of the same technical effect objectively and identifiably for the person skilled in the art is fundamentally not embraced by the extent of protection of the patent.

Fundamentally in accordance with the aforesaid, the courts in the United Kingdom also, in infringements cases, examine whether the specialist public may expect and rely on the decisive factor being precise compliance with the wording of the patent claim according to the patent (*cf.* the so-called third *Catnic* question; on the harmonized law of the Patents Court, 1989 F.S.R. 181, 1993 GRUR Int. 245 [21 **IIC** 860 (1990)]—*Improver Corporation v. Remington Consumer Products Ltd.* (*Epilady* case); Court of Appeal, 1995 R.P.C. 585, 1997 GRUR Int. 374 [28 **IIC** 114 (1997)]—*Kastner v. Rizla Ltd.*). Applied to an individual feature of the patent claim, the decisive factor is whether the feature in question appears to the person skilled in the art as a feature that can only be used literally if the claimed teaching for technical action is to be complied with. Such an interpretation may in particular be applicable to figures and measurements [citations omitted].

As with other elements of the patent claim, the effect according to the claim may not be determined without consideration of the figures and dimensions contained in the claim. Consequently, it is not as a matter of principle sufficient for the inclusion of different embodiments within the scope of protection that, according to the interpretation of the person skilled in the art, the effect according to the invention also occurs independently of compliance with the figures. If the person skilled in the art does not identify different figures as being equivalent to the figures according to the claim, the extent of protection does not extend beyond the essential meaning of the patent claim in this aspect. The effect according to the claim of a feature determined numerically is in such event determined, according to the interpretation of the person skilled in the art, by (precise) compliance with a figure, and can therefore necessarily not be achieved by a different figure. In such a case, it is not sufficient for the person skilled in the art to recognize a teaching abstracted from the figures as being technically reasonable.

The applicant will not always recognize and exhaust the full technical contents of the invention; nor is he—irrespective of the question whether it is legally possible for him—obliged by the law to do such. If, considered objectively, the patent is restricted to a narrower wording of the claim than would be appropriate according to the technical content of the invention and as compared with the state of the art, experts can rely on the fact that protection is restricted accordingly. The patentee is then prevented from claiming protection subsequently for something that he has not protected. This applies even if the person skilled in the art realizes that the effect according to the invention as such (in the narrower sense set out above) could be achieved beyond the range protected in the patent claim.

4. The appeal court took into account all the relevant aspects and, in a manner that cannot be contested on appeal on the law, found that at the time of priority the person skilled in the art regarded the lower value of the angle range of 9° to 12° as not being a rigid limit, and could identify embodiments where the angle marginally falls below that of 9° as being of the same effect. The reasoning of the appeal court on the effect of the slight bending of the blades to the relevant radius, as protected in the patent at issue, which led to a different cutting geometry as compared with the state of the art, shows that the essential technical meaning, as identified by the person skilled in the art, of the acute angle defined more closely by the range 9° to 12° to the relevant radius of the base piece, is to be found in this cutting geometry determined by the angle and expressed in the claim through the specification of the angle. However, the appeal court could also rightly come to the conclusion that the person skilled in the art, applying considerations focusing on the essential meaning of the patent claim including the angle specified in feature 4c), could identify the slightly smaller angle, objectively and undisputedly of the same effect, of the contested embodiment as being of the same effect in such a way that he considered the contested embodiment as being the equivalent solution to the problem underlying the patent at issue.

5. The argument in the appeal on the law that, by referring to the general tolerance, the appeal court contradicted its own assumption that in the interpretation of the person skilled in the art production tolerances had already been taken into account in the specification of the range 9° to 12° is unfounded. It is clear that this assumption was merely intended to state that the essential technical meaning of the angle range 9° to 12° should not, in the interpretation of the person skilled in the art, be further extended to 8° 40 to 12° 20 by a tolerance range. This does not exclude the examination of the question whether the contested embodiment could be identified by the person skilled in the art as being of the same effect taking into

account the extent of the deviation from the wording of the claim within the limits of usual tolerance.

6. Nor can the further objection be upheld that the patent at issue was limited in the opposition appeal proceedings by the inclusion of the angle range 9° to 12°, thereby excluding a further extension of protection beyond these limits.

On this point the appeal court held that the restriction did not deny the patent at issue the extent of protection that it would have had if it had been filed (and granted) in the now applicable version. This is correct, and the appeal court also did not thereby ignore, as contended in the appeal on the law, the fact that the patent at issue was "doubly" restricted, namely first by the inclusion of the feature of the acute angle from granted claim 6 and then by the specified angle range from granted claim 7. It is true that this prevents every acute angle being regarded as equivalent, but does not prevent the assumption that the person skilled in the art would identify an angle slightly below 9° as being of no detriment to the effect of the invention.

Notes & Questions

1. Both the House of Lords and the German Supreme Court emphasized that the ability of an ordinary person skilled in the art of the invention to understand the meaning of claim terms in light of the specifications and drawings. Did the German Supreme Court already take account of equivalents when it interpreted the numerical range limit from the perspective of an ordinarily skilled person?

2. Would Lord Hofmann's conception of purposive claim construction (without any equivalent) protect an invention that is infringed upon by after-arising technologies? Consider how Lord Hoffmann would have handled the infringement issue before him if the alleged infringer had inserted a human erythropoietin gene into a protein machine that produced proteins corresponding to the inserted gene. Assume that this protein-making machine was invented around 1995, and is itself the subject of many patents. Would Lord Hoffmann have decided that the protein machine included a "host cell?"

ASIA

The patent law in Asian countries often has a provision similar to EPC Article 69. For example, Japanese law provides:

Article 70

Technical Scope of Patented Invention

(1) the technical scope of a patented invention must be determined by the description of claims which are accompanied with an application.

(2) In conducting the determination set forth in the preceding paragraph, the meaning of the terms in claims must be interpreted in light of the description in the specification and drawings that are accompanied with an application.

Article 70 does not mention equivalents with respect to claims. Nevertheless, Japanese courts may apply the doctrine of equivalents to find infringement even if they have already found no literal infringement.

TSUBAKIMOTO SEIKO CO. LTD. v. THK K.K.

Supreme Court of Japan

1998 CASRIP Newsletter Issue 1, February 24, 1998

Holding of This Court

The Tokyo High Court Judgment must be reversed. This case must be remanded to the Tokyo High Court.

Reasons

Concerning the reasons of this *joukoku* appeal advanced from the representative of *Joukoku* Appellant, Mr. Youhei Kinoshita:

I. This case relates to the appellant's alleged infringement of the appellee's patent and the appellee's request for compensatory damages. The facts found by the Tokyo High Court are as follows:

1. The appellee owns a patent right for the invention entitled "a ball spline bearing for infinite sliding" (the filing date: April 26, 1971; the publication date for opposition: July 7, 1978; and the issuance date: May 3, 1980) (Patent No. 999,139) (hereunder, the said patent right is called "this patent right" and the invention of this patent right is called "this invention").

2. The claim of the specification included in the patent application (hereinafter, it is called "this specification") reads as follows:

A ball spline bearing for infinite sliding, provided by assembling an outer tube with a holder wherein:

(A) said outer tube (to be addressed as "the element A" hereinafter) is provided on the inner wall thereof with torque transfer loaded ball guide grooves having a U-shape cross section and torque transfer unloaded ball guide grooves; said loaded ball guide grooves and said unloaded ball guide grooves being alternatively provided in the axial direction; said outer tube further provided on the both ends thereof with grooves having the same depth as the deeper grooves extending in the periphery direction;

(B) said holder (to be addressed as "the element B" hereinafter) includes thick wall portions and thin wall portions; said thick wall portions and thin wall portions being so structured as to correspond with said loaded ball guide grooves and said unloaded ball guide grooves that are alternatively provided in the axial direction on the inner wall of s aid outer tube; a through hole provided on the separating wall between said thick and thin wall portions; and an infinite orbit groove for providing a smooth ball transfer to unloaded ball guide grooves provided on said thick wall portions;

(C) said bearing is further comprised of a spline shaft (to be addressed as "the element C" herein after) provided with plural protruding portions in the axial direction thereof, and

(D) said plural protrusions being structured to correspond to the plurality of space defined by said holder and balls provided in said outer tube (to be addressed as "the element D" hereinafter).

3.   The appellee commercially manufactured and sold the accused device (please note that a step of 50 micron exists between the unload ball guide grooves and the tube portion, i.e. the portion in the peripheral direction 7) specified in the appendix to the judgment of the Tokyo High Court during the period of January 1983 to October 1988.

II.   The appellee alleged that the accused device falls within the technical scope of this invention because the appellant's device had infringed this invention literally or under the doctrine of equivalents. The Tokyo High Court determined the following and awarded the appellee damages for patent infringement.

1.   The elements C, D, and E of this invention read on the appellant's device.

2.   Regarding the element A, the claim recites "U-shaped cross section" and "grooves provided in the axial direction." In contrast, the structures corresponding to these limitations in the appellant's device are "half-circle cross-section" and "the peripherally extending steps 7".

3.   Regarding the element B, the holder of this invention is structured in one piece, providing functions to balls for infinite sliding guide, maintaining balls in the bearing

when the spline shaft is removed, and providing space for receiving the protruding portions on the shaft. In contrast, in the appellant's device, three discrete members, including the upper part of the protruding portions in the loaded ball guide grooves provided on the outer tube, plate members 11 and a pair of return caps 31, cooperate together to provide the functions of the holder of this invention as discussed above. Thus, with respect to these features, this invention and the appellant's device are different.

4. However, the object to be solved by the invention, the fundamental technical idea to solve the object, and the effect resulting from the adoption of structures to solve the object are common to this invention and the appellant's device. Regarding the structure of the holder recited as the element B, the court found that the structure adopted by the appellant was interchangeable with the structure of this invention, and that one skilled in the art would have known the interchangeability as of the application date of this patent. Regarding the element A, there is no technically substantial difference between "U-shaped cross-section" and "grooves provided in the axial direction" of this invention and "half-circle cross-section" and "the peripherally extending steps 7" in the appellant's device. Therefore, it is proper to determine that the appellant's device is within the technical scope of this invention.

III. However, we cannot affirm the judgment of the Tokyo High Court for the following reasons:

1. In determining whether a product or process adopted by an accused infringer (to be addressed as "an accused product" hereinafter) falls within the technical scope of a patented invention, courts must ascertain the technical scope of the patented invention in light of the description in the specification accompanying an application (Patent Law, Article 70, Paragraph 1). If there is any claimed element which is different from the corresponding structure of the accused product, the accused product does not fall within the technical scope of the patented invention. However, even if some claimed elements are different from the corresponding structures of the accused product, the accused product may fall within the technical scope of the patented invention for having equivalents to the structures recited in the claim if the following conditions are met: (1) the elements are not an essential portion of the patented invention; (2) the objective of the patented invention can be attained even if the elements are replaced with the structures in the accused product, and thus the accused

product results in the identical functions and effects as the patented invention; (3) a person with ordinary skill in the field of the patented invention (the person will be addressed as "one skilled hereinafter) would have readily conceived the interchangeability between the claimed portion and the replaced structures in the accused product as of the time of exploitation, such as the manufacturing of the accused product by the accused infringer; (4) the accused product is novel and would not have been able to be conceived by one skilled as of the application time of the patented invention; and (5) the accused product was not intentionally removed from the technical scope of the claim by the applicant during the patent prosecution. This is because (1) it is very difficult to describe claims to cover all possible infringing embodiments of the patented invention. If a competitor can escape from patent enforcement, including injunction, etc., by simply replacing some claimed elements with materials, technical means, etc. that are developed after the patent application, incentive for innovation is significantly reduced, which conflicts with the goal of the patent system to contribute to industrial developments through the protection and encouragement of inventions. Further, such an interpretation of law to allow competitors to escape from the charge of infringement would be unfair to the sense of justice in the society and conflict with the concept of fairness. (2) In considering these points, the substantial value of a patented invention extends to a structure which would have been readily conceived by a third party from the structure recited in the claim as being substantially identical to a patented invention. It is proper to assume that a third party must anticipate such an extension of the patent protection. (3) On the other hand, the technical scope of a patent cannot extend to an accused product which is part of the state of the art as of the application time of the patented invention, or would have been readily conceived by one skilled from the state of art, because no one could have obtained a patent on such accused product (Patent Law, Article 29). (4) Additionally, under the rule of estoppel, a patentee is prevented, during the patent prosecution, from claiming a patent right on an accused product which was intentionally removed by an applicant from the claim scope where the applicant admitted that the accused product did not fall within the technical scope of the patented invention or the applicant's behavior indicated such removal of the accused product from the claim scope.

2. Applying the aforementioned rules to this case, the Tokyo High Court found that some limitations of the claimed elements A and B were different from the corresponding structures in the appellant's device, but concluded that the appellant's device fell within the technical scope of this invention because the claimed elements and the structures adopted by the appellant were interchangeable and the interchangeability was known to one skilled. However, the Tokyo High Court found the following facts: (1) A ball spline bearing consisting of an outer tube, spline shaft and an holder was publicly known prior to the application time of this invention. "Said bearing is further comprised of a spline shaft (to be addressed as "the element C" hereunder) provided with plural protruded portions in the axial direction thereof; and said plural protrusions being structured to correspond to the plurality of space defined by said holder and balls provided in said outer tube" is a conventional structure to provide a shaft for a ball spline bearing; (2) (i) The holder of this invention is structured in one piece to provide functions for infinite sliding guide of the balls, to maintain balls in the bearing when the spline shaft is removed, and to provide space for receiving the protruding portions on the shaft (the element B). In contrast, the holder of the appellant's device consists of three discrete members, including the protruding portions in the loaded ball guide grooves provided on the outer tube 25, 27 and 29, plate members 11 and a pair of return caps 31, and these members cooperate together to provide the functions discussed above. (ii)The holder consisting of discrete members in the appellant's device which includes the three plate members 11 and a pair of return caps 31 is discussed in a ball spline bearing for infinite sliding disclosed in the specification of U.S. Patent No. 3,360,308, which was a publication distributed prior to the application time of this invention. (iii) To maintain balls by a holder consisting of discrete members, it is necessary to provide protrusions in the loaded ball guide grooves provided on the outer tube. Such protrusions, however, are discussed in the ball bearing disclosed in the U.S. Patent No. 3,398,999, which was a publication distributed prior to the application time of this invention. Based on the above facts, the appellant's holder which consists of discrete members and has the protrusions in the loaded ball guide grooves provided in the outer tube was disclosed in a ball spline bearing, which was published prior to the application time of this invention

In addition, the Tokyo High Court found that the appellant's device was identical to this invention in that unloaded balls slid in the axial direction and an angular contact structure of a plurality of lines was adopted so that the space of the spline shaft was structured to sandwich balls in the torque transfer loaded ball guide grooves. The court, however, recognized that unloaded balls for sliding in the axial direction and an angular contact of a plurality of lines were disclosed in detail in Japanese Patent Publication Shouwa 44–2361, German Patent No. 1,450,060, and U.S. Patent No. 3,494,148, which had been distributed prior to the application time of this invention. Based on these findings, it seems that adopting these features in a ball spline bearing was publicly known prior to the application time of this invention.

Accordingly, assuming that the technical idea for a ball spline bearing which included unloaded balls for sliding in the axial direction and an angular contact structure of a plurality of lines were published before the application time of this invention, because the Tokyo High Court found that the difference in the structure of having the balls contact with the wall resulted in no substantial difference in the structure of the holder, the appellant's device was simply a combination of a ball spline bearing provided with publicly known structures of unloaded balls for sliding in the axial direction and an angular contact structure having plural lines and a holder of discrete members. If one skilled would have readily conceived the combination, the appellant's device would have been conceived by one skilled from the state of the art prior to the application date of this invention. This means that it is improper to find equivalents between the structure recited in the claim included in the specification and the appellant's product. Therefore, the technical scope of this invention should not be understood to include the appellant's device.

In this case, as discussed earlier, some elements recited in the claim are different from the corresponding structures in the appellant's device. The Tokyo High Court focused its analysis mainly on the questions of whether the claimed elements and the corresponding structures were interchangeable and whether one skilled would have readily conceived the interchangeability but did not examine the relationship between the appellant's device and the state of the art as of the application time of this invention, which resulted in a conclusion that the appellant's device was equivalent to the structure recited in the claim and thus fell within the technical scope of this invention. Therefore, without reaching the question whether the Tokyo High Court properly found equivalency between the claimed elements and the structures in the appellant's device with respect to the interchangeability and the readiness of conceiving the inter-changeability, it is clear that the court improperly interpreted and applied the patent statute.

IV. As discussed above, the Tokyo High Court erroneously interpreted and applied the patent statute, which resulted in an unlawful judgment because it was based on an improper finding of facts and provided inappropriate reasons. These errors clearly affected the conclusion of the judgment of the Tokyo High Court.

Appellant's reasons for this appeal are lawful as pointed out in the discussions above. Therefore, the judgment of the Tokyo High Court must be reversed. This case must be remanded to the Tokyo High Court for further examination of the points discussed above. In conclusion, all judges unanimously agreed to the disposition of this case as indicated above

Notes & Questions

1. Although the Supreme Court of Japan has endorsed the application of the doctrine of equivalents to find infringement, Japanese courts are very reluctant to apply the doctrine. The first requirement of a non-essential element is most frequently cited to reject the application of the doctrine of equivalents. It is widely believed that the House of Lords in Catnic adopted purposive construction to avoid the necessity of determining whether an element was essential. Why do you think the Japanese Supreme Court adopted this requirement in 1998?

2. Unlike many European countries, Japanese courts apply prosecution history estoppel extensively. In many cases, Japanese courts have found a failure to meet the first requirement when they apply the fourth requirement of disclaimer. Is an amended claim element by definition an essential element? If so, did the Japanese Supreme Court adopt the absolute bar rule adopted by the Federal Circuit in *Festo*? Makoto Endo, *Comparative Study on Prosecution History Estoppel in the U.S. and Japan: What Can Japan Learn From the Chaos in Warner–Jenkinson and Festo?* 2002 CASRIP Newsletter Issues 3 (2002).

3. Is the third requirement comparable to the inventive step test? The German Federal Court also uses a similar test focusing on the capability of a skilled person to identify the substituted element which produces the same effect as that of the claim element. In determining the

scope of surrender by amendment, the Federal Circuit also suggested that there is a strong argument that an equivalent cannot be both non-obvious and insubstantial. Some scholars propose applying the inventive step or nonobviousness test to determine the insubstantial difference for finding equivalents. Toshiko Takenaka, Interpreting Patent Claims: The United States, Germany and Japan (1995).

C. INDIRECT INFRINGEMENT

Many European countries adopted provisions in the Community Patent Convention with respect to indirect infringement, even though the Convention was never ratified or came into force.

Article 26

Prohibition of Indirect Use of the Invention

> 1. A Community patent shall also confer on its proprietor the right to prevent all third parties not having his consent from supplying or offering to supply within the territories of the Contracting States a person, other than a party entitled to exploit the patented invention, with means, relating to an essential element of that invention, for putting it into effect therein, when the third party knows, or it is obvious in the circumstances, that these means are suitable and intended for putting that invention into effect.
>
> > 1. Paragraph 1 shall not apply to when the means are staple commercial products, except when the third party induces the person supplied to commit acts prohibited by Art 25 (Direct Infringement).
> >
> > 2. Persons performing the acts referred to in Art 27(a) to (c) shall not be considered to be parties entitled to exploit the invention within the meaning of paragraph 1.

It is unclear from the language of Article 26 what constitutes an essential element. In the following case, the German Federal Court very broadly interpreted the essential element.

IMPELLER FLOW METER (FLÜGELRADZÄHLER)

Federal Supreme Court of Germany
[2005] IIC 963, May 4, 2004

Facts:

The plaintiff has filed an action against the defendant for an injunction, rendering of accounts and a finding of damages on the basis of a license contract with the patent holder deriving from European Patent 388736 issued with effect for the Federal Republic of Germany (plaintiff's patent). . . .

The plaintiff markets impeller flow meters and housings for impeller flow meters, in part intended for concealed installation, in part intended for surface installation, with an interior thread dimension that only it uses. The defendant markets measuring capsules under the name "N." that can be screwed into the plaintiff's housings and undisputedly have in fact been screwed into the plaintiff's concealed housings.

The plaintiff regards the marketing of the measuring capsules as an indirect infringement of its patent. The district court dismissed its action; the appeal was dismissed.

In its admitted appeal on the law, the plaintiff pursues its petitions. The defendant contests the appeal.

Findings:

The admissible appeal is upheld and the case is returned to the appeal court for rehearing.

I.   The patent at issue concerns an impeller flow meter with which the through-put quantity of liquids can be recorded and which can in particular be used to meter water consumption. The impeller flow meter has a housing with an inlet and an outlet and surrounds a measuring cup in which there is an impeller connected to a meter. The measuring cup, impeller and meter form a single unit that can be removed from the housing. This unit can accordingly be replaced separately and calibrated if necessary, while the housing with the connections for the liquids to be measured remains in place, for instance in the wall.

The plaintiff's patent specification explains that it is regarded as desirable to be able to use the same meter for pipes installed at different depths in the wall. The bridging of considerable depths of installation using a T-shaped insert separating an inlet and outlet was known, and involved cutting to the desired length, in advance or on site, a connecting pipe in which the insert and hence the inlet and outlet channels are laid side by side. However, this solution was both comparatively complex and did not permit the tangential-radial activation of the impeller, which was desirable in certain applications, and led to the impeller being unevenly driven.

A further disadvantage of the known impeller flow meters, according to the plaintiff's patent specification, was the deposit of lime and other contamination that affected not only the hydrodynamic conditions but above all rendered the replacement of the measuring unit difficult, since it tended to stick tight at the joint between the insert and the measuring unit.

The plaintiff's patent specification qualifies the function of the invention as creating an inexpensive hydrodynamically improved impeller flow meter whose design is less susceptible to caking and is nevertheless suitable for high through-flow rates even with water pipes installed at a medium depth. Accordingly, the appeal court regarded the technical problem underlying the invention as being the improvement of the hydrodynamics of the water intake in the sense that the activation of the impeller should be as even and turbulence-free as possible, the risk of the measuring unit caking should be reduced, and the design of the housing should be suitable for water pipes installed at medium depth and be less expensive than the depth compensation implemented in the state of the art. This is not contested in the appeal on the law or by the respondent, nor does it disclose any error at law.

The invention's solution to this technical problem consists in the following combination of features:

1. The impeller flow meter has a housing

    1.1 with an inlet and an outlet, and

    1.2 in which there is an insert.

2. A (measuring) unit is provided which:

    2.1 has a measuring cup surrounded by the housing,

    2.2 an impeller located in the measuring cup, and

    2.3 a meter connected t the impeller.

3. The (measuring) cup unit can be removed from the housing.

4. The housing has a flow surface that

    4.1 connects at the inlet

    4.2 is at an angle, and

    4.3 points towards the measuring cup.

5. The measuring cup supports itself sealingly against the insert.

The drawing reproduced below (Exhibit K 14) shows such a measuring capsule inserted in the plaintiff's housing.

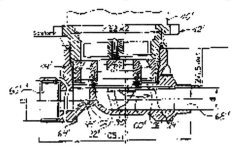

Fig. 5 of the plaintiff's patent specification reproduced below shows a partially exploded cross-section of an impeller flow meter according to the invention when assembled.

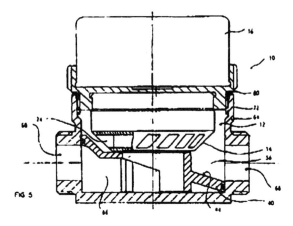

II. Since the contested measuring capsules that the defendant puts into circulation only constitute the measuring unit within the sense of feature 2, there is no direct infringement of the plaintiff's patent, as the plaintiff acknowledges. However, the plaintiff successfully contests the assumption by the appeal court that the defendant had not committed an indirect infringement within the meaning of the prohibition resulting from Sec. 10 of the Patent Act against supplying or offering to supply within the territory to which the Patent Act applies a person other than a person entitled to exploit the invention with means relating to an essential element of such invention for putting it into effect therein, when the supplier knows that these means are suitable and intended for putting that invention into effect.

* * *

2. The question left undecided by the appeal court is to be answered to the benefit of the plaintiff on the basis of the findings adopted by the appeal court; the defendant's measuring capsules constitute means relating to an essential element of the invention. . . .

a) The concept of an indirect patent infringement was developed by case law and was encoded for the first time in Sec. 10 of the Patent Act. Since this provision is based on the corresponding provision in the Community Patent Convention (Art. 30 of the 1975 Community Patent Convention = Art. 26 of the 1989 Community Patent Convention), the case law on the old German patent law cannot be used automatically to interpret this provision. In particular, the criterion of the adaptation of the means supplied to the inventive concept ("functional individualisation for the invention") that is decisive for the scope of the prohibition of the indirect patent infringement as developed by the courts has not been included in the Act [citation omitted].

Before it was regulated by statute, the indirect patent infringement was regarded as a particular form of participation in a patent infringement by another, which accordingly required a direct patent infringement as the "main offence" (**see e.g.** decision of the Federal Supreme Court, X ZR 70/80—**Rigg** [13 IIC 645 (1982)]. In contrast, the independent tort of Sec. 10(1) of the Patent Act does not require a direct infringement of the patent by the purchaser supplied with a means relating to an essential element of the invention [citation omitted]. Notwithstanding the aforesaid, Sec. 10 of the Patent Act does not extend the subject matter of the property right—as defined by the patent claim—(decision of the Federal Supreme Court, X ZR 37/90—**Heatable Breathing Air Hose** [24 IIC 259 (1993)], the use of which is exclusively reserved to the patent holder, but is intended to protect the patent holder in advance of a threatening infringement against the interference in this protected object. The tort of Sec. 10(1) of the Patent Act can for this reason also be referred to as the tort of patent endangerment [citations omitted]. The focus of its protection becomes particularly apparent in the light of the fact that Sec. 10(1) of the Act does not contain an absolute prohibition on the supply of the means relating to an essential element of the invention, but only applies if the means are not only suitable for putting the invention into effect but are also intended for this purpose. For the same reason, the means must be supplied for the purpose of the exploitation of the invention within the territory to which the Patent Act applies; only then is it capable of jeopardising the patent holder's right of prohibition derived from Sec. 9 of the Patent Act.

b) Against the background of this statutory purpose, the feature of "means relating to an essential element of the invention" restricts the preliminary prohibition to the delivery of such means that, by virtue of their effect, are capable of resulting in an interference in the subject matter of protection. It is (only) to this extent that there is functional agreement with the "individualised means for the function of the invention" of the previous case law.

The Act does not implement this restriction in the adaptation of the means itself, but rather in its relationship to the invention. This is shown in particular by Sec. 10(2) of the Patent Act, according to which means that are staple commercial products and hence not typically adapted to the invention can be means within the meaning of subsection (1). Section 10(2) of the Act does not simply exclude such means from the prohibition in subsection (1), but merely tightens the requirements of the subjective element, since the prohibition on staple commercial products only applies if the third party deliberately induces the purchaser to commit acts prohibited according to the second sentence of Sec. 9 of the Act. Means relate to an essential element of the invention if they are capable of interacting functionally with such an element in the implementation of the protected inventive concept. It is this capacity that leads to the particular risk, independent of the form of the means themselves, that the supply of the means will contribute to and encourage an interference in the subject matter of the patent protection. The privilege of Sec. 10(2) of the Patent Act, in this context, can be explained by the consideration that the supplier of objects that are traded generally and independently of a particular use cannot be expected to monitor the intentions of his purchasers even if in the individual case the intention to use them according to the invention is obvious. . . .

c) The criterion of the suitability of the means to interact functionally with an essential element of the invention in the implementation of the protected inventive idea excludes such means that—such as the energy needed for the operation of a protected device—might be suitable for being used in the exploitation of the invention but which contribute nothing to the implementation of the technical teaching of the invention. If a means makes such a contribution, it will, on the other hand, generally not depend on the feature or features of the patent claim that interact with the means. For, what is an element of the patent claim is, as a rule for this reason alone, also an essential element of the invention. The patent claim defines the protected invention and limits the protection granted to the patent holder to forms of exploitation that implement all the features of the invention. As a mirror image of each individual feature's function to limit protection in this way, each individual feature is fundamentally also an appropriate point of reference for the prohibition on the supply of means within the meaning of Sec. 10 of the

Patent Act. In particular, it is not possible to determine the essential elements of an invention according to whether they distinguish the subject matter of the patent claim from the state of the art. It is not infrequently the case that all the features of a patent claim as such are known in the state of the art. For this reason, this does not provide a suitable criterion for differentiation.

d) In the case at issue, the defendant's measuring capsules constitute means relating to an essential element of the invention according to the plaintiff's patent. They are designed in accordance with feature 2, and are suitable and intended for interacting with the housings supplied by the plaintiff, which, as must be assumed in the appeal on the law, implement features 1 and 4; they are mounted on these housings in accordance with feature 3, and supported by the latter in accordance with feature 5. It is only the combination of housing and measuring device that results in the protected impeller flow meters.

3.   The appeal court held that there had not been an indirect patent infringement. The plaintiff rightly objects that this is an error at law. . . .

a) There is no need to determine whether the putting into circulation of the plaintiff's concealed housings exhausts the plaintiff's right of prohibition with respect to these housings pursuant to Sec. 10 of the Patent Act. For, as the respondent concedes, this does not exhaust the plaintiff's exclusive right to the subject matter of its patent, allowing the plaintiff to prohibit any third party from making or putting on the market the impeller flow meters according to the invention without its consent (Sec. 9, second sentence, No. 1 of the Patent Act). If the combination of the (plaintiff's) housing and the (defendant's) measuring capsule create the protected impeller flow meter for the first time, the patent right is not exhausted [citations omitted].

i) The appeal court wrongly based its contrary point of view on the decision of this Court in [29 IIC 207 (1998)]—**Prospekthalter**. . . .

ii) It does not follow from the appeal court's findings that the plaintiff consented to the making of the product according to the invention by combining its concealed housings with the defendant's measuring capsules. Such a consent need not, however be issued expressly, but can also be given by implication [citation omitted]. The mere fact that the plaintiff expressly refers to its patent protection, however, is just as insufficient for this purpose as the public's expectation, as cited by the appeal court, that when installing concealed or wall-mounted connecting housings it can retain the possibility of a change of product or supplier given the considerable follow-up costs for the installation and replacement of measuring capsules. While this expectation may generally exist and be justified, it is unfounded if such a switch is impossible without the patent holder's consent precisely because of the protection applying to a specific impeller flow meter. It is for the patent holder to decide whether to issue such consent; it is this power that constitutes the essential content of his exclusive right. Admittedly, this does not exclude a consideration of the public's expectations in the appreciation of how the patent holder's declarations and conduct will be interpreted in good faith by those to whom they are addressed; nevertheless this does not eliminate the need for a finding of at least implied consent.

b) Nor, however, can the appeal court's decision be upheld for the cases in which the plaintiff's purchasers acquired complete impeller flow meters and replaced the plaintiff's measuring unit by the defendant's contested measuring capsule when it became necessary to replace the measuring unit.

In such cases, the purchasers are admittedly persons who acquired a product according to the invention put into circulation with the patent holder's consent, with respect to which the patent right is exhausted and which they are entitled to use according to its purpose, with the consequence that the purchasers are also entitled to exploit the invention within the meaning of Sec. 10 of the Patent Act. By replacing the measuring capsules, however, the purchasers exceed the limits of a use as intended and make the total product according to the invention again; the supply of measuring capsules to such purchasers is therefore likewise prohibited pursuant to Sec. 10 of the Patent Act.

i) It is true that the use of a patented product as intended also includes the maintenance and re-establishment of usability if the function or performance of the specific product is impaired or lost in whole or in part by wear or damage or on other grounds. However, there can no longer be a question of a re-establishment of the lost or impaired usability of a product put into circulation with the patent holder's consent if the

measures taken in fact amount to making the patented product again [citations omitted].

ii) Accordingly, the distinction between a (permissible)
repair and a (prohibited) remaking depends on whether the measures taken maintain the identity of the
specific patented product already put into circulation
[citation omitted], or are the equivalent of the creation
of a new product according to the invention. As a rule,
this can only be determined in the light of the particular nature of the subject matter of the invention and a
balancing of the conflicting interests.

Where the re-establishment or replacement of individual parts of a protected total device is involved,
older case law in this context took particular account
of whether the parts in question were parts individualised for the function of the invention. As individual
elements of the protected total device they did not
enjoy any independent patent protection, but nevertheless they were entitled to the same protection [cita-
tion omitted]. Accordingly, even the production of
such parts was regarded as an infringement of the
patent [citation omitted]. However, this is incompatible with the definition of the subject matter of protection in the patent claim [citation omitted]. Accordingly, as early as the **Rigg** decision, this Court held that
there was only a direct infringement of a combination
patent if the form of the infringement made use of the
totality of the combination features; at best only narrowly limited exceptions could be permitted to this
principle if the contested embodiment contained all
the essential features of the protected invention and
required for its completion at most the addition of
obvious elements of secondary importance for the
technical teaching of the invention. Only then could it
be irrelevant whether the last act of assembling the
total device, an act of no importance for the creative
effort, was taken by third parties (decision of the
Federal Supreme Court, X ZR 70/80—**Rigg** [13 IIC
645 (1982)]. Accordingly, the decisive factor for the
distinction between use as intended and the making of
the (new) protected object is always the total combination.

On the other hand, this does not mean that only
quantitative criteria apply to the question of when a
replacement of parts of a device can be regarded as
making it again. On the contrary, it is necessary to

balance the protectable interest of the patent holder in the commercial exploitation of the invention on the one hand and the interests of the purchasers in the unrestricted use of the patented product put into circulation on the other hand, while taking into account the individual nature of the patented product [citations omitted]. In this, it may be of importance, firstly, whether the parts concerned are ones that must usually be expected to be replaced during the working life of the device. Secondly, however, it also depends on the extent to which the parts replaced reflect the technical effects of the invention. Accordingly, the replacement of a wearing part that usually must be replaced—possibly several times—during the expected working life of a machine as a rule does not constitute a new making of the product. The situation may be different, however, if this part embodies essential elements of the invention [citation omitted]. For, if the replacement of this part implements the technical or commercial benefit of the invention a second time, it cannot be said that the patent holder has already drawn the benefits to which he is entitled from the invention as a result of the first putting into circulation of the device as a whole (**see also** the question worded by Lord Hoffmann in the case of **United Wire v. Screen Repair** [2000 ENPR 324] "whether, having regard to the nature of the patented article, the defendant could be said to have made it").

iii) The findings of fact necessary for this consideration have already been adopted by the appeal court in the case at issue. Since further findings are neither necessary nor to be expected, this Court can itself make a definitive assessment [citation omitted]. Accordingly, it follows that the replacement of the measuring unit in the impeller flow meter by a measuring capsule not originating from the patent holder constitutes the making of the impeller flow meter within the meaning of Sec. 9, second sentence, No. 1 of the Patent Act.

The measuring capsule contains a number of elements of the overall protected device in the form of the measuring cup, the impeller located therein and the meter (feature 2). A thread is cut into the capsule wall allowing the capsule to be mounted on the housing according to feature 3, and the capsule is fitted with a sealing ring so that the measuring cup is supported tight against the housing and the insert inside it (feature 5). It is true that the housing (features 1 and 1.1) with the insert (feature 1.2), the design of which together with a flow surface in accordance with feature 4 is an excellent solution to the problem underlying the invention, is not replaced. However, as already stated, the measuring capsule interacts directly with the housing (insert) designed in this way. As the appeal court rightly held, the advantages of the solution according to the invention are implemented on and in the corresponding measuring capsule such that it achieves an even and turbulence-free activation of the measuring cup (**i.e.** the impeller inside it) and reduces the risk of the measuring capsule and housing caking together. At the same time, the increased stress on the impeller bearings, held by the plaintiff's patent to be a fault in the state of the art, is avoided. The use of a new measuring capsule creates a new impeller flow meter with these advantages; only the patent holder and persons authorised by it can put it into circulation.

The appeal court's view that the assembly of the measuring capsule and housing was a technical and system-related addition, which did not affect the inventive concept and hence the patent holder's right, ignores the interaction between the housing and the measuring unit. Accordingly, the further fact cited by the appeal court that the plaintiff's patent naturally presupposed that the measuring unit could be replaced constitutes no more an aspect of relevance to the conclusion than the understandable desire of purchasers of the impeller flow meter according to the invention to be able on the occasion of the necessary replacement of the measuring unit to have recourse to suppliers other than those entitled to use the plaintiff's patent.

III. Nevertheless, this Court cannot reach a final decision on the dispute, since the appeal court has not adopted sufficient findings as to whether the combination of the plaintiff's concealed housings and the defendant's measuring capsules falls within the scope of protection of the plaintiff's patent, nor did it find whether and if so to what extent the wall-mounted housings are fitted with the contested measuring capsules by the purchasers. For this reason, the case is returned to the appeal court for rehearing.

If the appeal court should come to the conclusion that there are both a patented and a patent-free use of the defendant's measuring capsules, it will have to examine whether this can be taken into account by means of a correspondingly restricted prohibition [citations omitted].

If the appeal court should find that the defendant is liable for damages, it will have to take into account the fact that the plaintiff can only be entitled to a claim for damages of its own as asserted in its petition if it has a right to the patent that excludes other parties from using it, as might for instance result from an exclusive license [citations omitted]. The appeal court has as yet not adopted any findings as to such a right.

Notes & Questions

1.   35 USC § 271(c) requires that the "component of a patented machine, manufacture, combination or composition" or the "material or apparatus for use in practicing a patented process" constitute "a material part of the invention." However, the Federal Circuit does not apply this requirement independently from the other requirements in § 271(c). Thus, the Federal Circuit interprets the "material part" requirement as broadly as the German Supreme Court interprets the "essential element." In contrast, the language of Japanese Patent Law suggests a more restrictive interpretation. Japanese Patent Law provides two types of indirect infringement: (1) assignment etc. of a component exclusively used for producing a patented product or practicing a patented process; and (2) assignment etc. of a component which is used for producing a patented product or practicing a patented process and is essential for the solution of the problem to be solved by the patented invention with the knowledge that the product or process is patented and the component is used for direct infringement of the patented invention. Tokyo District Court held that the indispensable component must be novel and inventive part of the patented invention. Judgment of Tokyo District Court April 23, 2004, Hanrei Jiho No. 1892, 89.

2.   Is direct infringement requisite for indirect infringement? How does the German Federal Court answer this question in the *Impeller Flow Meter* case? The U.S. Supreme Court answered this question affirmatively in *Aro I*, stating "there can be no contributory infringement in the absence of a direct infringement." *Aro Mfg. Co. v. Convertible Top Replacement Co.,* 365 U.S. 336 (1961). There are two lines of doctrines to support indirect infringement. One doctrine aims to punish a participation of an indirect infringer in a subsequent direct infringement. The other doctrine aims to effectively prevent direct infringement by cutting off the infringer's necessary supplies that allow the infringement, and hence the damage to take place. If the patent law of a jurisdiction subscribes to the latter doctrine, direct infringement is not a requisite. Alison Firth, *Direct and Indirect Patent*

Infringement, Toshiko Takenaka ed., Patent Law and Theory 463 (2008).

D. EXCEPTIONS TO INFRINGEMENT

TRIPS Article 30 allows member states to provide limited exceptions to the exclusive rights of a patent as long as such exceptions do not unreasonably conflict with a normal exploitation of the patent and do not unreasonably prejudice the legitimate interests of the patent owner. An example of such an exception is the use of a patented invention for experimental purposes. The EU Directive 2004/27/EC relating to medicinal products for human use provides such an experimental use exception:

Article 10

Conducting the necessary studies and trials with a view to the application of paragraphs 1, 2, 3 and 4 and the consequential practical requirements shall not be regarded as contrary to patent rights or to supplementary protection certificates for medicinal products.

This exception applies only to clinical trials used to develop data for obtaining regulatory approval in the EU market. Many EPC member states have adopted the general experimental use exception provision in the Community Patent Convention Article 27(b). For example, Article 11(1) of the German Patent Act provides "The rights of a patent shall not extend to acts done for experimental purposes relating to the subject matter of the patented invention." Very similar language was adopted in U.K. Patents Act Section (5)(b). Japanese Patent Law Article 69(1) also includes language similar to that of the German Patent Act. Korean and Chinese Patent Acts also include similar experimental use exception provisions.

The majority of these countries limit the application of the exception to acts carried out on or into the invention. However, some countries apply the exception to acts carried out with or using the invention. The result of these types of provisions is to make the such patenting of research tools meaningless.

Further, it is often difficult to apply the exception if the defendant is engaged in the alleged infringement with multiple purposes. The following excerpt indicates a challenge to set a boundary in applicability of the exception.

COREVALVE INC. v. EDWARDS LIFESCIENCES A.G.

[2009] EWHC 6(Pat), January 9, 2009

Mr. Peter Prescott QC

The "Experimental Use" Defence

66. Section 60(5)(b) of the Patents Act 1977 provides that an act which would otherwise infringe a patent shall not do so if "it is done for experimental purposes relating to the subject-matter of the invention".

67. This point is somewhat hypothetical, in that I have held that CoreValve are not using the invention. If they were, they would be supplying a product different from what they are using in reality. It would be cylindrical instead of bulbous. The statutory exception does not permit a patented invention to be used for experimental acts relating to a different invention.

68. I can state the relevant facts briefly. At present CoreValve does not supply its product to all comers, but only to selected hospital sites in Europe (not the USA). This is part of a formidable clinical programme, referred to in the evidence as the Registry, an important feature of which is that cardiologists are carefully trained in the use of the product, and then train others—a sort of pyramid apprenticeship scheme, as it were. As will become more apparent later, it is highly important that there should be professional confidence in these products if they are to take off commercially. This scheme helps to establish that confidence.

CoreValve obtained a CE Mark [i.e. regulatory] approval for its product in May 2007 for the treatment of aortic stenosis in elderly high risk patients. The current product is Generation 3 so far as physical design is concerned. However, and according to its CEO Mr. Michiels:

The main aims of the Registry are (1) to investigate and confirm the safety and efficacy of the procedure and valve function on a *long-term* basis and in a *large number* of patients; (2) to monitor unwanted effects under *expanded use*, and (3) to investigate and understand the effectiveness of the training/certification program in anticipation of larger scale expansion of such a program. In particular, the information that is being learned through use of the Registry database is giving CoreValve a much more detailed understanding of the risks and challenges of the procedure according to patients' anatomy. Furthermore, this data is directly guiding CoreValve's decisions on future design generations, and is leading to a tighter delineation of the patient selection criteria. The

Registry also serves to fulfil NSAI's post-surveillance data requirements. Finally, the Registry database is designed to provide the clinical data detail that will be necessary to establish the parameters for future randomized clinical trials with a view to extending the *ReValving*® treatment to other classes of patients who would benefit from the procedure, but are ineligible for treatment under the current, narrow selection criteria.

70. Apart from the reference to decisions on future design generations, which is rather vague, and would have applied to Henry Ford when he first introduced his Model T automobile, all of these investigations are about cardiological procedures, and do not concern trying modifications to the hardware as such.

71. CoreValve do not supply their product gratis; on the contrary, they invoice a very substantial amount for each unit.

72. It is well settled (*Monsanto v. Stauffer* [1985] RPC 515, C.A.) that mere field trials which are intended to demonstrate the efficacy of the product for the purposes of regulatory approval do not qualify for the exception set for in s.60(5)(b) of the Act. In general, the purpose of this defence is to encourage scientific research while protecting the legitimate interests of the patentee. This involves a balance.

73. Section 60(5)(b) is based on Article 27(b) of the Community Patent Convention. The Federal Supreme Court of Germany considered the equivalent provision in *Klinische Versuche (Clinical Trials) I* [1997] RPC 623. The only part of the court's official headnote that is relevant for present purposes is as follows (English translation):

An act for experimental purposes which is related to the subject-matter of the invention and therefore legitimate can exist if a patented pharmaceutically active substance is used in clinical trials with the aim of finding whether and, where appropriate, in what form the active substance is suitable for curing or alleviating certain other human diseases.

74. In that case the substance in question (an interferon) was known for use in the treatment of rheumatoid arthritis and the defendants were conducting clinical trials to see if that substance could be used for treating other diseases such as cancer, AIDS and hepatitis. The invention—the thing that was claimed in the patent—was the substance as such. I can see that those clinical trials were squarely within the purpose of the exception, for their immediate purpose was to generate scientific information by experimenting with the substance that was the subject of the patent claim.

75. However, there must surely be an outward limit to that principle. Suppose the defendants in the German case had been

selling a pharmaceutical that was fairly new to the market and their defence had been that, by so doing, they were gaining valuable information that was not otherwise available—contraindications, for instance, which could be stated in the product literature. Would that be acts done for 'experimental' purposes?

76. A defendant could always say, and with some truth, that by putting his product on the market (general or special) he was gaining valuable information that might even prompt him to modify his device in future. I have referred to Henry Ford's Model T car. I dare say that vehicle went through various modifications in the light of experience on the roads of early twentieth century America, and that is usually the case with any engineering product.

77. I acknowledge that the mere fact that the purpose of the defendant is commercial is no rebuttal of the statutory defence. After all, most pharmaceutical research organisations are commercial. They do research because they hope to make money one day. However, in the present case it cannot be denied that an immediate and present purpose of CoreValve is to generate revenue—which was not so in the German case.

78. I therefore think that a more complete statement of the principle—it did not arise in the German case—should involve the consideration whether the immediate purpose of the transaction in question is to generate revenue.

79. The relevant statutory phrase is "acts done for experimental purposes". The difficulty arises where the defendant has mixed purposes. I would reject the extreme proposition that, so long as one of the defendant's purposes is to generate information of scientific or technical value, it is irrelevant that another of his purposes is to generate ready cash. There may be no help for it but to consider the defendant's preponderant purposes.

80. On the evidence in this case I would hold that CoreValve's purposes are threefold: (1) to establish confidence in their product within the relevant market; (2) to generate immediate revenue of a substantial character; and (3) to gain information about clinical indications and, possibly, future modifications to be made to the physical structure of the device in the light of experience. I do not find that purpose (3) was their preponderant purpose.

81. I have not found this point easy, but on the whole I would hold that, on the assumption that the CoreValve device falls within Claim 1 of the patent in suit, section 60(5)(b) of the Patents Act 1977 is not a valid defence on the facts of this case.

Notes & Questions

1. The Supreme Court of Japan interpreted its experimental exception provision under Article 69(1) and did not prevent the defendant

from claiming the exception despite the commercial purpose out of the clinical trials. The Court looked into the patent policy of securing freedom to exploit inventions after the expiration of a patent and the Drug Regulation Law to ensure drug safety. The Court emphasized the extension of patent terms if it did not find that the trials were covered by the exception as a reason for applying the exception to clinical trials, which would lead to a conflict with the patent policy. Would this be a good reason to apply the exception to acts with multiple purposes?

2. In the United States, *Madey v. Duke University,* 307 F.3d 1351 (Fed. Cir. 2002) suggests there is effectively no common law general experimental use exception beyond the statutory exception under 35 USC § 271(e). Lawrence M. Sung & Claire M. Maisano, *Piercing the Academic Veil: Disaffecting the Common Law Exception to Patent infringement Liability and the Future of a Bona Fide Research Use Exemption after Madey v. Duke University,* 6 J. Health Care L. & Pol.y 256 (2003). What kind of problems do you anticipate will arise if no experimental use exception is available? Are U.S. courts better off without a general experimental use exception?

E.   REPAIR VERSUS RECONSTRUCTION

The owner of a patented product's right to repair is a doctrine used to limit the exclusive right of a patent that is closely related to the exhaustion doctrine (which will be discussed in Chapter 8). Although Japanese Patent Law does not specifically mention a right to repair, Japanese courts reject a claim of infringement if the acts of the owner fall within the scope of the right to repair the product. This doctrine is also available in European countries such as the U.K. and Germany.

CANON K.K. v. RECYCLE ASSIST K.K.

Supreme Court of Japan
2009 CASRIP Newsletter Issue 1, November 8, 2008

Holding of the Court

The present petition is rejected.

Fees for the petition are to be borne by Petitioner.

Reasons

4. Petitioner [Recycle Assist] argues that the decision below employed an illegal standard to determine whether the patent right could be exercised, and that its judgment in reliance on that standard not to restrict the patent right violated the law. We cannot adopt this argument. The reasons are as follows.

(1) In the case where the patentee or its licensee (hereinafter, both are referred to as "the patentee") sells a patented article

within Japan, the patent has fulfilled its purpose and is deemed exhausted with respect to that article, so the patent's effect no longer applies to the use, sale etc ... of the article. (Here and below, this phrase includes the use, sale etc ..., export or import, or offer to sell etc ..., as stated in art. 2, sec. 3, para. 1 of the Patent Act.) When the patentee has made such sale, the patentee should not be permitted to exercise the patent right with respect to that article. If the patentee's permission were required every time the patented article is sold, this would obstruct the article's fluid circulation on the market, causing instead more harm to the patentee's own interests and ultimately contravening the goals of the Patent Act as stated in article 1 of the Act. At the same time, the patentee has already had the opportunity to secure its reward for publishing the invention, so when the patentee sells the patented article it is not necessary to let him benefit twice in the course of its circulation. **Id.** This type of exhaustion is expressly provided for in art. 12, sec. 3 of the Semiconductor Integrated Circuit Design Act, and art. 21, sec. 1, para. 4 of the Seeds and Seedlings Act. We think the exercise of patent rights should be restricted in the same way.

Still, exhaustion operates to limit the patent only for the specific article sold by the patentee in Japan. Therefore, when an article sold in Japan by the patentee is modified or its parts are replaced, and because of this a new instance of the patented article having a new identity is created, the patentee should be permitted to exercise the patent with respect to the new article. Moreover, in order to determine whether a new instance of the patented article was constructed, it is appropriate to consider the totality of the circumstances including the attributes of the patented article, the content of the patented invention, the manner in which the article was modified or its parts replaced, as well as the actual conditions of the commercial transaction, etc. The attributes of the patented article should include the article's functions, structure and materials, intended uses, lifespan, and the manner in which it is used. The manner in which the article was modified or its parts were replaced should include the state of the patented article when it was modified, the nature and degree of the modification etc ..., the lifespan of the replaced parts, and the technical function and economic value of those parts within the article.

(2) On the other hand, in the case where the holder of a Japanese patent or one regarded as such (collectively the "the patentee") sells a patented article in a foreign country, the patentee should not be allowed to exercise the patent with respect to that article within Japan against the buyer (unless

patentee agreed with the buyer to exclude Japan from the article's territory of sale or use), or against a third party or subsequent purchaser who acquired the article from the buyer (unless such agreement was reached with the buyer and this is also clearly marked on the article). **Id.** This principle limits the patent only with respect to the specific article sold overseas by the holder of the Japanese patent, but it is no different from the case where the patentee sold the article in Japan. Therefore, when an article sold by the patentee in a foreign country is modified or its parts are replaced, and because of this a new instance of the patented article having a new identity is created, the patentee should be permitted to exercise the patent with respect to the new article within Japan. Moreover, the determination of whether a new instance of the patented article was constructed should follow the same standard as when an article sold in Japan is modified or its parts are replaced.

(3) We turn now to the present case. According to the facts given above, when Respondent [Canon]'s ink tanks are refilled with ink and reused, this can cause problems such as reduced print quality and malfunction of the printer itself. Thus, Respondent warns, its articles are for single use only and should be replaced with new items. For this reason Respondent's products do not have holes for adding ink, and this structure makes it necessary to open holes in the cartridges in order to refill the ink. Indeed, in the course of refurbishing them to make Petitioner's products, a hole is opened on the top surface of the cartridge's liquid storage reservoir and is closed after the ink is injected. In this light, the nature of the modification etc. performed to make Petitioner's products goes beyond simply refilling consumable ink: It is nothing less than a physical alteration of the ink tank cartridge to make it refillable.

Furthermore, according to the facts described above, it is the ink itself in Respondent's products which performs the technical function of becoming the barrier in the compressed interface to stop the flow of air. Thus, once the ink is consumed to a certain degree, some or all of the compressed interface loses its ability to hold ink. Moreover, when Respondent's used products are removed from the printer, the residual ink inside them hardens in about one week to ten days. Thus, if the ink tanks are refilled while in this state, the ink cannot create the barrier to stop the flow of air, even if the entire liquid storage reservoir is filled with ink and the negative pressure chamber is also filled to a point above the compressed interface where the negative pressure generating members meet. In Petitioner's products, however, the insides of the cartridges are cleaned to wash away the hardened ink and restore the ability to create the barrier along the compressed interface that stops the flow of air and the ink is also filled to the same level as Respondent's articles before they were used. These steps return the ink tank to the state where ink can be held along the entirety of the compressed interface no matter what position the ink tank may be in.

For this reason, we can say that the manner in which the ink tanks are modified etc. goes beyond simply refilling consumed ink. The cartridges are reused in a manner whereby objects that had ceased to possess structures embodying essential parts of the present invention (Limitation H and Limitation K) were made to possess these structures for a second time. We see no choice but to hold that this re-creates the substantive value of the present invention, and enables the articles for a second time to achieve the operational effect of the present invention, which is the preventing of ink leakage before the package is opened.

Additionally, when we consider **in toto** the circumstances of the commercial transactions involving the ink tanks along with the other circumstances appearing in the facts described above, Petitioner's products should be viewed as new instances of the patented article having different identities from Respondent's products before the modifications took place. The present patent right, therefore, should not be restricted with respect to those products of Petitioner that were made using Respondent's used cartridges that were sold in Japan by the patentee, or sold overseas by the holder of the Japanese patent. Therefore, since Respondent is the holder of this patent right, Respondent may seek an order based on the patent to enjoin the importation, sale etc . . . of these articles and ordering their disposal.

5.   As stated above, the decision below is correct in its conclusion with respect to the points discussed above. We cannot adopt the argument of this appeal.

NOW, THEREFORE, this Court has unanimously decided what was stated in the disposition of this decision.

Notes & Questions

1.   The U.S. Supreme Court gives a lawful owner of a patented product an expansive scope of right to repair. In *Aro Mfg. Co. v. Convertible Top Replacement Co.*, 365 U.S. 336 (1961), the Court held "reconstruction of a patented entity, comprised of unpatented elements, is limited to such a true reconstruction of the entity as to 'in

fact make a new article' [Citation Omitted] after the entity, viewed as a whole has become spent. In order to call the monopoly, conferred by the patent grant, into play for a second time, it must, indeed, be a second creation of the patented entity, as, for example, in Cotton–Tie Co. v. Simmons, supra. Mere replacement of individual unpatented parts, one at a time, whether of the same part repeatedly or different parts successively, is no more than the lawful right of the owner to repair his property.'' Following this instruction from the Supreme Court, the great majority of Federal Circuit cases addressing the repair doctrine do not find infringement. Please compare the Canon case with Hewlett–Packard Co. v. Repeat–O–Type Stencil Mfg. Corp., 123 F.3d 1445 (Fed. Cir. 1997). How would the Federal Circuit have found the refilling act of the defendant in the *Canon* case?

2.   Is the doctrine of a right to repair part of the exhaustion doctrine? Japan's IP High Court has incorporated the doctrine as a limitation to the exhaustion doctrine, holding that exhaustion does not occur if the product lost its function due to being worn out or (2) the replacement of all or any elements of the patented product, which elements constitute an essential part of the invention. The Supreme Court did not use the same format but discussed the exhaustion doctrine in relation to the repair doctrine. The *Quanta* opinion suggests that the U.S. Supreme Court views the two doctrines as separate defenses.

Chapter 8

REMEDIES

A. INJUNCTIONS

TRIPS Article 44 provides that, "[t]he judicial authorities shall have the authority to order a party to desist from an infringement, *inter alia* to prevent the entry into the channels of commerce in their jurisdiction of imported goods...." that involve the infringement of an intellectual property right. The essence of the patent right is the ability to exclude others from practicing the claimed invention. However, as the U.S. Supreme Court has recognized, the right to exclude does not necessarily translate into an absolute right to enjoin infringing activity in all cases. *eBay v. MercExchange, L.L.C.*, 547 U.S. 388 (2006) (requiring consideration of a four-factor test prior to the entry of a permanent injunction).

Subsection 2 of TRIPS Article 44, includes two specified exclusions. The first sentence allows members to limit remedies for "use by governments, or by third parties authorized by a government" to a monetary remedy as described in subparagraph (h) of Article 31.[1] One example of such a statute is 28 U.S.C. § 1498, which authorizes the U.S. government and those that the government authorizes to use a patented invention upon the payment of adequate compensation. Under this statute, an injunction against patent infringement by the U.S. government use is unavailable. *See Zoltek Corp. v. United States*, 442 F.3d 1345 (Fed. Cir. 2006).

The second sentence of Article 44 states, "[i]n other cases, the remedies under this Part shall apply or, where these remedies are inconsistent with a Member's law, declaratory judgments and ade-

---

1. Article 31, subsection (h), specifies that "Where the law of a Member allows for other use of the subject matter of a patent without the authorization of the right holder, including use by the government or third parties authorized by the government, the following provisions shall be respected.... the right holder shall be paid adequate remuneration in the circumstances of each case, taking into account the economic value of the authorization."

quate compensation shall be available." One source acknowledges that "[t]he drafting of this art. 44(2) and especially the second sentence is infelicitous." Daniel Gervais, THE TRIPS AGREEMENT 452 (3rd ed. 2008). Applying accepted principles of treaty interpretation, Prof. Gervais concludes that this sentence allows a member to limit remedies to declaratory judgments and compensation for intellectual property "other than patents and integrated circuits and copyright" where the infringement constitutes "use by or authorised bona fide by [the] government." *Id.*

Under the U.S. Supreme Court's *eBay* decision, a court's ability to grant an injunction against future infringement requires consideration of equitable factors, and an injunction may be denied unless those factors weigh in the patentee's favor. *See Innogenetics, N.V. v. Abbott Laboratories*, 512 F.3d 1363 (Fed. Cir. 2008) (applying *eBay*, reversing a permanent injunction). Is the *eBay* standard consistent with TRIPS Article 44?

B. COMPULSORY LICENSES

A compulsory license is granted by a government to compel the patentee to transfer to a third party a right to produce a patented product or to use a patented process. Some reasons that a government may authorize a compulsory license include:

1) allowing a producer to practice an invention where the patentee does not work the patent;

2) where there is an important public interest at stake; and

3) a patentee's abuse of the patent, for example as a remedy for a patentee's antitrust violation.

See generally Michael Halewood, *Regulating Patent Holders: Local Working Requirements and Compulsory Licenses at International Law*, 35 OSGOODE HALL L.J. 243, 260 (1997). In the first two of these examples, the third party must pay a license fee to the licensee at a rate set by the government.

Both the Paris Convention and the TRIPS Agreement discuss compulsory licensing. Specifically, the Paris Convention section 5(A)(2), states that, "[e]ach country ... shall have the right to take legislative measures providing for the grant of compulsory licenses to prevent the abuses which might result from the exercise of the exclusive rights conferred by the patent, for example, failure to work." Consider how the term "abuses" within this section can be interpreted. Does this term mean that a patentee's failure to work *is* an abuse of a patent? Alternatively, does this section condition the availability of a compulsory license on some *separate* abuse, such as an antitrust violation, that stems from a failure to work?

The TRIPS Agreement includes several sections relating to compulsory licenses. As an initial matter, Article 30 states, "[m]embers may provide limited exceptions to the exclusive rights conferred by a patent, provided that such exceptions do not unreasonably conflict with a normal exploitation of the patent and do not unreasonably prejudice the legitimate interests of the patent owner. . . ." As a WIPO panel explained, ". . . Article 30's very existence amounts to a recognition that the definition of patent rights contained in Article 28 would need certain adjustments." *Canada— Patent Protection of Pharmaceutical Products*, WT/DS114/R para. 7.26 (17 March 2000). Further, TRIPS Article 8 states that members may "adopt measures to protect public health and nutrition, and to promote the public interest in sectors of vital importance to their socio-economic and technological development. . . ."

The TRIPS Agreement outlines specific restrictions on a member's ability to grant compulsory licenses. For example, blanket authorizations are not permitted; rather, "authorization of such use shall be considered on its individual merits." TRIPS, Art. 31(a). Such uses must be limited in scope or duration, be non-exclusive and also non-assignable. *Id.* at Art. 31(c, d & e). Non-governmental users must first seek a license from the patentee, although a government may excuse this requirement "in the case of a national emergency or other circumstances of extreme urgency." *Id.* at Art. 31(b). A decision to authorize use and all remuneration decisions must be subject to review by a judicial or higher authority. *Id.* at Art. 31(i & j).

One important limitation on a government's ability to grant a compulsory license is Article 31(f), which states that any compulsory license "shall be authorized predominantly for the supply of the domestic market of the Member authorizing such use." An illustration from the pharmaceutical industry highlights an important dimension to this language. This geographical limitation, as originally drafted, creates a disadvantage for a country that does not have any capability to manufacture pharmaceuticals within its borders. This is because Article 31(f)'s geographic limitation prevents countries with drug manufacturing capabilities from generating significant exports to developing countries that lack them.

Why was Article 31(f) drafted in this manner? As a practical matter, this provision prevents "arbitrage," a practice that can interfere with an inventive drug company's ability to recoup the significant cost of drug development if they are to successfully engage in the development of new medicines. Generally, arbitrage exists when:

> . . . wholesalers in a low-price country divert supplies through international trade channels to nations in which the manufac-

turer is attempting to maintain high prices, undermining the high prices (and their contribution to research and development expenditures) in the wealthier nations and, if quantitatively substantial, inhibiting the manufacturer's willingness to supply at low prices in the low-income nation.

F.M. Scherer & Jayashree Watal, *Post–TRIPS Options for Access to Patented Medicines in Developing Nations*, 5 J. INT'L ECON. L. 913, 928 (2002).

Why do drug companies charge different prices for the same prices in different nations? As a practical matter, customers for pharmaceuticals within different nations differ in their ability to pay for treatment. Citizens of poorer nations may be completely unable to pay for products. As one commentator explains:

> Purchasing AIDS drugs at U.S. prices is not an option for the vast majority of these people. The per capita annual cost of a popular first-line ARV [antiretroviral for treating HIV/AIDS] in the United States is $7215, and the recently introduced Fuzeon (enfuvirtide) costs $20,000 per year. The annual per capita health expenditures in sub-Saharan Africa averages $29.30 and range from $12 (Malawi) to $253 (South Africa). Radically reducing the price of AIDS medications for the poor is thus a necessary condition to extending ARV treatments to millions of afflicted persons worldwide. Indeed, for many patients, the drugs must be free.

Kevin Outterson, *Pharmaceutical Arbitrage: Balancing Access and Innovation in International Prescription Drug Markets*, 5 YALE J. HEALTH POL'Y L. & ETHICS 193, 252 (2005). Some companies attempt to compensate for income disparity between nations by engaging in price discrimination. In short, companies charge more in wealthier countries, and less in poorer nations, for the same product. Under this practice, called price discrimination, wealthier nations bear a greater share of the cost for pharmaceutical companies that engage in drug development. Patents place these companies in the best position to maximize profit by enabling those companies to control prices where their products are sold.

Arbitrage interferes with a patent holder's ability to price discriminate. To illustrate, reduced-price HIV treatment drugs intended for use in Africa were intercepted and diverted for sale in Europe. *See HIV Drugs for Africa Diverted to Europe; Probe Targets Wholesalers*, THE WASH. POST, Oct. 3, 2002, at A10 (noting that the drugs "did not have special packaging or markings to differentiate them from medicines offered for sale in Europe."). These diverted drugs, which were obtained at a low price, will compete with the same HIV treatment drugs intended for sale at a higher price in the wealthier region. In this case, the drug maker cannot obtain the same level of profit anticipated to be earned in Europe, and might be unable to recoup the full cost of developing the HIV treatment. Indeed, some drug makers may elect to reduce or entirely forgo sales in poorer nations, in part to reduce the risk of arbitrage. In short, when fewer products are distributed in poorer nations, fewer products will become available to divert elsewhere. Instead, those companies may want to focus on the more affluent segment of the population in these countries to maximize the profitability of sales made there even though that segment may represent only a minority. Peter K. Yu, *The International Enclosure Movement*, 82 IND. L. J. 827, 844–45 (2007). As a result, some pharmaceuticals solutions are not available in some nations.

TRIPS Article 31(f) seeks to prevent arbitrage by proscribing that products made under a compulsory license "shall be authorized predominantly for the supply of the domestic market of the Member authorizing such use." This limitation prevents a government from authorizing a manufacturer within a poorer country from exporting goods to wealthier nations, undercutting the patent holder's more profitable sales there. In operation, Article 31 strikes a compromise between concerns over arbitrage and those of governments concerned about public health. When a government authorizes a compulsory license under Article 31(f), local drug manufacturers can make another's patented formulation so long as reasonable remuneration payments are made to the patentee. At the same time, these licensed products cannot be used to compete with the patentee's sales in wealthier countries.

TRIPS Article 31 provides very limited assistance to countries that have no manufacturing capability to make products for domestic use. Further, Article 31(f)'s limit on government issued licenses "for the supply of the domestic market" effectively prevents countries with manufacturing capacity to export needed drugs to poorer nations. This problem is particularly acute for "neglected diseases" that impact only the poorer nations, such as African sleeping sickness and African river blindness. Such diseases typically obtain very little research attention. *See* World Health Organization, Report of the Commission on Intellectual Property Rights, INNOVATION AND PUBLIC HEALTH, PUBLIC HEALTH, INNOVATION AND INTELLECTUAL PROPERTY RIGHTS 13 (2006) (describing "very neglected diseases" that affected poorer companies disproportionately, noting that "[s]uch diseases receive extremely little R & D, and essentially no commercially based R & D in the rich countries.). To address these concerns, WTO members have engaged in discussions that have resulted in the actions discussed in the next section.

C. TRIPS, DOHA AND COMPULSORY LICENSES

During the Fourth WTO Ministerial Meeting in Doha, Qatar in 2002, WTO members adopted the Declaration on the TRIPS Agreement and Public Health, known at the "Doha Declaration." World Trade Org., Declaration on the TRIPS Agreement and Public Health, WT/MIN(01)/DEC/2, 41 I.L.M. 755 (2002). Paragraph 5(b) provides that "[e]ach member has the right to grant compulsory licences and the freedom to determine the grounds upon which such licences are granted." Paragraph 6 states:

> We recognize that WTO members with insufficient or no manufacturing capacities in the pharmaceutical sector could face difficulties in making effective use of compulsory licensing under the TRIPS Agreement. We instruct the Council for TRIPS to find an expeditious solution to this problem and to report to the General Council before the end of 2002.

Most recently, the WTO member states accepted a protocol of amendment, which sought to add a new Article 31*bis* to the TRIPS Agreement. In reviewing this excerpt of the Annex to this provision, consider whether this proposal adequately addresses the interests for all parties concerned.

DECISION OF THE GENERAL COUNCIL, AMENDMENT OF THE TRIPS AGREEMENT, ANNEX TO THE PROTOCOL AMENDING THE TRIPS AGREEMENT (ARTICLE 31*BIS*)

WT/L/641 (Dec. 6, 2005)

1. For the purposes of Article 31bis and this Annex:

(a) "pharmaceutical product" means any patented product, or product manufactured through a patented process, of the pharmaceutical sector needed to address the public health problems as recognized in paragraph 1 of the Declaration on the TRIPS Agreement and Public Health (WT/MIN(01)/DEC/2). It is understood that active ingredients necessary for its manufacture and diagnostic kits needed for its use would be included;

(b) "eligible importing Member" means any least-developed country Member, and any other Member that has made a notification to the Council for TRIPS of its intention to use the system set out in Article 31bis and this Annex ("system") as an importer, it being understood that a Member may notify at any time that it will use the system in whole or in a limited way, for example only in the case of a national emergency or other circumstances of extreme urgency or in cases of public non-commercial use. It is noted that some Members will not use the system as importing Members and that some other Members have stated that, if they use the system, it would be in no more than situations of national emergency or other circumstances of extreme urgency;

(c) "exporting Member" means a Member using the system to produce pharmaceutical products for, and export them to, an eligible importing Member.

2. The terms referred to in paragraph 1 of Article 31*bis* are that:

(a) the eligible importing Member(s) has made a notification to the Council for TRIPS, that:

> (i) specifies the names and expected quantities of the product(s) needed;

> (ii) confirms that the eligible importing Member in question, other than a least developed country Member, has established that it has insufficient or no manufacturing capacities in the pharmaceutical sector for the product(s) in question in one of the ways set out in the Appendix to this Annex; and

> (iii) confirms that, where a pharmaceutical product is patented in its territory, it has granted or intends to grant a compulsory licence in accordance with Articles 31 and 31*bis* of this Agreement and the provisions of this Annex;

(b) the compulsory licence issued by the exporting Member under the system shall contain the following conditions:

> (i) only the amount necessary to meet the needs of the eligible importing Member(s) may be manufactured under the licence and the entirety of this production shall be exported to the Member(s) which has notified its needs to the Council for TRIPS;

> (ii) products produced under the licence shall be clearly identified as being produced under the system through specific labelling or marking. Suppliers should distinguish such products through special packaging and/or special colouring/shaping of the products themselves, provided that such distinction is feasible and does not have a significant impact on price; and

> (iii) before shipment begins, the licensee shall post on a website7 the following information:

> —the quantities being supplied to each destination as referred to in indent (i) above; and

—the distinguishing features of the product(s) referred to in indent (ii) above;

(c) the exporting Member shall notify the Council for TRIPS of the grant of the licence, including the conditions attached to it. The information provided shall include the name and address of the licensee, the product(s) for which the licence has been granted, the quantity(ies) for which it has been granted, the country(ies) to which the product(s) is (are) to be supplied and the duration of the licence. The notification shall also indicate the address of the website referred to in subparagraph (b)(iii) above.

3.   In order to ensure that the products imported under the system are used for the public health purposes underlying their importation, eligible importing Members shall take reasonable measures within their means, proportionate to their administrative capacities and to the risk of trade diversion to prevent re-exportation of the products that have actually been imported into their territories under the system. In the event that an eligible importing Member that is a developing country Member or a least-developed country Member experiences difficulty in implementing this provision, developed country Members shall provide, on request and on mutually agreed terms and conditions, technical and financial cooperation in order to facilitate its implementation.

4.   Members shall ensure the availability of effective legal means to prevent the importation into, and sale in, their territories of products produced under the system and diverted to their markets inconsistently with its provisions, using the means already required to be available under this Agreement. If any Member considers that such measures are proving insufficient for this purpose, the matter may be reviewed in the Council for TRIPS at the request of that Member. . . .

Notes and Questions

1.   If Article 31*bis* is ratified by two-thirds of the WTO membership, this new provision would relieve certain members of the territorial limits of Article 31(f). Do these terms address the concerns of patentees? Of lesser-developed nations? How? Do you believe that industrialized nations, including the U.S., should support its adoption?

2.   Some commentators have been critical of the Doha arrangement, arguing that the arrangement would undermine the uniform global system of protection that TRIPS was intended to establish. Alan Sykes recognizes that, prior to TRIPS, less developed nations had few incentives to enact strong intellectual property protection. *See* Alan O. Sykes, *TRIPS, Pharmaceuticals, Developing Countries, and the Doha*

"Solution," 3 Chi. J. Int'l L. J. 47 (2002). As Sykes describes, during this time, patent protection had "been a matter of national (not international) law and could thus be changed at any time without international penalties." *Id.* at 65. Sykes writes that, pre-TRIPS:

> [E]ach nation may be tempted not to afford patent protection, secure in the knowledge that it will reap the full benefits of lower domestic drug prices as a result, while its policy will have only modest impact on global research incentives. Put differently, each nation will reap all the benefits from a decision not to afford patent protection, while the costs will be borne by developing countries as a whole. . . .

> The TRIPS Agreement has the potential to change this situation dramatically. Once the transition periods for developing countries expire, all WTO members will be required to afford full patent rights on pharmaceuticals (although it would allow them to permit parallel imports). The requirement is backed by standard WTO sanctions for non-compliance. Thus, after the transition, TRIPS is, in principle, a vehicle for overcoming at least part of the collective action problem.

> However, the Doha Declaration does much to undermine its effectiveness in this regard. Any pharmaceutical company contemplating research on diseases of particular interest to developing nations is now on notice that in the event a successful new drug is developed, developing country customers may declare a "national emergency" and thereafter award compulsory licenses without prior negotiation, and at a royalty rate that may be minimal depending on the eventual interpretation of the "adequate remuneration" standard in Article 31. Even if such behavior is not in the collective interest of developing nations, the temptation to engage in it on an individual country basis may be great because the costs to others are externalized.

Id. at 65–66. Do you agree with Sykes that 31*bis* reduces incentives to invent? Is Sykes correct that lesser-developed countries better off with weaker patent laws, compared to those enforced in industrialized nations? If so, will patentees in industrialized nations adjust their expectations—and their behavior—accordingly?

3. Thomas Cotter disagrees with Sykes' analysis and instead argues that developing countries are unlikely to abuse 31*bis*:

> . . . a variety of practical constraints should limit the ability of developing countries to engage in the excessive use of compulsory licensing. Conceivably, the TRIPs Declaration might embolden some countries to consider compulsory licensing that they otherwise would forego, out of fear of having to incur litigation costs to defend themselves before the WTO. . . . [E]ven post-Doha, a nation must still comply with the other provisions of article 31. Thus, if the desire to avoid litigation costs is paramount, it should continue to play a role in ensuring that developing countries provide adequate remuneration, an opportunity for judicial review, and so on.

These safeguards should work to reduce, even if they do not eliminate, the potential for abuse. In addition, a country that abuses its ability to engage in compulsory licensing might suffer diplomatic or other repercussions. . . .

Sykes may be on firmer ground when he argues that compulsory licensing may reduce the pharmaceutical industry's incentive to undertake research into diseases that are endemic principally to the developing world. That consequence would be perverse, but again a little dose of reality is helpful. Even in the presence of strong patent rights, the developing nations' willingness to pay may be so constrained that little incentive will exist anyway for the pharmaceutical companies to engage in much of this type of research and development. Indeed, most observers who have considered this issue have concluded that it will take much more than strong patent rights to induce this type of research. . . .

Thomas F. Cotter, *Market Fundamentalism and the TRIPS Agreement*, 22 CARDOZO ARTS & ENT. L. J. 307, 335–36 (2004) (footnotes omitted). In your view, who has the better argument between Sykes and Cotter?

4. Consider this proposal by Jean Olson Lanjouw, who suggests that pharmaceutical innovators who research diseases that affect all nations be permitted patent protection in either wealthy or poor nations:

> The proposed mechanism involves a straightforward change in legislation in rich countries, and in the rare cases that it might require enforcement, it would use the existing infrastructure in those countries. The mechanism imposes no regulatory burden on developing countries. The idea is this: Whenever patent owners are dealing with a pharmaceutical innovation related to a listed global disease, the mechanism effectively requires owners to choose either protection in the rich countries or protection in the poor countries, but not both. Given this choice, such patentees would obviously choose to maintain patent protection in rich country markets and allow competition in the poor countries.

Jean Olson Lanjouw, *Beyond TRIPS: A New Global Patent Regime*, CENTER FOR GLOBAL DEVELOPMENT (August 2002) available at http://www.cgdev.org. Lanjouw defines "poor countries" as those with a poor capita domestic product of less than $500 U.S. dollars per person. Arguing that "compromise is unavoidable," Lanjouw further explains:

> The policy utilizes firms' knowledge of the relative importance of markets. For example, suppose that AIDS were a listed global disease but that there were a particular form of AIDS specific to Africa or, alternatively, a drug-delivery system particularly suited to African conditions. For products treating this specific form of AIDS, or for products related to this delivery system, inventors could choose to protect their markets in Africa, and any profits available to support innovation would be preserved.

Does an economic incentive approach to the problem make sense? Do you prefer Lanjouw's approach to the proposed Article 31*bis*?

D. CASE STUDY: DOHA AND CANADA'S ACCESS TO MEDICINES REGIME

In 2004, Canada relied on Doha to enact the Canadian Access to Medicines Regime ("CAMR"). This statute provides a procedural mechanism whereby Canada's drug makers can export pharmaceuticals to developing nations with little or no manufacturing ability. The CAMR includes schedules that list eligible nations, as well as a list of patented products that may be used to address public health problems afflicting developing and least-developed countries. Additionally, the CAMR provides a method for applicants to seek the Canadian government's approval for the manufacture of a qualifying product to a qualifying nation that has issued a compulsory license. More specifically, the statute provides several requirements, including that:

(3) The Commissioner [of Patents] shall authorize the use of the patented invention only if

(a) the applicant has complied with the prescribed requirements, if any;

(b) the Minister of Health has notified the Commissioner that the version of the pharmaceutical product that is named in the application meets the requirements of the Food and Drugs Act and its regulations, including the requirements under those regulations relating to the marking, embossing, labelling and packaging that identify that version of the product as having been manufactured

(i) in Canada as permitted by the General Council Decision, and

(ii) in a manner that distinguishes it from the version of the pharmaceutical product sold in Canada by, or with the consent of, the patentee or patentees, as the case may be;

Moreover, an applicant must provide a declaration stating that, at least thirty days before filing the application, the applicant sought a license to manufacture and sell the pharmaceutical product for export to the country named in the application on reasonable terms and conditions and that such efforts have not been successful. Additionally, the applicant's declaration must state either: 1) the products is not patented in a WTO member nation; or 2) that the importing country has granted, or intends to grant, a compulsory license to the relevant patent under Article 31 of the TRIPS Agreement.

In 2007, Canada's Commissioner of Patents issued its first authorization under the CAMR to drug maker Apotex, Inc., for the export of a drug, Apo–TriAvir, a triple combination HIV/AIDS drug, to Rwanda. This formulation included molecules patented by a third party, pharmaceutical maker GlaxoSmithKline, Inc. Canada's authorization was limited to a specified number of tablets and a two-year duration. Apotex shipped product for roughly one year. However, Apotex has indicated a reluctance to continue, because the CAMR process is too cumbersome and difficult. *See* Press Release, CAMR Federal Law Needs to Be Fixed If Life–Saving Drugs for Children Are to Be Developed (May 29, 2009), available at http://www.apotex.com/ca/en/aboutapotex/pressreleases/20090514.asp (quoting Apotex President Jack Kay, stating, "We invested millions in the research and development of the product, legal costs in negotiating with the brand companies and made no profits in this process. We did it because it was the right thing to do," but that CAMR "in its current form . . . [was] not workable").

Whether Article 31*bis* will be ratified is far from assured. Even if it is, it is unclear whether the provision will be widely used by such drug manufacturers.

E. COMPULSORY LICENSES AT THE NATIONAL LEVEL

Although TRIPS provides safeguards and a mechanism for granting compulsory licenses, individual member nations must still grapple with whether such rights *should* be granted in particular circumstances. Recall that under U.S. law, the *eBay v. MercExchange, L.L.C.*, 547 U.S. 388 (2006), decision sets forth a four-factor test for assessing whether an injunction should be granted: 1) that the plaintiff has suffered an irreparable injury; 2) that remedies available at law, such as monetary damages, are inadequate to compensate for that injury; 3) that considering the balance of hardships between the plaintiff and defendant, a remedy in equity is warranted; and 4) the public interest would not be disserved by a permanent injunction. A court's decision to deny an injunction, subject to a running royalty, can resemble a compulsory license in the very broadest sense of the word. *See* Innogenetics, N.V. v. Abbott Laboratories, 512 F.3d 1363, 1381 (Fed. Cir. 2008) (referring to a post-trial running royalty as a "compulsory license").

Other nations have implemented statutes. For example, the German Patent Act's Section 24(1), analyzed in the Federal Supreme Court's *Polyferon* opinion below, states as follows:

> A non-exclusive authorization to commercially exploit an invention shall be granted by the Patent Court in individual cases in accordance with the following provisions (compulsory license) if

1. the applicant for a license has unsuccessfully endeavored during a reasonable period of time to obtain from the patentee consent to exploit the invention under reasonable conditions usual in trade; and

2. public interest commands the grant of a compulsory license.

As you read the *Polyferon* decision, consider how the term "public interest" from this statute is defined and applied.

GERMANY: PATENTS—COMPULSORY LICENCE: POLYFERON

German Federal Supreme Court
1996 GRUR 190, 28 IIC 242 (1997)[2]

The first defendant is the holder of German patent No. 32 38 554 published on November 23, 1989, and of European patent No. 0 077 670 with effect inter alia for the Federal Republic of Germany, the grant of which was published on June 28, 1989. The German translation of the version of Claim No. 1 of the European patent as valid for Germany as a contracting state reads as follows:

Human immune interferon with the amino-acid sequence depicted in Fig. 5 and alleles thereof, free from other protein with which it is ordinarily associated.

The second defendant is the sole licensee in the territory of the Federal Republic of Germany for the contested patent. The defendants collaborate at international level in the development and testing of pharmaceuticals containing the active ingredient interferon (IFN)-gamma.... On May 24, 1991, the second defendant had requested approval from the Ethics Commission of the University of Freiburg for a clinical study to investigate tolerance and effect of a long-term "Imukin" treatment on patients with clinically active rheumatoid arthritis (RA) resistant to non-steroidal antiphlogistics. An application for approval of "Imukin" for the treatment of this indication has not yet been submitted.

The plaintiff, B., manufactured a pharmaceutical under the name "Polyferon 20" and "Polyferon 50" using the effective ingredient interferon-gamma (human re-combined), which it obtained from abroad, for the treatment of "classical rheumatoid arthritis (chronic polyarthritis) with clinical symptoms of activity and an insufficient reaction to non-steroidal antiphlogistics." It supplied this pharmaceutical to R.A., which was then responsible for distribution. The pharmaceutical was granted approval by the Federal Health Agency for the said field of application in a ruling dated

January 24, 1989. It is currently the only pharmaceutical containing the active ingredient IFN-gamma approved in Germany for the treatment of chronic polyarthritis.

From 1984 on, B. had submitted a series of patent applications to the German and the European Patent Offices concerning the use of IFN-gamma (human re-combined) for certain therapeutic fields of application. Some of these applications resulted in the grant of patents, including German patent No. 34 36 638 concerning the use of preparations containing IFN-gamma for the treatment of rheumatic complaints.

In a letter dated March 20, 1990, B. unsuccessfully requested a license from the first defendant for the two contested patents for the manufacture and sale of "Polyferon" in return for an appropriate remuneration and lodging of security.

With its present action, B. requests the grant of a compulsory license. It has submitted that it is in the public interest to grant it permission to manufacture and sell "Polyferon" using the contested patents in return for the payment of a suitable remuneration. The public interest derives from the fact that the Federal Health Agency prematurely granted restricted approval for "Polyferon" in accordance with Sec. 28(3) of the Drugs Law. Irrespective of the aforesaid, "Polyferon" is urgently needed as the only pharmaceutical containing the active ingredient IFN-gamma for the treatment of rheumatoid arthritis....

The Federal Patent Court held that there was a public interest. It granted B. limited approval for the territory of the Federal Republic of Germany to use the contested patents, against payment of a license fee of 8%, for the permitted indication of classical rheumatoid arthritis (chronic polyarthritis) with clinical symptoms of activity and an insufficient reaction to non-steroidal antiphlogistics, dismissing the remainder of the action against the first defendant and the action against the second defendant.

The first defendant and B. appealed against the decision....

The first defendant argued inter alia that the license rate assumed by the Federal Patent Court was too low, a license of 40% of the current net selling price being appropriate....

FROM THE OPINION:

II.

1.   The term "public interest" as used in Sec. 24(1), first sent., of the Patent Act is an indefinite term that must be given concrete meaning by case law. There can be no universally valid definition of public interest. On the contrary, this term, like any general term, is subject to change. The assessment of the balancing of the interests

of the patent holder and of the general public is subject to varying points of view. The decision depends entirely on the circumstances of the individual case. Public interest cannot be established merely on the basis of the exclusive position enjoyed by the patent holder, even if the latter enjoys an actual monopoly on the market. As a reward for the publication of his invention and the efforts, risk and costs involved, the patent holder is granted by law an exclusive right which he is able to exploit irrespective of the competitive position. For this reason, public interest can only be affected if there are particular circumstances that subordinate the unrestricted recognition of the patent holder's exclusive right and interests to the interest of the general public in the exploitation of the patent by the party seeking a license. Only then is there justification for a major impairment of the patent holder's rights against his will in the form of a compulsory license. . . .

b) Contrary to the first defendant's opinion, neither the Constitution nor Art. 5A(2) of the Paris Convention requires Sec. 24 of the Patent Act to be constructed in such a way that public interest always presupposes abusive use of the patent, and that this alone prevents the grant of a compulsory license in any other circumstances . . . [W]here the patent holder refuses to grant permission, the party seeking a license shall be given authority to exploit the patented invention if permission is indispensable in the public interest. If these conditions are met, the patent holder must accept this impairment of his right without there being any infringement of his basic rights under Art. 14 of the Constitution.

Nor does Art. 5A of the Lisbon version of the Paris Convention reveal that it is a binding requirement for the existence of a public interest in accordance with Sec. 24(1), first sent, that the patent holder is abusing his legal position. Article 5A of the Paris Convention merely regulates the case of a compulsory license in the absence of any or sufficient exploitation of the patent, but not, however, the case of the grant of a compulsory license by virtue of public interest, with the effect that the national legislature was unrestricted in its regulation of other cases of compulsory licenses, particularly by virtue of public interest. Furthermore, Art. 5A(2) of the Paris Convention leaves open the question of what specifically is meant by the abuses that are to be prevented. There is no conflict with the principle that the Act must be construed in line with the Convention.

c) Nor does the Agreement on Trade–Related Aspects of International Property Law permit a construction that allows the grant of a compulsory license only in the case of abuse. According to Art. 30, the member states may provide limited exceptions to the exclusive rights conferred by a patent provided that such exceptions do not unreasonably conflict with a normal exploitation of the patent and do not unreasonably prejudice the legitimate interests of the patent owner, taking account of the legitimate interests of third parties. The German legislature has complied with the above condition by subjecting the grant of a compulsory license in Sec. 24 of the Patent Act to the requirement that the impairment of the right granted to the patent holder is only lawful if it is "indispensable" in the public interest.

d) Special circumstances that justify the assumption of public interest, in addition to the abusive exploitation of patent rights, may therefore also include other circumstances, particularly of a technical, economic, socio-political and medical nature. Account must thereby be taken of the well-being of the general public, particularly in the field of general health care. The question of the requirements to substantiate a public interest that make indispensable the grant of a compulsory license specifically to this party depends on the circumstances of the individual case and is to be decided in each case by balancing the patent holder's protectable interests against all the relevant points of view concerning the interests of the general public. Since the grant of a compulsory license represents a significant encroachment on the patent holder's legal and constitutionally protected exclusive rights, the balancing of interests must be subjected to the principle of reasonableness. For this reason, a compulsory license in a pharmaceutical cannot be granted if the public interest can be satisfied with other more or less equivalent alternative products. . . .

2.   a) It is not disputed that the scope of both patents extends to the use of the patented ingredient interferon-gamma (human recombined) for the treatment of rheumatoid arthritis identified by B. and embodied in the approved pharmaceutical "Polyferon."

b) Nor does the approval of the pharmaceutical "Polyferon" by the ruling of the Federal Health Agency dated January 24, 1989, justify the assumption that there is a public interest within the meaning of Sec. 24(1), first sent., of the Patent Act. The Federal Health Agency investigates the approval exclusively from the pharmaceutical law point of view. Given the purpose of the Pharmaceuticals Act, the issue turns on the public's interest in the approval of a pharmaceutical and not on the disputed question whether public interests require an encroachment on a private patent right by means of a compulsory license.

c) Nor are there any indications for assuming that the defendants do not exploit or do not intend to exploit their patents in the Federal Republic of Germany. Since September 1984, the second defendant, as exclusive licensee in the Federal Republic of Germany, has been carrying out clinical studies of IFN-gamma and supplying the necessary quantities of this active ingredient for this purpose....

4. Contrary to the plaintiff's argument, it has as yet not been found with certainty that there is a significant improvement in the therapeutic possibilities for rheumatoid arthritis as a result of "Polyferon" as compared with traditional medicaments....

b) ... In the absence of comparative clinical studies between interferon-gamma and second-choice standard medicaments, the expert was not able to determine whether the therapeutic chances of a treatment with interferon-gamma are greater or at least the same as with other well-known second-choice medicaments, and whether a long-term effect of the substance can be assumed.

5. The plaintiff has failed to prove that from the medical point of view there is no other preparation with a comparable effect for the treatment of rheumatoid arthritis in those possible exceptional cases where the use of "Polyferon" is necessary and beneficial.

Notes and Questions

1. How might a U.S. court assess the facts of the *Polyferon* case under the *eBay* standard?

2. Patents to pharmaceuticals and medical diagnostics have proven to be controversial, implicating governmental interests in access to affordable health care. For example, France enacted a statutory compulsory licensing provision that reads as follows:

> Where the interests of public health demand, patents granted for medicines or for processes for obtaining medicines, for products necessary in obtaining such medicines or for processes for manufacturing such products may be subject to ex officio licenses in accordance with Article L. 613–17 in the event of such medicines being made available to the public in insufficient quantity or quality or at abnormally high prices, by order of the Minister responsible for industrial property, at the request of the Minister responsible for health.

Law No. 2004–1338 of December 8, 2004, Journal Officiel de la République Française [J.O.] [Official Gazette of France], December 9, 2004, Art. 613–16. Does this statute create any conflict with the Paris Convention? With TRIPS?

This article is said to have been prompted, at least in part, by an anticipated conflict with Myriad, a patent holder who claimed rights to diagnostic testing for genes indicative of a tendency to manifest breast cancer. According to an attorney who represented the Institut Curie, a French organization involved in cancer research:

> Not only was Myriad asking for two thousand five hundred Euros for the first family test and forty Euros for subsequent tests, but the company was also demanding that the analyses be carried out

in their laboratories in Salt Lake City. The reason was that if they carried out the test themselves, on the basis of a pre-defined scheme, this would guarantee that the results could be faithfully reproduced. This was contrary to practices in French cancer centres which do not have a uniform protocol.

Needless to say, this caused an uproar. Social Security could not meet such a high cost. The Ministry for Research feared that since such analyses could not be carried out in France, this would result in a major scientific loss to our laboratories, despite the fact that there were still mutations to detect and numerous statistical studies to pursue.

Jacques Warcoin, Remarks *The Struggle Against the Patenting of a Gene*, L'Ecole de Paris du Management (2/16/2005), available at http://ecole.org/orateurs/OR0202.

Assuming that no non-infringing alternative existed for the breast cancer gene test, how would these facts be analyzed under the French statute, as enacted? Under Germany's statute and *Polyferon*? Under the U.S. *eBay* standard? To what degree should a conflict with a single patent holder impact governmental policies with all patent holders within a field?

3. Most western industrialized countries have a statutory system in place to authorize a compulsory license under specified conditions. *See* Friedrich–Karl Beier, *Exclusive Rights, Statutory Licences and Compulsory Licences in Patent and Utility Model Law*, 30 INT'L REV. OF INTELL. PROP. AND COMPETITION L. 251 (1999). Professor Beier explains:

> [T]he existence of these [compulsory licensing] provisions cannot disguise the fact that the grant of a compulsory license remains a rare exception in all these countries. Compulsory licenses are rarely applied for and it is even rarer for such a license to be granted ...

> It appears as though the institution of the compulsory license has outlived itself and—at least in industrialized countries—has lost its practical significance. However, it is generally assumed that in many cases the mere existence of a provision on compulsory licenses is sufficient to cause a patent owner to grant a voluntary license on reasonable terms to a potential compulsory license applicant.

> Irrespective of the assessment of the effectiveness of compulsory licenses, two elements must be borne in mind: their exceptional nature and the fact that compulsory licenses, through their mere existence as well as through the apprehension of compulsory license proceedings are liable to increase the willingness of a patent owner to grant a voluntary license.

Id. at 260 (footnotes omitted). The U.S. does not have the broader compulsory licensing provisions parallel to those in force within Germany and elsewhere.

F. PRELIMINARY INJUNCTIONS

The ability to seek court intervention to issue a preliminary injunction is available in many countries. However, the standard for assessing the availability within each varies. In this vein, consider the standards applied in the following opinion.

F. HOFFMANN–LA ROCHE LTD. v. CIPLA LTD.

High Court of Delhi at New Delhi

[2008 (37) PTC 71]

Mr. Justice S. Ravindra Bhat

1. The Plaintiffs in this suit seek permanent injunction restraining infringement of their patent rights in the drug Erlotinib, rendition of accounts, damages and delivery up of the infringing goods.

2. The first Plaintiff is a company organized and existing under the laws of Switzerland [that] ... jointly owns a patent with Pfizer Products Inc. in respect of a small drug molecule, medically termed as a Human Epidermal Growth Factor Type–1/Epidermal Growth Factor Receptor (HER/EGFR) inhibitor, popularly known as Erlotinib. It is claimed that this drug marked a major breakthrough and innovation in the treatment of cancer; it is used to destroy some types of cancer cells while causing little harm to normal human cells....

4. The Defendant, CIPLA, is the second biggest pharmaceutical company in India. It is incorporated under the Indian Companies Act, 1956; it has its registered office at Mumbai. In December 2007 and January 2008, various news reports appeared in the print as well as the electronic media about the defendants['] plans to launch a generic version of Erlotinib in India and also for exporting it to various countries. One such report appeared on 11.1.2008 in an English daily Mint published by the Hindustan Times Group. The Plaintiffs claim their knowledge of the Defendants plans to infringe their rights in the patent, from such reports. They have filed the present action seeking permanent injunction and damages.

5. It is averred by the Plaintiffs that Erlotinib was developed after long, sustained and substantial research, and after incurring enormous expenditure for the tests, mandatorily conducted to establish its efficacy and safety. It is submitted that this innovation is duly protected under the provisions of law and no person except those authorized to exercise the legal rights associated with the patented drug can be allowed or permitted to copy/simulate and/or recreate it in any manner or in any other name. They allege that the Defen-

dant is following an illegal course to offer a generic version of the patented drug. . . .

22.   The Plaintiff, as well as the Defendant, relied upon the celebrated English decision reported as American Cyanamid Co v. Ethicon Ltd 1975 (1) All. ER 504 to say what are the guiding principles which courts have to adopt in cases involving infringement of patent and copyright cases. The Court had in that case enumerated the salient considerations which weigh with a court while granting or refusing interim injunction, in actions complaining infringement of patents; it was held as follows: As to that, the governing principle is that the court should first consider whether, if the plaintiff were to succeed at the trial in establishing his right to a permanent injunction, he would be adequately compensated by an award of damages for the loss he would have sustained as a result of the defendant's continuing to do what was sought to be enjoined between the time of the application and the time of the trial. If damages in the measure recoverable at common law would be adequate remedy and the defendant would be in a financial position to pay them, no interlocutory injunction should normally be granted, however strong the plaintiff's claim appeared to be at that stage. If, on the other hand, damages would not provide an adequate remedy for the plaintiff in the event of his succeeding at the trial, the court should then consider whether, on the contrary hypothesis that the defendant were to succeed at the trial in establishing his right to do that which was sought to be enjoined, he would be adequately compensated under the plaintiff's undertaking as to damages for the loss he would have sustained by being prevented from doing so between the time of the application and the time of the trial. If damages in the measure recoverable under such an undertaking would be an adequate remedy and the plaintiff would be in a financial position to pay them, there would be no reason upon this ground to refuse an interlocutory injunction. It is where there is doubt as to the adequacy of the respective remedies in damages available to either party or to both, that the question of balance of convenience arises. . . .

80.   [Editor's note: The court considered that the defendant had raised a credible challenge to the plaintiffs' patent as nonobvious.] It would now be relevant to consider the various factual aspects other than the patent claims of the plaintiff. It is asserted on its behalf that the drug has been made available since the year 2006 by it and has till date recorded sales worth Rs. 13.2 crores.[3] The plaintiff does not have a manufacturing facility in India; it imports Tarceva. It is unclear—since no claim in that regard has been

---

3. Editor's note. The abbreviation "Rs." refers to the rupee, the monetary unit used in India. The "crore" equals ten million. "Rs. 13.2 crores" equals 13,-200,00 rupees.

made, as to the marketing arrangements of the plaintiff for its product or its advertisement and other incidental expenses for Tarceva. The plaintiff asserts that one of its tablet costs Rs.3200/- and that the effective treatment with the drug involves its use for two months, the patient taking the tablet once a day. The Defendant contests this and has produced packaging of the plaintiff and copies of bills disclosing the particulars of Tarceva, as costing Rs. 48,000/-per strip of 10 tablets. It has also produced bills from three pharmacists in different cities i.e. Chennai, Ahmedabad and Mumbai showing that the maximum retail price of its product Erlocip is Rs.1600/-per tablet. The defendant has also produced a copy of the Central Government Standard Drug Control Organization permission in Form 46 under the Trade and Cosmetics Act, dated 19.10.2007 permitting it to manufacturing Erlocip for the treatment of nonsmall lung cancer. . . .

84.   The plaintiff's counsel had at some stage argued eloquently about the country's entry into the TRIPS regime and its commitment to integrate with the global patent regime. He discounted the price differential between the plaintiffs Tarceva and the defendant's product Erlotinib as being dangerous and jingoistic. As noticed with reference to the two judgments cited above, price differential in the case of a life saving drug—or even a life improving drug in the case of a life threatening situation, is an important and critical factor which cannot be ignored by the court. The materials before the Court in the form of documents undoubtedly show that the plaintiff does not have any manufacturing unit in India, for producing Tarceva. The defendant, on the other hand, manufactures and markets it. The plaintiff has not—apart from blandly asserting in its affidavit about the volume of sales being Rs. 13.2 crores—disclosed by any independent, objective material about its sales. Even if, its assertions are accepted, roughly 1000 patients have perhaps benefited from its drug on a rough conclusion so far. This is on the basis that the cost of the monthly doses being Rs. 1.28 lakhs; the course of treatment involving two months as against the total sale figure claimed as to be 13.2 crores. The defendant's product Erlotinib, on the other hand, is marketed at a third of the cost of Tarceva; it costs Rs. 1600/-per tablet.

85.   Undoubtedly, India entered into the TRIPS regime, and amended her laws to fulfill her international obligations, yet the court has to proceed and apply the laws of this country, which oblige it to weigh all relevant factors. In this background the Court cannot be unmindful of the right of the general public to access life saving drugs which are available and for which such access would be denied if the injunction were granted. The degree of harm in such eventuality is absolute; the chances of improvement of life expectancy; even chances of recovery in some cases would be

snuffed out altogether, if injunction were granted. Such injuries to third parties are un-compensatable. Another way of viewing it is that if the injunction in the case of a life saving drug were to be granted, the Court would in effect be stifling Article 21 so far as those would have or could have access to Erloticip are concerned. It is precisely this consideration that was emphasized as a relevant and significant factor in American Cyanamid and Roussel Uclaf. Even the United States Supreme Court was not unmindful of such considerations when recently it disavowed the liberal practice, of granting injunctions, and underlining the necessity of weighing relevant factors, including public interest, in *eBay* [v. MercExchange, L.L.C., 547 U.S. 388 (2006)]. In another decision, Cordis Corporation v. Boston Scientific Corporation 2004 US App. LEXIS 11557, the US Court of Appeals for Federal Circuit affirmed the refusal to enjoin the defendant, in a patent infringement action where the product was a drug-eluting stent. The court held that such injunction would inhibit a broad choice of availability of such stents. The court compared the public interest in protection of the patentees right with the broader public interest in availability of the product, and held: While crediting the validity of this point, this court also acknowledges that it cannot control in every case, without obliterating the public interest component of the preliminary injunction inquiry. Thus, for good reason, the courts have refused to permanently enjoin activities that would injure the public health.

86.   The last and also significant factor that has to be examined is the question of irreparable hardship. Strangely, the plaintiff did not even address the court on this issue—presumably on its assumption that an injunction would follow once a prima facie case was established. As discussed earlier, in the section concerning balance of convenience, irreparable hardship is a separate distinct head which the Court of necessity has to examine and be satisfied about, while considering interlocutory applications for injunction. The crucial aspect here is whether refusal of injunction would cause such irreparable hardship to the plaintiff as cannot be later compensated in mandatory terms. The suit itself contains the averment that the defendant is a pharmaceutical giant in India. The plaintiff too claims to be holding a large number of patents for a wide variety of drugs, particularly life saving drugs. Neither party has produced any evidence as to the number of patients suffering from small cell lung cancer. Yet in one of the Newspaper articles produced by the plaintiff, states that about 90,000 men and 79,000 women in India suffer annually from lung cancer. The National Cancer Registry Report released by the Indian Medical Council in 2007 states that every hour 50 persons are diagnosed of cancer in the country. The same report states that 24% of all cancer incidents, are in relation to lung cancer. The figures of those suffering

from the ailment that Tarceva and Erlocip seek to alleviate therefore, are significant. There is no empirical material, or statistical method by which the Court can deduce the numbers of such patients who would be using the plaintiff's product if injunction is refused; on the other hand, it is plain that a large number of them would be deprived of access to a life saving drug if injunction is granted. Therefore, this Court is of the opinion that as between the two competing public interests, that is, the public interest in granting an injunction to affirm a patent during the pendency of an infringement action, as opposed to the public interest in access for the people to a life saving drug, the balance has to be tilted in favour of the latter. The damage or injury that would occur to the plaintiff in such case is capable of assessment in monetary terms. However, the injury to the public which would be deprived of the defendants product, which may lead to shortening of lives of several unknown persons, who are not parties to the suit, and which damage cannot be restituted in monetary terms, is not only uncompensatable, it is irreparable. Thus, irreparable injury would be caused if the injunction sought for is granted.

87. The result of the above discussion is that the plaintiff is not entitled to claim an ad interim injunction, in the terms sought. . . .

Notes and Questions

1. In *Hoffmann–La Roche*, the High Court of Delhi relied on the United Kingdom decision *American Cyanamid Co. v. Ethicon Ltd.* [1975] 2 WLR 316 for setting the standard for assessing a request for a preliminary injunction in a patent case. Similarly to *Hoffmann–La Roche*, the *American Cyanamid* court examined claims against a generic source, Ethicon, which was poised to enter a market for medical sutures established by American Cyanamid, the patentee. The *American Cyanamid* court focused on the balance of the hardships between the parties, rather than the public interest, in assessing whether a preliminary injunction should be granted to prevent Ethicon from selling the patented sutures:

> . . . Ethicon's sutures XLG were not yet on the market; so they had no business which would be brought to a stop by the injunction; no factories would be closed and no workpeople would be thrown out of work. . . . If Ethicon were entitled also to establish themselves in the market for PHAE absorbable surgical sutures until the action is tried, which may not be for two or three years yet, and possibly thereafter until the case is finally disposed of on appeal, Cyanamid, even though ultimately successful in proving infringement, would have lost its chance of continuing to increase its share in the total market in absorbable surgical sutures which the continuation of an uninterrupted monopoly of PHAE sutures would have gained for it by the time of the expiry of the patent in

1980. It is notorious that new pharmaceutical products used exclusively by doctors or available only on prescription take a long time to become established in the market, that much of the benefit of the monopoly granted by the patent derives from the fact that the patented product is given the opportunity of becoming established and this benefit continues to be reaped after the patent has expired.

Did the High Court of Delhi in *Hoffmann–La Roche* address any of these concerns? Ultimately, this High Court ruling was upheld on appeal, and Roche's application to India's Supreme Court dismissed with an order to expedite the trial on the merits. See "Breaking News: Supreme Court Dismisses Roche 'Tarceva' Petition," Spicy IP (Aug. 28, 2009) available at http://spicyipindia.blogspot.com/2009/08/breaking-news-supreme-court-dismisses.html. Does this adequately address the patent holder's concerns?

2. The High Court of Delhi's *Hoffmann–La Roche*, includes a citation to the U.S. Supreme Court's eBay Inc. v. MercExchange, L.L.C., 547 U.S. 388 (2006). Note that the U.S. Federal Circuit has considered the patentee's drug discovery costs in a post-*eBay* decision, *Sanofi–Synthelabo v. Apotex, Inc.*, 470 F.3d 1368, 1383–84 (Fed. Cir. 2006). In that case, the Federal Circuit affirmed a district court's entry of a preliminary injunction, explaining:

> The district court relied on [expert] testimony.... in finding that the average cost of developing a blockbuster drug is $800 million. Importantly, the patent system provides incentive to the innovative drug companies to continue costly development efforts. We therefore find that the court did not clearly err in concluding that the significant public interest in encouraging investment in drug development and protecting the exclusionary rights conveyed in valid pharmaceutical patents tips the scales in favor of Sanofi. (internal quotations omitted).

Generally, pharmaceutical companies have maintained that the cost of drug development justifies strong measures against patent infringement. Can the patent system be implemented in a manner that considers both large research costs and public health?

G. MONETARY RELIEF

Unlike the jury system in the U.S., other nations rely on judges to determine the amount of monetary relief. The following excerpt is one court's consideration of a damages award under the reasonable royalty rubric.

ULTRAFRAME (UK) LTD. v. EUROCELL BUILDING PLASTICS LTD.

[2006] EWHC 1344 (Pat) (Eng.)

THE HONOURABLE MR JUSTICE KITCHIN

The claimant ("Ultraframe") is one of the market leaders and sells a number of modular systems, one of which is called Ultralite 500. Until 2002, the defendants (collectively "Eurocell") were one of the largest distributors of Ultralite 500 systems. In that year they began to make and sell their own system called Pinnacle 500.

In 2004 Ultraframe developed a new product called Elevation. It contends it took this step to compete with Pinnacle 500 and in an attempt to recapture some of the market and mitigate its loss. It says that having attempted, over a period of time, to meet the competition by advertising and promotional activity, it really had no alternative. In the circumstances it was forced to develop a new design and it duly did so.

Ultraframe contends that every sale of Pinnacle 500 is a lost sale of Ultralite 500 because Pinnacle 500 was designed to compete directly with Ultralite 500 and was a virtually identical product.

Eurocell say this argument is too simplistic and ignores a number of important factors.

[Plaintiff's expert] Mr Hall split the Pinnacle 500 sales into three categories:

> i) Pinnacle 500 sales made to customers who had previously bought Ultralite 500 from Eurocell;

> ii) Pinnacle 500 sales made to customers who had previously bought Ultralite 500 from Ultraframe; and

> iii) Pinnacle 500 sales to customers not in either of the categories above, that is to say new customers.

[Defendants' expert] Mr Plaha accepted, in the end, that Ultraframe would have made all the sales falling in categories i) and ii) but only a proportion of those in category iii). As to this latter category, he assumed that only a proportion (some 60%) represent lost Ultralite 500 sales based upon an adjusted market share estimate. He arrived at a total figure for lost sales of 100,637 SQM. Thus the difference between the experts is only some 34,000 SQM.

To my mind all of these points illustrate the inherently difficult and uncertain nature of the exercise both experts were seeking to perform. At the end of the day I have to make an assessment based upon my impressions of the evidence as a whole.

As to the proportion of these that represent lost sales, I will adopt the same position as the experts in relation to categories i) and ii) and assume that these all represent lost sales. As to category iii) I consider that a larger percentage of these would have been made by Ultraframe than Mr Plaha has allowed and estimate the figure at 52,500 (or just under 80% of the sales in category iii). Overall therefore I estimate that 120,000 SQM of the sales of Pinnacle 500 represent lost sales of Ultralite 500.

I have found that Eurocell sold 135,000 SQM of Pinnacle 500 and that 120,000 SQM represents lost sales of Ultralite 500. Ultraframe is therefore entitled to a royalty on the remaining 15,000 SQM.

Eurocell suggest a royalty rate of 5%. Ultraframe suggest it should be 15–17.5%.

It is fair to say that this is a mechanical patent type of case and that royalty rates for such patents are commonly about 5%. Further I think it relevant that not all the Pinnacle 500 products infringe— certain ancillary items do not. The non infringing items include such things as the white plastic firrings. Nevertheless Eurocell accept the royalty is to be calculated on them all.

There are, however, certain factors which point to a higher rate. The product was obviously the market leader and, before the infringement, unique. Looking at the profits available, Ultraframe says that a 50:50 split of gross profits would likely be agreed between a willing licensor and willing licensee bearing in mind the nature of the product and the market in issue. This, Mr Wallis says, would produce a rate of 15–17.7%.

I have reached the conclusion that a willing licensor and willing licensee would have agreed a figure closer to that contended for by Eurocell. It must be remembered that the royalty is only on sales that Ultraframe would not have made. Further, I think that a 50:50 split of profits estimated at 35% is not realistic. Overall, I think a reasonable figure for the royalty is 8%.

I reached the conclusion that the presence and pricing of Pinnacle 500 was one of the causes of the price depression of Ultralite 500. Eurocell directly targeted Pinnacle 500 at Ultralite 500 from its position as a distributor. But for the infringement the price of Ultralite 500 in each of the years 2003–2005 would have been higher than it was. Ultraframe was obliged to reduce its prices to retain its market share. In the circumstances I believe that Ultraframe has suffered a loss on sales of Ultralite 500 which is recoverable from Eurocell. That loss was both foreseeable and caused by the infringement. It amounts to the difference between the price Ultraframe achieved on sales of Ultralite 500 and the price it would have achieved but for the infringement.....

Notes and Questions

1. What standard does the court use to calculate lost profits? How does the analysis set forth in *Ultraframe* compare with the standards applied by the U.S. courts?

2. What is the basis of the reasonable royalty rate determined by the *Ultraframe* court? How does this compare with the U.S. analysis? *See* Georgia–Pacific Corp. v. United States Plywood Corp., 318 F.Supp. 1116, 1120 (S.D.N.Y. 1970), *modified and aff'd*, 446 F.2d 295 (2d Cir. 1971) (describing a multi-factor test to determine a reasonable royalty rate). Note that the *Ultraframe* court examined the market for comparable technologies, rather than the parties' prior licensing agreement, in setting the royalty figure. Why do you suppose that *Ultraframe* did not place more weight on the parties' negotiated rate?

3. Why did *Ultraframe* reject the patentee's efforts to recover development costs for Elevation, a new design intended to compete with the infringer's product? Are there instances where development costs might be recoverable under UK law, or does *Ultraframe* close the door to compensation for such costs? Is it consistent with the purposes of a patent system to permit such recovery?

4. Under U.S. law, monetary damages have a compensatory purpose whether awarded as lost profits, reasonable royalty or a combination of both. *See* 35 U.S.C. section 284 (setting damages for infringement at a level "adequate to compensate for the infringement"). Additionally, U.S. law allows a patentee to collect up to three times the compensatory amount in exceptional cases, such as where the infringer acted willfully. *Id.*; *see In re* Seagate Tech., LLC, 497 F.3d 1360 (Fed. Cir. 2007) (en banc) (holding that willfulness requires a showing that the infringer acted with an objectively high likelihood that its actions constituted infringement of valid patent). The United States eliminated recovery based on the disgorgement of a defendant's profits during the 1940's. *See* Amy L. Landers, *Let the Games Begin: Incentives to Innovation in the New Economy of Intellectual Property Law*, 46 SANTA CLARA L. REV. 307 (2006) (tracing the history of U.S. patent remedies).

German law differs by allowing a patentee to demonstrate damages by showing the patentee's actual loss, a license rate, or disgorgement of the defendant's profits. *See* Volker Behr, *Punitive Damages in American and German Law—Tendencies Towards Approximation of Apparently Irreconcilable Concepts*, 78 CHI.-KENT L. REV. 105, 137 (2003). Additionally, a court can limit damages owed by an infringer who acts with only slight negligence to an amount between the actual damages suffered and the gain achieved. *Id.* at 139; German Patent Act, § 139(1).

In adopting the IP Right Enforcement Directives (Directive 2004/4/48/EC), EU member states enhanced measures to obtain evidence for establishing patent infringement and increased monetary relief for the compensation of damages. German courts are criticized for awarding limited damages in most cases because damages are equivalent to legally negotiated license royalty rates. In implementing the directive, German courts began to award an increased royalty rate in exceptional cases where the infringer takes an unfair advantage over legally negotiated licensees despite knowledge of the patent. The courts also increased the award for damages in the form of defendant's profits by refusing to deduct indirect costs, such as overhead costs.

Japanese courts followed German tradition by calculating damages using a royalty rate in the majority of cases. Alarmed by a huge gap between damages awarded by U.S. as opposed to Japanese courts, the Japanese Government revised Japanese patent law to help patentees establish damages by codifying the *Panduit* test established under U.S. case law. *Panduit Corp. v. Stahlin Bros. Fibre Works, Inc.*, 575 F.2d 1152 (6th Cir. 1978). However, the impact of the revision has been much smaller than expected. Toshiko Takenaka, *Harmonizing Patent Infringement Damages: A Lesson from Japanese Experiences*, Wolrad Prinz zu Waldeck und Pyrmont et al, Patent and Technological Progress in a Global World 463 (2008). A similar revision has since been introduced in Korean patent law.

However, some patent systems do not authorize punitive damages for willful infringement. *See* Paul M. Janicke, *Do We Really Need So Many Mental And Emotional States In United States Patent Law?*, 8 TEX. INTELL. PROP. L.J. 279, 287–88 (2000) (noting that punitive damages are not available under the German patent statute); Mindy L. Kotler & Gary W. Hamilton, U.S. DEP'T OF COMMERCE, A GUIDE TO JAPAN'S PATENT SYSTEM, 35 (1995) ("enhanced damages are unavailable in Japan.").

5.   Unlike U.S. law, some countries authorize criminal actions against patent infringement. For example, the German Patent Act authorizes criminal penalties for patent infringement, including an imprisonment term that ranges up to five years in length. German Patent Act, § 142; *see also* Code de la Propriété Intellectuelle, art. 615–14 (France) (providing for a prison term and fine for knowing patent infringement). One report details some limited active enforcement of the German statute, stating that authorities raided dozens of booths at a consumer electronics show held in Hannover, Germany, and that "cell phones, navigation devices, and other gear that allegedly infringe on patents" were confiscated. Anne Broache, "Patent Police Raid Booths at CeBit Trade Show," CNET NEWS BLOG (3/6/09), available at: http://news.cnet.com/8301–10784_3–9887955–7.html. Note that the Hannover raid was based on complaints of patent infringement at an investigatory stage, rather than after a court-entered finding of infringement. Are such seizures authorized under U.S. law? Further, what are the positive and/or negative implications for adding criminal enforcement to the patent system?

6.   The U.S. Patent Act, 35 U.S.C. § 287 precludes a damage award where a patentee fails to mark a patented product, although damages

are recoverable beginning from the time that "the infringer was notified of infringement and continued to infringe thereafter." Compare Section 62(1) of the United Kingdom Patents Act, which states "patent damages shall not be awarded, and no order shall be made for an account of profits, against a defendant ... who proves that at the date of the infringement he was not aware, and had no reasonable grounds for supposing, that the patent existed...." This section further provides that marking a product with a designation "patent" or "patented," is not sufficient to establish knowledge "unless the number of the patent accompanied the word or words in question."

How does this standard compare with the United States' 35 U.S.C. section 287? Consider the following interpretation of the United Kingdom's standard:

> The words "had no reasonable grounds for supposing" impose an objective test. The existence of reasonable grounds must be judged in the light of all the circumstances at the time of infringement. Marking with the patent number and sale and exhibition on a large scale would be important factors, as would be actual copying of the goods.

Texas Iron Works Inc.'s Patent, [2000] R.P.C. 207, 235 (PCC). Are there situations where damages would be awarded under the United States law but not the United Kingdom's? In formulating your response, consider this explanation of United Kingdom statute:

> ... if it was intended that marking with the patent number was always to be conclusive against such infringer, the section would have said so.... Circumstances might, however, exist in which only a few examples of the plaintiffs' patented goods, though marked with a patent number, had been made and sold at the time of the infringement in question and the defendant might not have seen any of them. If so, it might well not be right to hold that at that time there had been sufficient notification to amount to the existence of reasonable grounds for supposing that a patent existed.'

Lancer Boss Ltd. v. Henley Forklift Co. Ltd., [1975] R.P.C. 307, 314. Is this standard meaningfully different from that implemented in the United States? See *Maxwell v. J. Baker*, Inc., 86 F.3d 1098 (Fed. Cir. 1996) (continuous efforts to ensure marking of patented goods was sufficient to support a damage award, although five percent of goods sold were unmarked).

Chapter 9

PATENTS & COMPETITION LAW AND POLICY

A. UNITED STATES ANTITRUST LAW

The relationship between patents and competition law is an old one that can be traced back to at least 1623 with the enactment of the Statute Against Monopolies by English Parliament. The Statute placed limitations on the grant of exclusive rights by the Crown to inventors or discoverers for the production and distribution of products, processes, and services. Patent grants, however, were permitted but could not be "contrary to the law nor mischievous to the state by raising prices of commodities at home, or hurt of trade, or generally inconvenient." In a few words, the Statute initiated a debate that continues on through today: to what extent is patent law consistent with competition law and policy?

Within the United States, competition law and policy is defined by the Antitrust Laws, which were initiated by the enactment of the Sherman Antitrust Act in 1890, followed by the Clayton Act and Federal Trade Commission Act of 1914. The Sherman Act has two principal provisions. Section one outlaws contracts and combinations in restraint of trade, meaning agreements among two or more competitors that restrict competition. Section two outlaws acts by a single company that monopolize or tend to monopolize a market. The Clayton Act was enacted to provide some guidance to these two provisions with more rule-like and focused provisions attempting to clarify what acts should be subject to scrutiny. Initially the primary enforcer of the Antitrust Laws was the Department of Justice, with some private enforcement. With the enactment of the Federal Trade Commission Act, a new agency, the Federal Trade Commission, shares responsibility with the Department of Justice for enforcement of the Antitrust Laws. The Federal Trade Commission Act outlaws unfair methods of competition and unfair or deceptive business practices. These methods and practices include acts prohibited by the Sherman and Clayton Acts, but may also include more.

Licensing and other business uses of patents can raise antitrust scrutiny. The readings below provide an overview of the seminal issues at the intersection of patent law and antitrust. The cases highlight current legal issues pertaining to competition law and antitrust. Our goal is to educate about the broader debates and to introduce the reader to some important doctrinal issues. As far as the larger debates, ask yourself the following question. Should patents be exempted from antitrust enforcement or should the market exclusivity invite antitrust scrutiny? The case for exemption is based on patent's role in promoting innovation and competition in the long run, which might require antitrust law to create an exception so as not to interfere with the dynamic growth of the market. On the other hand, patent exclusivity may prevent the entry of new firms and corresponding new ideas and products which can promote competition. How can antitrust and patent law coexist? In answering these questions, think about the exceptions created by the Statute Against Monopolies with respect to raising prices and hurting trade. Has the law made any progress since this pronouncement? Before we work on answering these questions the student must understand the unique American doctrine of patent misuse and its relations to American antitrust law.

1. MISUSE AND PATENT–ANTITRUST

In the United States a violation of the antitrust laws by the patentee may constitute a defense to a suit for patent infringement under the equitable doctrine of patent misuse, at least until the adverse effects of the misuse are purged by the patentee. The patent misuse doctrine is not easy to understand because it provides a specific remedy for a litigant who brings a substantive misuse violation to the attention of the court during infringement litigation. These activities frequently are, but need not be antitrust violations.

The doctrinal development of substantive patent misuse began with a series of cases where the patent owner brought suit for contributory infringement against a manufacturer who was selling unpatented supplies, used by licensees of patented machines in violation of their license. The manufacturer defended on the ground that the patent owner was trying to monopolize an unpatented product. Hence, the court should not enforce the patent against it. The classic case was the decision of the Sixth Circuit written by Judge Taft (later President Taft and then Chief Justice Taft) in *Heaton–Peninsular Button–Fastener Co. v. Eureka Specialty Co.*, 77 F. 288 (6th Cir.1896). This opinion manifests a sophisticated approach to the economics of tying practices. The opinion recognized that permitting a patentee to control the supplies used in the operation of its patented machines merely measured the intensity of use of the patented machine and did not constitute improper monopolization and an unpatented product. However, this approach did not survive the passage of the Clayton Act for in 1917 the Supreme Court, while it did not rely on the Clayton Act, refused to enforce a patent against a contributory infringer who was selling movies used in connection with licensed patented projectors, *Motion Picture Patents Co. v. Universal Film Mfg. Co.*, 243 U.S. 502 (1917).

Motion Picture Patents was followed by a series of cases involving the refusal of courts to enforce patents against contributory infringers who were selling unpatented components that were either used with or were part of, but not the complete, patented combination or process. This line of cases culminated in *Mercoid Corp. v. Mid–Continent Investment Co.*, 320 U.S. 661 (1944) (Mercoid I) and *Mercoid Corp. v. Minneapolis–Honeywell Regulator Co.*, 320 U.S. 680 (1944) (Mercoid II). Mercoid I and II extended the doctrine against suits for contributory infringement to all unpatented components even if they were the essence of the patented combination or process. Moreover, they may have gone even further, precluding a suit for contributory infringement even if the patentee was not trying to control any unpatented component, but was merely trying to conveniently use a manufacturer of unpatented components as a collector of royalties for use of the patented combination.

However, all of these cases which discussed the patentee's extending his monopoly to unpatented components were suits against sellers of such components. Thus, the courts recognized no separate doctrine of patent misuse until 1942. However, defendants sued for contributory infringement could allege that the suit should fail because the lawsuit represented the patentee's attempt to monopolize unpatented components. Then the dam burst as two years before the Mercoid cases, the Court created the doctrine of patent misuse in **Morton Salt Co. v. G. S. Suppiger Co.**, 314 U.S. 488 (1942), where the Court held that any alleged infringer could raise as an equitable defense a claim that the patent owner was misusing the asserted patent and therefore it would be inequitable for the American courts to enforce such a patent even if the alleged wrongful activities did not in any way harm the alleged infringer. The authors know of no other field of law where a defendant can ask the court to refuse to grant the plaintiff the relief it is entitled to because the plaintiff has taken some allegedly improper action that has harmed someone other than the defendant.

Morton Salt opened the floodgates to numerous misuse claims by accused infringers. Patent litigation was frequently marked by assertions that the patent owner was improperly extending its monopoly or engaging in conduct that amounted to an antitrust violation, even though the alleged infringer was itself unaffected by the challenged conduct. The majority of patent trials thus took on the flavor of antitrust trials as the courts condemned a wide variety of practices in the name of patent misuse. For example, courts held that it was misuse for a patentee to insist on collecting royalties based on unpatented goods or processes as a condition of a patent license. Moreover, the mere collection of royalties on unpatented goods or processes was argued to be a misuse. Likewise, a patentee could not insist that a licensee take a license on more than one patent, but a license under multiple patents ultimately was found not to constitute misuse if the patentee did not insist on that form of licensee. Patentees could include a grant-back clause in a license, but whether a patentee may insist upon a grant-back clause was unclear. Clauses that precluded the licensee from competing with the patentee with a product or process not covered by the license were held to be a misuse even where the parties voluntarily agreed to such clauses.

Perhaps the key to understanding all of these cases is that any sort of leveraging by the patentee could invoke the misuse penalty: refusal to enforce the patent until the misuse is purged, even if the conduct is not an antitrust violation. In addition, any antitrust violations relating to the patent could support the misuse remedy whether or not grounded on the improper use of leverage.

In 1952, Congress moved to overturn the extreme leveraging theory found in *Mercoid I and II* by passing § 271(d) which added three definitions of actions that are not to be treated as patent misuses with the clear intent to overrule the *Mercoid* decisions. The Court interprets those three definitions in **Dawson Chemical Co. v. Rohm and Haas Company, 448 U.S. 176 (1980). In the** 1988 Patent Misuse Reform Act Congress added two more definitions of conduct that was not to be considered patent misuse, 271(d)(4) and 271(d)(5). The basic question posed by 271(d) is whether the acts that cannot be classified as patent misuses may be antitrust violations. In *In re Independent Serv. Org. Antitrust Litig.*, 203 F.3d 1322 (Fed.Cir.2000), the Federal Circuit in the course of discussing whether Xerox's refusal to either sell spare parts or license its intellectual property covering such spare parts violated the antitrust laws suggested that the answer is "no". In the following case, the Supreme Court clarified the confusion over the relationship between patent misuse and antitrust law in holding that ownership of a patent did not create a presumption of market power for an antitrust tying claim.

ILLINOIS TOOL WORKS INC. v.
INDEPENDENT INK, INC.

547 U.S. 28 (2006)

JUSTICE STEVENS delivered the opinion of the Court.

[Author's summary: Illinois Tool owned patents on an ink jet printhead and an ink container which were components of its printing systems which it licensed to original equipment manufacturers of printers (OEM). The OEM's agreed to license the patents on the condition that they distribute the printers with Illinois Tool's unpatented, specially designed ink. Independent Ink developed and sold an ink that could be used with the OEM's printers. Independent Ink brought a declaratory judgment to invalidate Illinois Tool's patents and to claim that Illinois Tool was violating the Sherman Act by engaging in a tying arrangement in conditioning the licensing of the patents on the use of the ink. The district court found against Independent Ink on the Sherman Act claim on the grounds that Independent Ink failed to show that Illinois Tool had market power. The Federal Circuit reversed, citing language from Supreme Court precedent that ownership of a patent created a presumption of market power in tying claims. The Supreme Court reversed the Federal Circuit and clarified its precedent on patent ownership and market power and then after reviewing all of the relevant tying jurisprudence added the following with respect to 271(d).]

It is Congress' most recent narrowing of the patent misuse defense, however, that is directly relevant to this case. Four years after our decision in Jefferson Parish repeated the patent-equals-market-power presumption, 466 U.S., at 16, 104 S.Ct. 1551, Congress amended the Patent Code to eliminate that presumption in the patent misuse context, 102 Stat. 4676. The relevant provision reads:

> "(d) No patent owner otherwise entitled to relief for infringement or contributory infringement of a patent shall be denied relief or deemed guilty of misuse or illegal extension of the patent right by reason of his having done one or more of the following: . . .

> (5) conditioned the license of any rights to the patent or the sale of the patented product on the acquisition of a license to rights in another patent or purchase of a separate product, unless, in view of the circumstances, the patent owner has market power in the relevant market for the patent or patented product on which the license or sale is conditioned." 35 U.S.C. § 271(d)(5) (emphasis added).

The italicized clause makes it clear that Congress did not intend the mere existence of a patent to constitute the requisite "market power." Indeed, fairly read, it provides that without proof that Trident had market power in the relevant market, its conduct at issue in this case was neither "misuse" nor an "illegal extension of the patent right."

While the 1988 amendment does not expressly refer to the antitrust laws, it certainly invites a reappraisal of the per se rule announced in *International Salt*. A rule denying a patentee the right to enjoin an infringer is significantly less severe than a rule that makes the conduct at issue a federal crime punishable by up to 10 years in prison. See 15 U.S.C. § 1. It would be absurd to assume that Congress intended to provide that the use of a patent that merited punishment as a felony would not constitute "misuse." Moreover, given the fact that the patent misuse doctrine provided the basis for the market power presumption, it would be anomalous to preserve the presumption in antitrust after Congress has eliminated its foundation.* * *

2. LIMITED LICENSES AND PATENT EXHAUSTION

Another broad area of possible limitations on the exploitation of patents is in the area of limited licenses. Limited licenses are licenses that permit the licensee to carry out only certain of the acts controlled by the licensed patent. For example, a license that permits the licensee to manufacture and sell a patented product, but only at a particular price or to particular customers. The Antitrust Division in the 1970s targeted various forms of limited patent licenses accusing them of illegality under the antitrust laws and thus also patent misuse since any violation of the antitrust laws causes any patent that facilitates that violation to be unenforceable under *Morton Salt*. This crusade against limited patent licenses ultimately collapsed under the weight of the Division's defeat in **United States v. Studiengesellschaft Kohle**, 670 F.2d 1122 (D.C. Cir. 1981). A species of limited licensing goes under the name of patent exhaustion. Patent exhaustion is the doctrine that indicates that even if a patent owner sells a patent product with only a limited license expressly stated for resale, that provision is ignored at least for the purposes of patent law. In the 19th century the Court had expressly stated that such a provision is to be ignored, *Keeler v. Standard Folding Bed*, 157 U.S. 659 (1895). Nevertheless, in **Mallinckrodt Inc. v. Medipart Inc.**, 976 F.2d 700 (Fed. Cir. 1992) the Federal Circuit expressly held that cases such as *Keeler* were all overruled by *General Talking Pictures Corp. v. Western Electric Co.*, 304 U.S. 175, *aff'd on reh'g*, 305 U.S. 124 (1938). But then in 2008, in the following case, the Court announced that there were limits on how far down the chain of distribution a patent owner could impose licensing restrictions on users of patented technology.

QUANTA COMPUTER, INC. v. L.G. ELECTRONICS, INC.

553 U.S. 617 (2008)

JUSTICE THOMAS delivered the opinion of the Court.

For over 150 years this Court has applied the doctrine of patent exhaustion to limit the patent rights that survive the initial authorized sale of a patented item. In this case, we decide whether patent exhaustion applies to the sale of components of a patented system that must be combined with additional components in order to practice the patented methods. The Court of Appeals for the Federal Circuit held that the doctrine does not apply to method patents at all and, in the alternative, that it does not apply here because the sales were not authorized by the license agreement. We disagree on both scores. Because the exhaustion doctrine applies to method patents, and because the license authorizes the sale of components that substantially embody the patents in suit, the sale exhausted the patents.

I

* * *LGE licensed a patent portfolio to Intel Corporation (Intel). The cross-licensing agreement (License Agreement) permits Intel to manufacture and sell microprocessors and chipsets that use the LGE Patents (the Intel Products). The License Agreement authorizes Intel to " 'make, use, sell (directly or indirectly), offer to sell, import or otherwise dispose of' " its own products practicing the LGE Patents. Notwithstanding this broad language, the License Agreement contains some limitations. Relevant here, it stipulates that no license " 'is granted by either party hereto . . . to any third party for the combination by a third party of Licensed Products of either party with items, components, or the like acquired . . . from sources other than a party hereto, or for the use, import, offer for sale or sale of such combination.' " * * *

The License Agreement purports not to alter the usual rules of patent exhaustion, however, providing that, " '[n]otwithstanding anything to the contrary contained in this Agreement, the parties agree that nothing herein shall in any way limit or alter the effect of patent exhaustion that would otherwise apply when a party hereto sells any of its Licensed Products.' * * *

In a separate agreement (Master Agreement), Intel agreed to give written notice to its own customers informing them that, while it had obtained a broad license " 'ensur[ing] that any Intel product that you purchase is licensed by LGE and thus does not infringe any patent held by LGE,' " the license " 'does not extend, expressly or by implication, to any product that you make by combining an Intel product with any non-Intel product.' " * * *

Petitioners, including Quanta Computer (collectively Quanta), are a group of computer manufacturers. Quanta purchased microprocessors and chipsets from Intel and received the notice required by the Master Agreement. Nonetheless, Quanta manufactured computers using Intel parts in combination with non-Intel memory and buses in ways that practice the LGE Patents. Quanta does not modify the Intel components and follows Intel's specifications to incorporate the parts into its own systems.

LGE filed a complaint against Quanta, asserting that the combination of the Intel Products with non-Intel memory and buses infringed the LGE Patents. The District Court granted summary judgment to Quanta, holding that, for purposes of the patent exhaustion doctrine, the license LGE granted to Intel resulted in forfeiture of any potential infringement actions against legitimate purchasers of the Intel Products.* * *The court found that, although the Intel Products do not fully practice any of the patents at issue, they have no reasonable noninfringing use and therefore their authorized sale exhausted patent rights in the completed computers under *United States v. Univis Lens Co.*, 316 U.S. 241, 62 S.Ct. 1088, 86 L.Ed. 1408 (1942).* * * The Court of Appeals for the Federal Circuit affirmed in part and reversed in part. It agreed that the doctrine of patent exhaustion does not apply to method claims. In the alternative, it concluded that exhaustion did not apply because LGE did not license Intel to sell the Intel Products to Quanta for use in combination with non-Intel products.* * * We granted certiorari.

II

The longstanding doctrine of patent exhaustion provides that the initial authorized sale of a patented item terminates all patent rights to that item. This Court first applied the doctrine in 19th-century cases addressing patent extensions on the Woodworth planing machine. Purchasers of licenses to sell and use the machine for the duration of the original patent term sought to continue using the licenses through the extended term. The Court held that the extension of the patent term did not affect the rights already secured by purchasers who bought the item for use "in the ordinary pursuits of life." *Bloomer v. McQuewan*, 14 How. 539, 549, 14 L.Ed. 532 (1853).* * * In *Adams v. Burke*, 17 Wall. 453, 21 L.Ed. 700 (1873), the Court affirmed the dismissal of a patent holder's suit alleging that a licensee had violated postsale restrictions on where patented coffin-lids could be used. "[W]here a person ha[s] purchased a patented machine of the patentee or his assignee," the Court held, "this purchase carrie[s] with it the right to the use of that machine so long as it [is] capable of use." Id., at 455.

Although the Court permitted post sale restrictions on the use of a patented article in *Henry v. A.B. Dick Co.*, 224 U.S. 1, 32 S.Ct. 364, 56 L.Ed. 645 (1912), that decision was short lived. In 1913, the Court refused to apply A.B. Dick to uphold price-fixing provisions in a patent license. See *Bauer & Cie v. O'Donnell*, 229 U.S. 1, 14–17, 33 S.Ct. 616, 57 L.Ed. 1041 (1913). Shortly thereafter, in *Motion Picture Patents Co. v. Universal Film Mfg. Co.*, 243 U.S. 502, 518, 37 S.Ct. 416, 61 L.Ed. 871 (1917), the Court explicitly overruled *A.B. Dick*. In that case, a patent holder attempted to limit purchasers' use of its film projectors to show only film made under a patent held by the same company. The Court noted the "increasing frequency" with which patent holders were using A.B. Dick-style licenses to limit the use of their products and thereby using the patents to secure market control of related, unpatented items. 243 U.S., at 509, 516–517, 37 S.Ct. 416. Observing that "the primary purpose of our patent laws is not the creation of private fortunes for the owners of patents but is 'to promote the progress of science and useful arts,' " id., at 511, 37 S.Ct. 416 (quoting U.S. Const., Art. I, § 8, cl. 8), the Court held that "the scope of the grant which may be made to an inventor in a patent, pursuant to the [patent] statute, must be limited to the invention described in the claims of his patent." 243 U.S., at 511, 37 S.Ct. 416. Accordingly, it reiterated the rule that "the right to vend is exhausted by a single, unconditional sale, the article sold being thereby carried outside the monopoly of the patent law and rendered free of every restriction which the vendor may attempt to put upon it." Id., at 516, 37 S.Ct. 416

This Court most recently discussed patent exhaustion in *Univis*, 316 U.S. 241, 62 S.Ct. 1088, 86 L.Ed. 1408, on which the District Court relied. Univis Lens Company, the holder of patents on eyeglass lenses, licensed a purchaser to manufacture lens blanks by fusing together different lens segments to create bi-and tri-focal lenses and to sell them to other Univis licensees at agreed-upon rates. Wholesalers were licensed to grind the blanks into the patented finished lenses, which they would then sell to Univis-licensed prescription retailers for resale at a fixed rate. Finishing retailers, after grinding the blanks into patented lenses, would sell the finished lenses to consumers at the same fixed rate. The United States sued Univis under the Sherman Act, 15 U.S.C. §§ 1, 3, 15, alleging unlawful restraints on trade. Univis asserted its patent monopoly rights as a defense to the antitrust suit. The Court granted certiorari to determine whether Univis' patent monopoly survived the sale of the lens blanks by the licensed manufacturer and therefore shielded Univis' pricing scheme from the Sherman Act.

The Court assumed that the Univis patents containing claims for finished lenses were practiced in part by the wholesalers and finishing retailers who ground the blanks into lenses, and held that the sale of the lens blanks exhausted the patents on the finished lenses. *Univis*, 316 U.S., at 248–249, 62 S.Ct. 1088. The Court explained that the lens blanks "embodi[ed] essential features of the patented device and [were] without utility until ... ground and polished as the finished lens of the patent." Id., at 249, 62 S.Ct. 1088. The Court noted that:

> "where one has sold an uncompleted article which, because it embodies essential features of his patented invention, is within the protection of his patent, and has destined the article to be finished by the purchaser in conformity to the patent, he has old his invention so far as it is or may be embodied in that particular article." Id., at 250–251, 62 S.Ct. 1088.

In sum, the Court concluded that the traditional bar on patent restrictions following the sale of an item applies when the item sufficiently embodies the patent-even if it does not completely practice the patent-such that its only and intended use is to be finished under the terms of the patent.

With this history of the patent exhaustion doctrine in mind, we turn to the parties' arguments.

III

A

* * *Nothing in this Court's approach to patent exhaustion supports LGE's argument that method patents cannot be exhausted.* * *Eliminating exhaustion for method patents would seriously undermine the exhaustion doctrine. Patentees seeking to avoid patent exhaustion could simply draft their patent claims to describe a method rather than an apparatus.* * *This case illustrates the danger of allowing such an end-run around exhaustion. On LGE's theory, although Intel is authorized to sell a completed computer system that practices the LGE Patents, any downstream purchasers of the system could nonetheless be liable for patent infringement. Such a result would violate the longstanding principle that, when a patented item is "once lawfully made and sold, there is no restriction on [its] use to be implied for the benefit of the patentee." *Adams*, 17 Wall., at 457, 21 L.Ed. 700. We therefore reject LGE's argument that method claims, as a category, are never exhaustible.

B

We next consider the extent to which a product must embody a patent in order to trigger exhaustion.* * *Just as the lens blanks in *Univis* did not fully practice the patents at issue because they had not been ground into finished lenses, Quanta observes, the Intel Products cannot practice the LGE Patents-or indeed, function at all-until they are combined with memory and buses in a computer system. If, as in *Univis*, patent rights are exhausted by the sale of the incomplete item, then LGE has no postsale right to require that the patents be practiced using only Intel parts. Quanta also argues that exhaustion doctrine will be a dead letter unless it is triggered by the sale of components that essentially, even if not completely, embody an invention. Otherwise, patent holders could authorize the sale of computers that are complete with the exception of one minor step-say, inserting the microprocessor into a socket-and extend their rights through each downstream purchaser all the way to the end user.

LGE, for its part, argues that *Univis* is inapplicable here for three reasons. First, it maintains that Univis should be limited to products that contain all the physical aspects needed to practice the patent. On that theory, the Intel Products cannot embody the patents because additional physical components are required before the patents can be practiced. Second, LGE asserts that in *Univis* there was no "patentable distinction" between the lens blanks and the patented finished lenses since they were both subject to the same patent.* * *In contrast, it describes the Intel Products as "independent and distinct products" from the systems using the LGE Patents and subject to "independent patents."Finally, LGE argues that Univis does not apply because the Intel Products are analogous to individual elements of a combination patent, and allowing sale of those components to exhaust the patent would impermissibly "ascrib[e] to one element of the patented combination the status of the patented invention in itself." *Aro Mfg. Co. v. Convertible Top Replacement Co.*, 365 U.S. 336, 344–345, 81 S.Ct. 599, 5 L.Ed.2d 592 (1961).

We agree with Quanta that *Univis* governs this case. As the Court there explained, exhaustion was triggered by the sale of the lens blanks because their only reasonable and intended use was to practice the patent and because they "embodie[d] essential features of [the] patented invention." 316 U.S., at 249–251, 62 S.Ct. 1088. Each of those attributes is shared by the microprocessors and chipsets Intel sold to Quanta under the License Agreement.

First, *Univis* held that "the authorized sale of an article which is capable of use only in practicing the patent is a relinquishment of the patent monopoly with respect to the article sold." Id., at 249, 62

S.Ct. 1088. The lens blanks in *Univis* met this standard because they were "without utility until [they were] ground and polished as the finished lens of the patent." Ibid. Accordingly, "the only object of the sale [was] to enable the [finishing retailer] to grind and polish it for use as a lens by the prospective wearer." Ibid. Here, LGE has suggested no reasonable use for the Intel Products other than incorporating them into computer systems that practice the LGE Patents. Nor can we can discern one: A microprocessor or chipset cannot function until it is connected to buses and memory. And here, as in *Univis*, the only apparent object of Intel's sales to Quanta was to permit Quanta to incorporate the Intel Products into computers that would practice the patents.

Second, the lens blanks in *Univis* "embodie[d] essential features of [the] patented invention." Id., at 250–251, 62 S.Ct. 1088. The essential, or inventive, feature of the Univis lens patents was the fusing together of different lens segments to create bi-and tri-focal lenses. The finishing process performed by the finishing and prescription retailers after the fusing was not unique.* * *Like the Univis lens blanks, the Intel Products constitute a material part of the patented invention and all but completely practice the patent. Here, as in *Univis*, the incomplete article substantially embodies the patent because the only step necessary to practice the patent is the application of common processes or the addition of standard parts. Everything inventive about each patent is embodied in the Intel Products. They control access to main and cache memory, practicing the '641 and '379 patents by checking cache memory against main memory and comparing read and write requests. They also control priority of bus access by various other computer components under the '733 patent. Naturally, the Intel Products cannot carry out these functions unless they are attached to memory and buses, but those additions are standard components in the system, providing the material that enables the microprocessors and chipsets to function. The Intel Products were specifically designed to function only when memory or buses are attached; Quanta was not required to make any creative or inventive decision when it added those parts. Indeed, Quanta had no alternative but to follow Intel's specifications in incorporating the Intel Products into its computers because it did not know their internal structure, which Intel guards as a trade secret. Intel all but practiced the patent itself by designing its products to practice the patents, lacking only the addition of standard parts.

We are unpersuaded by LGE's attempts to distinguish *Univis*. First, there is no reason to distinguish the two cases on the ground that the articles in *Univis* required the removal of material to practice the patent while the Intel Products require the addition of components to practice the patent.* * *[W]e think that the nature of the final step, rather than whether it consists of adding or deleting material, is the relevant characteristic. In each case, the final step to practice the patent is common and noninventive: grinding a lens to the customer's prescription, or connecting a microprocessor or chipset to buses or memory. The Intel Products embody the essential features of the LGE Patents because they carry out all the inventive processes when combined, according to their design, with standard components.* * *

C

Having concluded that the Intel Products embodied the patents, we next consider whether their sale to Quanta exhausted LGE's patent rights. Exhaustion is triggered only by a sale authorized by the patent holder. *Univis*, 316 U.S., at 249, 62 S.Ct. 1088.

* * *Nothing in the License Agreement restricts Intel's right to sell its microprocessors and chipsets to purchasers who intend to combine them with non-Intel parts. It broadly permits Intel to " 'make, use, [or] sell' " products free of LGE's patent claims. To be sure, LGE did require Intel to give notice to its customers, including Quanta, that LGE had not licensed those customers to practice its patents. But neither party contends that Intel breached the agreement in that respect. In any event, the provision requiring notice to Quanta appeared only in the Master Agreement, and LGE does not suggest that a breach of that agreement would constitute a breach of the License Agreement. Hence, Intel's authority to sell its products embodying the LGE Patents was not conditioned on the notice or on Quanta's decision to abide by LGE's directions in that notice.* * *

The License Agreement authorized Intel to sell products that practiced the LGE Patents. No conditions limited Intel's authority to sell products substantially embodying the patents. Because Intel was authorized to sell its products to Quanta, the doctrine of patent exhaustion prevents LGE from further asserting its patent rights with respect to the patents substantially embodied by those products.

IV

The authorized sale of an article that substantially embodies a patent exhausts the patent holder's rights and prevents the patent holder from invoking patent law to control postsale use of the article. Here, LGE licensed Intel to practice any of its patents and to sell products practicing those patents. Intel's microprocessors and chipsets substantially embodied the LGE Patents because they had no reasonable noninfringing use and included all the inventive aspects of the patented methods. Nothing in the License Agreement limited Intel's ability to sell its products practicing the LGE Patents. Intel's authorized sale to Quanta thus took its products outside the scope of the patent monopoly, and as a result, LGE can no longer assert its patent rights against Quanta. Accordingly, the judgment of the Court of Appeals is reversed.

3. PATENT SETTLEMENTS

IN RE CIPROFLOXACIN HYDROCHLORIDE ANTITRUST LITIGATION

544 F.3d 1323 (Fed. Cir. 2008)

PROST, CIRCUIT JUDGE.

This case under the Hatch–Waxman Act presents the issue of whether a settlement agreement between a patent holder and a generic manufacturer violates the antitrust laws. The agreements here involve a reverse payment from the patent holder to the generic manufacturer, but do not implicate the 180–day exclusivity period. Indirect purchasers of Cipro and several advocacy groups ("appellants") appeal the grant of summary judgment of their federal antitrust claims and dismissal of their state antitrust claims against the patent holders and brand-name manufacturers, Bayer AG and Bayer Corp. (collectively "Bayer"), and the generic manufacturers, Barr Labs., Inc. ("Barr"), Hoechst Marion Roussel, Inc. ("HMR"), The Rugby Group, Inc. ("Rugby"), and Watson Pharmaceuticals, Inc. ("Watson") (collectively "generic defendants"). The United States District Court for the Eastern District of New York granted Bayer's and the generic defendants' motion for summary judgment, holding that any anti-competitive effects caused by the settlement agreements between Bayer and the generic defendants were within the exclusionary zone of the patent, and thus could not be redressed by federal antitrust law.* * *For the reasons set forth below, we affirm.

I

A

Bayer is the owner of U.S. Patent No. 4,670,444 ("the '444 patent").* * * [T]he patent is directed to ciprofloxacin hydrochloride, the compound that is the active ingredient in Cipro® ("Cipro").* * * The patent issued on June 2, 1987, and Bayer's predecessor obtained approval from the Food and Drug Administration ("FDA") to market Cipro in October 1987. The FDA granted Bayer an additional six-month period of marketing exclusivity (pediatric exclusivity) following the expiration of the patent on December 9, 2003.

In October 1991, Barr filed an abbreviated new drug application ("ANDA") for a generic version of Cipro. The ANDA included a Paragraph IV certification indicating that Barr sought to market its generic drug before expiration of the '444 patent on the grounds that the patent was invalid and unenforceable. Specifically, Barr asserted that the patent was invalid based on obviousness under 35 U.S.C. § 103 and obviousness type double patenting under 35 U.S.C. § 101, and unenforceable due to inequitable conduct. Under the Hatch–Waxman Act, the first filer of a Paragraph IV ANDA is automatically entitled to a 180–day period of market exclusivity, which, in the version of the Act in effect at the time, begins to run either on the date that the first ANDA filer begins to market its drug or on the date of a final court decision finding the patent to be invalid or not infringed, whichever is earlier. 21 U.S.C. § 355(j)(4)(B)(iv) (1988). Thus, as the first Paragraph IV ANDA filer, Barr was entitled to the 180–day exclusivity period.

On January 16, 1992, Bayer sued Barr for patent infringement in the Southern District of New York. Barr answered and counterclaimed for a declaratory judgment that the '444 patent is invalid and unenforceable and that its generic ciprofloxacin would not infringe the '444 patent. In 1996, Rugby (a subsidiary of HMR) and Barr entered into the "Litigation Funding Agreement," in which Rugby agreed to help Barr fund its litigation against Bayer in exchange for half of any profits realized from Barr's sale of ciprofloxacin. Also, in 1996, Bayer entered into settlement discussions with HMR and Barr.

Just before trial, Bayer, Barr, HMR, and Rugby entered into [four agreements]. The first three agreements provided that Barr, HMR, Rugby, Apotex, and Bernard Sherman would not challenge the validity or enforceability of the '444 patent. Pursuant to the Barr Settlement Agreement, Barr agreed to convert its Paragraph IV ANDA to a Paragraph III ANDA, thus certifying that it would not market its generic version of Cipro until after the '444 patent expired. See 21 U.S.C. § 355(j)(2)(A)(vii)(III). In exchange, Bayer agreed to make a settlement payment to Barr of $49.1 million.

Under the [fourth agreement], Bayer agreed to either supply Barr with Cipro for resale or make quarterly payments (referred to as "reverse payments" or "exclusion payments") to Barr until December 31, 2003. In return, Barr agreed not to manufacture, or have manufactured, a generic version of Cipro in the United States. Beginning at least six months before the '444 patent expired, Bayer agreed to allow Barr to sell a competing ciprofloxacin product. ayer and Barr then entered into a consent judgment, whereby Barr affirmed the validity and enforceability of the '444 patent and admitted infringement.

On July 25, 1997, Bayer filed for reexamination. Bayer cancelled and amended certain claims, and the validity of the remaining claims of the '444 patent was reaffirmed by the Patent and Trademark Office ("PTO") in the reexamination certificate. In particular, the patentability of claim 12, directed to ciprofloxacin hydrochloride, was confirmed.* * *

III

[In 2000 and 2001, direct and indirect purchasers of Cipro and advocacy groups filed several antitrust actions in federal courts challenging the Agreements.]

The appellants allege that the district court erred in its determination that the Agreements did not constitute an unreasonable restraint of trade in violation of section 1 of the Sherman Act, and in its grant of Bayer's and the generic defendants' motions for summary judgment on Counts I–IV, as follows: (1) by not finding the Agreements to be per se unlawful, or at least applying a proper rule of reason analysis; (2) by finding the Agreements to be lawful because they fell within the "exclusionary zone" of the '444 patent; (3) by not considering the law of the regional circuits and government agencies in evaluating the Agreements.* * * We address each asserted error in turn.

A

According to the appellants, the Agreements allowed Bayer to exclude a horizontal competitor from the market not by enforcing its rights as a patentee, but instead by ceasing to enforce its rights and paying the competitor $398 million. The appellants contend that the district court should have concluded that the Agreements were per se unlawful or should have applied a proper rule of reason analysis. At a minimum, the appellants assert, the court should not have resolved the case on summary judgment, but instead should have presented it to a fact-finder to determine whether the Agreements constituted an unreasonable restraint on trade.

The Sherman Act provides that "[e]very contract, combination in the form of trust or otherwise, or conspiracy, in restraint of trade or commerce among the several States, or with foreign nations, is declared to be illegal." 15 U.S.C. § 1. Although by its terms, the Act prohibits any "restraint of trade," the Supreme Court "has long recognized that Congress intended to outlaw only unreasonable restraints." *State Oil Co. v. Khan*, 522 U.S. 3, 10, 118 S.Ct. 275, 139 L.Ed.2d 199 (1997). Courts will presumptively apply a "rule of reason" analysis to determine whether an agreement imposes an unreasonable restraint on competition. *Texaco, Inc. v. Dagher*, 547 U.S. 1, 5, 126 S.Ct. 1276, 164 L.Ed.2d 1 (2006). nly agreements that have a "predictable and pernicious anticompetitive effect, and ... limited potential for procompetitive benefit" are deemed to be per se unlawful under the Sherman Act. *State Oil*, 522 U.S. at 10, 118 S.Ct. 275. A finding of per se unlawfulness "is appropriate '[o]nce experience with a particular type of restraint enables the Court to predict with confidence that the rule of reason will condemn it.'" Id. (quoting *Arizona v. Maricopa County Med. Soc'y*, 457 U.S. 332, 344, 102 S.Ct. 2466, 73 L.Ed.2d 48 (1982)). The Supreme Court has expressed reluctance to adopt per se rules where the economic impact is not immediately obvious. Id.

Since there was no basis for the district court to confidently predict that the Agreements at issue here would be found to be unlawful under a rule of reason analysis, we find no error by the court in declining to find them to be per se unlawful. Instead, the court properly went through a rule of reason analysis to determine whether the Agreements were in fact an unreasonable restraint of trade.

First, the plaintiff bears the initial burden of showing that the challenged action has had an actual adverse effect on competition as a whole in the relevant market. Then, if the plaintiff succeeds, the burden shifts to the defendant to establish the pro-competitive redeeming virtues of the action. Should the defendant carry this burden, the plaintiff must then show that the same pro-competitive effect could be achieved through an alternative means that is less restrictive of competition. *Clorox Co. v. Sterling Winthrop, Inc.*, 117 F.3d 50, 56 (2d Cir.1997) (citations and internal quotations omitted). Typically, the starting point is to define the relevant market, *Geneva Pharms. Tech. Corp. v. Barr Labs., Inc.*, 386 F.3d 485, 495–96 (2d Cir.2004), and to determine whether the defendants possess market power in the relevant market. *United States v. Visa U.S.A., Inc.*, 344 F.3d 229, 238 (2d Cir.2003). Although the precise role that market power plays in the rule of reason analysis is unclear, it may be a highly relevant factor. Id. at 238 n. 4.

Contrary to the contentions of the appellants, the court did undertake a full rule of reason analysis. It first determined that the relevant market is ciprofloxacin and that Bayer had market power within that market.* * * It then determined that there was no evidence that the Agreements created a bottleneck on challenges to the '444 patent or otherwise restrained competition outside the "exclusionary zone" of the patent.* * * Thus, the court concluded that the plaintiffs had failed to demonstrate that the Agreements had an anti-competitive effect on the market for ciprofloxacin beyond that permitted by the patent. Id. Because the court concluded that the plaintiffs failed to meet their burden under the first step of the rule of reason analysis, it did not find it necessary to consider the second or third steps of the analysis.* * *

B

The appellants assert, however, that the district court erred in concluding that the Agreements were within the "exclusionary zone" of the '444 patent, in essence treating them as per se legal. According to the appellants, the patentee's right to exclude competition is not defined by the facial scope of the patent, but rather is limited to the right to exclude others from profiting from the patented invention. Under the Agreements, the appellants argue, Bayer is seeking not simply to enforce its patent rights, but to insulate itself from competition and avoid the risk that the patent is held invalid.

The district court did not treat the Agreements as per se legal. Rather, the court simply recognized that any adverse anti-competitive effects within the scope of the '444 patent could not be redressed by antitrust law.* * * This is because a patent by its very nature is anticompetitive; it is a grant to the inventor of "the right to exclude others from making, using, offering for sale, or selling the invention...." 35 U.S.C. § 154(a)(1); *Dawson Chem. Co. v. Rohm & Haas Co.*, 448 U.S. 176, 215, 100 S.Ct. 2601, 65 L.Ed.2d 696 (1980) ("[T]he essence of a patent grant is the right to exclude others from profiting by the patented invention."). Thus, "a patent is an exception to the general rule against monopolies and to the right of access to a free and open market." *Precision Instrument Mfg. Co. v. Auto. Maint. Mach. Co.*, 324 U.S. 806, 816, 65 S.Ct. 993, 89 L.Ed. 1381 (1945). The district court appreciated this underlying tension between the antitrust laws and the patent laws when it compared the anti-competitive effects of the Agreements with the "zone of exclusion" provided by the claims of the patent. See *In re Tamoxifen*, 466 F.3d at 201–02; *Andrx Pharms., Inc. v. Elan Corp.*, 421 F.3d 1227, 1235 (11th Cir.2005); *Schering–Plough Corp. v. FTC*, 402 F.3d 1056, 1066 (11th Cir.2005); *Valley Drug*, 344 F.3d at 1312. Because the court found no anti-competitive effects outside the exclusionary zone of the patent, it concluded that the Agreements were not violative of section 1 of the Sherman Act.* * *

We find no error in the court's analysis. Pursuant to the Agreements, the generic defendants agreed not to market a generic version of Cipro until the '444 patent expired and not to challenge the validity of the '444 patent, and Bayer agreed to make payments and optionally supply Cipro for resale. Thus, the essence of the Agreements was to exclude the defendants from profiting from the patented invention. This is well within Bayer's rights as the patentee. Furthermore, there is a long-standing policy in the law in favor of settlements, and this policy extends to patent infringement litigation. *Flex–Foot, Inc. v. CRP, Inc.*, 238 F.3d 1362, 1368 (Fed. Cir.2001); *Foster v. Hallco Mfg. Co.*, 947 F.2d 469, 477 (Fed.Cir. 1991). Settlement of patent claims by agreement between the parties-including exchange of consideration-rather than by litigation is not precluded by the Sherman Act even though it may have some adverse effects on competition. *Standard Oil Co. v. United States*, 283 U.S. 163, 171 & n. 5, 51 S.Ct. 421, 75 L.Ed. 926 (1931).

We disagree with the appellants that the fact that the generic defendants agreed not to challenge the validity of the '444 patent renders the Agreements violative of the antitrust laws. According to the appellants, there is a vital public interest in patent validity challenges to ensure that consumers are not burdened by unwarranted patent monopolies. Appellants assert that Congress underscored this public interest by providing in 35 U.S.C. § 282 that an issued patent carries only a rebuttable presumption of validity, which can be challenged in court. In fact, appellants argue, at the preliminary injunction stage, the patentee has the burden of establishing the likelihood of success on the merits of the patent's validity. Furthermore, the appellants contend, in the Hatch–Waxman Act, Congress provided the incentive of a 180–day exclusivity period to the first generic manufacturer to challenge a patent.* * *

C

The appellants urge this court to consider the legal standards applied by the regional circuits and government agencies in addressing Agreements involving exclusion payments in the context of the Hatch–Waxman Act, all of which, they assert, encompass greater antitrust scrutiny than the standard adopted by the district court. In particular, the appellants point to the Sixth Circuit's decision in *In re Cardizem CD Antitrust Litigation*, 332 F.3d 896 (6th Cir.2003), upholding a summary judgment ruling by the district court that a reverse payment agreement is per se illegal. Further, the appellants assert that although the Eleventh Circuit in *Valley Drug* reversed the district court's ruling of per se illegality, it provided a more extensive analytical framework within which to review the settlement agreements on remand. And, in *Schering–Plough*, the appellants assert the Eleventh Circuit adhered to the standard in *Valley Drug* and recognized the need to evaluate the strength of the patent in determining whether reverse payments are unlawful. The appellants contend that the Federal Trade Commission ("FTC") advocates a rule of reason inquiry focusing on the amount of the payment and several other factors, although not requiring consideration of the validity of the patent. Finally, the appellants note that the Solicitor General has suggested that a reverse payment should be evaluated using a rule of reason approach and that "the strength of the patent as it appeared at the time at which the parties settled" should be considered in the analysis. According to the appellants, only the Second Circuit in *In re Tamoxifen*, has concluded that a settlement between a patent holder and an alleged infringer in Hatch–Waxman litigation does not violate the antitrust laws provided the litigation is not baseless, although it recognized that such an approach shields settlement agreements involving "fatally weak" patents. Therefore, the appellants assert, the district court's treatment of the Agreements here was not in line with that of the other circuits, the FTC, and the Solicitor General, and we should reject the district court's approach in lieu of those other standards.

We find, however, the district court's analysis to be sound. As noted above, the district court applied a rule of reason analysis in assessing the lawfulness of the Agreements. In that analysis, it considered whether there was evidence of sham litigation or fraud before the PTO, and whether any anticompetitive effects of the Agreements were outside the exclusionary zone of the patent. The application of a rule of reason analysis to a settlement agreement involving an exclusion payment in the Hatch–Waxman context has been embraced by the Second Circuit, and advocated by the FTC and the Solicitor General. And, although the Sixth Circuit found a per se violation of the antitrust laws in *In re Cardizem*, the facts of that case are distinguishable from this case and from the other circuit court decisions. In particular, the settlement in that case included, in addition to a reverse payment, an agreement by the generic manufacturer to not relinquish its 180–day exclusivity period, thereby delaying the entry of other generic manufacturers. *In re Cardizem*, 332 F.3d at 907. Furthermore, the agreement provided that the generic manufacturer would not market non-infringing versions of the generic drug. Id. at 908 n. 13. Thus, the agreement clearly had anticompetitive effects outside the exclusion zone of the patent.* * * To the extent that the Sixth Circuit may have found a per se antitrust violation based solely on the reverse payments, we respectfully disagree.

The Eleventh Circuit in *Valley Drug* reversed a finding by the district court that settlement agreements constituted a per se violation of the antitrust laws because the court failed to consider the exclusionary power of the patent in its antitrust analysis. 344 F.3d at 1306, 1312. Although it rejected the court's condemnation of the agreements as a per se antitrust violation, it did not advocate application of a rule of reason analysis, finding such an analysis to be inappropriate given that the anticompetitive effects of the exclusionary zone of a patent are not subject to debate. Id. at 1312 n. 27. In so holding, it emphasized that the subsequent declaration of invalidity did not render the patent's potential exclusionary effects irrelevant to the antitrust analysis. Id. at 1309. It did leave open the possibility, however, that an antitrust violation could be found in the extreme situation where there was evidence of fraud on the PTO or sham litigation. Id. at 1309 & n. 21. On remand, it ordered the district court to consider the exclusionary potential of the patent, the extent to which provisions of the settlement agreement exceeded the scope of the patent, and the anticompetitive effects of those provisions. Id. at 1312.* * *

We conclude that in cases such as this, wherein all anticompetitive effects of the settlement agreement are within the exclusionary power of the patent, the outcome is the same whether the court begins its analysis under antitrust law by applying a rule of reason approach to evaluate the anti-competitive effects, or under patent law by analyzing the right to exclude afforded by the patent. The essence of the inquiry is whether the agreements restrict competition beyond the exclusionary zone of the patent. This analysis has been adopted by the Second and the Eleventh Circuits and by the district court below and we find it to be completely consistent with Supreme Court precedent. See *Walker Process Equip., Inc. v. Food Mach. & Chem. Corp.*, 382 U.S. 172, 175–77, 86 S.Ct. 347, 15 L.Ed.2d 247 (1965) (holding that there may be a violation of the Sherman Act when a patent is procured by fraud, but recognizing that a patent is an exception to the general rule against monopolies).

In addition, we agree with the Second and Eleventh Circuits and with the district court that, in the absence of evidence of fraud before the PTO or sham litigation, the court need not consider the validity of the patent in the antitrust analysis of a settlement agreement involving a reverse payment. The FTC has also rejected the application of a post hoc analysis of the validity of the patent as part of the antitrust analysis.* * * Accordingly, we find the analysis by the district court to be fully supported in law and to demonstrate that it was cognizant of the legal standards applied by the regional circuits and government agencies in addressing agreements involving exclusion payments in the context of the Hatch–Waxman Act.

B. EUROPEAN UNION COMPETITION LAW

Competition law in the European Union addresses many of the same policies that arise in United States Antitrust law. One key difference is the commitment to the free movement of goods across borders in the European Union. Much of the law originates from the Treaty of Rome, establishing the European Community in 1958. The Treaty also provides the foundation for the European Union. Two key provisions from the treaty are Article 81 and Article 82. The first deals with industry cartels and is analogous to Section One of the Sherman Act. Article 82 deals with abuse of a dominant position in a market and is analogous to Section Two of the Sherman Act.

1. ABUSE OF DOMINANT POSITION

JUDGMENT OF THE GENERAL COURT (SIXTH CHAMBER, EXTENDED COMPOSITION)

1 July 2010

relating to a proceeding under Article 82 of the EC Treaty and Article 54 of the EEA Agreement (Case COMP/A. 37.507/F3 AstraZeneca)

Background to the dispute

1 Astra AB was a company incorporated under Swedish law established in Södertälje (Sweden) and was the parent company of a pharmaceutical group including, inter alia, AB Hässle and Astra Hässle AB, two wholly-owned subsidiaries established in Mölndal (Sweden). With effect from 6 April 1999, Astra merged with Zeneca Group plc to form AstraZeneca plc, the second applicant in this case, a holding company established in London (United Kingdom). As a result of that merger, Astra, which was wholly owned by AstraZeneca plc, acquired the name AstraZeneca AB, the first applicant in this case, and became a research and development, marketing and production company. The companies which belonged to the Astra group and those now in the AstraZeneca plc group will be called 'AZ'. However, in so far as AstraZeneca plc and AstraZeneca AB are being referred to in their capacity as parties to these proceedings, they will be called together 'the applicants'.

2 AZ is a pharmaceutical group active, worldwide, in the sector of inventing, developing and marketing innovative products. Its business is focused on a number of pharmaceutical areas including, in particular, that of gastrointestinal conditions. In that regard, one of the major products marketed by AZ is known as 'Losec', a brand name used in most European markets for that omeprazole product.

3 On 12 May 1999, Generics (UK) Ltd and Scandinavian Pharmaceuticals Generics AB ('the complainants') lodged a complaint pursuant to Article 3 of Regulation No 17 of the Council of 6 February 1962, First Regulation implementing Articles [81 EC] and [82 EC] (OJ, English Special Edition 1959–1962, p. 87) against Astra, by which they complained of AZ's conduct aimed at preventing them from introducing generic versions of omeprazole on a number of European Economic Area (EEA) markets. * * *

7 On 15 June 2005, the Commission adopted a decision relating to a proceeding under Article 82 [EC] and Article 54 of the EEA Agreement (Case COMP/A.37.507/F3—AstraZeneca) ('the contested decision'), by which it found that AstraZeneca AB and

AstraZeneca plc had committed two abuses of a dominant position, in breach of Article 82 EC and Article 54 of the EEA
Agreement.

8   The first alleged abuse consisted of a pattern of allegedly
misleading representations made before the patent offices in
Germany, Belgium, Denmark, Norway, the Netherlands and the
United Kingdom, and before the national courts in Germany
and Norway (Article 1(1) of the contested decision). The second
alleged abuse consisted of the submission of requests for deregistration of the marketing authorisations for Losec capsules in
Denmark, Norway and Sweden combined with the withdrawal
from the market of Losec capsules and the launch of Losec
MUPS tablets in those three countries (Article 1(2) of the
contested decision).

9   The Commission imposed on the applicants jointly and severally
a fine of EUR 46 million and on AstraZeneca AB a fine of EUR
14 million (Article 2 of the contested decision).* * *

Law

23   By their action, the applicants call in question the lawfulness
of the contested decision as regards the definition of the
relevant market, the assessment of the dominant position, the
first abuse of a dominant position, the second abuse of a
dominant position and the amount of the fines imposed. The
Court will examine in turn the pleas put forward by the
applicants in the context of each of these issues. * * *

2.   Findings of the Court

239   It should be noted at the outset that it is settled case-law that
a dominant position under Article 82 EC concerns a position
of economic strength held by an undertaking which enables it
to prevent effective competition from being maintained on the
relevant market by giving it the power to behave to an
appreciable extent independently of its competitors, its customers and, ultimately, consumers. In general the existence of
a dominant position derives from a combination of various
factors which, taken separately, are not necessarily decisive
(Case 27/76 *United Brands and United Brands Continentaal*
v. *Commission* [1978] ECR 207, paragraphs 65 and 66, and
Case 85/76 *Hoffmann–La Roche* v. *Commission* [1979] ECR
461, paragraphs 38 and 39).* * *

b) Price levels

255   The applicants and the EFPIA dispute that the higher prices
charged by AZ for Losec amounted to evidence of the existence of AZ's market power.

256   As regards the EFPIA's argument that prices are the result of
      or are strongly influenced by decisions of public authorities,
      the Court would point out that it is apparent from the
      contested decision, which has not been challenged by the
      applicants and the EFPIA on that point, that pharmaceutical
      undertakings which offer for the first time products with a
      high added therapeutic value as a result of their innovative-
      ness are able to extract from public authorities higher prices
      or reimbursement levels than those of existing products. In
      this respect, it has been observed that national authorities
      which set reimbursement levels or prices of medicines are
      encouraged, on account of their public interest mission, to
      ensure the inclusion in their health systems of products
      which contribute significantly to the improvement of public
      health.

257   Since prices or reimbursement levels of medicines are neces-
      sarily set by public authorities as a result of a dialogue with
      pharmaceutical undertakings, at the very least in so far as the
      latter must provide them with relevant information for this
      purpose, the Commission was entitled to take the view that
      pharmaceutical undertakings had bargaining power vis-à-vis
      the national authorities, which varied according to the added
      therapeutic value that their products offer in comparison with
      pre-existing products. Furthermore, it is also apparent from
      the contested decision, which has not been challenged on that
      point, that, in certain cases, it may be in the strategic interest
      of pharmaceutical undertakings not to market their products
      on certain markets, where the prices which national authori-
      ties are prepared to pay do not meet their expectations * * *.

258   The EFPIA emphasises that pricing decisions are adopted
      unilaterally by public authorities. It recognises however that
      prices or reimbursement levels of medicines are set according
      to their innovative value and, consequently, that a product
      offering a significant added therapeutic value will be granted
      a price or reimbursement level higher than that of products
      not offering such therapeutic value. It is therefore common
      ground that, although the price or reimbursement level stems
      from a decision adopted by the public authorities, the ability
      of a pharmaceutical undertaking to obtain a high price or
      reimbursement level depends on the innovative value of the
      product.

259   In the present case, the Court observes that, as the first
      undertaking to offer a PPI, namely omeprazole, whose ther-
      apeutic value was much higher than that of the existing
      products on the market, AZ was able to obtain a higher
      price from public authorities. By contrast, such higher prices

were not so easy to obtain for pharmaceutical undertakings marketing other PPIs, the 'me-too' products, such as lansoprazole, pantoprazole and rabeprazole. The applicants themselves explained to the Commission that reimbursement bodies tended to view 'me-too' products, product line extensions and new formulations of existing products more sceptically since such products offered only limited added therapeutic value* * *.

260   The Court therefore takes the view that AZ's ability to obtain higher prices or reimbursement levels reflects the advantages that it derived from its first-mover status on a market which it pioneered. That first-mover status is an important factor in AZ's leading competitive position, which the Commission took into account in* * * the contested decision. It is that first-mover status which is in part the cause of the undisputed strength of AZ's omeprazole in terms of market share, in comparison with competitors which marketed other PPIs.

261   Furthermore, as the Commission claimed in reply to the questions put by the Court, the fact that AZ was able to maintain a much higher market share than those of its competitors while charging prices higher than those charged for other PPIs is a relevant factor showing that AZ's behaviour was not, to an appreciable extent, subject to competitive constraints from its competitors, its customers and, ultimately, consumers. The fact that the higher prices charged by AZ are due in part to the setting of high reimbursement thresholds does not affect that finding.

262   In this respect, the Court would point out that the Commission is justified in finding* * * that the health systems which characterise markets for pharmaceutical products tend to reinforce the market power of pharmaceutical companies, since costs of medicines are fully or largely covered by social security systems, which to a significant extent makes demand inelastic. That is more particularly the case where a pharmaceutical undertaking, which is the first to offer a new product with an added therapeutic value in relation to existing products, is able to obtain a higher reimbursement level than that which will subsequently be granted to 'me-too' products. Vis-à-vis undertakings which enjoy first-mover status, the reimbursements paid by social security systems are set at relatively high levels in comparison with 'me-too' products and enable the pharmaceutical company which enjoys such status to set its price at a high level without having to worry about patients and doctors switching to other less costly products.* * *

c) The existence and use of intellectual property rights

270 As regards the grounds of complaint regarding the relevance attached to intellectual property rights and rights conferred by pharmaceutical regulation, the Court would point out, first of all, that it cannot be argued that intellectual property rights do not constitute a relevant factor for the purposes of determining the existence of a dominant position. Although the mere possession of intellectual property rights cannot be considered to confer such a position, their possession is none the less capable, in certain circumstances, of creating a dominant position, in particular by enabling an undertaking to prevent effective competition on the market (see, to that effect, *Magill*, paragraph 229 above, paragraphs 46 and 47).

271 In the present case, the applicants and the EFPIA do not call in question the Commission's finding that, as the first PPI to be introduced on the market, Losec enjoyed particularly strong patent protection, on the basis of which AZ brought a series of legal actions which enabled it to impose significant constraints on its competitors Takeda, Byk Gulden and Eisai and to dictate to a large extent market-entry terms to them. *[confidential]* Similarly, Eisai was forced to pay compensation to AZ for sales of rabeprazole and to give it access to certain technologies which could be used for future formulations of omeprazole* * *.

272 The fact, noted by the applicants, that the patent proceedings brought by AZ and the ensuing amicable settlements were in no way unlawful does not affect the Commission's finding that the patent protection enjoyed by Losec enabled AZ to exert significant pressure on its competitors, which was, in itself, a relevant indicator of its dominant position. Thus, contrary to what the applicants seem to suggest, it is in no way necessary that the terms of the 'settlement agreements' be abusive in order to find that they constitute evidence of a dominant position. As the Commission observes, the applicants' argument stems from confusion between the notions of dominance and abuse.

273 Lastly, the Court must reject the assertion that the taking into account of intellectual property rights and of their exercise, even if not abusive, in order to establish the existence of a dominant position is liable to reduce any incentive to create innovative products. The Court would point out that innovation is in any event rewarded by the exclusivity that intellectual property rights confer on the author of the innovation. To the extent that, as in the present case, the possession and exercise of those intellectual property rights may be relevant

evidence of the dominant position, it should be recalled that such a position is not prohibited *per se*; only the abuse of such a position is so proscribed. In this respect, where the holder of the intellectual property right is regarded as enjoying a dominant position, the requirement that use of that right be non-abusive cannot be regarded as insufficient reward in the light of the incentives for innovation.

274   In addition, as regards the applicants' argument that lansoprazole and pantoprazole entered the German market in 1993 and 1994 respectively, the Court observes that, to be a relevant factor, the existence of solid protection by means of intellectual property rights does not necessarily have to be such as to exclude all competition on the market.

275   The Court therefore finds that the Commission did not commit a manifest error of assessment in taking into consideration the existence and use of AZ's intellectual property rights when assessing its competitive position on the market.

   d) AZ's first-mover status

276   In * * *the contested decision, the Commission outlined the competitive advantages which could be derived from first-mover status and incumbency on the PPI market.

277   The applicants dispute however the relevance of AZ's first-mover status, in the light, in particular, of the fact that pantoprazole had acquired a 20.66% market share in 1995 in Germany after only two years of presence on the market.

278   The Court observes, first of all, that the Commission based its assessment of AZ's dominant position on a series of factors, foremost of which was its much higher market share than those of its competitors. Next, in view (i) of the specific features of the markets for pharmaceutical products, which are characterised by 'inertia' on the part of prescribing doctors, and (ii) of the difficulties encountered by pharmaceutical undertakings to enter a market which increase in line with the number of competitors and products already on that market, difficulties that are demonstrated by a study of the Organisation for Economic Co-operation and Development (OECD) which was taken into account by the Commission, the latter was entitled to take the view that first-mover status was an appreciable competitive advantage. That competitive advantage is also borne out by AZ's internal documents, which show that Losec enjoyed a solid brand image and reputation on account of its status of 'first product on the market', and had the most experience behind it.

279   None the less, the Commission did not state that the competitive advantages related to AZ's extended presence on the PPI market precluded competitor sales growth in all circumstances. Thus, the fact that pantoprazole was able to obtain a 20.66% market share in Germany cannot call in question the competitive advantages that AZ derived from its first-mover status, either on the German market or on the other relevant geographic markets, where AZ's position was sometimes overwhelmingly strong. The Court also observes that pantoprazole was not able to challenge Losec's status as the largest selling PPI in Germany.

280   Similarly, the fact that generic products were in a position to undermine AZ's dominant position does not call in question the fact that its first-mover status conferred on it appreciable competitive advantages. The Court would also point out that, during the periods selected by the Commission during which AZ was in a dominant position, generic products had not undermined AZ's dominant position on the relevant geographic markets.

281   As regards, next, the EFPIA's argument that the vulnerability of a pharmaceutical product to the entry of innovative products negates the relevance of first-mover status, suffice it to note, as the Commission observes, that neither the applicants nor the EFPIA make any mention of the market entry of innovative products which challenged AZ's dominant position on the PPI market.

282   Lastly, the fact that AZ concluded licensing agreements with certain competitors cannot negate the relevance of its incumbency on the market in the present case. Moreover, as the Commission observes, the regulatory framework does not at all facilitate the market entry of manufacturers of generic products seeking to market their products, since data communicated by manufacturers of original products for the purpose of obtaining marketing authorisations are protected for a period of between 6 and 10 years (see Point 8(a)(iii) of the third paragraph of Article 4 of Council Directive 65/65/EEC of 26 January 1965 on the approximation of provisions laid down by law, regulation or administrative action relating to proprietary medicinal products (OJ, English Special Edition 1965–1966, p. 24, as amended at the material time)), so that, during that period, manufacturers of generic products who wish to obtain marketing authorisations may not refer to those data and must carry out their own tests.

283   The Court therefore finds that the Commission did not commit a manifest error of assessment in also taking into ac-

count, in its overall assessment, AZ's first-mover status on the PPI market.* * *

804   It should be observed that the preparation by an undertaking, even in a dominant position, of a strategy whose object it is to minimise erosion of its sales and to enable it to deal with competition from generic products is legitimate and is part of the normal competitive process, provided that the conduct envisaged does not depart from practices coming within the scope of competition on the merits, which is such as to benefit consumers.

805   In the contested decision, the Commission does not express a view on the compatibility with Article 82 EC of the series of actions envisaged in the framework of the three principles at the centre of the LPP Strategy. The abuse of a dominant position identified by the Commission consists solely in the deregistration of the Losec capsule marketing authorisations in Denmark, Norway and Sweden, in combination with the conversion of sales of Losec capsules to Losec MUPS, that is to say the launch of Losec MUPS and the withdrawal from the market of Losec capsules (see recital 860 of the contested decision). Thus, the applicants' arguments seeking to defend the conformity with Article 82 EC of the series of actions envisaged overall in the LPP Strategy are irrelevant inasmuch as they do not relate to the conduct objected to. * * *

806   As regards, next, the abusive nature of the conduct in question, it should be recalled that the conduct classified by the Commission as an abuse of a dominant position consists in the deregistration of the Losec capsule marketing authorisations in Denmark, Norway and Sweden, in combination with the conversion of sales of Losec capsules to Losec MUPS, that is to say the withdrawal from the market of Losec capsules and the introduction on the market of Losec MUPS.

807   As the Commission stated in reply to the Court's questions and at the hearing, although it defined the abuse of a dominant position as the combination of those elements, the central feature of the abuse consists in the deregistration of the Losec capsule marketing authorisations, the conversion of sales of Losec capsules to Losec MUPS being the context in which the deregistrations of the marketing authorisations were carried out.

808   In this respect, the Court observes that the conversion of sales of Losec capsules to Losec MUPS, namely the withdrawal from the market of Losec capsules and the introduction on the market of Losec MUPS, was not capable, in itself, of

producing the anticompetitive effects alleged by the Commission in the present case, namely the creation of regulatory obstacles to the market entry of generic omeprazole and to parallel imports of Losec capsules.

809   As regards generic medicinal products, the Court of Justice has held that, for the grant of a marketing authorisation on the basis of the abridged procedure provided for in point 8(a)(iii) of the third paragraph of Article 4 of Directive 65/65, it is only necessary that all the particulars and documents relating to the reference medicinal product remain available to the competent authority concerned by the marketing authorisation, and it is not necessary that the reference medicinal product be actually marketed (*AstraZeneca*, paragraph 617 above, paragraph 27). Thus, the fact that the reference medicinal product has been withdrawn from the market does not preclude the use of the abridged procedure provided for in point 8(a)(iii) of the third paragraph of Article 4 of Directive 65/65. Similarly, the launch of Losec MUPS cannot preclude the use of the abridged procedure in respect of pharmaceutical products which are essentially similar to Losec capsules.

810   Furthermore, with respect to parallel imports, the Court observes that, in the contested decision, the Commission did not consider that the withdrawal from the market of Losec capsules and the introduction on the market of Losec MUPS was such as to lead the national authorities to revoke the parallel import licences for Losec capsules. On the other hand, the Commission observed* * * that parallel import licences have traditionally relied on the existing market authorisations of the proprietary medicinal product in question. Consequently, only deregistration of marketing authorisations could, by hypothesis, be such as to induce national authorities to withdraw parallel import licences. It is apparent from the contested decision that that was the case in Finland and Sweden, where the national authorities revoked the parallel import licences as a result of the deregistration of the marketing authorisations.

811   Thus, in view of the fact that, in the present case, the conduct that may be classified as an abuse of a dominant position consists essentially in deregistration of the marketing authorisations, which is, by hypothesis, the sole element which could be capable of producing the anticompetitive effects alleged by the Commission, the applicants' arguments are irrelevant inasmuch as they assert, in essence, that, first, Losec MUPS was introduced on the market because it was a better product and, second, Losec capsules were withdrawn from the market because the local marketing companies con-

sidered, inter alia as a result of several market studies and a study on consumer preferences, that it was preferable to maintain just one product on the market. In the present case, there is no reason to reproach AZ either for launching Losec MUPS or for withdrawing Losec capsules from the market, since those acts were not such as to raise the legal barriers to entry complained of by the Commission that were capable of delaying or preventing the introduction of generic products and parallel imports.

812 By contrast, the deregistration of the Losec capsule marketing authorisations cannot be regarded as within the scope of competition on the merits. [T]hat conduct was not based on the legitimate protection of an investment designed to contribute to competition on the merits, since AZ no longer had the exclusive right to make use of the results of the pharmacological and toxicological tests and clinical trials. Furthermore, the applicants adduce no evidence to permit the inference that those deregistrations were necessary, or even useful, for the introduction on the market of Losec MUPS, or for the conversion of sales of Losec capsules to Losec MUPS. Thus, without prejudice to the question whether the Commission has established to the requisite legal standard that the objective context in which the impugned conduct took place permitted the inference that that conduct was such as to restrict competition, the deregistration of the Losec capsule marketing authorisations was the sole aspect of the conduct identified by the Commission which would be capable of creating obstacles to the market entry of generic products and to parallel imports.

813 The applicants repeatedly claim that there is no documentary evidence expressly indicating that AZ applied a 'malevolent' or 'intentional' strategy in Denmark, Norway and Sweden seeking to deregister the marketing authorisations in order to delay the market entry of generic products and to prevent parallel imports. In this respect, it is sufficient to note that the concept of abuse of a dominant position is an objective concept and does not require that an intention to cause harm be established* * *. It is common ground that AZ carried out those deregistrations in Denmark, Norway and Sweden. The alleged absence of any malevolent intention underlying that conduct cannot therefore preclude the Commission's classification of that conduct as an abuse of a dominant position where it is established that, in view of the objective context in which that conduct took place, the conduct was such as to delay or prevent the introduction of generic products and parallel imports.

814   In any event, it is quite clear from the documents on which the Commission relied that AZ intended, by means of those deregistrations, to obstruct the introduction of generic products and parallel imports. It is apparent inter alia from the document of 3 October 1997 setting out the MUPS strategy* * *, and from the memorandum of 22 October 1997 on the consequences of the MUPS strategy* * *, that AZ was aware of the utility that the deregistration of the Losec capsule marketing authorisations might have for the purposes of raising barriers to entry of a regulatory nature, with regard both to the introduction on the market of generic products and to parallel imports. Those documents also show that AZ was aware that the envisaged action might be caught by the European rules on competition and free movement of goods. The Commission further observed, in recital 302 of the contested decision, that the Norwegian LPP Strategy document indicates that AZ intended to deregister the Losec capsule marketing authorisations in order to bring an end to parallel imports and to make them 'virtually non existing from February 1, 1999' (see paragraph 788 above).

815   The applicants further claim that an obligation must not be imposed on AZ to protect the interests of companies marketing generics or of parallel importers by maintaining the marketing authorisations.

816   However, the Court observes that the fact that an undertaking in a dominant position is under no obligation to protect the interests of competitors does not make practices implemented solely to exclude competitors compatible with Article 82 EC. The mere desire of an undertaking in a dominant position to protect its own commercial interests and to guard against competition from generic products and parallel imports does not justify recourse to practices falling outside the scope of competition on the merits.* * *

Conclusion

864   In the light of all the foregoing, the Court holds that the Commission did not err in finding that AZ's deregistration of the Losec capsule marketing authorisations in Denmark, Norway and Sweden, in conjunction with the swing in AZ's sales from Losec capsules towards Losec MUPS in those countries, amounted to an abuse of a dominant position, inasmuch as it was such as to restrict access to the market of generic products in those countries. Similarly, the Commission did not err in taking the view that that conduct constituted an abuse of a dominant position in Sweden, inasmuch as it was

such as to restrict parallel imports of Losec capsules in that country.

865   The second plea must however be upheld to the extent that it alleges an error by the Commission inasmuch as it considered that the conduct objected to constituted an abuse of a dominant position in Denmark and in Norway in so far as it restricted parallel trade in Losec capsules. The Commission has failed to establish to the requisite legal standard that the deregistration of the Losec capsule marketing authorisations was capable of restricting parallel imports of Losec capsules in those two countries.

MERCK v. PRIMECROWN
European Court of Justice, 1997
1 C.M.L.R. 83

* * *

3.   Merck claims that Primecrown has infringed its United Kingdom patents for a hypertension drug marketed under the trade mark Innovace in the United Kingdom and under the trade mark Renitec elsewhere, for a drug prescribed in prostrate treatment, marketed under the trade mark Proscar, and for a glaucoma drug marketed under the trade mark Timoptol. It complains that Primecrown has carried out parallel imports of those products into the United Kingdom. Renitec and Proscar have been imported from Spain whilst Timoptol has been imported from Portugal.

4.   Beecham has brought an action against Europharm for infringing its United Kingdom patents covering an antibiotic called Augmentin in the United Kingdom and Augmentine in Spain. Beecham complains that Europharm has imported this product from Spain into the United Kingdom with a view to applying to the competent authorities for an import licence which would allow it to import more of the product.

5.   Merck and Beecham consider that they are entitled to oppose parallel imports of a drug for which they hold patents when, as in these cases, those imports come from a Member State where their products are marketed but were not patentable there.

6.   Primecrown and Europharm refer, for their part, to the case-law of the Court on Articles 30 and 36 of the Treaty and in particular to the principle of the exhaustion of rights, as interpreted by the Court in its judgment in Case 187/80 Merck v. Stephar and Exler ([1981] ECR 2063, hereinafter Merck v. Stephar' or Merck'). They deduce from Merck v. Stephar that, upon expiry of the transitional periods laid down in Articles 47 and 209 of the Act of Accession, they are entitled to import the products in question

from Spain and Portugal where they have been marketed by, or with the consent of, the patent holders.

7.   In Merck v. Stephar, the Court referred to its case-law on Articles 30 and 36 of the Treaty according to which the proprietor of an industrial and commercial property right protected by the legislation of a Member State may not rely on that legislation to oppose the importation of a product which has been lawfully put on the market in another Member State by, or with the consent of, the proprietor of that right himself. The Court held that this case-law also applied where the product concerned was put on the market by, or with the consent of, the proprietor in a Member State where the product was not patentable.* * *

26.   [T]he national court asks whether Articles 30 and 36 of the Treaty preclude application of national legislation which grants the holder of a patent for a pharmaceutical product the right to oppose importation by a third party of that product from another Member State in circumstances where the holder first put the product on the market in that State after its accession to the European Community but before the product could be protected by a product patent in that State. In this regard, the national court mentions certain specific circumstances and asks what relevance they have.

27.   In substance, the High Court is seeking to ascertain whether it is necessary to reconsider the rule in Merck v. Stephar or whether, having regard to the specific circumstances mentioned, its scope should be limited.

28.   Merck and Beecham consider that there are weighty reasons for departing from the rule in Merck v. Stephar. They point out first of all that an important change in the situation has occurred since Merck. At the time when the Court gave that judgment, it was the exception rather than the rule for pharmaceutical products to be patentable in Europe. Nowadays, such products are patentable in all the countries of the European Economic Area, with the exception of Iceland. Similarly, the Community institutions have emphasized the importance of patents in the pharmaceutical sector, in particular by the adoption of Council Regulation (EEC) No 1768/92 of 18 June 1992 concerning the creation of a supplementary protection certificate for medicinal products (OJ 1992 L 182, p. 1). Merck and Beecham then point to the increasingly serious financial consequences of maintaining the rule in Merck which, in their view, appreciably reduce the value of patents granted in the Community. Finally, they argue that the specific subject-matter of a patent can be exhausted only if the product in question is marketed with patent protection and that Merck is incompatible with the later case-law of the Court.* * *

29.   It is first necessary to recall the Court's reasoning in Merck.

30. In that judgment, the Court referred to its judgment in Case 15/74 *Centrafarm v. Sterling Drug* [1974] ECR 1147 in which it held, in paragraphs 8 and 9, that as an exception, on grounds of the protection of industrial and commercial property, to one of the fundamental principles of the common market, Article 36 of the Treaty admitted such derogation only in so far as it was justified for the purpose of safeguarding rights constituting the specific subject-matter of that property, which, as regards patents, is, in particular, in order to reward the creative effort of the inventor, to guarantee that the patentee has the exclusive right to use an invention with a view to manufacturing industrial products and putting them into circulation for the first time, either directly or by the grant of licences to third parties, as well as the right to oppose infringements.

31. In paragraphs 9 and 10 of Merck, the Court then stated that it followed from the definition of the specific purpose of a patent that the substance of a patent right lies essentially in according the inventor an exclusive right to put the product on the market for the first time, thereby allowing him a monopoly in exploiting his product and enabling him to obtain the reward for his creative effort without, however, guaranteeing such reward in all circumstances.

32. The Court held, finally, in paragraphs 11 and 13 of Merck that it was for the holder of the patent to decide, in the light of all the circumstances, under what conditions he would market his product, including the possibility of marketing it in a Member State where the law did not provide patent protection for the product in question. If he decides to do so, he must then accept the consequences of his choice as regards free movement of the product within the common market, this being a fundamental principle forming part of the legal and economic circumstances which the holder of the patent must take into account in determining how to exercise his exclusive right. Under those conditions, to permit an inventor to invoke a patent held by him in one Member State in order to prevent the importation of the product freely marketed by him in another Member State where that product was not patentable would cause a partitioning of national markets contrary to the aims of the Treaty.

33. For the reasons set out below, the arguments for reconsideration of the rule in Merck are not such as to call in question the reasoning on which the Court based that rule.

34. It is true, as Merck and Beecham point out, that it is now the norm for pharmaceutical products to be patentable. However, such a development does not mean that the reasoning underlying the rule in Merck is superseded.

35.   The same is true in relation to the arguments based, first, on the efforts made by the Community institutions to give enhanced protection to holders of patents for pharmaceutical products and, second, on the consequences of maintaining that rule for research and development by the pharmaceutical industry.

36.   There can be no doubt now, any more than at the time when the judgment in Merck was given, that if a patentee could prohibit the importation of protected products marketed in another Member State by him or with his consent, he would be able to partition national markets and thereby restrict trade between the Member States. By the same token, if a patentee decides, in the light of all the circumstances, to put a product on the market in a Member State where it is not patentable, he must accept the consequences of his choice as regards the possibility of parallel imports.

37.   The arguments put forward in the present cases have not shown that the Court was wrong in its assessment of the balance between the principle of free movement of goods in the Community and the principle of protection of patentees' rights, albeit that, as a result of striking that balance, the right to oppose importation of a product may be exhausted by its being marketed in a Member State where it is not patentable.

39.   Furthermore, the situations addressed by the ruling in Merck are set to disappear since pharmaceutical products are now patentable in all the Member States. If, upon accession of new States to the Community, such situations were to recur, the Member States could adopt the measures considered necessary, as was the case when the Kingdom of Spain and the Portuguese Republic acceded to the Community.

40.   Finally, Merck's and Beecham's argument that judgments given by the Court after Merck, in particular those in Case 19/84 *Pharmon v. Hoechst* ([1985] ECR 2281) and in Case 158/86 *Warner Brothers and Metronome Video v. Christiansen* ([1988] ECR 2605), support their point of view must be rejected.

41.   Contrary to their contention, the judgment in Pharmon shows that the Court confirmed the principles laid down in Merck. In Pharmon, the Court emphasized the importance of the patentee's consent to the product in question being put into circulation. At paragraph 25 it held that, where the authorities of a Member State grant a third party a compulsory licence allowing him to carry out manufacturing and marketing operations which the patentee would normally have the right to prevent, the patentee cannot be deemed to have consented to those operations and he may therefore oppose importation of products made by the holder of the compulsory licence.

42. Unlike the cases now under consideration, Warner Brothers concerned legislation of the importing State which allowed the author of a musical or cinematographic work not only to control the initial sale but also to oppose the hiring out of videos of that work for as long as he refused specific consent for such hiring out. In that judgment, the Court held that, since there was a specific market for hiring out distinct from the market for sales, such a specific right would lose its substance if the proprietor of the work were unable to authorize hiring out, even in the case of video cassettes already put into circulation with his consent in another Member State whose legislation allowed the author to control the initial sale without giving him the right to prohibit hiring out.

43. Since none of the arguments for re-examining the rule in Merck which the Court has thus far considered have been accepted, the Court must next determine whether, having regard to the specific circumstances mentioned by the national court, the scope of that rule must be restricted.

44. The first question to be considered is whether the rule in Merck also applies where the patentee has a legal or ethical obligation to market or to continue to market his product in the exporting State. Here the national court is concerned to know what importance is to be attached to a requirement of that State's legislation or of Community legislation that, once the product has been put on the market in that State, the patentee must supply and continue to supply sufficient quantities to satisfy the needs of domestic patients.

45. The second question is whether the rule in Merck applies where the legislation of the exporting State not only grants to its authorities the right, which they exercise, to fix the sale price of the product but also prohibits the sale of the product at any other price. Here the national court is concerned to know whether it is relevant that those authorities have fixed the price of the products at a level such that substantial exports of the product to the Member State of importation are foreseeable.

46. Merck and Beecham maintain in particular that, in the circumstances mentioned in the order for reference, their right to decide freely on the conditions in which they market their products is removed or considerably reduced. In their view, it follows from Pharmon that the rule in Merck does not apply in the present cases.

47. As to that, although the imposition of price controls is indeed a factor which may, in certain conditions, distort competition between Member States, that circumstance cannot justify a derogation from the principle of free movement of goods. It is well settled that distortions caused by different price legislation in a Member

State must be remedied by measures taken by the Community authorities and not by the adoption by another Member State of measures incompatible with the rules on free movement of goods (see Case 16/74 Winthrop [1974] ECR 1183, paragraph 17; Joined Cases 55/80 and 57/80 Musik–Vertrieb Membran and K-tel International v. GEMA [1981] ECR 147, paragraph 24; and Joined Cases C–427/93, C–429/93 and C–436/93 Bristol–Myers Squibb and Others [1996] ECR I–3457, paragraph 46).

48.   The next question which must be examined is how far the rule in Merck applies where patentees are legally obliged to market their products in the exporting State.

49.   In answering that question it is to be remembered, first, that in Merck the Court emphasized the importance of the fact that the patentee had taken his decision to market his product freely and in full knowledge of all relevant circumstances and, second, that it follows from Pharmon that a patentee who is not in a position to decide freely how he will market his products in the exporting State may oppose importation and marketing of those products in the State where the patent is in force.

50.   It follows that, where a patentee is legally bound under either national law or Community law to market his products in a Member State, he cannot be deemed, within the meaning of the ruling in Merck, to have given his consent to the marketing of the products concerned. He is therefore entitled to oppose importation and marketing of those products in the State where they are protected.

51.   It is for the patentee to prove, before the national court from which an order prohibiting imports is sought, that there is a legal obligation to market the product concerned in the exporting State. He must in particular show, for example by reference to decisions of the competent national authorities or courts or of the competent Community authorities, that there is a genuine, existing obligation.

52.   According to the information given to the Court in these proceedings and as the Advocate General observes in points 152 and 153 of his Opinion, such obligations can hardly be said to exist in the case of the imports in question.

53.   Finally, as regards the argument that ethical obligations may compel patentees to provide supplies of drugs to Member States where they are needed, even if they are not patentable there, such considerations are not, in the absence of any legal obligation, such as to make it possible properly to identify the situations in which the patentee is deprived of his power to decide freely how he will market his product. Such considerations are, at any rate in the present context, difficult to apprehend and distinguish from commercial considerations. Such ethical obligations cannot, therefore,

be the basis for derogating from the rule on free movement of goods laid down in Merck.

54.   In view of the foregoing, the answer to be given to the third question must be that Articles 30 and 36 of the Treaty preclude application of national legislation which grants the holder of a patent for a pharmaceutical product the right to oppose importation by a third party of that product from another Member State in circumstances where the holder first put the product on the market in that State after its accession to the European Community but before the product could be protected by a patent in that State, unless the holder of the patent can prove that he is under a genuine, existing legal obligation to market the product in that Member State.

2.   PATENTS AND INDUSTRY STANDARDS

ORANGE BOOK STANDARD

Federal Court of Justice (Germany) Judgment of 6 May 2009
KZR 39/06

[Author's Summary: Philips Electronics is the owner of several patents in Germany and other countries related to the manufacture of writable compact disks. The technology patented serves as the basis for the industry standard. The defendant made and sold writable compact disks that used the patented technology without a license from Philips, which sought an injunction for patent infringement in Germany. The Regional Court and the Court of Appeal found for Philips. The Federal Court of Justice upheld the injunction in an opinion that provided useful analysis on abuse of dominant position and licensing.]

* * *1.   The appellate court assumed that the plaintiff did not violate the prohibition of discrimination according to Sec. 20 Para. 1 GWB [*Law against Restraints on Competition*]. According to the appellate court, it is true that the plaintiff is the addressee of this law, because according to its own submission, everyone who manufactures customary CD–R and CD–RW has to comply with the standard comprised of the specifications listed in the so-called Orange Book, and therefore inevitably has to use the patent in suit; the grant of licenses under the patent in suit therefore objectively constitutes an independent market which is controlled by the plaintiff as the only supplier. The grant of licenses is moreover a kind of commerce that is usually accessible to companies of the same kind, because the plaintiff has granted various licenses. Yet according to the appellate court, the plaintiff does not discriminate the defendants against other companies of the same kind. The defendants did not submit that there are or were licensees with

whom the plaintiff had concluded license agreements which provided for the payment of a royalty of 3% of the net sales price, which was the percentage considered reasonable by the defendants. According to the appellate court, the defendants made an ample statement regarding the fact that the plaintiff does not sufficiently monitor the compliance with its license agreements, does not enforce its rights, makes repayments and tolerates so-called "underreporting", so that the agreed minimum royalty per blank CD sold was actually not being paid. Yet the appellate court considers that there is nothing in the defendants' submission to prove that the actual and mutual handling of a license agreement which had formerly been concluded on different terms would now lead to only 3% of the net sales price being paid to the plaintiff.

2.   The criticism of this assessment raised in the appeal on points of law does not need to be discussed, because there are other reasons why the defendants cannot claim that the plaintiff has an obligation to grant a license under the patent in suit.

a) Still, a defendant who has been sued based on a patent is generally able to defend himself against the patent proprietor's claim for injunctive relief by submitting that the plaintiff who refuses to conclude a patent license agreement, inequitably prevents him from taking part in a commerce that is usually accessible to similar companies, or discriminates him against other companies, thus abusing its dominating position on the market.

aa) In its "Standard–Spundfass" decision (BGHZ 160, 67, 81 f.), the present court left the question as to whether a claim based on Sec. 33 Para. 1 GWB in conjunction with Art. 82 EC or Secs. 19, 20 GWB can be raised against the claim for injunctive relief based on Sec. 139 Para. 1 PatG unanswered. The courts of the first instance and literature have a controversial opinion about this question.

To the extent that the "compulsory license defence under cartel law" is accepted (in favour: LG Düsseldorf WuW/E DE–R 2120, 2121; Heinemann, ZWeR2005, 198, 2001; Kühnen in Festschrift für Tilmann, p. 513, 523; Schulte/Kühnen, PatG, 8th edition Sec. 24 no. 66 f.; Meinberg, Zwangslizenzen im Patent—und Urheberrecht als Instrument der kartellrechtlichen Missbrauchsaufsicht im deutschen und europäischen Recht (2006), p. 196; Benkard/Scharen, PatG, 10th edition Sec. 9 no. 73; Wirtz/Holzhäuser, WRP 2004, 683, 693 f.), it is based on the consideration that, although the party wishing to take a license acts unlawfully when using the patent without the consent of the patent proprietor, the patent proprietor can still not sue him for injunctive relief, because with the request to cease and desist, he would ask for something he would have to immediately give back (in the form of the grant of a license) (dolo petit, qui petit quod statim redditurus est), thus violating the principle of good faith (Sec. 242 BGB).

According to the opposite opinion (OLG Düsseldorf InstGE 2, 168, no. 27; OLG Dresden GRUR 2003, 601, 603 f.; Jaecks/Dörmer in Festschrift für Säcker, p. 97, 106 ff.; Maaïen, Normung, Standardisierung und Immaterialgüterrechte (2006), p. 257 f.; Graf von Merveldt, WuW 2004, 19 ff.; Rombach in Festschrift für Günter Hirsch, p. 311, 321 f.), the compulsory license plea is not successful in infringement proceedings, because the prerequisites of a right to "self-help" pursuant to Sec. 229 BGB are not met, and because the grant of the license only has an effect for the future—as in the case of Sec. 24 PatG; as long as the proposed licensee has not enforced his right to a license by filing an action or a counterclaim, he is liable to cease and desist. In addition to that, Art. 31 of the TRIPS Agreement requires an act of a higher authority for a compulsory license to be granted.

bb) Generally, we agree with the first-mentioned opinion.

If a company with a dominant position on the market discriminates the company seeking a license in a commerce usually accessible to similar companies, or if it inequitably obstructs the proposed licensee by refusing to conclude a patent license agreement it has been offered, the enforcement of the patent-law claim for injunctive relief constitutes an abuse of its dominant position on the market, because the dominant company prevents the other company from gaining the very access to the market that it is obliged grant by entering into the license agreement. The enforcement of the claim for injunctive relief is therefore just as prohibited as the refusal to conclude the license agreement that would annihilate the claim for injunctive relief. However, the public courts cannot order a behaviour that contravenes cartel law.

Art. 31 of the TRIPS Agreement does not say anything different, because this provision generally permits the grant of a right to use the subject matter of a patent without the authorization of the right holder, provided the authorization of such use shall be considered on its individual merits. The further precondition, according to which the proposed user must have made efforts to obtain authorization from the right holder on reasonable commercial terms and conditions, and such efforts have not been successful, (Art. 31 lit. b)) is not binding on the member states according to Art. 31 lit. k), if the use is permitted in order to remedy a practice determined after judicial or administrative process to be anti-competitive. Moreover, this precondition is also met if the infringer of the patent in suit has unsuccessfully tried to obtain a license on non-discriminatory terms prior to taking up the use of the patent. It does not matter if the Agreement requires the member states to grant the right of use conferred by cartel law through a higher authority, as the plaintiff wants to infer from Art. 31 lit. a) and i) in its reply to the appeal on points of law with reference to Rombach (ibid., p. 322), because a judicial review in infringement proceedings alone is sufficient for this, establishing in a binding manner if and to which extent the user of the invention has a right to be granted a license.

b) However, the patent proprietor who asserts a claim for injunctive relief based on his patent, although the defendant is entitled to be granted a license under the patent in suit, only abuses his dominant position on the market and only acts in bad faith if two conditions are met: Firstly, the party wishing to obtain a license must have made an unconditional offer to conclude a license agreement which the patent proprietor cannot reject without unreasonably obstructing the party wishing to take a license or without violating the prohibition of discrimination, and the proposed licensee must stay bound by this offer. And secondly, the proposed licensee has to comply with the obligations on which the use of the licensed subject matter depends according to the license agreement still to be concluded, if he already uses the subject matter of the patent before the patent proprietor has accepted his offer. This means in particular that the proposed licensee has to pay the royalties resulting from the contract or ensure their payment.

aa) The fact that the proposed licensee must have made an offer on acceptable contracting terms that the patent proprietor cannot refuse without discriminating the proposed licensee against similar companies without objective reason or without unduly obstructing him, is, to our knowledge, generally recognized, because the patent proprietor with a dominant position on the market is not obliged to offer to permit the use of the invention; only if he declines an offer to conclude an agreement on non-restraining or discriminating terms, does he abuse his dominant position on the market. He does not have to tolerate the use of his patent by a company who is not ready to enter into a license agreement on such terms and conditions.

The present case does not warrant a detailed discussion of what kind of terms and conditions such a license offer has to include in detail. If the proposed licensee makes an offer on customary terms and conditions, the patent proprietor is only able to claim that he does not have to accept individual contract terms if he offers other terms instead, which agree with his obligations under cartel law.

It likewise results from what has been said above that an abuse of a dominant position on the market is not present if the proposed licensee only makes a conditional license offer, i.e. if he offers to conclude an agreement only on the condition that the infringement court affirms the infringement of the patent in suit by the attacked embodiment that he denies. The patent proprietor does not have to accept such an offer under other circumstances, either; it can therefore not be used as a defence against his claim for injunctive relief.

bb) Yet the unconditional, acceptable contract offer is not sufficient in order to make the "compulsory license defence" effective against the patent proprietor's request for injunctive relief. The grant of a license generally only has an effect for the future (Rombach ibid. p. 322). The licensee is not authorized to use the subject matter of the license agreement until he has been granted the license; at the same time, every act of use (unless a consideration has been agreed that is independent of use) establishes a claim of the licensor to the contractual consideration which—as in the case at issue—is typically a unit or sales-related royalty. The proposed licensee who starts using the patent in suit in anticipation of the license to be granted to him must not only "anticipate" his contractual rights, but also his contractual obligations. He is able to raise the *dolo-petit* defence against the request for injunctive relief only if he has not just made an offer to the patent proprietor that the patent proprietor must not reject, but if he likewise behaves as if the patent proprietor had already accepted his offer. In this case he would not only be entitled to use the subject matter of the patent, but he would in particular be obliged to account for the use on a regular basis and to pay the royalties resulting from his accounts to the patent proprietor. On the other hand, the patent proprietor neither commits and abuse nor an act of bad faith if he asserts claims based on the patent against someone who claims a licensee's authorization to use the patent, but does not pay the consideration that the licensee would be obliged to pay according to a non-discriminatory or non-restrictive license agreement.* * *

C. COMPARATIVE LICENSING PRACTICE

As many of the cases discussed in this chapter show, licensing practices are often the basis for assertions of anticompetitive conduct by patent owners. Because of the uncertainties that these assertions can create for the dissemination of technology and for licensing practice more broadly, competition policy makers in the United States and the European Union have enacted guidelines for determining when licensing practices cross the line into conduct that violates the competition laws. Below are excerpts from the Intellectual Property Licensing Guidelines propagated by the United States Department of Justice and the Federal Trade Commission in 1995 and the European Commission Regulations on Technology

Transfer Agreements (available at http://europa.eu/legislation_summaries/competition/firms/l26108_en.htm). The excerpts below were selected to give you a flavor of how the two jurisdictions address anticompetitive licensing issues.

ANTITRUST GUIDELINES FOR THE LICENSING OF INTELLECTUAL PROPERTY
Issued by the US Department of Justice and the Federal Trade Commission
April 6, 1995

1. Intellectual property protection and the antitrust laws

1.0   These Guidelines state the antitrust enforcement policy of the U.S. Department of Justice and the Federal Trade Commission (individually, "the Agency," and collectively, "the Agencies") with respect to the licensing of intellectual property protected by patent, copyright, and trade secret law, and of know-how. By stating their general policy, the Agencies hope to assist those who need to predict whether the Agencies will challenge a practice as anticompetitive. However, these Guidelines cannot remove judgment and discretion in antitrust law enforcement. Moreover, the standards set forth in these Guidelines must be applied in unforeseeable circumstances. Each case will be evaluated in light of its own facts, and these Guidelines will be applied reasonably and flexibly.* * *

The intellectual property laws and the antitrust laws share the common purpose of promoting innovation and enhancing consumer welfare. The intellectual property laws provide incentives for innovation and its dissemination and commercialization by establishing enforceable property rights for the creators of new and useful products, more efficient processes, and original works of expression. In the absence of intellectual property rights, imitators could more rapidly exploit the efforts of innovators and investors without compensation. Rapid imitation would reduce the commercial value of innovation and erode incentives to invest, ultimately to the detriment of consumers. The antitrust laws promote innovation and consumer welfare by prohibiting certain actions that may harm competition with respect to either existing or new ways of serving consumers.

2. General principles

2.0   These Guidelines embody three general principles: (a) for the purpose of antitrust analysis, the Agencies regard intellectual property as being essentially comparable to any other form of property; (b) the Agencies do not presume that intellectual property creates market power in the antitrust context; and (c) the Agencies recognize that intellectual property licensing allows firms to combine complementary factors of production and is generally procompetitive.

2.1 Standard antitrust analysis applies to intellectual property

The Agencies apply the same general antitrust principles to conduct involving intellectual property that they apply to conduct involving any other form of tangible or intangible property. That is not to say that intellectual property is in all respects the same as any other form of property. Intellectual property has important characteristics, such as ease of misappropriation, that distinguish it from many other forms of property. These characteristics can be taken into account by standard antitrust analysis, however, and do not require the application of fundamentally different principles.

Although there are clear and important differences in the purpose, extent, and duration of protection provided under the intellectual property regimes of patent, copyright, and trade secret, the governing antitrust principles are the same. Antitrust analysis takes differences among these forms of intellectual property into account in evaluating the specific market circumstances in which transactions occur, just as it does with other particular market circumstances.

Intellectual property law bestows on the owners of intellectual property certain rights to exclude others. These rights help the owners to profit from the use of their property. An intellectual property owner's rights to exclude are similar to the rights enjoyed by owners of other forms of private property. As with other forms of private property, certain types of conduct with respect to intellectual property may have anticompetitive effects against which the antitrust laws can and do protect. Intellectual property is thus neither particularly free from scrutiny under the antitrust laws, nor particularly suspect under them.

The Agencies recognize that the licensing of intellectual property is often international. The principles of antitrust analysis described in these Guidelines apply equally to domestic and international licensing arrangements. However, as described in the 1995 Department of Justice and Federal Trade Commission Antitrust Enforcement Guidelines for International Operations, considerations particular to international operations, such as jurisdiction and comity, may affect enforcement decisions when the arrangement is in an international context.

2.2 Intellectual property and market power

Market power is the ability profitably to maintain prices above, or output below, competitive levels for a significant period of time. The Agencies will not presume that a patent, copyright, or trade secret necessarily confers market power upon its owner. Although the intellectual property right confers the power to exclude with respect to the specific product, process, or work in question, there will often be sufficient actual or potential close substitutes for such product, process, or work to prevent the exercise of market power. If a patent or other form of intellectual property does confer market power, that market power does not by itself offend the antitrust laws. As with any other tangible or intangible asset that enables its owner to obtain significant supracompetitive profits, market power (or even a monopoly) that is solely "a consequence of a superior product, business acumen, or historic accident" does not violate the antitrust laws. Nor does such market power impose on the intellectual property owner an obligation to license the use of that property to others. As in other antitrust contexts, however, market power could be illegally acquired or maintained, or, even if lawfully acquired and maintained, would be relevant to the ability of an intellectual property owner to harm competition through unreasonable conduct in connection with such property.

2.3   Procompetitive benefits of licensing

Intellectual property typically is one component among many in a production process and derives value from its combination with complementary factors. Complementary factors of production include manufacturing and distribution facilities, workforces, and other items of intellectual property. The owner of intellectual property has to arrange for its combination with other necessary factors to realize its commercial value. Often, the owner finds it most efficient to contract with others for these factors, to sell rights to the intellectual property, or to enter into a joint venture arrangement for its development, rather than supplying these complementary factors itself.

Licensing, cross-licensing, or otherwise transferring intellectual property (hereinafter "licensing") can facilitate integration of the licensed property with complementary factors of production. This integration can lead to more efficient exploitation of the intellectual property, benefiting consumers through the reduction of costs and the introduction of new products. Such arrangements increase the value of intellectual property to consumers and to the developers of the technology. By potentially increasing the expected returns from intellectual property, licensing also can increase the incentive for its creation and thus promote greater investment in research and development.

Sometimes the use of one item of intellectual property requires access to another. An item of intellectual property "blocks" another when the second cannot be practiced without using the first. For example, an improvement on a patented machine can be blocked by the patent on the machine. Licensing may promote the coordinated development of technologies that are in a blocking relationship.

Field-of-use, territorial, and other limitations on intellectual property licenses may serve procompetitive ends by allowing the licensor to exploit its property as efficiently and effectively as possible. These various forms of exclusivity can be used to give a licensee an incentive to invest in the commercialization and distribution of products embodying the licensed intellectual property and to develop additional applications for the licensed property. The restrictions may do so, for example, by protecting the licensee against free-riding on the licensee's investments by other licensees or by the licensor. They may also increase the licensor's incentive to license, for example, by protecting the licensor from competition in the licensor's own technology in a market niche that it prefers to keep to itself. These benefits of licensing restrictions apply to patent, copyright, and trade secret licenses, and to know-how agreements.

. . . .

5.   Application of general principles

5.0   This section illustrates the application of the general principles discussed above to particular licensing restraints and to arrangements that involve the cross-licensing, pooling, or acquisition of intellectual property. The restraints and arrangements identified are typical of those that are likely to receive antitrust scrutiny; however, they are not intended as an exhaustive list of practices that could raise competitive concerns.* * *

5.3   Tying arrangements

A "tying" or "tie-in" or "tied sale" arrangement has been defined as "an agreement by a party to sell one product . . . on the condition that the buyer also purchases a different (or tied) product, or at least agrees that he will not purchase that [tied] product from any other supplier." *Eastman Kodak Co. v. Image Technical Services, Inc.*, 112 S. Ct. 2072, 2079 (1992). Conditioning the ability of a licensee to license one or more items of intellectual property on the licensee's purchase of another item of intellectual property or a good or a service has been held in some cases to constitute illegal tying. Although tying arrangements may result in anticompetitive effects, such arrangements can also result in significant efficiencies and procompetitive benefits. In the exercise of their prosecutorial discretion, the Agencies will consider both the anticompetitive effects and the efficiencies attributable to a tie-in. The Agencies would be likely to challenge a tying arrangement if: (1) the seller has market power in the tying product, (2) the arrangement has an adverse effect on competition in the relevant market for the tied product, and (3) efficiency justifications for the arrangement do not outweigh the anticompetitive effects. The Agencies will not presume that a patent, copyright, or trade secret necessarily confers market power upon its owner.

Package licensing—the licensing of multiple items of intellectual property in a single license or in a group of related licenses—may be a form of tying arrangement if the licensing of one product is conditioned upon the acceptance of a license of another, separate product. Package licensing can be efficiency enhancing under some circumstances. When multiple licenses are needed to use any single item of intellectual property, for example, a package license may promote such efficiencies. If a package license constitutes a tying arrangement, the Agencies will evaluate its competitive effects under the same principles they apply to other tying arrangements.

6.   Enforcement of invalid intellectual property rights

The Agencies may challenge the enforcement of invalid intellectual property rights as antitrust violations. Enforcement or attempted enforcement of a patent obtained by fraud on the Patent and Trademark Office or the Copyright Office may violate section 2 of the Sherman Act, if all the elements otherwise necessary to establish a section 2 charge are proved, or section 5 of the Federal Trade Commission Act. . . . Inequitable conduct before the Patent and Trademark Office will not be the basis of a section 2 claim unless the conduct also involves knowing and willful fraud and the other elements of a section 2 claim are present. . . . Actual or attempted enforcement of patents obtained by inequitable conduct that falls short of fraud under some circumstances may violate section 5 of the Federal Trade Commission Act. Objectively baseless litigation to enforce invalid intellectual property rights may also constitute an element of a violation of the Sherman Act.

COMMISSION REGULATION (EC) NO 772/2004 OF 27 APRIL 2004 ON THE APPLICATION OF ARTICLE 81(3) OF THE TREATY TO CATEGORIES OF TECHNOLOGY TRANSFER AGREEMENTS

Whereas:* * *

(4) This Regulation should meet the two requirements of ensuring effective competition and providing adequate legal security for undertakings. The pursuit of these objectives should take account of the need to simplify the regulatory framework and its application. It is appropriate to move away from the approach of listing exempted clauses and to place greater emphasis on defining the categories of agreements which are exempted up to a certain level of market power and on specifying the restrictions or clauses which

are not to be contained in such agreements. This is consistent with an economics-based approach which assesses the impact of agreements on the relevant market. It is also consistent with such an approach to make a distinction between agreements between competitors and agreements between non-competitors.

(5) Technology transfer agreements concern the licensing of technology. Such agreements will usually improve economic efficiency and be pro-competitive as they can reduce duplication of research and development, strengthen the incentive for the initial research and development, spur incremental innovation, facilitate diffusion and generate product market competition.

(6) The likelihood that such efficiency-enhancing and pro-competitive effects will outweigh any anti-competitive effects due to restrictions contained in technology transfer agreements depends on the degree of market power of the undertakings concerned and, therefore, on the extent to which those undertakings face competition from undertakings owning substitute technologies or undertakings producing substitute products.* * *

(12) There can be no presumption that above these market-share thresholds technology transfer agreements do fall within the scope of Article 81(1). For instance, an exclusive licensing agreement between non-competing undertakings does often not fall within the scope of Article 81(1). There can also be no presumption that, above these market-share thresholds, technology transfer agreements falling within the scope of Article 81(1) will not satisfy the conditions for exemption. However, it can also not be presumed that they will usually give rise to objective advantages of such a character and size as to compensate for the disadvantages which they create for competition.

(18) In order to strengthen supervision of parallel networks of technology transfer agreements which have similar restrictive effects and which cover more than 50% of a given market, the Commission should be able to declare this Regulation inapplicable to technology transfer agreements containing specific restraints relating to the market concerned, thereby restoring the full application of Article 81 to such agreements.

HAS ADOPTED THIS REGULATION:

Article 2
Exemption

Pursuant to Article 81(3) of the Treaty and subject to the provisions of this Regulation, it is hereby declared that Article 81(1) of the Treaty shall not apply to technology transfer agreements entered into between two undertakings permitting the production of contract products.

This exemption shall apply to the extent that such agreements contain restrictions of competition falling within the scope of Article 81(1). The exemption shall apply for as long as the intellectual property right in the licensed technology has not expired, lapsed or been declared invalid or, in the case of know-how, for as long as the know-how remains secret, except in the event where the know-how becomes publicly known as a result of action by the licensee, in which case the exemption shall apply for the duration of the agreement.

Article 3
Market-share thresholds

1.   Where the undertakings party to the agreement are competing undertakings, the exemption provided for in Article 2 shall apply on condition that the combined market share of the parties does not exceed 20% on the affected relevant technology and product market.

2.   Where the undertakings party to the agreement are not competing undertakings, the exemption provided for in Article 2 shall apply on condition that the market share of each of the parties does not exceed 30% on the affected relevant technology and product market.

3.   For the purposes of paragraphs 1 and 2, the market share of a party on the relevant technology market(s) is defined in terms of the presence of the licensed technology on the relevant product market(s). A licensor's market share on the relevant technology market shall be the combined market share on the relevant product market of the contract products produced by the licensor and its licensees.

Article 4
Hardcore restrictions

1.   Where the undertakings party to the agreement are competing undertakings, the exemption provided for in Article 2 shall not apply to agreements which, directly or indirectly, in isolation or in combination with other factors under the control of the parties, have as their object:

(a) the restriction of a party's ability to determine its prices when selling products to third parties;

(b) the limitation of output, except limitations on the output of contract products imposed on the licensee in a non-reciprocal agreement or imposed on only one of the licensees in a reciprocal agreement;

(c) the allocation of markets or customers except:

(i) the obligation on the licensee(s) to produce with the licensed technology only within one or more technical fields of use or one or more product markets,

(ii) the obligation on the licensor and/or the licensee, in a non-reciprocal agreement, not to produce with the licensed technology within one or more technical fields of use or one or more product markets or one or more exclusive territories reserved for the other party,

(iii) the obligation on the licensor not to license the technology to another licensee in a particular territory,

(iv) the restriction, in a non-reciprocal agreement, of active and/or passive sales by the licensee and/or the licensor into the exclusive territory or to the exclusive customer group reserved for the other party,

(v) the restriction, in a non-reciprocal agreement, of active sales by the licensee into the exclusive territory or to the exclusive customer group allocated by the licensor to another licensee provided the latter was not a competing undertaking of the licensor at the time of the conclusion of its own licence,

(vi) the obligation on the licensee to produce the contract products only for its own use provided that the licensee is not restricted in selling the contract products actively and passively as spare parts for its own products,

(vii) the obligation on the licensee, in a non-reciprocal agreement, to produce the contract products only for a particular customer, where the licence was granted in order to create an alternative source of supply for that customer;

(d) the restriction of the licensee's ability to exploit its own technology or the restriction of the ability of any of the parties to the agreement to carry out research and development, unless such latter restriction is indispensable to prevent the disclosure of the licensed know-how to third parties.

2.   Where the undertakings party to the agreement are not competing undertakings, the exemption provided for in Article 2 shall not apply to agreements which, directly or indirectly, in isolation or in combination with other factors under the control of the parties, have as their object:

(a) the restriction of a party's ability to determine its prices when selling products to third parties, without prejudice to the possibility of imposing a maximum sale price or recommending a sale price, provided that it does not amount to a fixed or minimum sale price as a result of pressure from, or incentives offered by, any of the parties;

(b) the restriction of the territory into which, or of the customers to whom, the licensee may passively sell the contract products, except:

(i) the restriction of passive sales into an exclusive territory or to an exclusive customer group reserved for the licensor,

(ii) the restriction of passive sales into an exclusive territory or to an exclusive customer group allocated by the licensor to another licensee during the first two years that this other licensee is selling the contract products in that territory or to that customer group,

(iii) the obligation to produce the contract products only for its own use provided that the licensee is not restricted in selling the contract products actively and passively as spare parts for its own products,

(iv) the obligation to produce the contract products only for a particular customer, where the licence was granted in order to create an alternative source of supply for that customer,

(v) the restriction of sales to end-users by a licensee operating at the wholesale level of trade,

(vi) the restriction of sales to unauthorised distributors by the members of a selective distribution system;

(c) the restriction of active or passive sales to end-users by a licensee which is a member of a selective distribution system and which operates at the retail level, without prejudice to the possibility of prohibiting a member of the system from operating out of an unauthorised place of establishment.

3.   Where the undertakings party to the agreement are not competing undertakings at the time of the conclusion of the agreement but become competing undertakings afterwards, paragraph 2 and not paragraph 1 shall apply for the full life of the agreement unless the agreement is subsequently amended in any material respect.

Article 5
Excluded restrictions

1.   The exemption provided for in Article 2 shall not apply to any of the following obligations contained in technology transfer agreements:

(a) any direct or indirect obligation on the licensee to grant an exclusive licence to the licensor or to a third party designated by the licensor in respect of its own severable improvements to or its own new applications of the licensed technology;

(b) any direct or indirect obligation on the licensee to assign, in whole or in part, to the licensor or to a third party designated by the licensor, rights to its own severable improvements to or its own new applications of the licensed technology;

(c) any direct or indirect obligation on the licensee not to challenge the validity of intellectual property rights which the licensor holds in the common market, without prejudice to the possibility of providing for termination of the technology transfer agreement in the event that the licensee challenges the validity of one or more of the licensed intellectual property rights.

2. Where the undertakings party to the agreement are not competing undertakings, the exemption provided for in Article 2 shall not apply to any direct or indirect obligation limiting the licensee's ability to exploit its own technology or limiting the ability of any of the parties to the agreement to carry out research and development, unless such latter restriction is indispensable to prevent the disclosure of the licensed know-how to third parties.

Notes and Questions

1. Patents provide its owners a right to exclude others from using, making, selling, offering to sell, and importing the patented invention. This right to exclude, however, does not necessarily lead to market power. The economic and legal notion of market power is the right to affect the market price of a product through one's conduct. If a firm unilaterally raises its price, this decision will not affect the market price if there are many other firms in the marketplace. Consumers will simply stop purchasing from the firm with the higher price. The right to exclude, however, can prevent entry of firms into a marketplace. A patent owner's decision not to license its patent to a willing licensee means that the licensee cannot make the patented invention and therefore one fewer firm is in the market to make and sell the patented invention. However, the denied licensee might be able to invent around the patented invention and make a close substitute to the patented invention which would be just as good from a consumer perspective. The *Illinois Tool* decision makes perfect sense from this perspective.

2. The use of tying arrangements involving a patent used to be viewed with suspicion as the *Illinois Tool* decision illustrates. However, a contractual requirement in a patent license requiring the purchase of an additional product or service makes sense from the perspective of monitoring quality and usage of the patented invention. How about other restrictions in a patent license? The *Quanta* decision suggests that there might be some limits on what a patent owner can place as a condition on a patent license, particularly if those conditions are meant to affect third parties. The analogy to conditions in patent licenses is to servitudes on real property. The common law places restrictions on when such servitudes ran with the land. The first sale doctrine is the

analogy in patent law to conditions on patent licenses, which will not always run with the patented invention as it continues through the stream of commerce.

3.   Pharmaceuticals have been an important industry promoted by patent law. However, as the Federal Circuit's decision in *Cipro* and the European Commission's decision in *AstraZeneca* illustrate, antitrust law places some limits on the right of patent owner. Compare and contrast the United States and the European approaches. The U.S. takes a categorical approach, which applies a rule of reason approach to the business practices of patent owners except for some narrow instances which are deemed per se illegal. The European approach recognizes abuse of dominant position more readily than the United States. Furthermore, the European approach relies more on enforcement of competition laws by government agencies like the European Commission while the United States relies on private enforcement by competitors as well as government enforcement.

4.   The *Orange Book* case illustrates how courts deal with standard setting by patent owners, particularly cases in which the patent owner works with competitors to set an industry standard which is covered by a patent. The German Federal Court adopts an approach favorable to the patent owner, while recognizing some situations in which an injunctive remedy would constitute an abuse of dominant position. In the United States, the enforceability of a patent incorporated into an industry standard will rest on whether the patent owner has met whatever disclosure obligation it had as a member of a standard setting body. On the issue of standard setting and patent licensing in the United States, see *Qualcomm Inc. v. Broadcom Corp.*, 548 F.3d 1004 (Fed. Cir. 2008) (patent owner's duty to disclose was found to extend to patents that might reasonably be found to extend to practicing the standard); *Rambus, Inc. v. FTC*, 522 F.3d 456 (D.C.Cir. 2008) (conduct of owner of patents incorporated into a standard was held not to be exclusionary under Sherman Antitrust Act). For an analysis of rule of reason in the context of patent pools involving a license, see Princo Corp. v. ITC, 563 F.3d 1301 (Fed. Cir. 2009).

5.   The last section of the chapter presents guidelines used in the United States and the European Union to determine the treatment of intellectual property licenses under the respective antitrust and competition laws. The United States approach is to follow a rule of reason, except for certain conduct that is deemed per se illegal. The European approach is more categorical, mixing per se rules with more flexible standards. Rethink the *Quanta* decision. Is the Supreme Court's approach consistent with the rule of reason? Or is it more of a mixed standard as represented by the European approach?

Chapter 10

PATENTS AND TERRITORIAL BORDERS

A. FOREIGN JURISDICTION AND TERRITORIALITY

Patentees may find enforcement against international actors challenging. Generally speaking, patents are effective within the issuing nation or territory. Jurisdictional rules limit any particular nation's ability to reach non-citizens.

These tensions have long arisen in patent disputes between actors within various European nations. Recall that many European nations are members of the European Patent Convention, which has harmonized patent law among its members to some degree. The Brussels Convention, adopted originally in 1968 and subsequently embodied in European Communities Regulation Number 44/2001, governs various aspects of the litigation of civil and commercial disputes among members of the European Communities. At one time, some courts within Europe were willing to adjudicate patent disputes involving parties domiciled in different nations. For example, courts in the Netherlands promulgated the "spider in the web" doctrine, whereby multiple related corporate defendants could be sued if the principle defendant was based there. *See* Pierre Véron, *Thirty Years of Experience with the Brussels Convention in Patent Infringement Litigation*, 84 J. Pat. & Trademark Off. Soc'y 431 (2002). The following two decisions consider the degree to which relief across Europe can be granted in any court of a single nation today.

ROCHE NEDERLAND BV v. PRIMUS

[2006] ECR I–6535

JANN, P

. . .

2.   The reference was made in the course of proceedings between Roche Nederland BV and eight other companies in the Roche group, on the one hand, and Drs Primus and Goldenberg, on the other, in respect of an alleged infringement of the latter's rights in a European patent of which they are the proprietors.

Legal background

The Brussels Convention

3.   Featuring in Title II, on the rules of jurisdiction, and Section I, entitled 'General Provisions', the first paragraph of Article 2 of the Brussels Convention states:

> 'Subject to the provisions of this convention, persons domiciled in a Contracting State shall, whatever their nationality, be sued in the courts of that State.'

. . .

5.   Article 6 of the Brussels Convention, which appears in Section 2 of Title II, entitled 'Special jurisdiction', states:

> '[A defendant domiciled in a Contracting State] may also be sued:
>
> > (1) where he is one of a number of defendants, in the courts for the place where any one of them is domiciled;

. . .

7.   Article Vd of the Protocol annexed to the Brussels Convention, which, pursuant to Article 65 of the latter, forms an integral part of the Convention, states:

> 'Without prejudice to the jurisdiction of the European Patent Office under the Convention on the Grant of European Patents, signed at Munich on 5 October 1973, the courts of each Contracting State shall have exclusive jurisdiction, regardless of domicile, in proceedings concerned with the registration or validity of any European patent granted for that State which is not a Community patent by virtue of the provisions of Article 86 of the Convention for the European Patent for the Common Market, signed at Luxembourg on 15 December 1975.'

8.   Article 22 of the Brussels Convention, which appears in Section 8 . . . provides that where related actions are brought in the courts

of different Contracting States, any court other than the court first seised may, while the actions are pending at first instance, stay its proceedings or, under certain conditions, decline jurisdiction. According to the third paragraph of that provision:

'For the purposes of this article, actions are deemed to be related where they are so closely connected that it is expedient to hear and determine them together to avoid the risk of irreconcilable judgments resulting from separate proceedings.'

. . .

12. As regards the rights conferred on the proprietor of a European patent, Article 64(1) and (3) of [the Munich C]onvention provides:

'(1) A European patent shall . . . confer on its proprietor from the date of publication of the mention of its grant, in each Contracting State in respect of which it is granted, the same rights as would be conferred by a national patent granted in that State.

(3) Any infringement of a European patent shall be dealt with by national law.'

The main proceedings and the questions referred for a preliminary ruling

13. Drs Primus and Goldenberg, who are domiciled in the United States of America, are the proprietors of European patent No 131 627.

14. On 24 March 1997, they brought an action before the Rechtbank te s'—Gravenhage against Roche Nederland BV, a company established in the Netherlands, and eight other companies in the Roche group established in the United States of America, Belgium, Germany, France, the United Kingdom, Switzerland, Austria and Sweden ('Roche and Others'). The applicants claimed that those companies had all infringed the rights conferred on them by the patent of which they are the proprietors. That alleged infringement consisted in the placing on the market of immunoassay kits in countries where the defendants are established.

15. The companies in the Roche group not established in the Netherlands contested the jurisdiction of the Netherlands' courts. As regards the substance, they based their arguments on the absence of infringement and the invalidity of the patent in question. . . .

The questions referred for a preliminary ruling

18. . . . [T]he national court asks essentially whether Article 6(1) of the Brussels Convention must be interpreted as meaning that it

is to apply to European patent infringement proceedings involving a number of companies established in various Contracting States in respect of acts committed in one or more of those States and, in particular, where those companies, which belong to the same group, have acted in an identical or similar manner in accordance with a common policy elaborated by one of them.

19.   By way of derogation from the principle laid down in Article 2 of the Brussels Convention, that a defendant domiciled in a Contracting State is to be sued in the courts of that State, in a case where there is more than one defendant, Article 6(1) of the Convention allows a defendant domiciled in one Contracting State to be sued in another Contracting State where one of the defendants is domiciled.

20.   In the judgment in Case 189/87 Kalfelis [1988] ECR 5565, paragraph 12, the Court held that for Article 6(1) of the Brussels Convention to apply there must exist, between the various actions brought by the same plaintiff against different defendants, a connection of such a kind that it is expedient to determine the actions together in order to avoid the risk of irreconcilable judgments resulting from separate proceedings.

21.   The requirement of a connection does not derive from the wording of Article 6(1) of the Brussels Convention. It has been inferred from that provision by the Court in order to prevent the exception to the principle that jurisdiction is vested in the courts of the State of the defendant's domicile laid down in Article 6(1) from calling into question the very existence of that principle (Kalfelis, paragraph 8). . . .

22.   The formulation used by the Court in Kalfelis repeats the wording of Article 22 of the Brussels Convention, according to which actions are deemed to be related where they are so closely connected that it is expedient to hear and determine them together to avoid the risk of irreconcilable judgments resulting from separate proceedings. Article 22 was interpreted in Case C–406/92 Tatry [1994] ECR I5439, paragraph 58, to the effect that, in order to establish the necessary relationship between the cases, it is sufficient that separate trial and judgment would involve the risk of conflicting decisions, without necessarily involving the risk of giving rise to mutually exclusive legal consequences. . . .

27.   . . . [I]n the situation referred to by the national court in its first question referred for a preliminary ruling, that is in the case of European patent infringement proceedings involving a number of companies established in various Contracting States in respect of acts committed in one or more of those States, the existence of the same situation of fact cannot be inferred, since the defendants are

different and the infringements they are accused of, committed in different Contracting States, are not the same.

28. Possible divergences between decisions given by the courts concerned would not arise in the context of the same factual situation....

30. In particular, it is apparent from Article 64(3) of the Munich Convention that any action for infringement of a European patent must be examined in the light of the relevant national law in force in each of the States for which it has been granted.

31. It follows that, where infringement proceedings are brought before a number of courts in different Contracting States in respect of a European patent granted in each of those States, against defendants domiciled in those States in respect of acts allegedly committed in their territory, any divergences between the decisions given by the courts concerned would not arise in the context of the same legal situation.

32. Any diverging decisions could not, therefore, be treated as contradictory.

33. In those circumstances, even if the broadest interpretation of 'irreconcilable' judgments, in the sense of contradictory, were accepted as the criterion for the existence of the connection required for the application of Article 6(1) of the Brussels Convention, it is clear that such a connection could not be established between actions for infringement of the same European patent where each action was brought against a company established in a different Contracting State in respect of acts which it had committed in that State.

34. That finding is not called into question even in the situation referred to by the national court in its second question, that is where defendant companies, which belong to the same group, have acted in an identical or similar manner in accordance with a common policy elaborated by one of them, so that the factual situation would be the same.

35. The fact remains that the legal situation would not be the same ... and therefore there would be no risk, even in such a situation, of contradictory decisions.

36. Furthermore, although at first sight considerations of procedural economy may appear to militate in favour of consolidating such actions before one court, it is clear that the advantages for the sound administration of justice represented by such consolidation would be limited and would constitute a source of further risks.

37. Jurisdiction based solely on the factual criteria set out by the national court would lead to a multiplication of the potential heads of jurisdiction and would therefore be liable to undermine the

predictability of the rules of jurisdiction laid down by the Convention, and consequently to undermine the principle of legal certainty, which is the basis of the Convention.

38.   The damage would be even more serious if the application of the criteria in question gave the defendant a wide choice, thereby encouraging the practice of forum shopping which the Convention seeks to avoid and which the Court, in its judgment in Kalfelis, specifically sought to prevent....

41.   Having regard to all of the foregoing considerations, the answer to the questions referred must be that Article 6(1) of the Brussels Convention must be interpreted as meaning that it does not apply in European patent infringement proceedings involving a number of companies established in various Contracting States in respect of acts committed in one or more of those States even where those companies, which belong to the same group, may have acted in an identical or similar manner in accordance with a common policy elaborated by one of them....

GESELLSCHAFT FUR ANTRIEBSTECHNIK MBH & CO. KG v. LAMELLEN UND KUPLUNGSBAU BETEILIGUNGS KG (GAT v. LUK)

[2006] ECR I–6509

Jann, P.

. . .

2.   The reference has been made in the course of proceedings between Gesellschaft fur Antriebstechnik mbH & Co. KG ('GAT') and Lamellen und Kupplungsbau Beteiligungs KG ('LuK') concerning the marketing of products by the first of those companies which, according to the second, amounts to an infringement of two French patents of which it is the proprietor.

3.   Article 16 of the Brussels Convention, which constitutes Section 5 ('Exclusive jurisdiction') of Title II, concerning the rules of jurisdiction, states:

> 'The following courts shall have exclusive jurisdiction, regardless of domicile:
>
> 4.   in proceedings concerned with the registration or validity of patents, trade marks, designs, or other similar rights required to be deposited or registered, the courts of the Contracting State in which the deposit or registration has been applied for, has taken place or is under the terms of an international convention deemed to have taken place; ...

8.   GAT and LuK, companies established in Germany, are economic operators competing in the field of motor vehicle technology.

9. GAT made an offer to a motor vehicle manufacturer, also established in Germany, with a view to winning a contract to supply mechanical damper springs. LuK alleged that the spring which was the subject of GAT's proposal infringed two French patents of which LuK was the proprietor.

10. GAT brought a declaratory action before the Landgericht (Regional Court), Dusseldorf to establish that it was not in breach of the patents, maintaining that its products did not infringe the rights under the French patents owned by LuK and, further, that those patents were either void or invalid.

11. The Landgericht Dusseldorf considered that it had international jurisdiction to adjudicate upon the action relating to the alleged infringement of the rights deriving from the French patents. It considered that it also had jurisdiction to adjudicate upon the plea as to the alleged nullity of those patents. The Landgericht dismissed the action brought by GAT, holding that the patents at issue satisfied the requirements of patentability.

The question referred for a preliminary ruling

13. ... [T]he referring court seeks in essence to ascertain the scope of the exclusive jurisdiction provided for in Article 16(4) of the Convention in relation to patents. It asks whether that rule concerns all proceedings concerned with the registration or validity of a patent, irrespective of whether the question is raised by way of an action or a plea in objection, or whether its application is limited solely to those cases in which the question of a patent's registration or validity is raised by way of an action.

14. It should be recalled, in this connection, that the notion of proceedings 'concerned with the registration or validity of patents' contained in Article 16(4) of the Convention must be regarded as an independent concept intended to have uniform application in all the Contracting States.

15. The Court has thus held that proceedings relating to the validity, existence or lapse of a patent or an alleged right of priority by reason of an earlier deposit are to be regarded as proceedings 'concerned with the registration or validity of patents'.

16. If, on the other hand, the dispute does not concern the validity of the patent or the existence of the deposit or registration and these matters are not disputed by the parties, the dispute will not be covered by Article 16(4) of the Convention. Such would be the case, for example, with an infringement action, in which the question of the validity of the patent allegedly infringed is not called into question.

17.   In practice, however, the issue of a patent's validity is frequently raised as a plea in objection in an infringement action, the defendant seeking to have the claimant retroactively denied the right on which the claimant relies and thus have the action brought against him dismissed. The issue can also be invoked, as in the case in the main proceedings, in support of a declaratory action seeking to establish that there has been no infringement, whereby the claimant seeks to establish that the defendant has no enforceable right in regard to the invention in question. . . .

21.   In relation to the objective pursued, it should be noted that the rules of exclusive jurisdiction laid down in Article 16 of the Convention seek to ensure that jurisdiction rests with courts closely linked to the proceedings in fact and law.

22.   Thus, the exclusive jurisdiction in proceedings concerned with the registration or validity of patents conferred upon the courts of the Contracting State in which the deposit or registration has been applied for or made is justified by the fact that those courts are best placed to adjudicate upon cases in which the dispute itself concerns the validity of the patent or the existence of the deposit or registration. The courts of the Contracting State on whose territory the registers are kept may rule, applying their own national law, on the validity and effects of the patents which have been issued in that State. This concern for the sound administration of justice becomes all the more important in the field of patents since, given the specialised nature of this area, a number of Contracting States have set up a system of specific judicial protection, to ensure that these types of cases are dealt with by specialised courts.

23.   That exclusive jurisdiction is also justified by the fact that the issue of patents necessitates the involvement of the national administrative authorities.

24.   In relation to the position of Article 16 within the scheme of the Convention, it should be pointed out that the rules of jurisdiction provided for in that article are of an exclusive and mandatory nature, the application of which is specifically binding on both litigants and courts. Parties may not derogate from them by an agreement conferring jurisdiction or by the defendant's voluntary appearance. Where a court of a Contracting State is seised of a claim which is principally concerned with a matter over which the courts of another Contracting State have jurisdiction by virtue of Article 16, it must declare of its own motion that it has no jurisdiction. A judgment given which falls foul of the provisions of Article 16 does not benefit from the system of recognition and enforcement under the Convention.

25.   In the light of the position of Article 16(4) within the scheme of the Convention and the objective pursued, the view must be

taken that the exclusive jurisdiction provided for by that provision should apply whatever the form of proceedings in which the issue of a patent's validity is raised, be it by way of an action or a plea in objection, at the time the case is brought or at a later stage in the proceedings. . . .

30. The argument, advanced by LuK and the German Government, that under German law the effects of a judgment indirectly ruling on the validity of a patent are limited to the parties to the proceedings, is not an appropriate response to that risk. The effects flowing from such a decision are in fact determined by national law. In several Contracting States, however, a decision to annul a patent has erga omnes effect. In order to avoid the risk of contradictory decisions, it is therefore necessary to limit the jurisdiction of the courts of a State other than that in which the patent is issued to rule indirectly on the validity of a foreign patent to only those cases in which, under the applicable national law, the effects of the decision to be given are limited to the parties to the proceedings. Such a limitation would, however, lead to distortions, thereby undermining the equality and uniformity of rights and obligations arising from the Convention for the Contracting States and the persons concerned.

31. In the light of the foregoing, the answer to the question referred must be that Article 16(4) of the Convention is to be interpreted as meaning that the rule of exclusive jurisdiction laid down therein concerns all proceedings relating to the registration or validity of a patent, irrespective of whether the issue is raised by way of an action or a plea in objection. . . .

Notes and Questions

1. In *Roche v. Primus*, the Court of Justice determined that Article 6(1) of the Brussels Convention was insufficient to create jurisdiction for a suit alleging that related companies infringed a single European patent. The *Roche* Court determined that an assertion that the defendants were acting according to a common plan did not change the result. What concerns did the court express to support the ruling? If this action was filed today, where should the patentees file to obtain complete relief against all defendants for infringement of the European patent?

Note that a European Patent is granted by a single agency, the European Patent Office. Nonetheless, a European Patent provides "the same rights as would be conferred by a national patent granted in that State." EPC Art. 64(1). Further, the Convention provides that "[a]ny infringement of a European patent shall be dealt with by national law." *Id.* at 64(3). Thus, Contracting States have autonomy to vary patent law within certain parameters.

Thus, national law among the European Contracting States is not uniform. Two often-cited examples that illustrate the distinctions are the *Epilady* decisions, which concern two patents claiming an improved hair removal device granted to a single inventor from two different European nations, England and Germany. The patentee asserted infringement against a single defendant, Remington, asserting the British patent in the United Kingdom and the German patent in the German courts. After considering the patentee's infringement allegations, each nation's courts arrived at disparate results. Specifically, the British court found that the defendant Remington's hair removal product did not infringe. *Epilady U.K. I*, 21 INT'L REV. INDUS. PROP. & COPYRIGHT L. 860. However, the German court reached the opposite result. *Epilady Germany II*, 24 INT'L REV. INDUS. PROP. & COPYRIGHT L. 843. One patent attorney assessed these two results as follows:

> These examples illustrate how divergent policies underlying the application of patent laws have caused many of the difficulties in achieving uniform patent interpretation and enforcement across national borders. Unpredictable results, whereby foreign courts reach opposite conclusions with respect to the patent validity and infringement, further illustrate the problem of multinational patent enforcement. Without transnational administrative and adjudicative bodies to administer patent laws and patent policy, such divergent results will continue to confound commercial enterprises using patented technologies.

John Gladstone Mills III, *A Transnational Patent Convention for the Acquisition and Enforcement of International Rights*, 84 J. PAT. & TRADEMARK OFF. SOC'Y 83, 115 (2002). Note that the *Roche* opinion determined that considering infringement in a single court "undermine the principle of legal certainty." To what type of certainty does the *Roche* court refer? How is this different that the type of certainty referred to by attorney Mills in the above excerpt? Consider the following explanation by a former European jurist, who explained:

> It is true that national judges apply the same European rules, but there is no guarantee that they apply the same European rules in the same way. Divergences could emerge not only between judicial decisions in the various countries but also between national judicial decisions and the case law of the Boards of Appeal of the EPO. Unity of law and legal certainty are missing. Unity and legal certainty are not enhanced by the fact that national judges are only part of the national procedural laws vary from country to country in many ways.... The result is that inevitable differences exist as to the quality, the speed and the cost of patent litigation in Europe.

Jan J. Brinkhof, *Patent Litigation in Europe: Two Sides of the Picture*, 9 FED. CIR. B.J. 467, 468 (2000).

2. In *GAT v. LuK*, the court determined that the courts of the Contracting State had exclusive jurisdiction to adjudicate patent validity. Why are the reasons that the *GAT* court determined that the

German court should decline to consider validity of the French patent? In the wake of *Roche v. Primus* and *GAT v. LuK*, is there any room for pan-European patent litigation within the national courts? *See* Marketa Trimble, *Cross–Border Injunctions in U.S. Patent Cases and Their Enforcement Abroad*, 13 MARQ. INTELL. PROP. L. REV. 331, 360 (2009) (suggesting that foreign courts could stay infringement proceedings against a resident pending an validity determination by the issuing nation, or fully adjudicate cases in which validity is not disputed).

3. Compare the *Roche* and *GAT* decision to the U.S. Federal Circuit's *Voda v. Cordis Corp.*, 476 F.3d 887 (Fed. Cir. 2007), where the court determined that a district court could not establish jurisdiction over foreign patents under 28 U.S.C. § 1367:

> [T]here is no explicit statutory direction indicating that the district courts should or may exercise supplemental jurisdiction over claims arising under foreign patents, and the Paris Convention, PCT, and Agreement on TRIPS neither contemplate nor allow the extraterritorial jurisdiction of our courts to adjudicate patents of other sovereign nations. We have also noted the territorially limited nature of patent rights. . . .

> Patents and the laws that govern them are often described as complex. Indeed, one of the reasons cited for why Congress established our court was because it felt that most judges didn't understand the patent system and how it worked. As such, Cordis U.S. and one of the amicus curiae assert, and Voda does not dispute, that the foreign sovereigns at issue in this case have established specific judges, resources, and procedures to help assure the integrity and consistency of the application of their patent laws. Therefore, exercising jurisdiction over such subject matter could disrupt their foreign procedures.

Id. at 904–05 (quotations and citations omitted). Are these concerns consistent with those expressed by the European courts in *Roche* and *GAT*?

4. Consider the following critique of the limits on the litigation of transnational intellectual property disputes:

> With international harmonization of substantive law, the development of sophisticated information retrieval systems, the enhanced personal and professional interchange among judges, and the development of specialized courts-to name but a few-arguments about a lack of judicial competence are less persuasive. At the same time, the frequency of transborder disputes has made the cost of insisting on serial national litigation more substantial. The reality of international disputes about international markets makes partitioning of adjudication seem a costly and romantic hankering for the inefficiencies of a balkanized past.

Graeme B. Dinwoodie, *Developing a Private International Intellectual Property Law: The Demise of Territoriality?*, 51 WM. & MARY L. REV. 711, 770 (2009). Are Professor Dinwoodie's concerns well-founded? How should patentees proceed against a single infringer who is acting in several nations? How should the issues of foreign court competency, territoriality and efficiency be resolved?

B. A LOOK AHEAD: A UNIFIED EUROPEAN PATENT SYSTEM?

Some nations have developed specialized intellectual courts, tribunals or divisions that hear intellectual property cases. For example, Japan has designated certain courts to hear cases involving the alleged infringement of patents, utility model registrations, integrated circuit layout design rights, and computer program copyrights, and an Intellectual Property High Court to hear appeals. *See* Toshiko Takenaka, *Success or Failure? Japan's National Strategy on Intellectual Property and Evaluation of its Implication from the Comparative Law Perspective*, 8 WASH. U. GLOBAL STUD. L. REV. 379 (2009).

A significant example of a multinational organization that coordinates the filing, examination and administration of patents is the European Patent Office (EPO). The EPO is comprised of thirty-six (36) members, does not have any mechanisms to litigate patent infringement disputes. Rather, European Patents are litigated in the national courts, where they may be subject to interpretive variation during enforcement proceedings. As one former jurist explained:

> It is true that national judges apply the same European rules, but there is no guarantee that they apply the same European rules in the same way. Divergences could emerge not only between judicial decisions in the various countries but also between national judicial decisions and the case law of the Boards of Appeal of the EPO. Unity of law and legal certainty are missing. Unity and legal certainty are not enhanced by the fact that national judges are only part of the national procedural laws vary from country to country in many ways.... The result is that inevitable differences exist as to the quality, the speed and the cost of patent litigation in Europe.

Jan J. Brinkhof, *Patent Litigation in Europe: Two Sides of the Picture*, 9 FED. CIR. B.J. 467, 468 (2000). One study concludes that this fragmented system has led to higher patenting and managerial costs, as well added uncertainty, for patenting within Europe compared to other nations. Bruno van Pottelsberghe and Jérôme Danguy, *Economic Cost–Benefit Analysis of the Community Patent* (4/7/09), available at http://ec.europa.eu/internal_market/indprop/

patent/index_en.htm. This study suggests that this uncertainty may lead to a multiplicity of validity challenges:

> The high uncertainty induced by the fragmented patent system, in case of litigation, is due to the possibility of having different outcomes across countries. Patent validity can be challenged independently at both the European and national level. What makes the opposition process at the EPO especially attractive for the opponents is that the decision on European patent validity is effective in all the states where the European patent is to be enforced. A decision to uphold a European patent leaves the way open for further validity challenges before national courts.

Id. at 7.

For the past several years, the European Communities (EC) has been examining the possibility of coordinating the patent application and litigation system among its twenty-seven (27) members. Recently, the Council of the European Union proposed a regulation that details key aspects of the plan. These include a European Union patent ("EU patent") as an added option to the currently existing European patent and national patent alternatives. As currently envisioned, EU patents would be effective throughout the entire European Community. The plan anticipates that the EPO will be responsible for examining, granting and administering EU patents. Below is an excerpt of the European Council's Conclusions with respect to the creation of a unified European patent court, called the European and EU Patents Court ("EEUPC").

CONCLUSIONS ON AN ENHANCED PATENT SYSTEM IN EUROPE

Council of the European Union (12/4/09)

The Council adopted the following conclusions:

"THE COUNCIL OF THE EUROPEAN UNION

1.   RECALLING that enhancing the patent system in Europe is a necessary prerequisite for boosting growth through innovation and for helping European business, in particular SMEs, face the economic crisis and international competition;

2.   CONSIDERING that such an enhanced patent system is a vital element of the Internal Market and that it should be based on two pillars, i.e. the creation of a European Union patent (hereafter "EU patent") and the setting up of an integrated specialised and unified jurisdiction for patent related disputes thus improving the enforcement of patents and enhancing legal certainty;

3. ACKNOWLEDGING the considerable amount of work accomplished so far by the Council's preparatory bodies on the legal instruments needed to establish the above-mentioned two pillars;

4. AGREES that the following conclusions on the main features of the European and EU Patents Court (I) could form the basis of, while on the EU patent (II) they should form part of the overall final agreement on a package of measures for an Enhanced Patent System in Europe comprising the creation of a European and EU Patents Court (EEUPC), an EU patent, including the separate regulation on the translation arrangements . . ., an Enhanced Partnership between the European Patent Office and central industrial property offices of Member States and, to the extent necessary, amendments to the European Patent Convention; . . . .

I. MAIN FEATURES OF THE EUROPEAN AND EU PATENTS COURT THE EUROPEAN AND EU PATENTS COURT

10. The EEUPC should have exclusive jurisdiction in respect of civil litigation related to the infringement and validity of EU patents and European patents.

11. As outlined in the Draft Agreement, the EEUPC should comprise a Court of First Instance, a Court of Appeal and a Registry. The Court of First Instance should comprise a central division as well as local and regional divisions.

12. The European Court of Justice shall ensure the principle of primacy of EU law and its uniform interpretation.

THE COMPOSITION OF THE PANELS

13. In order to build up trust and confidence with users of the patent system and to guarantee the high quality and efficiency of the EEUPC's work, it is vital that the composition of the panels is organised in a way which makes best use of experience of patent litigation among judges and practitioners at national level through pooling of resources. Experience could also be acquired through theoretical and practical training which should be provided in order to improve and increase available patent litigation expertise and to ensure a broad geographic distribution of such specific knowledge and experience.

14. All panels of the local and regional divisions and the central division of the Court of First Instance should guarantee the same high quality of work and the same high level of legal and technical expertise. . . .

15. The allocation of judges should be based on their legal or technical expertise, linguistic skills and relevant experience. . . .

JURISDICTION IN RESPECT OF ACTIONS AND COUNTER-CLAIMS FOR REVOCATION

20. In order to ensure that local and regional divisions work in an expeditious and highly efficient way, it is vital that the divisions have some flexibility on how to proceed with counterclaims for revocation.

(a) Direct actions for revocation of patents should be brought before the central division.

(b) A counterclaim for revocation can be brought in the case of an action for infringement before a local or regional division. The local or regional division concerned may;

(i) proceed with the counterclaim for revocation; or,

(ii) refer the counterclaim to the central division and either proceed with the infringement action or stay those proceedings; or,

(iii) with the agreement of the parties, refer the whole case for decision to the central division....

THE ENHANCED PARTNERSHIP

41. The aim of the Enhanced Partnership is to promote innovation by enhancing the efficiency of the patent granting process through avoiding duplication of work, with the goal of more rapid delivery of patents which will increase speed of access to market for innovative products and services and reduce costs for applicants. Enhanced Partnership should both make use of central industrial property offices' existing expertise and strengthen their capacity to enhance the overall quality of the patent system in future.

42. Enhanced Partnership should enable the European Patent Office to make regular use, where appropriate, of the result of any search carried out by central industrial property offices of Member States of the European Patent Organisation on a national patent application the priority of which is claimed in a subsequent filing of a European patent application....

44. Enhanced Partnership should fully respect the central role of the European Patent Office in examining and granting European patents. Under the Enhanced Partnership the European Patent Office would be expected to consider but not be obliged to use the work provided by participating offices. The European Patent Office should remain free to carry out further searches. The Enhanced Partnership should not restrict the possibility for applicants to file their application directly at the European Patent Office.

45. Enhanced partnership would be subject to periodic reviews, adequately involving views of the users of the patent system. In addition, regular feed back from the European Patent Office to the participating offices on how search reports are utilised at the European Patent Office would be essential for the enabling of the

fine-tuning of the search process to the benefit of the optimal utilisation of resources.

Notes and Questions

1. What type of patentee is most likely to benefit from the creation of a Community-wide patent system? Will some patentees continue to grapple with nation-by-nation enforcement under the *Roche v. Primus* and *GAT v. LuK* decisions?

2. Is the ability to have the cases decided by technically qualified judges a desirable feature that should be integrated into U.S. law? Consider the following arguments in favor of such a proposal:

> First, it would eliminate forum shopping entirely, as there would be no possible alternative forum. Second, it would eliminate the inconsistency and unpredictability in patent case resolution that currently exists because of district court variations which would provide better guidance to competitors for primary behavior. Third, a specialized tribunal would develop expertise in patent law and the resolution of patent cases, increasing its accuracy and efficiency at resolving these cases.

Kimberly A. Moore, *Forum Shopping In Patent Cases: Does Geographic Choice Affect Innovation?* 79 N.C.L.R. 889, 932 (2001). Are there counterarguments that weigh against uniformity? Cf., Craig Allen Nard and John F. Duffy, *Rethinking Patent Law's Uniformity Principle,* 101 Nw. U. L. Rev. 1619 (2007). Is there a benefit to multiplicity, such as developing differing perspectives?

Observe that the EU's proposal focuses on the qualifications of judges as the decision makers. Should juries be introduced into the EU system? Note that juries play a key role in determining infringement and validity issues in U.S. courts, which is not the case in Europe currently.

3. The proposed EU system provides a mechanism to transfer invalidity disputes to a central division for resolution. What do you believe is the purpose of this procedure? On balance, are there features of a system that separates invalidity from infringement proceedings that outweigh any undesirable aspects?

C. PATENT ENFORCEMENT AT THE BORDER: AGENCIES AND IP ENFORCEMENT

TRIPS requires members to authorize judicial authorities to order provisional measures to prevent infringement "and in particular to prevent the entry into the channels of commerce in their jurisdiction of goods, including imported goods immediately after customs clearance." TRIPS art. 50(1). Additionally, TRIPS provides that members must enact procedures to allow copyright and trade-mark holders "to lodge an application in writing with competent authorities, administrative or judicial, for the suspension by the customs authorities of the release into free circulation of such goods." *Id.*, art 51. Why do you suppose that patents are absent from this obligation? Consider the following proposed explanation: "A reason to limit the application of the measure to 'visibly infringing' goods, is that certain customs authorities may not be equipped to properly identify goods which may infringe, e.g., a patent claim or layout-design of an integrated circuit." Daniel Gervais, THE TRIPS AGREEMENT: DRAFTING HISTORY AND ANALYSIS 475 (Third ed. 2008).

Furthermore, TRIPS excludes members from the obligation to enact administrative remedial relief for goods "in transit." TRIPS art. 51, nt. 13. Nonetheless, some authorities have enacted rules that cover both patent infringement *and* goods in transit. In the upcoming *Sosecal v. Sisvel*, issued from a court in The Netherlands, the issue concerns whether customs officials there may exercise control over in-transit goods accused of patent infringement. *Sosecal* examines the former and current European Communities regulation (referred to as the "Anti–Piracy Regulations," or APR therein). The customs detentions are temporary pending notification that the rights-holder has initiated a court proceeding to determine infringement. *See* Council Regulation (EC) 1383/03, art. 13. As you read *Sosecal*, consider what is at stake from the various parties' perspectives. What are the European Union's interests? What are the reasons that The Netherlands may wish to be involved? What are the interests of the nations that ship products and those that are designated to receive them?

SOSECAL v. SISVEL

Case No. 311378 / KG ZA 08–617 (The Hague District Court) (July 18, 2008)

. . .

2.2   Koninklijke Philips Electronics N.V., France Télécom, Télédif-fusion de France S.A. and Institut für Rundfunktechnik GmbH (Philips and others) are (co-) holders of the patents EP 0 660 540, EP 0 402 973 and EP 0 599 824 (the patents) that are valid in Austria, Belgium, Switzerland, Germany, Denmark, Spain, France, United Kingdom, Greece, Italy, Luxembourg, the Netherlands and Sweden. The patents regard MPEG Audio technology, such to include the MPEG Audio layer II and layer III (MP3) technology by means of which digital audio signals are compressed as a result of which more and/or longer audio fragments can be stored on a data carrier.

2.3 Philips and others granted a licence under the patents to Audio MPEG Inc. with the authority to grant a (sub-) licence to Sisvel, which authority has been used. Philips and others also granted an irrevocable power of attorney to Sisvel to act for and on their behalf in court on account of the patents, such to include the request for customs actions in pursuance of the applicable Anti–Piracy Regulation, the imposition of prejudgment attachments on goods detained by the Customs Authorities and the initiation of proceedings in order to determine as to whether the relevant goods infringe intellectual property rights of Philips and others or as to whether acts of wrong-doing are otherwise committed vis-à-vis Philips and others, Audio MPEG Inc. and/or Sisvel.

2.4 On 17 January 2008 the Customs Authorities detained a shipment of 6,000 MP4 players with MP3 functionality, provided with the brand indication "Mirage", in pursuance of article 9 of Regulation (EC) 1383/2003 (hereinafter referred to as the APR or the new APR) on the basis of a request for action from Sisvel ... which shipment KLM N.V. (KLM) had in its possession for transportation from Shenzhen, China, to Sao Paolo, Brazil (or further to Venezuela, as argued by Sosecal), whereby the customs status of the goods is such of customs warehousing.... Hence, it regards non-community goods....

2.6 On 14 February 2008 Sisvel—after having obtained permission of the Preliminary Injunction Court in Haarlem [in The Netherlands] and arguing that the detained MP4 players fall under the scope of protection of the patents and were manufactured and marketed without permission of Philips and others as a result of which the patents are infringed and as a consequence of which it would have been established that Council Regulation (EC) no. 1383/2003 of 22 July 2003 concerning customs action against goods suspected of infringing certain intellectual property rights and the measures to be taken against goods found to have infringed such rights these players fall under the application of the APR—had a prejudgment garnishment to deliver levied on this shipment of players under and (exclusively) at the expense of KLM. Also on 14 February 2008 Sisvel initiated proceedings on the merits against (only) KLM....

4.5 From a content point of view the parties are divided about the question as to whether in this framework the so called "manufacturing fiction" is to be assumed (i.e. that the MP4 players were manufactured in the Netherlands.... The manufacturing fiction implies that by way of fiction it is assumed that the MP4 players were manufactured in the Netherlands and it is then considered as to whether these devices then infringe the patents under Dutch patent laws.

4.6 In Dutch Supreme Court 19 March 2004, LJN AO 0903 (Philips/Princo) it was ruled with regard to the old APR (Regulation 3295/94) that the manufacturing fiction applies. . . .

4.7 In District Court of The Hague 13 July 2005, roll number 02–2947 (Philips/Princo), it was then ruled that the same applies to the new APR, also in consideration of recital 8[4] thereof. . . .

This should be seen in conjunction with article 10 APR:

The law in force in the Member State within the territory of which the goods are placed in one of the situations referred to in article 1 paragraph 1[5] shall apply when deciding whether an intellectual property right has been infringed under national law.

According to this judgment this manufacturing fiction comprises the question as to whether the allegedly infringing products are held to, according to Dutch law and assuming the fiction that there were manufactured here, would infringe the (. . .) (invoked) patents (. . .). Then none of the actions as intended by article 16 of the new APR can be performed with regard to these goods, such to include the placing under a suspensive procedure and re-export. . . .

4.11 Needlessly, it is considered that the [European] Commission also sees the APR in line with the elaborated established case-law when it comes to transit. In COM(2005) 479 . . . it is of the opinion, in section 3.1.1, that in pursuance of the APR the Customs Authorities "can stop suspected fakes during import, export, transit or *transhipment*" (own italics, President), which is also on a large scale applied in practice: 22,000 interventions in 2004 resulting in detainment of counterfeit goods (against 10,000 of these kinds of interventions in 2003). It thereby indicates that: "EU Customs legislation in this area is now reckoned to be among the strongest in the world (China has now adopted new legislation of a similar type) (. . .) With controls on all movements of goods, *especially during transhipment*, customs protect not only the EU but also other parts of the world and in particular the least developed countries which are often targeted by fraudsters (cf. seizures of fake medicines, condoms and parts stopped at EU borders on route

---

4. [Editor's note: Recital 8 reads as follows:

Proceedings initiated to determine whether an intellectual property right has been infringed under national law will be conducted with reference to the criteria used to establish whether goods produced in that Member State infringe intellectual property rights.]

5. [Editor's note: Generally, Article 1, paragraph 1 states that Council Regulation (EC) No 1383/2003 describes the conditions for action by the customs authorities when goods are suspected of infringing an intellectual property right either (a) when they are entered for release for free circulation, export or re-export; or (b) when they are found during checks on goods entering or leaving the Community customs territory].

to Africa"; italics again added, President). Interpretation in another sense would, in the provisional opinion of the Court, deprive the APR of a lot of its intended ... and meanwhile practical functioning. . . .

4.13   In this state of affairs there is no reason to in preliminary relief proceedings deviate from a doctrine deriving from established case-law on the basis of an interpretation founded on a judgment which was, in the provisional opinion of the Court, passed on different grounds and which would imply farreaching consequences where the intended and practical functioning of the APR is concerned. In other words: In the provisional opinion of the Court there are insufficient indications in this judgment that there would be question of a trend shift resulting in the Court ruling on the merits to decide that the manufacturing fiction could no longer be applied.

Notes and Questions

1.   Observe that, according to the opinion, the patentee did not have a patent in either the point of origin (China) or either of the potential destinations (Brazil or Venezuela). There are a number of reasons for this circumstance. First, a patentee may not have pursued patent protection in any of those countries. Second, the patent offices may have not yet acted, or perhaps, rejected applications filed by a patentee. Although TRIPS sets uniform, minimum standards, nations may apply these standards differently as a practical matter. *Sosecal* does not examine these potential reasons, instead focusing on whether the relevant authorities support the Dutch exercise of jurisdiction. Should the reason that the patentee lacks patent protection in the other nations matter to the inquiry? Should it make any difference whether the goods originated or were destined within the European Communities?

2.   In *Montex Holdings v. Diesel* [2006] ECR I–10881, a European Communities court considered in-transit seizures of goods accused of infringing a trademark. The *Montex* opinion determined that such seizures were appropriate "only if those goods are subject to the act of a third party while they are placed under the external transit procedure which necessarily entails their being put on the market in that Member State of transit."

In *Nokia Corporation v. Her Majesty's Commissioners of Revenue & Customs* (HMRC) [2009] EWHC 1903 (Ch), a United Kingdom court reached a similar result. In doing so, the Nokia court construed the Council Regulation (EC) 1383/03 (which Nokia called the "Counterfeit Goods Regulation") that was also construed by the *Sosecal* court:

> In this regard it will also be recalled that the definition of "infringing" goods and, more specifically, "counterfeit goods" is not limited to fakes. It extends to the use of the registered mark on any of

the goods the subject of the registration. It is not uncommon for the same mark to be owned and used quite legitimately by different proprietors in different territories in respect of the same goods. Yet if the manufacturing fiction applies, goods lawfully made in one territory and intended for lawful use in another but transhipped through a Member State in which that mark is registered in the name of a third party would be subject to seizure. It seems to me most unlikely that the Counterfeit Goods Regulation was ever intended to produce such a result.

Why might a court be reluctant to support in-transit seizures under trademark law? Is there a credible distinction between the trademark and patent laws that justifies the disparate treatment between *Montex* and *Nokia* on one hand, and *Sosecal* on the other? Consider this statement from *Montex* acknowledging authorities holding that "transit, which consists in transporting goods lawfully manufactured in a Member State to a non-member country by passing through one or more Member States, does not involve any marketing of the goods in question and is therefore not liable to infringe the specific subject-matter of the trade mark." Might there be similar arguments made for certain types of patent claims? On this point, see *Microsoft Corp. v. AT & T Corp.*, 550 U.S. 437, 455 (2007) (observing that U.S. patent law should not be presumed to encroach on the "different policy judgments about the relative rights of inventors, competitors, and the public in patented inventions" of foreign nations).

3.   Over the past several years, European customs authorities have engaged in several in-transit pharmaceuticals sent from India and Brazil. For example, in 2008 Dutch authorities seized drugs for a second-line treatment of HIV/AIDS shipped from India as part of a program implemented by the William J. Clinton Foundation on behalf of UNITAID in Nigeria. Another was a shipment of losartan, a hypertension treatment, made by a generic drug maker in India. Professor Abbott argues that such conduct may be contrary to the principles embodied in the General Agreement on Tariffs and Trade (GATT):

> Since 1947, Member States of the European Union have been members of the GATT, now the World Trade Organization (WTO). The EU is a Member of the WTO. The WTO provides the legal framework under which international trade is conducted. From its inception, the GATT/WTO has recognised in GATT art. V the principle of "freedom of transit" for goods moving through ports and airports in international trade. This fundamental principle has been so widely and consistently implemented that there has been virtually no controversy about it in the history of the GATT/WTO, despite the fact that goods are constantly moving in transit through its Members.

Frederick M. Abbott, *Seizure of Generic Pharmaceuticals in Transit Based on Allegations of Patent Infringement: A Threat to International Trade, Development and Public Welfare*, 1 W.I.P.O.J. 43, 45 (2009).

This area is expected to see more activity over the next several years. India has discussed filing a complaint before the WTO to challenge the seizures. See John W. Miller, *India Prepares EU Trade Complaint*, WALL STREET JOURNAL ONLINE (8/6/09), available at http://online.wsj.com/article/SB124949598103308449.html. The European Council is undertaking a review of Council Regulation (EC) 1383/03. *See* European Council Resolution 2009/C 71/01 (3/16/09). How would you propose moving those with competing perspectives toward a comprehensive solution?

†